FAMILY-BASED PREVENTION PROGRAMS FOR CHILDREN AND ADOLESCENTS

In addition to introducing readers to the field of family-based prevention science, *Family-Based Prevention Programs for Children and Adolescents* highlights the distinctive contributions of a set of exemplary programs in terms of their foundational theory, design, delivery mechanisms, performance, and unique opportunities for future research. It is organized into three sections to orient readers to: the existence of different types of family-based programs targeting families with children of different ages; the strategies and challenges that arise when attempting large-scale dissemination of prevention programs; and the emerging innovations that promise to push the field forward into uncharted territories. Each chapter is written by a preeminent program developer, including:

Gene H. Brody
Richard F. Catalano
Patricia Chamberlain
Thomas J. Dishion
Marion S. Forgatch

Kevin P. Haggerty
Cleve Redmond
Matthew R. Sanders
Richard L. Spoth
Carolyn Webster-Stratton

Contributors author review the state of the research and then provide a summary of their own program, including research and dissemination efforts. The authors also discuss take-home lessons for practitioners and policymakers, and provide their view of the future of program development and research in their area. As an important signpost signifying the noteworthy achievements of the field to date, as well as an arrow pointing the field toward significant growth in the future, this book is a must-have primary resource for graduate students in developmental or clinical psychology, counseling, family sciences, social work, or health policy, and an essential guide for practitioners and policymakers in the field of family-based prevention, family service delivery, or public health.

Mark J. Van Ryzin is a Research Scientist at the Oregon Social Learning Center and the Oregon Research Institute and faculty in the Department of Educational Methodology, Policy and Leadership in the College of Education at the University of Oregon.

Karol L. Kumpfer is a Professor in the University of Utah Department of Health Promotion and Education in the College of Health. She is also the Chair of the COH International Education and Research Committee in the College of Health at the University of Utah.

Gregory M. Fosco is an Assistant Professor of Human Development and Family Studies at Pennsylvania State University and founder of the Family Process Lab. In 2013 he was appointed the Karl R. and Diane Wendle Fink Early Career Professorship for the Study of Families.

Mark T. Greenberg is the Edna Peterson Bennett Endowed Chair in Prevention Research and Professor of Human Development and Family Studies at Pennsylvania State University. He is also the Founding Director of The Prevention Research Center.

FAMILY-BASED PREVENTION PROGRAMS FOR CHILDREN AND ADOLESCENTS

Theory, Research, and Large-Scale Dissemination

Edited by
Mark J. Van Ryzin, Karol L. Kumpfer,
Gregory M. Fosco, and Mark T. Greenberg

Psychology Press
Taylor & Francis Group
NEW YORK AND LONDON

First published 2016
by Psychology Press
711 Third Avenue, New York, NY 10017

and by Psychology Press
27 Church Road, Hove, East Sussex BN3 2FA

Psychology Press is an imprint of the Taylor & Francis Group, an informa business

© 2016 Taylor & Francis

The right of the editors to be identified as the authors of the editorial material, and of the authors for their individual chapters, has been asserted in accordance with sections 77 and 78 of the Copyright, Designs and Patents Act 1988.

All rights reserved. No part of this book may be reprinted or reproduced or utilized in any form or by any electronic, mechanical, or other means, now known or hereafter invented, including photocopying and recording, or in any information storage or retrieval system, without permission in writing from the publishers.

Trademark notice: Product or corporate names may be trademarks or registered trademarks, and are used only for identification and explanation without intent to infringe.

Library of Congress Cataloging-in-Publication Data
Family-based prevention programs for children and adolescents : theory, research, and large-scale dissemination / [edited by] Mark J. Van Ryzin,
Karol L. Kumpfer, Gregory M. Fosco, Mark T. Greenberg.
    pages cm
    Includes bibliographical references and index.
    1. Dysfunctional families—Services for.   2. Problem children—Services
    for.   3. Families—Psychological aspects.   4. Families—Health and
    hygiene.   5. Parent and child.   I. Ryzin, Mark J. Van, 1968-
    HV697.F3534 2015
    362.82'7—dc23   2015000004

ISBN: 978-1-84872-484-6 (hbk)
ISBN: 978-1-84872-485-3 (pbk)
ISBN: 978-1-315-76491-7 (ebk)

Typeset in Bembo
by Keystroke, Station Road, Codsall, Wolverhampton

Printed and bound in the United States of America by Publishers Graphics, LLC on sustainably sourced paper.

CONTENTS

List of Contributors	*ix*

1 Family-Based Approaches to Prevention: The State
  of the Field   1
  Mark J. Van Ryzin and Gregory M. Fosco

PART I
Family-Based Prevention Programs
Across Development   **21**

2 Family Foundations   23
  Mark E. Feinberg and Marni L. Kan

3 The Incredible Years® Series: A Developmental Approach   42
  Carolyn Webster-Stratton

4 Strengthening Families for Middle/Late Childhood   68
  Karol L. Kumpfer, Catia Magalhães, Henry Whiteside,
  and Jing Xie

5 The Family Check-Up Model as Prevention and Treatment
  of Adolescent Drug (Ab)Use: The Intervention Strategy,
  Outcomes, and Implementation Model   86
  Thomas J. Dishion and Anne Marie Mauricio

vi Contents

PART II
Large-Scale Dissemination of Family-Based Programs 111

6 Early Results from Implementing PMTO: Full Transfer
on a Grand Scale 113
Marion S. Forgatch, Laura A. Rains, and Margrét Sigmarsdóttir

7 The Triple P – Positive Parenting Program: A Community-
Wide Approach to Parenting and Family Support 134
Matthew R. Sanders, Karen M. T. Turner, and Jenna McWilliam

8 The PROSPER Delivery System and Implementation of the
Strengthening Families Program: For Parents and
Youth 10–14 160
*Cleve Redmond, Richard L. Spoth, Lisa M. Schainker,
and Mark E. Feinberg*

9 Scaling Up Treatment Foster Care Oregon: A Randomized
Trial of Two Implementation Strategies 186
Patricia Chamberlain and Lisa Saldana

PART III
Innovations and Adaptations of Family-Based Programs 207

10 Staying Connected With Your Teen® and the Promise
of Self-Directed Prevention Programs 209
*Kevin P. Haggerty, Tali Klima, Martie L. Skinner,
Richard F. Catalano, and Susan Barkan*

11 Families OverComing Under Stress (FOCUS): A Family-
Centered Preventive Intervention for Families Facing
Trauma, Stress, and Adversity: Implementation with
Military Families 229
*Patricia Lester, Lee Klosinski, William Saltzman,
Norweeta Milburn, Catherine Mogil, and William Beardslee*

12 Cultural and Gender Adaptations of Evidence-Based
Family Interventions 256
*Karol L. Kumpfer, Catia Magalhães, Jing Xie,
and Sheetal Kanse*

Contents **vii**

13 Family-Centered Prevention for Rural African Americans:
The Strong African American Families Program (SAAF),
the Strong African American Families–Teen Program
(SAAF–T), and the Adults in the Making Program (AIM) 282
Gene H. Brody

14 Thinking Systematically for Enduring Family Change 308
Gregory M. Fosco, Brian Bumbarger,
and Katharine T. Bamberger

Index *329*

CONTRIBUTORS

Katharine T. Bamberger, Department of Human Development and Family Studies, Pennsylvania State University

Susan Barkan, Social Development Research Group, University of Washington

William Beardslee, Judge Baker Children's Center, Harvard Medical School

Gene H. Brody, Center for Family Research, University of Georgia

Brian Bumbarger, Prevention Research Center for the Promotion of Human Development, Pennsylvania State University

Richard F. Catalano, Social Development Research Group, University of Washington

Patricia Chamberlain, Oregon Social Learning Center

Thomas J. Dishion, REACH Institute, Arizona State University

Mark E. Feinberg, Prevention Research Center for the Promotion of Human Development, Pennsylvania State University

Marion S. Forgatch, Oregon Social Learning Center

Gregory M. Fosco, Department of Human Development and Family Studies, Pennsylvania State University

x Contributors

Kevin P. Haggerty, Social Development Research Group, University of Washington

Marni L. Kan, RTI International

Sheetal Kanse, University of Utah

Tali Klima, Social Development Research Group, University of Washington

Lee Klosinski, Nathanson Family Resilience Center, University of California, Los Angeles

Karol L. Kumpfer, Department of Health Promotion and Education, University of Utah

Patricia Lester, Nathanson Family Resilience Center, University of California, Los Angeles

Catia Magalhães, Polytechnic Institute of Viseu

Anne Marie Mauricio, REACH Institute, Arizona State University

Jenna McWilliam, Triple P International

Norweeta Milburn, Nathanson Family Resilience Center, University of California, Los Angeles

Catherine Mogil, Nathanson Family Resilience Center, University of California, Los Angeles

Laura A. Rains, Implementation Sciences International, Inc.

Cleve Redmond, Partnerships in Prevention Science Institute, Iowa State University

Lisa Saldana, Oregon Social Learning Center

William Saltzman, Nathanson Family Resilience Center, University of California, Los Angeles

Matthew R. Sanders, Parenting and Family Support Centre, University of Queensland

Lisa M. Schainker, Partnerships in Prevention Science Institute, Iowa State University

Margrét Sigmarsdóttir, The Government Agency for Child Protection, Iceland

Martie L. Skinner, Social Development Research Group, University of Washington

Richard L. Spoth, Partnerships in Prevention Science Institute, Iowa State University

Karen M. T. Turner, Parenting and Family Support Centre, University of Queensland

Mark J. Van Ryzin, Oregon Research Institute, Oregon Social Learning Center, and University of Oregon

Carolyn Webster-Stratton, Professor Emeritus, University of Washington

Henry Whiteside, Lutra Group, Inc.

Jing Xie, Cultural and Health Research Center, University of Houston

1

FAMILY-BASED APPROACHES TO PREVENTION

The State of the Field

Mark J. Van Ryzin and Gregory M. Fosco

Introduction

This book was designed to provide the reader with an overview of the field of family-based prevention science. Family-based prevention programs focus on providing education to families, improving the quality of family relationships, and teaching key family management skills. The goal of these programs is to transform the way parents manage and monitor child behavior, the way the family negotiates conflicts and solves problems, and the affective quality of the family environment. These programs view the family as the most influential and malleable context from which to promote long-lasting behavioral and emotional adjustment among children and youth. By improving parenting practices and family relationships, these programs can promote positive outcomes by reducing salient risk factors and promoting more effective family functioning. Several systematic reviews and meta-analyses have found family-based programs to be effective at preventing or reducing a wide range of behavioral problems among children, including externalizing and disruptive behavior, attention deficit/ hyperactivity, and oppositional defiant disorder, while also promoting social competencies and academic performance (Maughan, Christiansen, Jenson, Olympia, & Clark, 2005; Nowak & Heinrichs, 2008; Reyno & McGrath, 2006; Sanders, Kirby, Tellegen, & Day, 2013; UNODC, 2010). Reviewers have drawn similar conclusions with regards to adolescents, finding significant reductions in behavioral problems such as delinquency, violence, substance abuse, depression/ anxiety, and HIV risk as well as enhancements to family and peer relations (Brody et al., 2010, 2012; Dusenbury, 2000; Farrington & Welsh, 2003; Foxcroft & Tsertsvadze, 2012; Kumpfer, Alvarado, & Whiteside, 2003; Lochman & van den Steenhoven, 2002; Petrie, Bunn, & Byrne, 2007; UNODC, 2010). Family-based programs have also been found to be effective at promoting a wide range of effective parent behaviors (Kazdin, 1997; Kumpfer et al., 2003; Sanders et al., 2013; UNODC, 2010) and preventing child maltreatment (Brook, McDonald & Yan, 2012; Lundahl, Nimer, & Parsons, 2006).

In addition to simple effectiveness, however, a range of research has established that family-based programs are often *more* effective than other approaches in terms of preventing behavioral and emotional problems. For example, in their meta-analysis, Stanton and Shadish (1996) found that family-based programs for substance use were more efficacious than individual counseling or peer group therapy. The Cochrane Reviews of substance abuse prevention also found that family-based prevention programs were more effective than youth-only programs (Foxcroft, Ireland, Lister-Sharp, Lowe, & Breen, 2003; Foxcroft & Tsertsvadze, 2012). Brestan and Eyberg (1998), in their review of effective psychosocial treatments for conduct-disordered children and adolescents, found that only two of 82 programs met their highest criteria for effectiveness, and both were family-based. Kumpfer and Alvarado's (2003) later systematic review for substance abuse and delinquency prevention identified seven family-based interventions with the highest level of effectiveness, all of which were independently replicated with large effect sizes. Research in the prevention and treatment of obesity has found that involvement of parents predicts a greater degree of success as compared to individualistic approaches (Kitzmann & Beech, 2006; Kitzman-Ulrich et al., 2010; Young, Northern, Lister, Drummond, & O'Brien, 2007). Finally, cost-benefit analyses have found family-based programs to be among the most cost effective at addressing a range of problem behavior despite having higher implementation costs (Miller & Hendrie, 2009).

This book was not intended to be a comprehensive collection of family-based programs, since such collections are available elsewhere; for example, the SAMHSA National Registry of Effective Programs and Policies (NREPP) and the Blueprints for Healthy Youth Development provide overviews of a wide range of effective programs. Instead, this book was intended to highlight the distinctive contributions of a set of exemplary programs in terms of their foundational theory, design, delivery mechanisms, performance, and unique opportunities for future research. This book is organized into three sections to orient readers to: (1) the existence of different types of family-based prevention programs targeting families with children in different developmental periods; (2) the strategies and challenges that arise when attempting large-scale dissemination of evidence-based programs; and (3) the emerging innovations that promise to push the field forward into uncharted territories. The first section is organized in a developmental sequence to showcase different family programs for infancy, early childhood, mid-to-late childhood, and adolescence. Chapters in this section (2–5) highlight the unique challenges and opportunities at different age levels and emphasize the need to tailor family-based programs to the specific ways in which parents can influence child behavior during different developmental periods (e.g., Van Ryzin, Fosco, & Dishion, 2012). Authors of these chapters were asked to describe the theoretical models underlying their programs, to report the quality of evidence from program trials, and to share insights regarding the resources needed to implement their programs successfully. In addition, authors were asked to share evidence related to the mediators and moderators of their program to shed light on *how* the programs work and *for whom* the programs are most effective.

The second section of the book offers a collection of chapters from leaders in the field of dissemination and implementation science. A long-standing and enduring challenge for the field is the translation of efficacious prevention and intervention models to successful, large-scale implementations in real-world settings. Chapters in this section (6–9) underscore the importance of leveraging our knowledge of family systems and prevention science to achieve a widespread public health impact (O'Connell, Boat, & Warner, 2009). Recent research has documented the many barriers that exist when attempting to implement and sustain evidence-based practices in community settings (Scheirer & Dearing, 2011), and the chapters in this section highlight the skillful efforts aimed at surmounting these barriers.

The third section (Chapters 10–13) presents recent efforts that attempt to extend the reach of existing family-based programs to traditionally underserved communities (e.g., ethnic minority groups, military families) and to expand our understanding of the complex interactions between the environment and the individual genotype in the context of family-based programs. These chapters draw on the vision of leading prevention scholars who discuss their recent efforts at introducing new and exciting innovations to the field of family-based prevention science.

Family Focus

Family-centered approaches arose out of a divergent view of mental health problems. Early family interventionists had to push a paradigm shift away from a mental illness perspective that emphasized a focus on individual disorder toward a conceptualization of an individual as functioning within a network of family relationships. Proponents of family-centered approaches to treatment re-cast children's emotional or behavioral problems as symptoms of an ailing family system, rather than mental illness contained within the individual (Minuchin & Fishman, 1981; Patterson, Chamberlain, & Reid, 1982). This framing helped redirect our attention away from a disordered individual and focused our attention on the family dynamics that caused or maintained problematic functioning in children and adolescents. At this point, there are now several models of family risk and protective processes that have been systematically developed to account for different processes that underlie child social, emotional, and behavioral problems (Ary et al., 1999; Dishion, Patterson, Stoolmiller, &

Skinner, 1991; Hawkins, Catalano, & Miller, 1992; Romer, 2003;Vakalahi, 2001). These models were developed using an iterative process in which developmental studies informed prevention programs, and tests of theorized prevention targets informed subsequent developmental studies; the result is a reciprocal process in which theory guides prevention and prevention studies inform theoretical models. Since we now recognize that the most effective programs are *theory-driven* (Nation et al., 2003), we sought to emphasize the theoretical principles that guide the diverse programs described in this book. As can be seen by the diversity of approaches, there are many ways to evoke lasting change in families. To orient the reader to this theoretical diversity, we provide a brief overview of three general frameworks that are prominent in family-centered prevention and intervention models today: behavioral parent training, family relationships/attachment promotion, and family systems.

Behavioral Parent Training

This approach to intervening typically focuses on working with parents alone, either individually or in groups, to target key parent management skills and promote cognitive, affective, or behavioral changes in the parent (Kumpfer & Alvarado, 2003). Behavioral parent training approaches stem largely from early work by Patterson and associates (e.g., Dishion, Patterson, & Kavanagh, 1992, Patterson et al., 1982; Patterson & Narrett, 1990; Wiltz & Patterson, 1974), which built upon behavioral evidence that highlighted coercive family processes (for reviews, see Dishion & Patterson, 2006; Patterson et al., 1982; Patterson, Reid, & Dishion, 1992; Reid, Patterson, & Snyder, 2002) and poor supervision and structure (see, e.g., Dishion & McMahon, 1998) as central risk processes for youth social, emotional, and behavioral problems. *Coercive family process* is characterized by the use of aversive behavior to control other family members. Coercive parenting includes power-assertive techniques, such as yelling, threats, or harsh punishments, and coercive child behavior may include angry, aversive behavior such as tantrums (in younger children) or yelling and aggressive posturing in older children, or the threat of such behaviors. The introduction of aversive behavior in the family environment may begin a conflict bout in which another family member responds in kind. These interactions are typically characterized by negative reciprocity and escalation of hostility until one family member's negative behavior terminates the bout, thereby "winning" the conflict. This process negatively reinforces the "winner's" aversive behavior, and can result in escape conditioning in which other family members are motivated to withdraw at the threat of a coercive interaction or to acquiesce early in the interaction sequence.

Another perspective informing behavioral parent training programs is a focus on reducing opportunities for experimentation with deviant behavior (Biglan, Flay, Embry, & Sandler, 2012). Unsupervised, unstructured time is a risk factor for engaging with a deviant peer group in a context of problem behavior (Ary et al., 1999; Dishion, Nelson, & Bullock, 2004; Duncan, Duncan, Biglan, & Ary, 1998; Griffin, Botvin, Scheier, Diaz, & Miller, 2000; Petraitis, Flay, & Miller, 1995; Svensson, 2000; Van Ryzin, Fosco, & Dishion, 2012). Some families exhibit a general deficit in parental monitoring, while others experience a deterioration in monitoring over time, in which coercive family interactions prompt parents to relinquish supervision and control, enabling youth to disengage from the family and engage with a deviant peer group (Dishion, Nelson, & Bullock, 2004).

Research in these behavioral family processes has led to the generation of parent training programs that typically focus on promoting parental monitoring and involvement, collaborative problem-solving, effective disciplinary techniques, and positive reinforcement for prosocial behavior (Patterson et al., 1982, 1992). These parenting practices can generate more positive, productive family interactions, increase positive child behavior, and short-circuit coercive interactions through non-emotional, contingent responding to children's aversive behaviors. Similarly, establishing clear rules, enforcing limits through effective discipline, and monitoring youth whereabouts serve to extinguish fledgling problem behaviors and minimize opportunities for experimentation with deviant behavior and involvement with deviant peer groups. Some exemplary program models that use behavioral parent training approaches include the Parent Management Training Oregon® Model (see Forgatch et al., this volume) and the Family Check-Up (see Dishion & Mauricio, this volume).

Family Relationships/Attachment Perspective

Another group of prevention and intervention programs have focused more intensively on the quality of family relationships or bonding/attachment to parents. Typically, these programs focus on promoting parental sensitivity, affection, and awareness of the child's needs, which includes contingent responding to the child's requests for support and expression of approval when the child exhibits positive behavior. Underlying theory and research emphasizes that this contingent parental responsiveness in infancy and childhood promotes the development of internal representations or working models that anticipate interpersonal interactions as a source of pleasure and safety; in contrast, children with a history of rejecting, neglecting, or inconsistent care develop models of others as unresponsive, unreliable, and potentially hurtful (Ainsworth, 1989; Bretherton, 2005; Sroufe, 1988; Sroufe & Fleeson, 1986). More positive or "secure" internal working models motivate child compliance and the internalization of prosocial values (e.g., Ainsworth, Bell, & Stayton, 1974; Kochanska, Barry, Stellern, & O'Bleness, 2009). A recent review by Buck and Dix (2014) describes 17 longitudinal studies that support the view that children's investment and security in the parent–child relationship can motivate children to behave in a manner consistent with parental guidance, which is linked with lower levels of antisocial behavior. Other work indicates that secure attachment, particularly in early childhood, guides more positive social development (Elicker, Englund, & Sroufe, 1992; Sroufe, Egeland, & Carlson, 1999), reduces risk for depression (Cummings & Cicchetti, 1990), and promotes better academic outcomes (Jacobsen & Hofmann, 1997; Moss & St-Laurent, 2001). Typically, programs that focus on attachment in families will train parents to respond sensitively to children's bids for attention, provide support for children's prosocial behavior, and may also attempt to change parents' representations of their relationships with their own parents, or with their children (Bakermans-Kranenburg, van Ijzendoorn, & Juffer, 2003; Diamond et al., 2010; Egeland, 2004). The Incredible Years® Program (see Webster-Stratton, this volume) is one example that has successfully incorporated an attachment focus.

Some programs have integrated behavioral parent training, child life and social skills training, and family relationship building components into an approach referred to as *Family Skills Training* (Kumpfer & Alvarado, 2003). These programs offer a multi-pronged approach that can be appealing to families. Often, family skills training programs will offer a family meal and have a strong emphasis on having families practice skills in the presence of trained group leaders before they go home, which builds on evidence from behavioral parent training programs that has found role-playing to be a crucial technique for evoking changes (Kaminski, Valle, Filene, & Boyle, 2008). Some researchers have even found that retention rates are higher for family skills training approaches as compared to parent-only groups (Kumpfer & Alvarado, 2003), possibly because it reduces barriers to participation, such as finding childcare, or it may be engaging to children, who will encourage parents to attend.

Family Systems

Some programs have incorporated family systems principles into their approach. We focus only on two examples: interdependency of family relationships, and family wholism. *Interdependency* refers to the view that family members and family relationships are interconnected, and effects to any subsystem within the family will have wide-reaching effects for the entire family (Minuchin, 1985). Guided by this principle, researchers have recently been attending to the potential for effects of a program that extend beyond the intended or targeted individuals. For example, a study of the Strong African American Families (SAAF) program found that program effects on parenting communication led to reductions in mothers' depressive symptoms (Beach et al., 2008). Similarly, family-based programs that reduce children's behavior problems can have

Family-Based Approaches to Prevention **7**

indirect effects on parents' life satisfaction and couple relationship quality (McEachern et al., 2013).

Considering the interdependent nature of family relationships has also shed light on the process in which affect is transferred from one relationship to another, often referred to as spillover or crossover (e.g., Erel & Burman, 1995). Of particular relevance to family-centered prevention programs is the interparental relationship. Considerable evidence now indicates that distressed couples who experience high levels of conflict are more likely to engage in less effective and more harsh or punitive parenting practices (e.g., Krishnakumar & Buehler, 2000). This body of evidence has led a prenatal prevention program to foster supportive couple communication (i.e., co-parenting) as parents adjust to the transition of having a new child (see Feinberg and Kan, this volume). There remains additional untapped potential for the integration of couple relationship dynamics into other family-centered programs.

Family *wholism* refers to the view that the "whole is greater than the sum of its parts" (Cox & Paley, 1997, p. 245). This concept calls researchers to think about the family system as an entity that is distinct from specific within-family relationships, and one that has an organization and emotional climate that offers unique predictive value for the functioning of those within it (e.g., Fosco & Grych, 2013). A whole-family approach introduces an important perspective for understanding how family-based programs can improve family functioning as compared to programs that focus on an individual. For example, a study by Szapocznik and colleagues (1989) compared structural family therapy and individual psychodynamic therapy in a small sample of Hispanic boys. Interestingly, both approaches were effective in reducing boys' emotional and behavioral symptoms, but the family-based program also improved overall family functioning, whereas boys in the individual therapy condition experienced deterioration in overall family functioning by 1-year follow-up. Thus, changes for the benefit of an individual, outside of the context of the family, may have unintended iatrogenic effects for the family and ultimately undermine individual functioning as a result. Evidence such as this argues for a more comprehensive family-based approach to intervening with youth, as well as broad assessments of family functioning to more completely understand how programs can influence children and their families. Moreover, programs that can promote healthy functioning at a family level can have long-lasting beneficial effects for children or adolescents (e.g., Fosco, Caruthers, & Dishion, 2012).

Although consideration of these family systems dynamics can be daunting, harnessing the power of family dynamics can prove quite advantageous. Because of the interdependent nature of family relationships, there are many inroads for prevention and intervention and many pathways to successful change. Perhaps it is this premise that is best captured in the diversity of approaches described in this volume, all of which lend support to the notion that there are many ways to evoke lasting change in families.

8 Mark J. Van Ryzin and Gregory M. Fosco

Level of Implementation

In addition to sharing a focus on the family, the programs described in this book target *universal* or *selective* levels of implementation, although some programs include *indicated* components for families with an identified need; in some cases, programs operate at all three levels, such as Triple-P (Sanders et al., this volume). The Institute of Medicine (1994) recommends that prevention programs be classified according to these three levels of implementation by considering the populations to whom the programs are directed. *Universal* or Tier 1 prevention programs are administered to all members of a target population in an attempt to reduce the likelihood of the onset of disorder. *Selective* or Tier 2 prevention programs are given to members of a subgroup of a population whose risk for disorder is deemed to be above average based upon defined assessments or screening protocols. *Indicated* or Tier 3 programs are provided to individuals who demonstrate minimal but detectable indicators of disorder. Beyond these three categories of prevention are highly intensive, tailored therapy programs that target individuals or families exhibiting definitive symptoms of disorder; such programs are beyond the scope of this book.

Universal programs (or universal components within multi-tiered programs) generally have a small footprint in terms of time and resources, and are designed to be broadly applicable to a wide variety of different kinds of families. Selective programs (or selective program components) are usually more customized and target specific profiles of family risk (e.g., divorced families, single parents, etc.). Given the at-risk nature of the target population, selective programs are often more intensive than universal programs in terms of the time and resources required for delivery. Indicated programs or components are generally the most intensive of the three categories and are often highly customized to address specific issues (e.g., a high degree of family conflict, runaway children, etc.) or to focus on specific parenting practices. Within each chapter in this book, program authors will classify their programs using these level(s) of implementation as the guiding framework.

Strength of Evidence

Another commonality among the programs in this book is that they are supported by strong evidence. Standards for evidence have evolved, starting with early definitions of the nature of empirical evidence for intervention programs by the American Psychological Association Task Force on Psychological Intervention Guidelines (1995) and including later efforts to differentiate among different levels of evidence (Chambless & Hollon, 1998). More recently, the Society for Prevention Research (SPR) created the Standards Committee, which set forth detailed criteria by which policymakers and service delivery organizations can weigh the accumulated evidence for prevention programs (Flay et al., 2005). The Committee defined criteria by which prevention programs can be judged to be *efficacious* (i.e., able to deliver significant effects under tightly controlled conditions), *effective* (i.e., sufficiently documented as to be deliverable by third parties and/or under non-optimal conditions) and *ready for dissemination* (i.e., systematically organized and supported to ensure program fidelity in large-scale, real-life implementations).

At the core of these criteria is the randomized controlled trial (RCT), which is the gold standard for scientific evidence. As the reader will soon realize, the programs in this book have been evaluated by means of large-scale RCTs, often more than once. The process of randomization in the RCT ensures that potentially confounding group differences (i.e., gender, ethnicity, socio-economic status, level of risk, etc.) are equalized across the intervention and control groups. Further, since the researcher controls the level of exposure to the prevention program across the groups, with the control group typically receiving no or minimal programming, causal inferences can be drawn regarding the efficacy of the program by simply comparing outcomes across groups (Shadish, Cook, & Campbell, 2002). The RCT has been, and remains, the dominant form of study design in the field of prevention science; in a recent meta-analysis of family-based programs for adolescent substance abuse, my colleagues and I found that, out of approximately 140 studies in our sample, more than 95% used some form of randomized design (Van Ryzin, Roseth, Fosco, Lee, & Chen, forthcoming).

However, although RCTs are important, there are additional criteria mandated by the Standards Committee before a prevention program can be considered to be *efficacious*. For example, the Standards Committee requires that at least two randomized trials be conducted, which serves to establish that effects can be replicated. The Committee also requires that the trials are conducted on a defined population; the study samples must be clearly delineated, and the researcher must discuss how well the samples represent the intended population. This requirement serves to establish external validity. Research must also use psychometrically sound measurement instruments (multiple measures for key outcome variables are recommended), valid data collection procedures, and appropriate statistical procedures for data analysis, all of which serve to establish internal validity. The analysis of program effects by subgroup within the sample (i.e., gender, ethnicity) is also recommended. Finally, the Committee requires that all trials demonstrate consistent positive effects on the outcomes of interest, without serious iatrogenic effects, and that researchers conduct at least one long-term follow-up to establish whether effects are maintained over long periods of time; the Committee recommends that follow-ups be at least 6 months after the conclusion of the program, but many studies cited in this book evaluate program effects many years later.

Once a program has been found to be efficacious, additional work must be done to establish that the program is *effective*. The leap from efficacious to effective requires that a program be implementable in community settings using delivery personnel that are not part of the core program development staff, so that findings more closely resemble the degree to which a program can be expected to produce effects under less controlled conditions. This sort of real-world demonstration is the first step in taking the program to scale. To be effective, a program must have a clear theory regarding its causal mechanism(s) and, ideally, this theory should be tested by means of mediational analysis, in which the hypothesized program processes are explicitly evaluated for their ability to transmit program effects. Programs must also be sufficiently manualized and supported by appropriate training and technical support to enable third parties to deliver the program, and must have established and tested procedures to measure the fidelity of program delivery and the engagement of the target audience. In addition, program effects must be demonstrated to be "practically significant" rather than just "statistically significant", which implies that effects (often measured as mean differences) are large enough to warrant the investment of time and money to implement the program.

Finally, a program that is both efficacious and effective can be deemed to be *ready for dissemination* if clear evidence exists regarding its ability to be implemented with a high degree of fidelity and with similar effect sizes across multiple trials in real-world settings. The program developer must provide an infrastructure for adequately managing and supporting the training of large numbers of implementation staff, including provisions for technical assistance when needed, and cost information must be made available to potential implementers, including a list of conditions and resources needed to support the long-term sustainability of the program. Finally, program developers must provide tools for monitoring of program outcomes to enable precise evaluation of program success and must provide feedback to the implementing staff on areas needing improvement.

Exploration of Programs Processes

In light of the SPR Standards Committee criteria for program effectiveness, which call for program developers to empirically evaluate program-level causal models, we can point to some notable weaknesses in the family-based prevention literature that deserve the attention of scientists and grantmakers. First, the research that summarizes the recent findings from the field has often been based upon conventional narrative reviews of the literature. Such reviews can be useful in terms of providing an overall status of the field and identifying emerging trends; however, since these reviews lack an empirical basis, they cannot provide an objective, quantifiable evaluation of program effectiveness while controlling for factors that can influence results, such as study design, sample demographics, attrition, and measurement tools. Further, since narrative reviews are inherently subjective, it can be difficult to determine the degree to which the conclusions reflect the inherent biases of the author(s).

There is also a lack of research that clarifies *why* family-based prevention programs have been successful. Although programs generally specify the theoretical foundations from which they were developed, few have explored the pathways through which they exert effects on child or youth behavior or family functioning. Indeed, Liddle (2004) has noted that although family-based programs have demonstrated favorable outcomes, we have a limited understanding of how these outcomes are achieved, and he called for more research on the exact "mechanisms of action" (p. 83). More recently, Sandler, Schoenfelder, Wolchik, and MacKinnon (2011) reviewed the literature on family-based programs and noted that only a few studies have examined the processes by which effects are achieved. Although there are some exceptions (e.g., Caruthers, Van Ryzin, & Dishion, 2014; Forgatch, Patterson, Degarmo, & Beldavs, 2009; Van Ryzin & Dishion, 2012), most family-based prevention programs lack a systematic program of research in which program processes are explored. In an era of increasing scarcity of resources, there is a critical need to more closely examine existing family-based programs to identify the most effective program components (Westen, Novotny, & Thompson-Brenner, 2004), which would enable programs to be streamlined and more precisely targeted to specific populations.

This issue is particularly salient given that recent research has questioned whether family-based factors exert similar effects across the entirety of adolescence. For example, using a longitudinal data set, Van Ryzin et al. (2012) found that parental monitoring in middle school exerted significant direct effects on substance use, but that monitoring had no direct effects on substance use in high school or early adulthood once peer influences were controlled; in contrast, parent–youth relationships were more salient to substance use in high school than in middle school. There also exists evidence of differential effectiveness of parenting constructs between genders; for example, monitoring has been found to be more effective at preventing substance use among males than females (Griffin et al., 2000). Indeed, Lochman and van den Steenhoven (2002) call for researchers to consider whether family-based programs "should address different parenting skills at different developmental periods" (p. 100); the authors suggest that programs may want to focus on disciplinary skills during childhood, and monitoring and communication during adolescence. However, before the field will consider such a proposal, evidence must be found that attests to the differential impact of family processes on child behavior across genders and at different developmental periods.

Some notable work has been done in the effort to streamline and optimize program composition and delivery. For example, Miller and Hendrie (2009) found in their cost-benefit analysis that particularly strong programs for teen drug prevention are those that are designed to strengthen bonds to family, school, and community, and facilitate participant development of skills, rather than just educating participants on the dangers of substance abuse. In addition, research suggests that family skills training, including interactive training such as role playing, group discussion, and homework assignments, is more effective than reading and lecturing (Kumpfer & Alvarado, 2003). The importance of family practice time was also confirmed by a CDC meta-analysis, which found that prevention programs including role playing were more successful because the skills became more natural and generalizable (Kaminski et al., 2008). However, although these findings are important and useful to the field, much work remains to be done.

To that end, we have undertaken a meta-analysis project in which we summarize the literature on family-based programs for the prevention of adolescent substance abuse (Van Ryzin et al., forthcoming). By applying meta-analytic techniques to this field of research, we can combine findings across studies, generate greater statistical power, and obtain results less affected by specific biases inherent in any given study. In addition, we have moved beyond the examination of complete treatment packages to focus our attention on program components (i.e., themes or topics). Our plan is to use the amount of time spent on each component to predict effect sizes on measures of adolescent substance use in an attempt to discern the components that are most consistently associated with larger effects. From a statistical point of view, we are testing whether variation in program components represents a source of variability in study outcomes (Miller & Pollock, 1994) when controlling for study factors such as research design and sample demographics. This approach is based upon that taken by Kaminski and colleagues (2008), who conducted a meta-analysis of family-based programs for behavioral problems in children. In their study, the authors moved beyond an examination of complete programs to evaluate program strategies and processes of change. Characteristics of program content and delivery method were used to predict effect sizes on measures of parenting and children's behavior, and their findings added significantly to our understanding of family-based programs for young children. In our project, we have applied this approach to substance use prevention research in adolescence, and have extended it by coding individual program components in terms of the amount of time spent on each by the various family-based programs, which can then be combined across programs and used to predict program effects.

The core of our work is the coding system by which we have decomposed and distilled each prevention program (Van Ryzin & Fosco, 2014). Our coding system includes 10 separate codes, each corresponding to a unique aspect of family-based prevention programs (see Table 1.1). For each program, we captured the amount of time spent on each code in terms of youth-only, parent-only, and whole-family time. We contend that this system enables us to capture systematic variance among different family-based prevention programs that

TABLE 1.1 Family-Based Program Coding System

Code	Description
1. Parental Monitoring and Behavior Management	Training (generally targeting parents) that develops skills for effective monitoring and management of child behavior.
2. Fostering School Success	Behavior that relates specifically to school, which includes parental actions aimed at fostering the family's involvement with school as well as youth actions that contribute to increased success in school, such as being productive and efficient with their time.
3. Positive Family Relationships	Training, activities, and experiences that are designed to promote a warm, friendly, engaged relationship between parents and youth, including skills related to emotional closeness, sharing, listening, and disclosure.
4. Substance Use Knowledge, Attitudes, and Values	Information and training that helps parents and youth to understand the facts regarding substance use and to clarify attitudes and values regarding substance use.
5. Self-Regulation and Stress Management	Training that enables parents and youth to cope with stress and anger.
6. Problem Solving	Training that assists parents and their youth with resolving ongoing problems and sources of conflict. This entails facilitating conversations about problems where all sides contribute their own point of view and an agreement is reached that is equitable to all sides.
7. Resisting Peer Risk	The development of skills and values that help youth to resist peer pressure to get involved in risky situations or engage in risky behavior. For parents, this code includes information and skills related to supporting their teen in avoiding or dealing with risky situations.
8. Psycho-Education	Information and training that provides parents with insight into biological, cognitive, and social development during childhood and/or adolescence.
9. Ethnic Identity	Activities designed to develop an awareness of or pride in one's ethnic identity. This also includes development of skills for dealing with racial discrimination.
10. Future Orientation	Envisioning dreams for the future and setting long-term goals related to these dreams. This includes youth working with their own goals, parents thinking about goals for their youth and how to help youth attain them, and parents supporting and encouraging youth with their own goals.

14 Mark J. Van Ryzin and Gregory M. Fosco

could potentially explain some of the variance in program outcomes that has been found in previous meta-analyses (e.g., Farrington & Welsh, 2003; Smit, Verdurmen, Monshouwer, & Smit, 2008). The codes in Table 1.1 correspond to the types of activities, training, and information that are typically provided as part of family-based prevention programs. We have found the system to be reliable, consistently generating high inter-rater reliability (> .90) across a variety of different types of family-based programs. We have also found that, in our sample (which encompasses many of the programs described in this book, as well as others from the field), more time is spent on Parental Monitoring and Behavior Management (*Median* = 175.5 minutes) and Problem Solving (*Median* = 96.0 minutes) than other areas, potentially reflecting the influence of Gerald Patterson and his colleagues and their parent training approach. At the same time however, the third-highest code in terms of time spent is Positive Family Relationships (*Median* = 82.5 minutes), suggesting that programs in the field of family-based prevention have grown and diversified to encompass theories of family relationships and family systems (for an in-depth discussion of this issue, see the section in this chapter entitled Family Focus). We found more evidence for this diversification when we conducted a latent profile analysis using the results of our coding; we found that no significant patterns emerged, suggesting that our sample of programs was homogeneous in terms of content, with no significant subgroups corresponding to specific theories or schools of thought. Overall, we are hopeful that our meta-analysis will provide not only a deeper understanding of how family-based programs work to prevent adolescent substance use, but also lay the groundwork for further systematic exploration of program processes in the field.

Conclusion

The field of family-based prevention has clearly achieved many of the goals that its early pioneers intended. There exist today a plethora of family-based programs, demonstrated to be effective through rigorous research, that can address a wide range of behavioral and emotional problems across many key developmental periods. At the same time, it is clear that much work remains to be done in terms of exploring program processes, more thoroughly integrating a whole-family approach, and exploring the biological, behavioral, and cultural conditions under which programs are most effective. We hope that this book serves as an important signpost signifying the noteworthy achievements of the field to date, as well as an arrow pointing the field toward significant growth in the future.

References

Ainsworth, M. D. S. (1989). Attachments beyond infancy. *American Psychologist, 44,* 709–716.

Family-Based Approaches to Prevention **15**

Ainsworth, M., Bell, S., & Stayton, D. (1974). Infant–mother attachment and social development: "Socialization" as a product of reciprocal responsiveness to signals. In M. Richards (Ed.), *The integration of a child into a social world* (pp. 99–135). London: Cambridge University Press.

American Psychological Association Task Force on Psychological Intervention Guidelines (1995). *Template for developing guidelines: Interventions for mental disorders and psychosocial aspects of physical disorders.* Washington, DC: American Psychological Association.

Ary, D.V., Duncan, T. E., Biglan, A., Metzler, C. W., Noell, J. W., & Smolkowski, K. (1999). Development of adolescent problem behavior. *Journal of Abnormal Child Psychology, 27*(2), 141–150.

Bakermans-Kranenburg, M. J., Van Ijzendoorn, M. H., & Juffer, F. (2003). Less is more: Meta-analyses of sensitivity and attachment interventions in early childhood. *Psychological Bulletin, 129*(2), 195–215.

Beach, S. R., Kogan, S. M., Brody, G. H., Chen, Y. F., Lei, M. K., & Murry, V. M. (2008). Change in caregiver depression as a function of the Strong African American Families Program. *Journal of Family Psychology, 22*(2), 241.

Biglan, A., Flay, B. R., Embry, D. D., & Sandler, I. N. (2012). The critical role of nurturing environments for promoting human well-being. *American Psychologist, 67*(4), 257–271.

Brestan, E. V., & Eyberg, S. M. (1998). Effective psychosocial treatments of conduct-disordered children and adolescents: 29 years, 82 studies, and 5,272 kids. *Journal of Clinical Child Psychology, 27*, 180–189.

Bretherton, I. (2005). In pursuit of the internal working model construct and its relevance to attachment relationships. In K. E. Grossmann, K. Grossmann, & E. Waters (Eds.), *Attachment from infancy to adulthood: The major longitudinal studies* (pp. 13–47). New York: Guilford.

Brody, G. H., Chen, Y.-f., Kogan, S. M., Murry, V. M., & Brown, A. C. (2010). Long-term effects of the Strong African American Families program on youths' alcohol use. *Journal of Consulting and Clinical Psychology, 78*(2), 281–285.

Brody, G. H., Chen, Y.-f., Kogan, S. M., Yu, T., Molgaard, V. K., DiClemente, R. J., & Wingood, G. M. (2012). Family-centered program to prevent substance use, conduct problems, and depressive symptoms in Black adolescents. *Pediatrics, 129*(1), 108–115.

Brook, J., McDonald, T. P., & Yan, Y. (2012). An analysis of the impact of the Strengthening Families Program on family reunification in child welfare. *Children and Youth Services Review, 34*, 691–695.

Buck, K. A., & Dix, T. (2014). Parenting and naturally occurring declines in the antisocial behavior of children and adolescents: A process model. *Journal of Family Theory & Review, 6*(3), 257–277.

Caruthers, A. S., Van Ryzin, M. J., & Dishion, T. J. (2014). Preventing high-risk sexual behavior in early adulthood with family interventions in adolescence: Outcomes and developmental processes. *Prevention Science, 15*, 59–69.

Chambless, D. L., & Hollon, S. D. (1998). Defining empirically supported therapies. *Journal of Consulting and Clinical Psychology, 66*, 7–18.

Cox, M. J., & Paley, B. (1997). Families as systems. *Annual Review of Psychology, 48*(1), 243–267.

Cummings, E. M., & Cicchetti, D. (1990). Toward a transactional model of relations between attachment and depression. In M. T. Greenberg & D. Cicchetti (Eds.), *Attachment in the preschool years: Theory, research, and intervention* (pp. 339–372). Chicago, IL: University of Chicago Press.

Diamond, G. S., Wintersteen, M. B., Brown, G. K., Diamond, G. M., Gallop, R., Shelef, K., & Levy, S. (2010). Attachment-based family therapy for adolescents with suicidal ideation: A randomized controlled trial. *Journal of the American Academy of Child & Adolescent Psychiatry*, *49*(2), 122–131.

Dishion, T. J., & McMahon, R. J. (1998). Parental monitoring and the prevention of child and adolescent problem behavior: A conceptual and empirical formulation. *Clinical Child and Family Psychology Review*, *1*, 61–75.

Dishion, T. J., Nelson, S. E., & Bullock, B. M. (2004). Premature adolescent autonomy: Parent disengagement and deviant peer process in the amplification of problem behavior. *Journal of Adolescence*, *27*(5), 515–530.

Dishion, T. J., & Patterson, G. R. (2006). The development and ecology of antisocial behavior in children and adolescents. In D. Cicchetti & D. J. Cohen (Eds.), *Developmental psychopathology, Vol. 3: Risk, disorder, and adaptation* (pp. 503–541). New York: Wiley.

Dishion, T. J., Patterson, G. R., & Kavanagh, K. (1992). An experimental test of the coercion model: Linking theory, measurement, and intervention. In J. McCord & R. Trembley (Eds.), *The interaction of theory and practice: Experimental studies of interventions* (pp. 253–282). New York: Guilford.

Dishion, T. J., Patterson, G. R., Stoolmiller, M., & Skinner, M. L. (1991). Family, school, and behavioral antecedents to early adolescent involvement with antisocial peers. *Developmental Psychology*, *27*, 172–180.

Duncan, S. C., Duncan, T. E., Biglan, A., & Ary, D. (1998). Contributions of the social context to the development of adolescent substance use: A multivariate latent growth modeling approach. *Drug and Alcohol Dependence*, *50*, 57–71.

Dusenbury, L. (2000). Family-based drug abuse prevention programs: A review. *Journal of Primary Prevention*, *20*, 337–352.

Egeland, B. (2004). Attachment-based intervention and prevention programs for young children. *Encyclopedia on Early Childhood Development* [online]. Montreal, Quebec: Centre of Excellence for Early Childhood Development, 1–7.

Elicker, J., Englund, M., & Sroufe, L. A. (1992). Predicting peer competence and peer relationships in childhood from early parent–child relationships. In R. D. Parke & G. W. Ladd (Eds.), *Family-peer relationships: Modes of linkage* (pp. 77–106). Hillsdale, NJ: Erlbaum.

Erel, O., & Burman, B. (1995). Interrelatedness of marital relations and parent–child relations: A meta-analytic review. *Psychological Bulletin*, *118*(1), 108–132.

Farrington, D. P., & Welsh, B. C. (2003). Family-based prevention of offending: A meta-analysis. *Australian & New Zealand Journal of Criminology*, *36*, 127–151.

Flay, B. R., Biglan, A., Boruch, R. F., Castro, F. G., Gottfredson, D., Kellam, S., et al. (2005). Standards of evidence: Criteria for efficacy, effectiveness and dissemination. *Prevention Science*, *6*, 151–175.

Forgatch, M. S., Patterson, G. R., Degarmo, D. S., & Beldavs, Z. G. (2009). Testing the Oregon delinquency model with 9-year follow-up of the Oregon Divorce Study. *Development and Psychopathology*, *21*, 637–660.

Fosco, G. M., Caruthers, A. S., & Dishion, T. J. (2012). A six-year predictive test of adolescent family relationship quality and effortful control pathways to emerging adult social and emotional health. *Journal of Family Psychology*, *26*(4), 565.

Fosco, G. M., & Grych, J. H. (2013). Capturing the family context of emotion regulation: A family systems model comparison approach. *Journal of Family Issues*, *34*(4), 557–578.

Foxcroft, D. R., Ireland, D., Lister-Sharp, D. J., Lowe, G., & Breen, R. (2003). Longer-term primary prevention for alcohol misuse in young people: A systematic review. *Addiction, 98*, 397–411.

Foxcroft, D. R., & Tsertsvadze, A. (2012). Universal alcohol misuse prevention programmes for children and adolescents: Cochrane systematic reviews. *Perspectives in Public Health, 132*, 128–134.

Griffin, K. W., Botvin, G. J., Scheier, L. M., Diaz, T., & Miller, N. L. (2000). Parenting practices as predictors of substance use, delinquency, and aggression among urban minority youth: Moderating effects of family structure and gender. *Psychology of Addictive Behaviors, 14*, 174–184.

Hawkins, J. D., Catalano, R. F., & Miller, J. Y. (1992). Risk and protective factors for alcohol and other drug problems in adolescence and early adulthood: Implications for substance abuse prevention. *Psychological Bulletin, 112*, 64–105.

Institute of Medicine (1994). *Reducing risks for mental disorders: Frontiers for preventive intervention research.* Washington, DC: The National Academies Press.

Jacobsen, T., & Hofmann, V. (1997). Children's attachment representations: Longitudinal relations to school behavior and academic competency in middle childhood and adolescence. *Developmental Psychology, 33*(4), 703–710.

Kaminski, J. W., Valle, L. A., Filene, J. H., & Boyle, C. L. (2008). A meta-analytic review of components associated with parent training program effectiveness. *Journal of Abnormal Child Psychology, 36*, 567–589.

Kazdin, A. E. (1997). Parent management training: Evidence, outcomes, issues. *Journal of the American Academy of Child and Adolescent Psychiatry, 36*, 1349–1356.

Kitzmann, K. M., & Beech, B. M. (2006). Family-based interventions for pediatric obesity: Methodological and conceptual challenges from family psychology. *Journal of Family Psychology, 20*, 175–189.

Kitzman-Ulrich, H., Wilson, D. K., St. George, S. M., Lawman, H., Segal, M., & Fairchild, A. (2010). The integration of a family systems approach for understanding youth obesity, physical activity, and dietary programs. *Clinical Child and Family Psychology Review, 13*, 231–253.

Kochanska, G., Barry, R. A., Stellern, S. A., & O'Bleness, J. J. (2009). Early attachment organization moderates the parent–child mutually coercive pathway to children's antisocial conduct. *Child Development, 80*, 1288–1300.

Krishnakumar, A., & Buehler, C. (2000). Interparental conflict and parenting behaviors: A meta-analytic review. *Family Relations, 49*, 25–44.

Kumpfer, K. L., & Alvarado, R. (2003). Family-strengthening approaches for the prevention of youth problem behaviors. *American Psychologist, 58*, 457–465.

Kumpfer, K. L., Alvarado, R., & Whiteside, H. O. (2003). Family-based interventions for substance use and misuse prevention. *Substance Use & Misuse, 38*, 1759–1878.

Liddle, H. A. (2004). Family-based therapies for adolescent alcohol and drug use: Research contributions and future research needs. *Addiction, 99*, 76–92.

Lochman, J. E., & van den Steenhoven, A. (2002). Family-based approaches to substance abuse prevention. *Journal of Primary Prevention, 23*, 49–114.

Lundahl, B. W., Nimer, J., & Parsons, B. (2006). Preventing child abuse: A meta-analysis of parent training programs. *Research on Social Work Practice, 16*, 251–262.

Maughan, D. R., Christiansen, E., Jenson, W. R., Olympia, D., & Clark, E. (2005). Behavioral parent training as a treatment for externalizing behaviors and disruptive behavior disorders: A meta-analysis. *School Psychology Review, 34*, 267–286.

McEachern, A. D., Fosco, G. M., Dishion, T. J., Shaw, D. S., Wilson, M. N., & Gardner, F. (2013). Collateral benefits of the family check-up in early childhood: Primary caregivers' social support and relationship satisfaction. *Journal of Family Psychology, 27*, 271–281.

Miller, N., & Pollock, V. E. (1994). Meta-analytic synthesis for theory development. In H. M. Cooper & L.V. Hedges (Eds.), *The handbook of research synthesis* (pp. 457–484). New York: Russell Sage Foundation.

Miller, T. A., & Hendrie, D. (2009). *Substance abuse prevention: Dollars and cents: A cost-benefit analysis.* Center for Substance Abuse Prevention (CSAP), SAMHSA. DHHS Pub. No. 07-4298, Rockville, MD.

Minuchin, P. (1985). Families and individual development: Provocations from the field of family therapy. *Child Development*, 289–302.

Minuchin, S., & Fishman, H. C. (1981). *Techniques of family therapy.* Cambridge, MA: Harvard University Press.

Moss, E., & St-Laurent, D. (2001). Attachment at school age and academic performance. *Developmental Psychology, 37*(6), 863–874.

Nation, M., Crusto, C., Wandersman, A., Kumpfer, K. L., Seybolt, D., Morrissey-Kane, E., & Davino, K. (2003). What works in prevention: Principles of effective prevention programs. *American Psychologist, 58*(6–7), 449.

Nowak, C., & Heinrichs, N. (2008). A comprehensive meta-analysis of Triple P-Positive Parenting Program using hierarchical linear modeling: Effectiveness and moderating variables. *Clinical Child and Family Psychology Review, 11*, 114–144.

O'Connell, M. E., Boat, T., & Warner, K. E. (Eds.). (2009). *Preventing mental, emotional, and behavioral disorders among young people: Progress and possibilities.* Washington, DC: National Academies Press.

Patterson, G. R., Chamberlain, P., & Reid, J. B. (1982). A comparative evaluation of parent training procedures. *Behavior Therapy, 13*, 638–650.

Patterson, G. R., & Narrett, C. M. (1990). The development of a reliable and valid treatment program for aggressive young children. *International Journal of Mental Health, 19*(3), 19–26.

Patterson, G. R., Reid, J. B., & Dishion, T. J. (1992). *Antisocial boys* (Vol. 4). Eugene, OR: Castalia.

Petraitis, J., Flay, B. R., & Miller, T. Q. (1995). Reviewing theories of adolescent substance use: Organizing pieces in the puzzle. *Psychological Bulletin, 117*, 67–86.

Petrie, J., Bunn, F., & Byrne, G. (2007). Parenting programmes for preventing tobacco, alcohol or drugs misuse in children <18: A systematic review. *Health Education Research, 22*, 177–191.

Reid, J. B., Patterson, G. R., & Snyder, J. E. (2002). *Antisocial behavior in children and adolescents: A developmental analysis and model for intervention.* Washington, DC: American Psychological Association.

Reyno, S. M., & McGrath, P. J. (2006). Predictors of parent training efficacy for child externalizing behavior problems: A meta-analytic review. *Journal of Child Psychology and Psychiatry, 47*, 99–111.

Romer, D. (2003). Prospects for an integrated approach to adolescent risk reduction. In D. Romer (Ed.), *Reducing adolescent risk: Toward an integrated approach* (pp. 1–8). Thousand Oaks, CA: Sage.

Sanders, M. R., Kirby, J. N., Tellegen, C. L., & Day, J. J. (2013). Towards a public health approach to parenting support: A systematic review and meta-analysis of the Triple P-Positive Parenting Program. *Clinical Psychology Review, 34*, 337–357.

Sanders, M. R., Nicholson, J. M., & Floyd, F. J. (1997). Couples' relationships and children. In W. K. Halford and H. J. Markman, (Eds.), *Clinical handbook of marriage and couples interventions* (pp. 225–253). Chichester: Wiley.

Sandler, I. N., Schoenfelder, E. N., Wolchik, S. A., & MacKinnon, D. P. (2011). Long-term effects of programs that promote effective parenting: Impressive effects but uncertain processes. *Annual Review of Psychology, 62*, 299–329.

Scheirer, M. A., & Dearing, J. W. (2011). An agenda for research on the sustainability of public health programs. *American Journal of Public Health, 101*, 2059–2067.

Shadish, W. R., Cook, T. D., & Campbell, D. T. (2002). *Experimental and quasi-experimental designs for generalized causal inference.* Independence, KY: Wadsworth Cengage Learning.

Smit, E., Verdurmen, J., Monshouwer, K., & Smit, F. (2008). Family interventions and their effect on adolescent alcohol use in general populations: A meta-analysis of randomized controlled trials. *Drug and Alcohol Dependence, 97*, 195–206.

Sroufe, L. A. (1988). The role of infant-caregiver attachment in development. In J. Belsky & T. Nezworski (Eds.), *Clinical implications of attachment* (pp. 18–38). Hillsdale, NJ: Erlbaum.

Sroufe, L. A., Egeland, B., & Carlson, E. A. (1999). One social world: The integrated development of parent–child and peer relationships. In W. A. Collins & B. Laursen (Eds.), *Relationships as developmental contexts: The Minnesota Symposium on Child Psychology* (Vol. 30, pp. 241–261). Mahwah, NJ: Erlbaum.

Sroufe, L. A., & Fleeson, J. (1986). Attachment and the construction of relationships. In W. Hartup & Z. Rubin (Eds.), *Relationships and development* (pp. 239–252). Hillsdale, NJ: Erlbaum.

Stanton, M. D., & Shadish W. R. (1996). Outcome, attrition, and family-couples treatment for drug abuse: A meta-analysis and review of the controlled, comparative studies. *Psychological Bulletin, 122*, 170–191.

Svensson, R. (2000). Risk factors for different dimensions of adolescent drug use. *Journal of Child and Adolescent Substance Abuse, 9*, 67–90.

Szapocznik, J., Rio, A., Murray, E., Cohen, R., Scopetta, M., Rivas-Vazquez, A., Hervis, O., Posada, V., & Kurtines, W. (1989). Structural family versus psychodynamic child therapy for problematic Hispanic boys. *Journal of Consulting and Clinical Psychology, 57*(5), 571–578.

United Nations Office on Drugs and Crime (UNODC, 2010). *Compilation of evidence-based family skills training programmes.* Vienna, Austria: United Nations Office of Drugs and Crime.

Vakalahi, H. F. (2001). Adolescent substance use and family-based risk and protective factors: A literature review. *Journal of Drug Education, 31*, 29–46.

Van Ryzin, M. J., & Dishion, T. J. (2012). The impact of a family-centered intervention on the ecology of adolescent antisocial behavior: Modeling developmental sequelae and trajectories during adolescence. *Development and Psychopathology, 24*, 1139–1155.

Van Ryzin, M. J., & Fosco, G. M. (2014). *The family-based prevention program coding system.* Unpublished manuscript, Oregon Social Learning Center, Eugene, Oregon.

Van Ryzin, M. J., Fosco, G. M., & Dishion, T. J. (2012). Family and peer predictors of substance use from early adolescence to early adulthood: An 11-year prospective analysis. *Addictive Behaviors, 37*, 1314–1324.

Van Ryzin, M. J., Roseth, C. R., Fosco, G. M., Lee, Y.-K., & Chen, I.-C. (forthcoming). *A component-based meta-analysis of family-based prevention programs for adolescent substance abuse.* Manuscript in preparation.

Westen, D., Novotny, C. M., & Thompson-Brenner, H. (2004). The empirical status of empirically supported psychotherapies: Assumptions, findings, and reporting in controlled clinical trials. *Psychological Bulletin, 130*, 631–663.

Wiltz, N. A., & Patterson, G. R. (1974). An evaluation of parent training procedures designed to alter inappropriate aggressive behavior of boys. *Behavior Therapy, 5*(2), 215–221.

Young, K. M., Northern, J. J., Lister, K. M., Drummond, J. A., & O'Brien, W. H. (2007). A meta-analysis of family-behavioral weight-loss treatment in children. *Clinical Psychology Review, 27*, 240–249.

PART I

Family-Based Prevention Programs Across Development

2

FAMILY FOUNDATIONS

Mark E. Feinberg and Marni L. Kan

Introduction

Although the family is the crucial proximal environment influencing early child development, achieving public health impact through universal, family-focused interventions has been difficult. The transition to parenthood is a critical phase in family development, fraught with strain and stress, and it can influence the course of family relationships and parent and child adjustment. Indicated and selected prevention programs targeting those families at elevated levels of risk during this phase have been developed, shown to be effective, and—in recent years—begun to be disseminated. The "public health paradox" is that the majority of new parents who experience relationship, adjustment, and mental health problems emerge from the lower- and moderate-risk strata that comprise the majority of the population (Rose, 1981). To date, no *universal* preventive programs designed to reach all parents expecting a first child have been tested in rigorous research, found to be effective, and disseminated widely.

Epidemiological data underscore a critical need for the diffusion of effective family interventions designed to reduce risk for child mental health and problem behaviors. Prevalence rates of youth mental health and problem behaviors— ranging from depression to substance use and violence to academic failure—are high (Carnegie Council on Adolescent Development, 1995; Spanier & Frank, 1998; Weissberg & Elias, 1993). Although genetic factors and extra-familial influences such as peer, school, and neighborhood factors may be important, it has long been known that familial processes are crucial in the early development of internalizing and externalizing behavior problems (Fosco & Grych, 2008; Offord, Boyle, & Racine, 1989; Tolan, Cromwell, & Brasswell, 1986) and in the development of competence and mental and behavioral health (Conger, Elder,

Lorenz, Simons, & Whitbeck, 1994; Hawkins, Catalano, & Miller, 1992; Mrazek & Haggerty, 1994; Resnick et al., 1997; Shedler & Block, 1990).

Early difficulties in parenting may lead to a negative developmental cascade. For example, one integrative model (Shaw & Bell, 1993) begins with the infant's general negative reaction to parent non-responsiveness in the attachment framework (Ainsworth, Bell, & Stayton, 1991; Sroufe, 1985; Stayton, Hogan, & Ainsworth, 1971), which leads to higher rates of child noncompliance. During the toddler period, parental difficulty in maintaining consistent limits and discipline may lead to the onset of coercive cycles (Patterson, 1982), which in turn may lead to generalized behavioral problems that impede positive relationships with peers and teachers, with negative implications for school performance. Children may also develop internalizing problems from a similar foundation of parental non-responsiveness, inconsistency, and harsh parenting behaviors. Given the high rate of child psychological and behavioral problems, and the importance of family factors early in life that have the potential to set off a negative cascade, we have focused on preventing such negative trajectories with modest preventive intervention dosage at the transition to parenthood.

Parenthood, with changes in roles, relations, routines, responsibilities, and identities (Levy-Shiff, Dimitrovsky, Shulman, & Har-Even, 1998), represents a paradigmatic life change. The Cowans have argued persuasively that the stresses and vulnerability of even "low-risk" couples have been underestimated; parents who are married, have good relationships, and are well-off in socio-economic terms can experience difficult strains as they enter parenthood and create an "emergent family system" (Cowan & Cowan, 2000; also see Belsky & Pensky, 1988). Evidence sometimes suggests that marital deterioration is similar across parents and non-parents (MacDermid, Huston, & McHale, 1990), although there is also evidence that deterioration is more precipitous and pervasive for parents (Cowan & Cowan, 1988; Kurdek, 1999; Lawrence, Rothman, Cobb, Rothman, & Bradbury, 2008; Lindahl, Malik, & Bradbury, 1997). Importantly, research suggests that the transition affects families in broadly different ways (Belsky & Hsieh, 1998). In a study of mothers over the first three years of parenthood, about 38% reported clinical depression at one to three of the five waves of data collection, and *an additional* 8% were clinically depressed at four or all five waves (NICHD Early Child Care Research Network, 1999). Problems in individual parent emotional health are probably reciprocally linked to the post-birth deterioration of couple relationship quality in many families (Kurdek, 1999; Shapiro, Gottman, & Carrere, 2000). Even if parents eventually recover good relationship quality and mental health, stressful family processes in these early years may affect children during sensitive developmental periods (Cowan & Cowan, 1992; Sollie & Miller, 1980; Wakschlag & Hans, 1999).

Theory and research suggest that the transition period is perhaps the best time to intervene because of parents' particular openness to change (Duvall, 1977; Elliott et al., 2000; Pryce, Martin, & Skuse, 1995) and the potential malleability of the newly developing family system. Building strong, positive, cohesive family relationships at the transition to parenthood can have long-term impact on family relations as well as children's developmental outcomes.

Need for universal family-focused prevention

Developing a range of preventive interventions across the spectrum of risk is a key goal of a public health approach to diseases, disorders, and health conditions (Mrazek, Haggerty, & United States Institute of Medicine, 1994). At the highest levels of risk, prevention can accompany clinical treatment interventions in order to prevent health problems from impacting a widening scope of areas of functioning and activity, as well as to limit recurrence of the problem. From a cost-benefit standpoint, given that high-risk individuals are quite likely to develop health conditions and problems, interventions for high-risk individuals and families can achieve cost effectiveness even if they take the form of intensive, high-dosage, high-cost approaches. For those at moderate risk, cost-benefit considerations lead to more moderate dosage and cost, and universal interventions that target the whole population (comprised largely of those at low risk) are most cost effective if the intensity and cost of the intervention is low.

Most of the existing, evidence-based preventive interventions for the transition to parenthood and early childhood consist of targeted approaches that focus on higher-risk families (e.g., Nurse Family Partnership®, The Incredible Years®). There are at least five important reasons for developing a *universal* framework for family-focused prevention: (1) the universal framework of the program will avoid the stigma often associated with parent training classes or therapeutic interventions; in fact, some programs include low-risk participants in order to avoid such stigmatization with the additional benefit that low-risk participants can model appropriate skills and behaviors; (2) a review of prevention strategy concludes that a universal program is an optimal first step, to be followed by referral to more intensive programs for non-responders (Offord, Kraemer, Kazdin, Jensen, & Harrington, 1998); (3) the family formation stage is stressful for nearly all parents, and reducing problems in low-risk as well as high-risk families should have positive effects for children, parents, and couple relations (Cowan & Cowan, 2000; Tolan, Quintana, & Gorman-Smith, 1998); (4) although some stability exists in pre/postpartum adjustment, predictive techniques would fail to account for at least half the variation over the transition, and thus determining families in need of intervention would not be successful (Tolan et al., 1998); (5) the absolute number of people in low-risk groups is generally large compared to high-risk groups, so despite the difference in probabilities of developing problems between the groups, the majority of individuals who develop problem behaviors emerge from low-risk groups (Offord et al., 1998).

The gap in universal family prevention at the transition to parenthood exists despite considerable federal resources spent on programs focusing on promoting healthy marriage and relationships over the past decade under the federal Healthy Marriage Initiative. This initiative was focused on couples at low to moderate income, a group typically associated with moderate to high levels of risk. A large, multi-site study known as Building Strong Families funded the adaptation of leading couple-relationship programs for low- and moderate-income couples at the transition to parenthood (Wood, Moore, Clarkwest, Killewald, & Monahan, 2012). The resulting manualized programs involved relatively high dosage, were supplemented by individual family caseworker support, and were costly to implement (the average implementation cost per family was $11,000). However, no overall effects were found for either intent-to-treat analyses or analyses limited to participants who received a minimum dosage of content. Some have pointed to moderately positive effects at one of the sites at post-test; however, given indications of iatrogenic effects at another site at post-test and yet another site at follow-up, as well as the overall cost of implementation, others have maintained that the positive effects at one site do not show promise (Hawkins et al., 2013; Johnson, 2012, 2013).

It is possible that beneficial program effects are difficult to obtain among lower income couples, and that programs targeting a broader socio-economic demographic may yield better outcomes. In fact, one of the earliest trials of a transition to parenthood program for couples does stand out as having been successful in helping couples navigate the transition to family life (Schulz et al., 2006). However, this early and innovative approach involved a large number of sessions, session content was somewhat based on group discussion with limited manualization of content, and groups were led by the program developers and graduate students. This model was not practical for dissemination and there have been no replications. Nonetheless, the success of that early effort paved the way for our own work, and we extend gratitude to the Cowans for their support and advice over the years.

Since the Cowans' work, a number of other studies have examined various programs aimed to support couples at the transition to parenthood. A meta-analysis of these studies showed that transition to parenthood programs in general showed some effects, although they were generally small (Pinquart & Teubert, 2010). In brief, there was no overall effect on couple adjustment; effects on couple communication and parenting were small at post-test, but were not significant at follow-up (at an average of one-year post-intervention across studies); and there was a small effect on parent mental health at post-test, which was large at follow-up (based on five studies). Moderator effects showed that programs of at least five sessions and those that included both pre- and post-natal components were generally stronger than shorter and more circumscribed programs.

Family Foundations

To address the aforementioned need for universal prevention programming with expectant parents, we created Family Foundations (FF). The key goal of

FF is to promote healthy family relationships and, through positive relationships, to promote child psychological and social well-being. More specifically, FF aims to promote healthy and cooperative coparenting relations as a foundation of positive couple romantic and parent–child relations. According to theory and our logic model (see Figure 2.1; Feinberg, 2002; Feinberg & Pettit, 2003), it is through positive coparenting that FF aims to reduce parental stress and depression, and enhance parents' confidence and patience. These positive effects on parents, couple relations, and parenting are expected to enhance children's sense of security, emotional health, self-regulatory ability, cooperation with parents, and positive relations with peers and teachers.

FF's focus on the coparenting dimension of the couple relationship is based on the view that coparenting is malleable, circumscribed, and exerts a causal influence on parenting and child outcomes (Feinberg, 2002). Indeed, research and theory indicate that coparenting is more closely linked to parenting and child outcomes than the overall couple relationship—especially early in childhood (Feinberg, Kan, & Hetherington, 2007; Frosch, Mangelsdorf, & McHale, 2000). Family systems theories suggest that the executive subsystem, which is composed of parents in their role as co-managers of family relationships and family members' behaviors, regulates family interactions and outcomes (Minuchin, 1974; Minuchin, 1985). Coparenting represents a bridge between the inter-parental subsystem and the parent–child subsystem, and addressing coparenting offers an opportunity to integrate prevention efforts that have traditionally focused separately on couple or parent–child relationships.

Part of the inspiration for focusing on coparenting relationship quality as a proximal intervention target relates to the abundant research on how couple relations, particularly conflict, affects children. Thirty years ago, researchers concluded that a strong familial predictor of child emotional and behavior problems was interparental discord (Emery & O'Leary, 1982; Hetherington, Cox, & Cox, 1982). In addition, the influence of couple relations on processes such as infant social referencing and attachment security emerges very early (Dickstein & Parke, 1988; Frosch et al., 2000; Vondra, Hommerding, & Shaw, 1999). Research over the past few decades has illuminated how hostile, dysregulated conflict between parents can disrupt calm, affectionate, competent parenting as well as child well-being (Erel & Burman, 1995; Whiteside & Becker, 2000). Further, couple conflict *concerning children*, which is a key dimension of coparenting, has been found to have particularly negative impact on children (Davies & Cummings, 1994).

A broad multidimensional model of coparenting underlies FF, which includes: (1) childrearing agreement, or the extent to which parents agree or disagree on discipline, children's emotional needs, educational standards, and other child-related topics; (2) division of duties, tasks, and responsibilities pertaining to child care, daily routines, and household tasks; (3) each parent's supportiveness versus undermining of each other's parenting competency, contributions, and decisions; and (4) management of family interactional

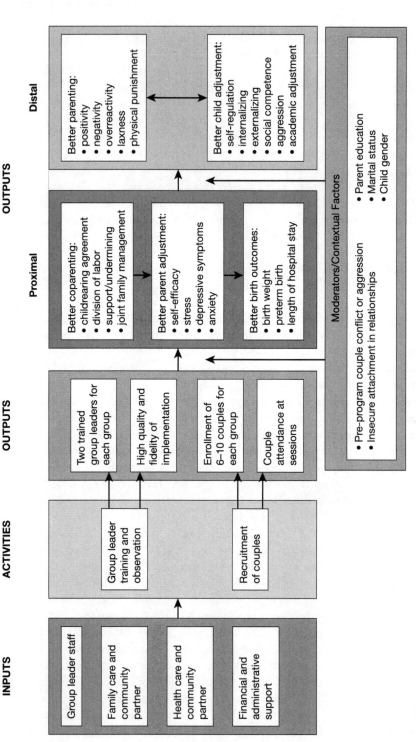

FIGURE 2.1 Logic Model

patterns, including conflict, coalitions, and balance. This conceptualization of coparenting lies at the center of an ecological model in which there are individual, family, and extrafamilial influences on coparenting, and the qualities of the coparenting relationship influence parenting and child adjustment, both directly and indirectly through parental adjustment (Feinberg, 2003). In fact, parental adjustment—including parental stress, efficacy, and depression—is likely a key mediator of the link between coparenting relations and parenting quality. Parents who do not feel supported but rather feel undermined by their partner have difficulty coordinating parenting roles, feel resentful about the division of labor, and likely experience elevated levels of negative affect and anger that undermine positive, sensitive, and attuned parenting.

FF is also based on an intervention framework that suggests that the transition to parenthood is an ideal time to intervene to enhance the coparenting relationship, given the newness of the coparenting relationship itself, the strains of this period for the family, and expectant and new parents' openness to education and support (Feinberg, 2002). Addressing coparenting during this period enables the intervention to integrate elements of couple- and parenting-focused programs in order to impact several domains of family functioning (i.e., parent adjustment, couple relationship quality, parenting, and child outcomes). A focus on coparenting also has the potential to reach couples who are not romantically involved, as coparenting relations remain important even if parents are no longer together. Finally, FF was developed with an eye toward successful implementation and dissemination, given that the ability of an intervention to impact public health in part depends on strong participant engagement and effective dissemination.

Implementation Structure

The original, standard version of FF targets couples in which partners are committed to raising the child together, are at least 18 years old, and are first-time parents (including couples in which a parent has another child with a different partner). Although the program can be implemented by a range of community, health, religious, corporate wellness, and other organizations, FF was originally developed in collaboration with childbirth educators to appeal to first-time, expectant parents and to ensure real-world viability. Indeed, the initial research focused on the program as delivered through childbirth education departments at local hospitals. This strategy was chosen because childbirth education is a non-stigmatizing educational framework and represents an existing institutional niche capable of facilitating dissemination.

FF was developed as a series of eight group sessions: four prenatal and four postnatal. Sessions last approximately two hours and take place weekly. Each group is designed to consist of 6–12 couples, and sessions are ideally led by a male–female team in order to offer a role model for each partner. The female leader is a childbirth educator. Group leaders receive three days of training, and ongoing observation of sessions facilitates regular supervision discussions. Sessions take place in hospitals, health center facilities, or other community facilities such as churches. If funding allows, a meal is provided at each evening session; child care is offered in a separate room during the postnatal classes. We have modified the original version of FF to integrate standard childbirth education into the class series; in this version, there is an additional prenatal session (thus a total of nine sessions overall), and the prenatal sessions are 2.5 to 3 hours in duration.

FF is a manualized program that utilizes a combination of didactic presentations, couple communication exercises, written worksheets, videotaped vignettes of other families, and group discussion. The program focuses on helping couples become aware of areas of coparental disagreement before parenthood and provides skills to manage disagreements through productive communication, problem solving, emotional self-management, and conflict management techniques. These topics are introduced and applied to issues such as dividing labor, facilitating emotional security, and providing stimulation. The program material prepares parents for the strains of the transition period by noting that many new parents experience a high level of stress and strain (see review in Sanders, Nicholson, & Floyd, 1997). The material on post-birth expectations introduces parents to the particular strains and difficulties they may experience after birth and the ways that these strains tend to affect coparenting. By providing information and video vignettes about other couples' experiences of parenthood, enhancing communication skills, and facilitating discussion of partner expectations for each other, FF aims to minimize the strains of the transition, increase coparental support, and decrease coparental undermining. Parenting strategies covered in the postnatal sessions include an understanding of infant temperament, fostering children's self-regulation, and promoting attachment security. The program also includes limited material on parent–child bonding, infant sleep, and nutrition, largely in the context of the coparenting relationship.

The unique aspect of FF with respect to most other similar programs is the focus on coparenting *per se*, rather than on the couple relationship, marriage promotion, father involvement, or parenting sensitivity. The bulk of the class material relates to enhancing the coparenting relationship, aligning parents' expectations of each other and of parenthood, and introducing positive childrearing strategies. The focus on coparenting—essentially asking couples to consider how they will work together supportively—permeates all material.

Research Evidence

Initial Efficacy Trial and Results

The first evidence for the efficacy of FF comes from a randomized trial involving two small U.S. cities embedded in rural areas. Adult couples who were living together (cohabiting or married) and expecting a first child were recruited through hospital childbirth education departments and other community and health provider channels. Consenting couples (N = 169) completed pretest questionnaires in a home visit before being randomized to control or intervention conditions. Post-test data, collected about six months after birth via mailed questionnaires, were followed by home visits at one and three years after birth. The prenatal and follow-up home visits included videotaped family interactions. Retention in the study was high; family participation rates ranged from 85% to 93% through three years after birth. Finally, at six years after birth, we attempted to re-contact the families for follow-up questionnaires with the parents and permission to obtain questionnaire ratings from the children's teachers. This follow-up wave was unfunded; without sufficient resources to find or compensate participants, and with the need to obtain first the cooperation of the family to contact the teacher and then the teacher as well, we were only able to recruit 79 of the children's teachers.

Eighty-two percent of couples were married at enrollment, and the majority of participants (91% of mothers and 90% of fathers) were non-Hispanic White. Median annual family income was $65,000 ($SD$ = $34,372), with a range of $2,500 to $162,500. Average educational attainment was 15.1 years for mothers (SD = 1.8) and 14.5 years for fathers (SD = 2.2), with a range of ninth grade to beyond college; 14.4% of mothers and 29.3% of fathers did not complete any postsecondary school education. Mean ages were 28.3 years (SD = 4.9) for mothers and 29.8 years (SD = 5.6) for fathers.

We examined program impacts at all follow-up waves on both proximal and distal targets in our logic model. With regard to proximal outcomes, intent-to-treat results indicated that compared to the control condition, the program enhanced coparental support and reduced coparental undermining through at least three years after birth, based on both parent report and video observation (Feinberg, Jones, Kan, & Goslin, 2010; Feinberg & Kan, 2008; Feinberg, Kan, & Goslin, 2009). Relative to the control condition, the program reduced parental stress and maternal depression and enhanced parent self-efficacy from post-test through three years after birth (Feinberg et al., 2010).

For distal outcomes, we found that parenting quality was better for those exposed to FF. At one year after birth, FF parents were rated as more warmly affectionate to children than control parents based on video observation; and, at three years, FF parents reported that they were less overreactive and less lax towards their child, and that they used less physical punishment than control parents (Feinberg et al., 2009). Moreover, children in families exposed to FF showed better adjustment than control children. At one year, FF children demonstrated greater capacity for self-soothing (by videotaped observation coding) than control children (Feinberg et al., 2009). At three years, FF children showed greater social competence, and boys showed fewer emotional and behavior problems relative to control children, according to parent report

(Feinberg et al., 2010). At age six, teachers reported that, compared to controls, FF children demonstrated fewer internalizing symptoms (d = .55), and boys demonstrated lower levels of externalizing behavior problems (d = .75; Feinberg, Jones, Roettger, Solmeyer, & Hostetler, 2014).

To further test the logic model, we examined the extent to which observed coparenting competition and positivity mediated program effects on child adjustment problems at age three (Solmeyer et al., 2014). In support of the model, coparenting competition significantly mediated effects of FF on adjustment for fathers with both sons and daughters and for mothers with sons. These effects accounted for between 39 and 55% of the intervention's impact on child adjustment problems.

Intervention effects are typically evaluated as we have just presented—as main effects on targeted outcomes. However, prevention can also be viewed as a supportive environmental factor that is intended to buffer the negative effects of risk factors on child outcomes. Indeed, our logic model includes several contextual factors and background characteristics that may moderate program effects. At six years after birth, we found that the program buffered children from the effects of a key risk factor: parents' level of couple conflict assessed during pregnancy. For academic adjustment, as well as internalizing and externalizing, children born to parents with higher levels of prenatal conflict benefited from the intervention more than those who were born to couples with lower levels of conflict. This is consistent with findings of prevention program impact in other areas in which the largest effects are often found for those at highest risk.

Moderation analyses also found differential effects of the program as a function of other parent characteristics and pre-program risk levels. At six-month follow-up, more positive effects of FF on maternal depression and coparenting were found for lower educated parents and for families with a father who reported higher levels of insecure attachment in close relationships (Feinberg & Kan, 2008). Effects from post-test through three years after birth on maternal depression were significant only for unmarried mothers; effects at age three on couple relationship satisfaction were significant only for parents of boys (Feinberg et al., 2010). We also found significant effects of FF on male-to-female partner aggression and mother-to-child aggression at child age three among couples with high levels of pre-program partner aggression (Kan & Feinberg, in press).

Effect sizes for significant outcomes ranged from 0.34 to 0.70 at six months, 0.28 to 0.60 at one year, and 0.16 to 0.81 at three-year follow-up. Notably, at age three, effects on parenting and child outcomes (distal outcomes in our logic model) appeared to be larger than effects on coparenting and parental adjustment (proximal outcomes). It may be that the intervention has an increasing impact over time, perhaps as a result of reducing family negativity that tends to cascade into more problematic situations over time as family members develop and reinforce negative attributions. It is also possible that the intervention's effects become stronger over time because of the compounding, mutually reinforcing effects across multiple interacting factors (e.g., parents' well-being, coparenting, parenting).

Since we launched the initial FF study, emerging research has accumulated documenting the links between maternal mental and emotional health, the physiological stress system, and poor birth outcomes such as low birth weight and preterm birth. Although not an original intervention target, given the impact of FF on mothers' stress and depression, we wondered if the program may also have an impact on pregnancy and childbirth outcomes. Analyses indicated that for mothers with medium to high levels of the stress hormone cortisol during pregnancy, assignment to FF program was linked to lower levels of preterm birth and greater birth weight, as well as a shorter average stay of the infant in the hospital after birth (Feinberg, Roettger, Jones, Paul, & Kan, 2014).

Second Randomized Trial of FF

A second randomized trial is underway, with a sample of 399 families. In this second trial, we have integrated the FF curriculum with standard childbirth education material. We hypothesize that the combination of material will provide an even higher level of impact than for FF delivered alone. Post-intervention data at child age 10 months has been collected and preliminary analyses support many of the effects found in the first trial. Although not measured in the first trial at post-test, family violence has been assessed in this second trial as an outcome. Preliminary results point to program impact on this important dimension of family life—both intimate partner violence and physically aggressive parenting behaviors to the infant. Preliminary analyses also point to beneficial impact on maternal depression and, for those at higher levels of risk, on some birth outcomes. Future reports will describe final results in more detail.

Implementation Fidelity

Several dimensions of implementation fidelity were measured in the first trial of FF, including adherence to the curriculum, group leader skill and connection with participants, and participant engagement and dosage. Raters from the project team completed observation forms for over 90% of intervention sessions. Group leaders completed feedback forms after each session and rated participant engagement at the end of each series of sessions (pre- and post-natal). Participants also completed feedback forms after every other session, and attendance logs were kept for each session. These fidelity materials are available to communities implementing the program.

Observer ratings indicated that FF was implemented as planned, with an average of 95% of curriculum content delivered. Leader ratings of participant

34 Mark E. Feinberg and Marni L. Kan

engagement averaged 3.6 for mothers and 3.5 for fathers on a 1 to 5 scale. Participants reported completing an average of 7.6 (mothers) and 7.3 (fathers) of the 14 homework assignments given across the eight sessions.

In the first trial, the average number of sessions couples attended was 5.5 (3.2 of four prenatal sessions, and 2.3 of four postnatal sessions). About two-thirds of couples attended five or more sessions overall (out of eight). Twelve percent of couples attended one or two sessions, and 3% of mothers and 5% of fathers attended no sessions. Couples almost always attended sessions together; only in a few cases did a parent attend a session when the partner was unavailable (e.g., because of work schedule or postpartum recovery).

Attendance data from the second trial indicate even stronger participant engagement. Couples attended an average of 6.5 of the nine classes; two-thirds of couples attended all five prenatal sessions. Couples also reported positive perceptions of the program on feedback questionnaires distributed after three of the sessions. On a 1 to 5 scale (with 5 indicating the most favorable response), average ratings of the perceived helpfulness and usefulness of the program averaged over 4.

Lessons for Implementation

During our randomized trials and dissemination efforts (through government-sponsored services in the United Kingdom, the Defense Department in the United States, and community agencies), we have learned several lessons regarding implementation.

First, the key to delivering high-quality program implementation is training and support. Although the Family Foundations manual is given positive feedback in terms of being clear, detailed, and easy to use, it is difficult to conduct high-fidelity sessions with an "out of the box" approach. We offer training for facilitators, and this training includes not only the content, but also the underlying approach taken by the program, which is key to maintaining fidelity—and maximizing impact—in implementation. Because the program involves significant group participation in the form of discussions and exercises, facilitators must respond continually to participant comments in ways that not only maintain engagement, but also promote the underlying themes and goals of the program. Further, a mechanical delivery of the program can be off-putting; the best facilitators are sufficiently familiar with the content such that they can respond to participant comments in ways that foreshadow future content. The best facilitators can also remind participants about their own goals and thoughts from earlier exercises and discussions, and can recall those participant comments in future sessions as ways to transition to new topics and provide linkages between earlier and later parts of the content. In order to weave participant comments into program delivery, facilitators must have a good command of the content and flow of the program. Such command requires both some degree of study of the curriculum, as well as experience in delivering the curriculum across multiple groups of couples.

Despite the clarity and structure of the manual, we find observation of new facilitators and feedback on their delivery of the sessions to be essential. Some trainees are highly experienced in leading groups, and some dislike the videotaped practice sessions we encourage them to engage in so that we can provide feedback. Nonetheless, we find it rare that a trainee is able to competently manage the flow of the curriculum, internalize the content and present it in an appealing and authentic manner, maintain connection with participants, manage group dynamics, handle the logistics of session materials, and coordinate with a co-facilitator all from the very beginning.

Second, the most variable aspect of program implementation is outreach and recruitment of parents. A program preparing couples to support each other in the family formation process is a novel idea for most expectant parents. And, despite some of the insecurities of pregnancy and knowledge of the risk of postpartum depression, many couples are excited about becoming parents and are unaware of the couple-level strains that parenthood can bring. In fact, the most positive reception to the idea of this program is expressed by the parents of the expectant couples—the grandparents—who are aware of the strains and difficulties that early family life can evoke.

Given that the program is novel and does not necessarily meet an already perceived need of expectant parents, finding ways to appeal to and engage expectant parents requires attention. For example, leaving pamphlets regarding the program in an ob/gyn office may not be a sufficient recruitment mechanism for a relatively unknown program. Instead, efforts to invite participation through letters, phone calls, and in-person contact during health care visits are helpful in achieving high levels of participation; reinforcing targeted recruitment through general community advertising (e.g., radio spots), newspaper articles, church newsletters, and fliers is also helpful. Moreover, recruitment messages should appeal to parents' goals of raising healthy, competent, successful children, as few expectant couples are sufficiently motivated to engage based on the theme of improving couple relationship quality and even coparenting *per se*. At this stage, expectant parents are most highly motivated by the well-being of their future child.

Adaptations of FF

We believe that there is a power in face-to-face interaction—and especially in the social support, modeling, and reinforcement that comes in group settings. However, many couples cannot be enticed to attend educational classes, whether because of work schedules, transportation issues (especially in rural areas), or simple preference. Thus, we have developed a DVD/ workbook version of the program (www.FamFound.net). In addition, we are developing an interactive, online version of the program for couples in which a partner is a member of the U.S. military reserve or a National Guard unit. These families are frequently geographically dispersed and thus do not have access to more centralized services offered to active duty personnel on military bases. Finally, we are currently disseminating FF for active-duty U.S. military personnel through a train-the-trainer model sponsored by the Department of Defense.

The focus on enhancing coparenting relations in our work is relevant for other populations, risk groups, and family configurations. For example, we are developing an enhanced version of the program for expectant couples at risk of future family violence. Our underlying hypothesis is that the enhanced material focused on violence prevention may be helpful, but the parents' own inherent motivations to provide the best upbringing for their children will be a strong motivation for adopting the perspectives and skills offered in the program. Through a focus on the importance of cooperative coparenting, we hope these at-risk couples will develop non-violent methods of communication and problem-solving that will reduce stress, provide mutual support, and enhance positive parenting.

From the beginning, we have considered coparenting to consist of the childrearing cooperation between any two adults involved in raising a child— including not just biological, step, or adoptive parents, but also potentially including grandparents, close friends, and non-parental romantic partners. This comprehensive definition has allowed us to broaden the scope of work. Thus, in a version of the FF program aimed at teen parents, issues of supportive involvement and interference by the teens' own parents (the new grandparents) becomes important. And, in a version of the program we are currently testing for parents involved in nurse home-visiting, the "father" may not always be the biological father.

Finally, in both the teen and home-visiting versions of the program, we hope that enhanced cooperative parenting relations will allow fathers to remain more engaged with their children even when romantic relationships between parents end (and the data indicates that romantic relationships among parents do frequently end, and this is particularly so among young and at-risk populations). Indeed, research from the Fragile Families study in the U.S., as well as other studies, indicate that young fathers are often involved early in their children's lives, but that difficulties in the relationship between the mother and father are linked to decreasing levels of involvement over time. By stressing the importance of cooperative coparenting for children, regardless of the state of the romantic relationship, we hope to support and increase the continuing positive involvement of fathers in children's lives. Such positive father involvement carries benefits for children's development, for mothers' stress and well-being, and for the fathers themselves.

Future Dissemination

As we continue to document the effects of Family Foundations, and to develop new versions for specific groups and populations, we are also exploring future dissemination possibilities. The key to disseminating Family Foundations, or one of the adapted versions for specific populations, will be the development of sustainable funding models. We envision four potential dissemination channels: preventive health care, government programs, corporate employers, and community initiatives.

The birth weight and maternal depression outcomes are particularly important in relation to the potential for health care financing. For example, health insurers, including public systems such as Medicaid and the military's TriCare, who recognize the health and financial benefits of effective prevention, may choose to cover program costs for couples.

Health and social service programs financed by state and federal governments—such as maternal and child health programs, family health initiatives, and relationship and father-involvement programs—may also sponsor dissemination of models like Family Foundations. For these potential government sponsors, reduced family violence, enhanced family relationship quality, and better child outcomes may be key goals.

Corporate employers may also choose to provide the program as a health and wellness offering for employees. In addition to the reduction in health care costs for covered employees and their children, reduction of stress, depression, family conflict, and child adjustment problems would all contribute to greater employee productivity and reduced absenteeism and turnover.

In the absence of large-scale dissemination through health insurers, government programs, or large employers, dissemination may depend on local community initiatives. Local health, social welfare, and child-focused coalitions may succeed in raising funds from a combination of sources (e.g., foundations, local fundraising, United Way, and other charitable giving brokers) in order to initiate program implementation in individual communities.

References

Ainsworth, M. D. S., Bell, S. M., & Stayton, D. J. (1991). Infant–mother attachment and social development: "Socialisation" as a product of reciprocal responsiveness to signals. In M. Woodhead & R. Carr (Eds.), *Becoming a person: Child development in social context, Vol. 1.* (pp. 30–55). London: Routledge.

Belsky, J., & Hsieh, K.-H. (1998). Patterns of marital change during the early childhood years: Parent personality, coparenting, and division-of-labor correlates. *Journal of Family Psychology, 12*(4), 511–528.

Belsky, J., & Pensky, E. (1988). Marital change across the transition to parenthood. *Marriage & Family Review, 12*(3–4), 133–156.

Carnegie Council on Adolescent Development. (1995). *Great transitions: Preparing adolescents for a new century.* New York: Carnegie Council of New York.

Conger, R. D., Elder, G. H., Jr., Lorenz, F. O., Simons, R. L., & Whitbeck, L. B. (Eds.). (1994). *Families in troubled times: Adapting to change in rural America*. Hawthorne, NY: Aldine de Gruyter.

Cowan, C. P., & Cowan, P. A. (1992). *When partners become parents: The big life change for couples*. New York: Basic Books.

Cowan, C. P., & Cowan, P. A. (2000). *When partners become parents: The big life change for couples*. Mahwah, NJ: Lawrence Erlbaum Associates.

Cowan, P. A., & Cowan, C. P. (1988). Changes in marriage during the transition to parenthood: Must we blame the baby? In G.Y. Michaels & W. A. Goldberg (Eds.), *The transition to parenthood: Current theory and research. Cambridge studies in social and emotional development* (pp. 114–154). New York: Cambridge University Press.

Davies, P. T., & Cummings, E. M. (1994). Marital conflict and child adjustment: An emotional security hypothesis. *Psychological Bulletin, 116*(3), 387–411.

Dickstein, S., & Parke, R. D. (1988). Social referencing in infancy: A glance at fathers and marriage. *Child Development, 59*(2), 506–511.

Duvall, E. C. (1977). *Marriage and Family Development*. Philadelphia, PA: Lippincott.

Elliott, S. A., Leverton, T. J., Sanjack, M., Turner, H., Cowmeadow, P., Hopkins, J., & Bushnell, D. (2000). Promoting mental health after childbirth: A controlled trial of primary prevention of postnatal depression. *British Journal of Clinical Psychology, 39*(3), 223–241.

Emery, R., & O'Leary, K. D. (1982). Children's perceptions of marital discord and behavior problems of boys and girls. *Journal of Abnormal Child Psychology, 10*, 11–24.

Erel, O., & Burman, B. (1995). Interrelatedness of marital relations and parent–child relations: A meta-analytic review. *Psychological Bulletin, 118*(1), 108–132.

Feinberg, M. E. (2002). Coparenting and the transition to parenthood: A framework for prevention. *Clinical Child & Family Psychology Review, 5*, 173–195.

Feinberg, M. E. (2003). The internal structure and ecological context of coparenting: A framework for research and intervention. *Parenting: Science and Practice, 3*, 95–132.

Feinberg, M. E., Jones, D. E., Kan, M. L., & Goslin, M. C. (2010). Effects of Family Foundations on parents and children: 3.5 years after baseline. *Journal of Family Psychology, 24*, 532–542.

Feinberg, M. E., Jones, D. E., Roettger, M. E., Solmeyer, A., & Hostetler, M. (2014). Long-term follow-up of a randomized trial of Family Foundations: Effects on children's emotional, behavioral, and school adjustment. *Journal of Family Psychology, 28*, 821–831.

Feinberg, M. E., & Kan, M. L. (2008). Establishing Family Foundations: Intervention effects on coparenting, parent/infant well-being, and parent–child relations. *Journal of Family Psychology, 22*(2), 253–263.

Feinberg, M. E., Kan, M. L., & Goslin, M. (2009). Enhancing coparenting, parenting, and child self-regulation: Effects of Family Foundations 1 year after birth. *Prevention Science, 10*, 276–285.

Feinberg, M. E., Kan, M. L., & Hetherington, E. M. (2007). The longitudinal influence of coparenting conflict on parental negativity and adolescent maladjustment. *Journal of Marriage and the Family, 69*, 687–702.

Feinberg, M. E., & Pettit, G. (2003). Promoting positive parenting. In T. Gullotta & M. Bloom (Eds.), *Encyclopedia of primary prevention*. New York: Kluwer Academic/ Plenum Press.

Feinberg, M. E., Roettger, M. E., Jones, D. E., Paul, I., & Kan, M. L. (2014). Effects of a psychosocial couple-based prevention program on adverse birth outcomes. *Maternal and Child Health Journal, 19*, 102–111.

Fosco, G. M., & Grych, J. H. (2008). Emotional, cognitive, and family systems mediators of children's adjustment to interparental conflict. *Journal of Family Psychology, 22*(6), 843–854.

Frosch, C. A., Mangelsdorf, S. C., & McHale, J. L. (2000). Marital behavior and the security of preschooler-parent attachment relationships. *Journal of Family Psychology, 14*, 144–161.

Hawkins, A. J., Stanley, S. M., Cowan, P. A., Fincham, F. D., Beach, S., Cowan, C. P., Rhoades, G. K., Markman, H. J., & Daire, A. P. (2013). A more optimistic perspective on government-supported marriage and relationship education programs for lower income couples. *American Psychologist, 68*(2), 110–111.

Hawkins, J. D., Catalano, R. F., & Miller, J. Y. (1992). Risk and protective factors for alcohol and other drug problems in adolescence and early adulthood: Implications for substance abuse prevention. *Psychological Bulletin, 112*(1), 64–105.

Hetherington, E. M., Cox, M., & Cox, R. (1982). Effects of divorce on parents and children. In M. E. Lamb (Ed.), *Nontraditional families*. Hillsdale, NJ: Erlbaum.

Johnson, M. D. (2012). Healthy marriage initiatives: On the need for empiricism in policy implementation. *American Psychologist, 67*, 296–308.

Johnson, M. D. (2013). Optimistic or quixotic? More data on marriage and relationship education programs for lower income couples. *American Psychologist, 68*, 111–112.

Kan, M. L., & Feinberg, M. E. (2014). Can a family-focused, transition-to-parenthood program prevent parent and partner aggression among young couples with young children? *Violence and Victims, 29*(6), 967–980.

Kurdek, L. A. (1999). The nature and predictors of the trajectory of change in marital quality for husbands and wives over the first 10 years of marriage. *Developmental Psychology, 35*(5), 1283–1296.

Lawrence, E., Rothman, A. D., Cobb, R. J., Rothman, M. T., & Bradbury, T. N. (2008). Marital satisfaction across the transition to parenthood. *Journal of Family Psychology, 22*(1), 41–50.

Levy-Shiff, R., Dimitrovsky, L., Shulman, S., & Har-Even, D. (1998). Cognitive appraisals, coping strategies, and support resources as correlates of parenting and infant development. *Developmental Psychology, 34*(6), 1417–1427.

Lindahl, K., Malik, N. M., & Bradbury, T. N. (1997). The developmental course of couples' relationships. In W. K. Halford & H. J. Markman (Eds.), *Clinical handbook of marriage and couples interventions.* New York: John Wiley.

MacDermid, S. M., Huston, T. L., & McHale, S. M. (1990). Changes in marriage associated with the transition to parenthood: Individual differences as a function of sex-role attitudes and changes in the division of household labor. *Journal of Marriage and the Family, 52*, 475–486.

Minuchin, P. (1985). Families and individual development: Provocations from the field of family therapy. *Child Development, 56*(2), 289–302.

Minuchin, S. (1974). *Families and family therapy.* Cambridge, MA: Harvard University Press.

Mrazek, P. J., & Haggerty, R. J. (1994). *Reducing risks for mental disorders: Frontiers for preventive intervention research* (Vol. xxvii). Washington, DC: National Academy Press.

NICHD Early Child Care Research Network. (1999). Chronicity of maternal depressive symptoms, maternal sensitivity, and child functioning at 36 months. *Developmental Psychology, 35*(5), 1297–1310.

Offord, D. R., Boyle, M. H., & Racine, Y. (1989). Ontario Child Health Study: Correlates of disorder. *Journal of the American Academy of Child & Adolescent Psychiatry, 28*(6), 856–860.

Offord, D. R., Kraemer, H. C., Kazdin, A. E., Jensen, P. S., & Harrington, R. (1998). Lowering the burden of suffering from child psychiatric disorder: Trade-offs among clinical, targeted, and universal interventions. *Journal of the American Academy of Child & Adolescent Psychiatry, 37*(7), 686–694.

Patterson, G. R. (1982). *Coercive family process*. Eugene, OR: Castalia.

Pinquart, M., & Teubert, D. (2010). Effects of parenting education with expectant and new parents: A meta-analysis. *Journal of Family Psychology, 24*(3), 316–327.

Pryce, C. R., Martin, R. D., & Skuse, D. (Eds.). (1995). *Motherhood in human and nonhuman primates: Biosocial determinants*. Basel, Switzerland: Karger.

Resnick, M. D., Bearman, P. S., Blum, R. W., Bauman, K. E., Harris, K. M., Jones, J., et al. (1997). Protecting adolescents from harm: Findings from the National Longitudinal Study on Adolescent Health. *Journal of American Medical Association, 278*(10), 823–832.

Rose, G. (1981). Strategy of prevention: Lessons from cardiovascular disease. *British Medical Journal (Clinical Research Ed.), 282*(6279), 1847–1851.

Schulz, M. S., Cowan, C. P., & Cowan, P. A. (2006). Promoting healthy beginnings: A randomized controlled trial of a preventive intervention to preserve marital quality during the transition to parenthood. *Journal of Consulting and Clinical Psychology, 74*, 20–31.

Shapiro, A. F., Gottman, J. M., & Carrere, S. (2000). The baby and the marriage: Identifying factors that buffer against decline in marital satisfaction after the first baby arrives. *Journal of Family Psychology, 14*(1), 59–70.

Shaw, D. S., & Bell, R. Q. (1993). Developmental theories of parental contributors to antisocial behavior. *Journal of Abnormal Child Psychology, 21*(5), 493–518.

Shedler, J., & Block, J. (1990). Adolescent drug use and psychological health: A longitudinal inquiry. *American Psychologist, 45*(5), 612–630.

Sollie, D. L., & Miller, B. C. (1980). The transition to parenthood as a critical time for building family strengths. In N. Stinnet, B. Chesses, J. DeFrain, & P. Kraus (Eds.), *Family strengths: Positive models of family life*. Lincoln, NE: University of Nebraska Press.

Solmeyer, A. R., Feinberg, M. E., Coffman, D. L., & Jones, D. E. (2014). The effects of the Family Foundations prevention program on coparenting and child adjustment: A mediation analysis. *Prevention Science, 15*(2), 213–223.

Spanier, C., & Frank, E. (1998). Maintenance interpersonal psychotherapy: A preventive treatment for depression. In J. C. Markowitz (Ed.), *Interpersonal psychotherapy* (pp. 67–98). Washington, DC: American Psychiatric Press.

Sroufe, L. A. (1985). Attachment classification from the perspective of infant–caregiver relationships and infant temperament. *Child Development, 56*, 1–14.

Stayton, D. J., Hogan, R., & Ainsworth, M. D. (1971). Infant obedience and maternal behavior: The origins of socialization reconsidered. *Child Development, 42*(4), 1057–1069.

Tolan, P. H., Cromwell, R. E., & Brasswell, M. (1986). Family therapy with delinquents: A critical review of the literature. *Family Process, 25*(4), 619–649.

Tolan, P. H., Quintana, E., & Gorman-Smith, D. (1998). Prevention approaches for families. In L. L'Abate (Ed.), *Family psychopathology: The relational roots of dysfunctional behavior* (pp. 379–400). New York: The Guilford Press.

Vondra, J., Hommerding, K. D., & Shaw, D. S. (1999). Stability and change in infant attachment in a low-income sample. In J. Vondra & D. Barnett (Eds.), *Atypical attachment in infancy and early childhood among children at developmental risk* (Vol. 64(3), pp. 119–209). Monographs of the Society for Research in Child Development.

Wakschlag, L. S., & Hans, S. L. (1999). Relation of maternal responsiveness during infancy to the development of behavior problems in high-risk youth. *Developmental Psychology, 35*, 569–579.

Weissberg, R. P., & Elias, M. J. (1993). Enhancing young people's social competence and health behavior: An important challenge for educators, scientists, policymakers, and funders. *Applied & Preventive Psychology, 2*(4), 179–190.

Whiteside, M. F., & Becker, B. J. (2000). Parental factors and the young child's postdivorce adjustment: A meta-analysis with implications for parenting arrangements. *Journal of Family Psychology, 14*(1), 5–26.

Wood, R. G., Moore, Q., Clarkwest, A., Killewald, A., & Monahan, S. (2012). *The long-term effects of building strong families: A relationship skills education program for unmarried parents*. Princeton, NJ: Mathematica Policy Research.

3

THE INCREDIBLE YEARS® SERIES

A Developmental Approach

Carolyn Webster-Stratton

Introduction

Rates of clinically significant behavioral and emotional problems are as high as 6–15% in children aged 3–12 years (Egger & Angold, 2006; Sawyer et al., 2000). These numbers are even higher for children from economically disadvantaged families (Webster-Stratton & Hammond, 1998).Young children with early-onset behavioral and emotional difficulties are at increased risk of developing severe adjustment difficulties, conduct disorders, school drop-out, violence, and substance abuse in adolescence and adulthood (Costello, Foley, & Angold, 2006; Egger & Angold, 2006). However, the good news is that research has consistently indicated that early intervention with evidence-based parent, teacher, and child programs can prevent and reduce the development of conduct problems, strengthen social and emotional competence and school readiness, and, in turn, prevent later development of secondary risk factors such as school underachievement and deviant peer groups (Kazdin & Weisz, 2010; Snyder, 2001).

Multiple risk factors contribute to young children's behavioral and emotional problems, including: ineffective parenting (e.g., harsh discipline, low parent involvement in school, neglect and low monitoring; Jaffee, Caspi, Moffitt, & Taylor, 2004); family risk factors (e.g., marital conflict, parental drug abuse, mental illness, and criminal behavior; Knutson, DeGarmo, Koeppl, & Reid, 2005); child biological and developmental risk factors (e.g., attention deficit hyperactivity disorders (ADHD), learning disabilities, and language delays); school risk factors (e.g., poor classroom management, high levels of classroom aggression, large class sizes, and poor school–home communication); and peer and community risk factors (e.g., poverty and gangs; Collins, Maccoby, Steinberg, Hetherington, & Bornstein, 2000). Effective interventions for preventing and reducing behavior problems ideally target multiple risk factors and are best offered as early as possible.

Need for Early Intervention

Extensive research over the past 30 years has consistently demonstrated the links between child, family, and school risk factors and the subsequent development of antisocial behaviors. Several prominent researchers (e.g., Dishion & Piehler, 2007; Dodge, 1993; Moffitt, 1993; Patterson, Reid, & Dishion, 1992; Patterson & Fisher, 2002) have helped coalesce this literature into strongly supported theories about the development of antisocial behaviors, which in combination with developmental theory have had some obvious implications for interventions. First, early intervention timed to key child developmental periods is critical. Treatment-outcome studies suggest that interventions for conduct disorders (CD) are of limited effect when offered in adolescence, after delinquent and aggressive behaviors are entrenched and secondary risk factors have developed, such as academic failure, school absence, substance abuse, and the formation of deviant peer groups (Dishion & Piehler, 2007; Offord & Bennet, 1994). Second, effective interventions need to target multiple risk factors across various settings. The increased treatment resistance in older CD probands results in part from delinquent behaviors becoming embedded in a broader array of reinforcement systems, including those at the family, school, peer group, neighborhood, and community levels (Lynam et al., 2000). Moreover, a recent Cochrane review by Furlong and colleagues (Furlong et al., 2010) showed that group-based parenting programs improve child behavior problems (whether measured independently or by parents) not only because they strengthen parenting skills but because they also improve parental mental health due to the support provided by the group. This suggests the added value of programs that reduce participant isolation and stigmatization and increase their support networks.

For these reasons, the Incredible Years® (IY) Series, a set of interlocking and comprehensive group training programs, was designed to prevent and treat behavior problems when they first begin (infancy–toddlerhood through middle childhood) and to intervene in multiple areas and settings through parent, teacher, and child training. Early intervention across multiple contexts can counteract malleable risk factors and strengthen protective factors, thereby helping to prevent a developmental trajectory toward increasingly aggressive and violent behaviors in later life. The model's hypothesis is that improving protective factors such as responsive and positive parent–teacher–child interactions and relationships as well as group support will lead to improved school readiness, emotion regulation, and social competence in young children. These short-term gains should, in turn, lead to increased academic achievement and reduced school drop-out, conduct disorders, and substance abuse problems in later life.

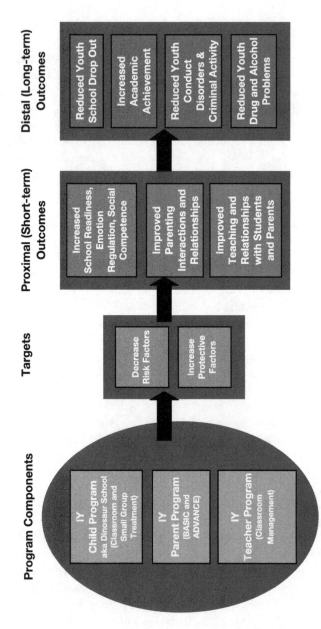

FIGURE 3.1 The Incredible Years® Parent, Child, and Teacher Programs. Source: www.incredibleyears.com

This chapter will focus on the underlying theoretical background for the IY Parent, Teacher, and Child Series. It will discuss four IY BASIC parent programs (baby, toddler, preschool, and school-age) that are considered "core" and a necessary component of the selective prevention model for young children. In addition it will discuss how the other IY adjunct parent, teacher, and child programs are added to address family risk factors and children's developmental issues as well as several IY programs designed for universal delivery. Information regarding IY program content and delivery methods will be briefly described, along with research evidence and ways to promote successful delivery of the programs. More information regarding specific program objectives can be found on the web site: http://incredibleyears.com/?s=objectives.

Theoretical Background for Incredible Years® (IY) Parent, Teacher, and Child Program Content and Methods

The main underlying theoretical background for the parent, teacher, and child programs includes:

- Cognitive social learning theory, and in particular Patterson's "coercion hypothesis" of negative reinforcement developing and maintaining deviant behavior (Patterson et al., 1992).
- Bandura's modeling and self-efficacy theories (Bandura, 1986).
- Piaget's developmental cognitive learning stages and interactive learning method (Piaget & Inhelder, 1962).
- Cognitive strategies for challenging angry, negative and depressive self-talk, and increasing parent self-esteem and self-confidence (Beck, 1979; D'Zurilla & Nezu, 1982; Jacobson & Margolin, 1979).
- Attachment and relationship theories (Ainsworth, 1974; Bowlby, 1980).

Program Content

Content goals for each individual parent, teacher, and child program will be described in more detail later in this chapter. However, it is important to note that all the IY programs include goals for promoting positive parent–teacher–child relationships and avoiding "coercion traps" by attending more to positive than negative child behavior, as first described by Patterson (Patterson, Reid, Jones, & Conger, 1975). The content taught in each program is adjusted according to children's cognitive developmental learning stage (Piaget & Inhelder, 1962). For example, program protocols for children aged 3–5 years focus more on coaching methods for enhancing social and emotional language and development, predictable routines, and school readiness skills. School-age protocols include incentives to motivate target behaviors, problem-solving training, and ways to support children's success in school. All the programs help

46 Carolyn Webster-Stratton

parents, teachers, and children learn how to challenge negative thoughts and replace them with more positive coping thoughts, positive imagery, and self-regulation strategies in order to build their self-confidence and self-efficacy (Bandura, 1989; Beck, 2005). All of the programs help build parent, teacher, or child support networks.

Program Methods

Bandura's (1977) cognitive social learning, modeling, and self-efficacy theories underlie the delivery method for all the IY programs. Advocates of video-based modeling techniques contend that observation of a model on video can support the learning of new skills. The IY programs make use of this teaching method by showing participants vignettes of parents, teachers, and children from different cultural backgrounds in a variety of home, school, and playground interactions. Some vignettes show effective interaction, while others represent less effective interactions. Trained group leaders use the vignettes to engage parti-cipants in focused group discussion, self-reflection, experiential practices, collaborative learning, and emotional support. During these discussions, group leaders help participants identify key "principles" from the vignettes, and apply them to their personal goals. Behavioral rehearsal is also a key component of the program; parents receive coaching while they practice new skills in scenarios that are tailored to their own goals and situations. Previous research indicates that participants tend to implement interventions with greater integrity when they are coached and given feedback on their use of the intervention strategies (Reinke, Stormont, Webster-Stratton, Newcomer, & Herman, 2012; Stormont, Smith, & Lewis, 2007). After learning and practicing new strategies in the group, participants make decisions about how they will apply the ideas to address their personal goals in their homes or classrooms.

All the IY programs use a group-based learning method that has several advantages. First, group intervention is more cost-effective than individual intervention. It also addresses important risk factors for children with behavior problems, including the family's isolation and stigmatization, the teacher's sense of frustration and blame, and children's feelings of loneliness or peer rejection. The group provides participants with a much needed support network. Another benefit of the group format is that it helps reduce resistance to the intervention through motivational interviewing principles (Miller & Rollnick, 2002) and use of the collective group wisdom. Rather than receiving information solely from an expert, participants are given the opportunity to interact with each other. When participants express beliefs counter to effective practices, the group leader draws on others to express other viewpoints. Through this discourse, the group leader is able to elicit change talk from the participants themselves, which makes it more likely they will follow through on intended changes. When group leaders position themselves in the "expert model" arguing for change, it is more likely to cement the attitudes of participants who are resistant to the intervention (see Miller & Rollnick, 2002). On the other hand, video vignettes allow group leaders to elicit behavioral principles from the participants' insights and serve as the stimulus for collaborative learning, practice exercises, and building self-efficacy.

Group leaders always operate within a collaborative context that is designed to ensure that the intervention is sensitive to individual cultural differences and personal values. The program is "tailored" to the individual needs and personal goals of each parent, teacher, or child, as well as to each child's personality, developmental ability, and behavior problems. The collaborative therapy process is also provided in a text for group leaders, titled *Collaborating with Parents to Reduce Children's Behavior Problems: A Book for Therapists Using the Incredible Years® Programs* (Webster-Stratton, 2012a).

Incredible Years® Core Parent Programs

The BASIC (core) parent training consists of four different curricula designed to fit the developmental stage of the child: Baby Program (4 weeks to 9 months), Toddler Program (1–3 years), Preschool Program (3–5 years), and School-Age Program (6–12 years). Each of these recently updated programs emphasizes developmentally appropriate parenting skills and includes age-appropriate video vignettes of culturally diverse families and children with varying temperaments and developmental issues. Trained and accredited IY group leaders/clinicians meet weekly for 2 hours with groups of 10–12 parents and use selected DVD vignettes to trigger discussions, problem solving, and practices. The number of weekly sessions ranges from 10 to 24 weeks, depending on which of the four curricula is selected and whether the group leader is following the prevention or high risk and treatment session protocols (see web site for protocols). The program protocol for high-risk populations such as socioeconomically disadvantaged families or those families whose children are diagnosed with Oppositional Defiant Disorder (ODD) or ADHD is longer than protocols for the prevention population. It is recommended that the group leader show at least the minimum number of recommended sessions for the population addressed and that they pace the learning according to family goals, needs, and progress. Frequently, several additional sessions are needed in order to complete the curriculum.

While participation in the group-based IY training program is highly recommended because of the support and learning provided by other parents, there is also a *Home-based Coaching Model* for each parenting program. These home-based sessions can be offered to parents who cannot attend groups, as make-up when parents miss a group session, or to supplement the group program for very high-risk families such as those referred by child welfare. Adding the individualized home-based program alongside the group delivery gives home coaches a chance to supplement group training with additional vignettes and to practice key skills in targeted parent–child interactions.

Goals of each the four programs are tailored specifically to the targeted age group and developmental stage of the child and include: (a) promoting parent competencies and strengthening families by increasing positive parenting, parent–child attachment, and parenting self-efficacy; (b) increasing parents' ability to use child-directed play interactions to coach children's social-emotional, academic, verbal, and persistence skills; (c) reducing critical and physically violent discipline and increasing proactive discipline strategies such as ignoring and redirecting, logical consequences, time-out to calm down, and problem solving; (d) increasing family support networks; and (e) strengthening home–school bonding and parents' involvement in school-related activities and connections with teachers.

The Incredible Years Parenting Pyramid® serves as the architectural plan for delivering content and is used to describe the program content structure. It helps parents conceptualize effective parenting tools and how these tools will help them achieve their goals. The bottom of the pyramid depicts parenting tools that are used liberally, as they form the foundation for children's emotional, social, and academic learning. The base of the pyramid includes tools such as positive parent attention, communication, and child-directed play interactions designed to build secure and trusting relationships. Parents also learn how to use specific academic, persistence, social, and emotional coaching tools to help children learn to self-regulate and manage their feelings, persist with learning despite obstacles, and develop friendships. One step further up the pyramid, parents are taught behavior-specific praise, incentive programs, and celebrations for use when goals are achieved. Next, parents discuss the use of predictable routines and household rules which scaffold children's exploratory behaviors and their drive for autonomy. The top half of the pyramid teaches parenting tools that are used more sparingly, to reduce specific targeted behaviors. These include proactive discipline tools such as ignoring inappropriate behaviors, distraction, and redirection. Finally, at the very top of the pyramid are more intrusive discipline tools such as time out to calm down and logical consequences. After the top of the pyramid is reached, the last part of the training focuses on how parents can come back down to the base of the pyramid. This refocuses parents on positive and proactive strategies for teaching children to problem solve, self-regulate, and manage conflict. At this point parents have all the necessary tools to navigate some of the challenging, but inevitable, aspects of their interactions with their children. A basic premise of the model is twofold: first, a positive relationship foundation must precede clear and predictable discipline strategies. This sequence of delivery of content is critical to the program's success. Second, attention to positive behavior, feelings, and cognitions should occur far more frequently than attention to negative behaviors, feelings, and cognitions. Tools from higher up on the pyramid only work when the positive foundation has been solidly constructed with secure scaffolding.

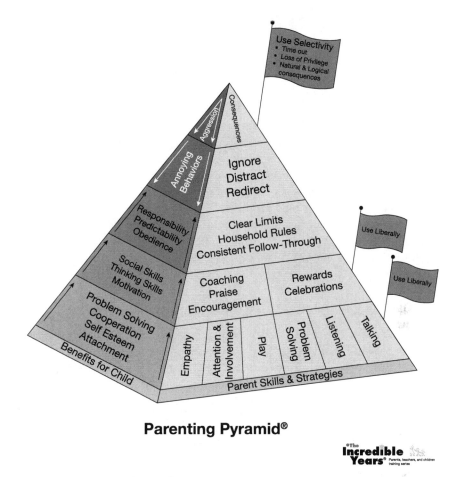

Parenting Pyramid®

FIGURE 3.2 Parenting Pyramid®. Source: www.incredibleyears.com

Incredible Years® Adjuncts to Parent Programs

In addition to the four core BASIC parenting programs, there are also supplemental or adjunct parenting programs which can be used in combination with BASIC for particular populations. The ADVANCE parenting program is offered after completion of the BASIC preschool or school-age programs (using selective and indicated protocols). The program is designed for selective high-risk populations such as child welfare-referred families and for indicated populations such as parents with children diagnosed with ODD and ADHD. This 10–12 week program focuses on parents' interpersonal risk factors such as anger and depression management, effective communication, ways to give and get support, problem solving between adults, and ways to teach children problem-solving skills. The content of both the BASIC and ADVANCE programs is also provided in the text that parents use for the preschool and school-age programs, titled *The Incredible Years: A Troubleshooting Guide for Parents* (Webster-Stratton, 2005; Webster-Stratton & Reid, 2006).

A second optional adjunct training is the *School Readiness Program* for children aged 3–4 years that was designed as a universal intervention to help parents support their children's preliteracy and interactive reading readiness skills. A third optional adjunct is the *Attentive Parenting Program* for children aged 2–8 years. This group program was also designed as a universal prevention program to teach all parents social, emotional, and persistence coaching, and ways to promote their children's reading skills, self-regulation skills, and problem-solving skills. The *Attentive Parenting Program* is not designed for parents of children with behavior problems, although can be used for this population after the BASIC Toddler or Preschool parenting program is completed and parents have learned the basic parenting tools. Finally, the most recent *Autism Program* is for parents of children on the autism spectrum or whose children have language delays. It can be used independently or in conjunction with the BASIC preschool program.

Incredible Years® Teacher Classroom Management Program

The Incredible Years® Teacher Classroom Management (IY-TCM) training program is a 6-day group-based program delivered monthly by accredited group leaders in small workshops (14–16 teachers) throughout the school year in order to provide teachers of children aged 3–8 years with ongoing support. There is also a program for teachers and day care providers of toddlers (1–3 years) called Incredible Beginnings. It is also recommended that trained IY coaches support teachers between workshops by visiting their classrooms, helping refine behavior plans, and addressing teacher goals. The goals of the teacher training program are: (a) improving teachers' classroom management skills, including proactive teaching approaches and effective discipline; (b) increasing teachers' use of academic, persistence, social, and emotional coaching with students; (c) strengthening teacher–student bonding; (d) increasing teachers' ability to teach social skills, anger management, and problem-solving skills in the classroom; (e) improving home–school collaboration, behavior planning, and parent–teacher bonding; and (f) building teachers' support networks. A complete and recently updated description of the content included in this curriculum is described in the book that teachers use for the course, titled *Incredible Teachers: Nurturing Children's Social, Emotional and Academic Competence* (Webster-Stratton, 2012b). More information about the training and delivery of the IY teacher program can be found elsewhere (Reinke et al., 2012; Webster-Stratton & Herman, 2010).

Incredible Years® Child Programs (Dinosaur Curricula)

There are two versions of the IY child program. In the universal prevention classroom version, teachers deliver 60+ social-emotional lessons and small group activities twice a week, with separate lesson plans for preschool to second grade. The second version is a therapeutic treatment group where accredited IY group leaders work with groups of 4–6 children in 2-hour weekly sessions. Children referred to this program may include those with externalizing or internalizing problems or developmental delays. The therapeutic version of the program can be offered in a mental health setting (often delivered at the same time as the BASIC parent program) or can be delivered as a pull-out program during the school day. Program content is delivered using a series of DVD programs (over 180 vignettes) that teach children feelings literacy, social skills, emotional self-regulation skills, the importance of following school rules, and problem solving. Large puppets are used to bring the material to life, and children are actively engaged in the material through role play, games, and activities. Organized to dovetail with the content of the parent training program, the program consists of seven main components: (1) Introduction and Rules; (2) Empathy and Emotion; (3) Problem Solving; (4) Anger Control; (5) Friendship Skills; (6) Communication Skills; and (7) School Skills. More information about the child programs can be found in other reviews (Webster-Stratton & Reid, 2003, 2004).

Evidence Supporting the Incredible Years® Parent Programs

Treatment and Indicated Populations

The efficacy of the IY BASIC parent treatment program for children (aged 2–8 years) diagnosed with ODD/CD has been demonstrated in eight published randomized control group trials (RCTs) by the program developer plus numerous replications by independent investigators (see review on web site http://incredibleyears.com/books/iy-training-series-book/).

In the early studies with indicated populations, the BASIC program was shown to improve parental confidence, increase positive parenting strategies, and reduce harsh and coercive discipline and child conduct problems compared to wait-list control groups (moderate to large effect sizes). The results were consistent for toddler, preschool, and school-age versions of the programs. The first series of RCTs evaluated the most effective training methods of bringing about parent behavior change. The video-based parent group discussion training approach (BASIC) was compared with the one-on-one personalized "bug in the ear" approach and a control group. Results indicated that the video-based discussion approach was as effective as the one-on-one parent–child training approach but far more cost-effective and had more sustained results at one-year follow-up (Webster-Stratton, 1984b). In the next study, treatment component analyses compared three training methods: group discussion alone without video led by a trained clinician, group discussion plus video with a trained clinician, self-administered video with no clinician, and a control group. Results indicated that the combination of group discussion, a trained clinician, and video modeling produced the most effective and lasting results (Webster-Stratton, Hollinsworth, & Kolpacoff, 1989; Webster-Stratton, Kolpacoff, & Hollinsworth, 1988). Next, the self-administered video program was compared with and without clinician consultation. Both programs showed significant improvements and there were few outcome differences, except that parent satisfaction was higher for the consultation condition (Webster-Stratton, 1992). Subsequently, a study was conducted to determine the added benefits of combining the ADVANCE program (focused on interpersonal parent problems such as depression and anger management) with the BASIC program (Webster-Stratton, 1994). Results indicated that the combined program had greater improvements in terms of parents' marital interactions and children's prosocial solution generation in comparison to the BASIC-only treatment condition families. As a result, the combined BASIC plus ADVANCE programs became the core treatment for parents of children diagnosed with ODD and/or ADHD, and has been used for treatment studies in the last two decades.

Other investigators have replicated the BASIC program's results with indicated and treatment populations in mental health clinics or doctors' offices with families of children diagnosed with conduct problems or high levels of behavior problems (Drugli & Larsson, 2006; Gardner, Burton, & Klimes, 2006; Lavigne et al., 2008; Perrin, Sheldrick, McMenamy, Henson, & Carter, 2014; Scott, Knapp, Henderson, & Maughan, 2001; Spaccarelli, Cotler, & Penman, 1992; Taylor, Schmidt, Pepler, & Hodgins, 1998). A recent meta-analytic review examined the IY parent training programs regarding disruptive and prosocial behavior in 50 studies where the IY intervention group was compared with a control or comparison group. Results were presented for treatment populations as well as indicated and selective prevention populations. Findings reported the program to be successful in improving child behavior in a diverse range of families, especially for children with the most severe problems, and the program was considered "well-established" (Menting, Orobio de Castro, & Matthys, 2013).

Several studies have also shown that IY treatment effects are durable 1–3 years post-treatment (Webster-Stratton, 1990). Two long-term follow-up studies evaluated families whose children were diagnosed with conduct problems and had received treatment with the IY parent program 8–12 years earlier. One study indicated that 75% of the teenagers were typically adjusted with minimal behavioral and emotional problems (Webster-Stratton, Rinaldi, & Reid, 2010). A recent study by an independent investigator reported that parents in the IY BASIC parent condition expressed greater emotional warmth and supervised their adolescents more closely than parents in the control condition who had received individualized "typical" psychotherapy offered at that time. Moreover, treatment children's reading ability was substantially improved in a standardized assessment compared with the "usual services" control condition children (Scott, Briskman, & O'Connor, 2014).

Selective Prevention Populations

Additionally, four RCTs have been conducted by the developer using the selective prevention version of the BASIC program with multiethnic, socioeconomically disadvantaged families in schools (Reid, Webster-Stratton, & Beauchaine, 2001; Webster-Stratton, 1998; Webster-Stratton, Reid, & Hammond, 2001a). Results showed that children whose mothers received the BASIC program showed fewer externalizing problems, better emotion regulation, and stronger parent–child bonding than mothers of control children. Mothers in the parent intervention group also showed more supportive and less coercive parenting than control mothers (Reid, Webster-Stratton, & Hammond, 2007).

At least six RCTs by independent investigators with selective prevention populations have found that the BASIC parenting program increases parents' use of positive and responsive attention (praise, coaching, descriptive commenting) and positive discipline strategies with their children, and reduces harsh, critical, and coercive discipline strategies (for review, see Webster-Stratton & Reid, 2010). These replications were "effectiveness" trials in applied mental health settings, schools, and doctors' clinical practices, not a university research clinic, and the IY group leaders were existing staff (nurses, social workers, and psychologists) at the centers or doctors' offices (Perrin et al., 2014). The program has also been found to be effective with diverse populations including those representing Latino, Asian, African American, and Caucasian background in the United States (Reid et al., 2001), and in other countries such as the United Kingdom, Ireland, Norway, Sweden, Holland, New Zealand, Wales, and Russia (Gardner et al., 2006; Hutchings et al., 2007; Larsson et al., 2009; Raaijmakers et al., 2008; Scott, Spender, Doolan, Jacobs, & Aspland, 2001; Scott et al., 2010). These findings illustrate the transportability of the BASIC parenting program to other cultures and countries.

To date, one RCT has been conducted by an independent investigator in Norway using a briefer version of the BASIC Preschool Program with a universal, non-high-risk population that has shown promising results (Reedtz, 2010). Another Norwegian study using the *Attentive Parenting Program* as a universal delivery is currently being evaluated. Finally, a pilot study in Wales evaluated the *School Readiness Program* as a universal program for parents in schools, with promising results (Pye, Bywater, & Hutchings, in preparation).

Evidence Supporting the Incredible Years® Child Programs as an Adjunct to IY Parent Programs

Indicated Prevention and Treatment Populations

Three RCTs have evaluated the effectiveness of combining the small-group child-training (CT) program with the parent training (PT) to reduce conduct problems and promote social and emotional competence in children diagnosed with ODD/CD (Webster-Stratton & Hammond, 1997; Webster-Stratton, Reid, & Hammond, 2004). Results indicated that children who received the CT-only condition showed greater improvements in problem-solving and conflict-management skills with peers compared to those in the PT-only condition (moderate to large effect sizes). On measures of parent and child behavior at home, the PT-only condition resulted in more positive parent–child behavioral interactions in comparison to interactions in the CT-only condition. One-year follow-up assessments indicated that all the changes noted immediately post-treatment were maintained over time. Moreover, child conduct problems at home had decreased over time. Analyses of the clinical significance of the results suggested that the combined CT + PT condition produced the most sustained improvements in child behavior at one-year follow-up. For this reason, the CT program was combined with the PT program in a recent study for children diagnosed with ADHD. Results replicated the earlier studies with children with ODD (Webster-Stratton, Reid, & Beauchaine, 2011). There has only been one RCT of the CT small-group program conducted by an independent investigator (Drugli & Larsson, 2006).

Selective Prevention Populations

One RCT has evaluated the classroom prevention version of the child program with Head Start families and primary grade classrooms in schools addressing economically disadvantaged populations. Matched schools were randomly assigned to intervention or control conditions. In the intervention classrooms, teachers offered the curriculum in biweekly sessions throughout the year. Results from multi-level models of reports and observations of 153 teachers and 1,768 students indicated that teachers used more positive management strategies and their students showed significant improvements in school readiness skills, emotional self-regulation, and social skills, and reductions in classroom behavior problems. Intervention teachers showed more positive involvement with parents than control teachers. Satisfaction with the program was high, regardless of the grade levels (Webster-Stratton, Reid, & Stoolmiller, 2008). A subsample of parents of indicated children (due to high levels of behavior problems by teacher or parent report) were selected and randomly offered either the combined parent program plus classroom intervention, classroom-only intervention, or control group. Mothers in the combined condition reported their children had fewer behavior problems and more emotional regulation than parents of children in the classroom-only or control conditions. Mothers in the combined condition had stronger mother–child bonding and were more supportive and less critical than the classroom-only or control conditions. Teachers reported that mothers in the combined condition were significantly more involved in school and their children had fewer behavior problems. This study indicates the added value of combining a social and emotional curriculum for students in the classroom with the IY parent program in schools (Reid et al., 2007).

Evidence Supporting Incredible Years® Teacher Classroom Management (IY-TCM) Program as an Adjunct to IY Parent Programs

The IY-TCM program has been evaluated in one treatment (Webster-Stratton et al., 2004) and two prevention RCTs (Webster-Stratton et al., 2001a; Webster-Stratton et al., 2008) and five RCTs by independent investigators (for review, see Webster-Stratton, 2012c). Research findings have shown that teachers who participated in the training used more proactive classroom management strategies, praised their students more, used fewer coercive or critical discipline strategies, and placed more focus on helping students to problem solve. Intervention classrooms were rated as having a more positive classroom atmosphere, higher levels of child social competence and school readiness skills, and lower levels of aggressive behavior (moderate to large effect sizes). In a study where BASIC parent alone treatment was compared with a treatment condition that combined BASIC with the IY-TCM teacher training program and with the combination of BASIC plus IY-TCM plus CT programs, the results indicated that combining IY-TCM and/or CT programs with BASIC parent training resulted in greater improvements in classroom behaviors as well as more positive parent involvement in their child's education. A recent study has replicated the benefits of the IY-TCM program alone for enhancing parent involvement in their children's education (Reinke et al., 2014).

Factors Affecting Intervention Outcomes

In addition to studying the specific training methods (group support vs. self-administered video vs. combined video plus group support) and the benefits of adding adjunct components to the IY Basic Parenting Series programs (advance parenting, teacher, and child training), over the past 30 years a number of studies have been conducted to determine mediators, moderators, and predictors of outcomes. For example, parental and familial factors such as life stress, depression, marital adjustment, socioeconomic status, parental age, ethnicity, and history of substance abuse (Beauchaine, Webster-Stratton, & Reid, 2005; Hartman, Stage, & Webster-Stratton, 2003; Reid et al., 2001; Webster-Stratton & Hammond, 1990), father involvement in treatment (Webster-Stratton, 1984a) and intergenerational family psychiatric history of antisocial behavior (Presnall, Webster-Stratton, & Constantino, 2014) have been analyzed in regard to treatment response. Additionally, child risk factors such as age, gender, psychiatric comorbidity, degree of externalizing problems, and comorbidity with attentional factors (Hartman et al., 2003; Webster-Stratton, 1996; Webster-Stratton, Reid, & Hammond, 2001b) and anxiety/depression (Beauchaine et al., 2005) as well as physiological measures of cardiac activity and reactivity (Beauchaine et al., 2013) were also analyzed. In general, results indicated the beneficial effectiveness of IY parent programs irrespective of family variables. Counter to expectation, one study showed better long-term child outcomes with younger mothers and those with a history of parental substance abuse (Beauchaine et al., 2005). Moreover, the IY programs were equally effective regardless of child gender, age, or comorbidity with attentional problems (Hartman et al., 2003) or anxious depression scores (Beauchaine et al., 2005). However, critical, harsh, and ineffective parenting both predicted and mediated outcomes at one-year follow-up (Beauchaine et al., 2005) and long-term follow-up (Webster-Stratton et al., 2010). These findings suggest that specific parenting goals should be achieved before the parent program is discontinued, or that parents who still have high levels of coercive parenting (despite improvements from baseline) should be selected for continued treatment with the advance parent program until therapeutic effectiveness has been achieved.

Implementation with Fidelity

An important aspect of a program's efficacy is fidelity in implementation. Indeed, if the program is not rigorously followed (for example, if session components are eliminated or program dosage is reduced, necessary resources are not available, or group leaders are not trained or supported with accredited mentors), then the absence of effects may be attributed not to the inefficacy of the program but to a lack of fidelity in its implementation (Hutchings et al. 2007). Recent research with the Incredible Years® BASIC parenting program shows that implementation with a high degree of fidelity not only preserves the anticipated behavior change mechanisms but is predictive of behavioral and relationship changes in parents, which, in turn, are predictive of social and emotional changes in the child as a result of the program (Eames et al., 2010).

One important aspect that facilitates the application of a program with fidelity is the standardization of program content, structure, processes, methods, and materials. In Incredible Years®, all components relating to the implementation of the program content are described in detail in DVDs and manuals, which also lay out the basic theoretical and empirical elements of each part of the program. For Weisz (2004), one of the main advantages of the Incredible Years® program, from the point of view of clinical practice, is precisely the program's accessibility for clinical use, along with its appealing nature and low abandonment rates.

In the context of implementation with fidelity, the training and supervision of group leaders warrants great attention (Webster-Stratton, 2004). First, carefully selected and motivated group leaders receive three days of training by accredited mentors before leading their first group of parents or teachers. Then, it is highly recommended they continue with ongoing consultation with IY coaches and/or mentors as they proceed through their first group. They are encouraged to start videotaping their sessions and to review these videos with their co-leader using the group leader checklist and peer review forms (Webster-Stratton, 2004). It is also recommended that they send these videos for outside coaching and consultation by an accredited IY coach or mentor as soon as possible. Group leaders find this video review immensely helpful and supportive.

The process of group leader accreditation is demanding, involving the leadership of at least two complete groups, video consultation, and a positive final video-based group assessment by an accredited mentor or trainer as well as satisfactory completion of group leader session protocols and weekly participant evaluations. This process ensures that leaders are delivering the program with fidelity, which includes both content delivery (required number of sessions, vignettes, role plays, brainstorms) and therapeutic skills. The whole process of coaching, consultation, and accreditation of new group leaders is carried out by a network of national and international accredited IY mentors and trainers. A recent RCT has shown that providing group leaders with ongoing consultation and coaching following the three-day workshop leads to increased group facilitator proficiency, program adherence, and delivery fidelity (Webster-Stratton, Reid, & Marsenich, 2014).

Planning and Implementation of IY Programs According to Risk Level of Population

The BASIC parent program (baby, toddler, preschool, or school-age version) is considered a mandatory or a "core" component of the prevention intervention training series. The ADVANCE program is offered in addition to the BASIC program for selective populations such as families characterized as depressed or with considerable marital discord, child-welfare referred families, or families living in shelters. For indicated children with behavior problems that are pervasive (i.e., apparent across settings both at home and at school), it is also recommended that the child Dinosaur program and/or teacher training program be offered in conjunction with the parent training program to assure changes at school or day care. For indicated children whose parents cannot participate in the BASIC program due to their own psychological problems, delivery of both the child and teacher program is optimal.

Again, the pyramid is used to depict the levels of intervention according to risk level of populations. As seen in Figure 3.3, Levels 1 and 2 are the foundation of the pyramid and recommend a series of programs that could be offered *universally* to all parents of young children (0–6 years). These programs could be offered in pediatricians' offices, Head Start programs, day care centers, preschools,

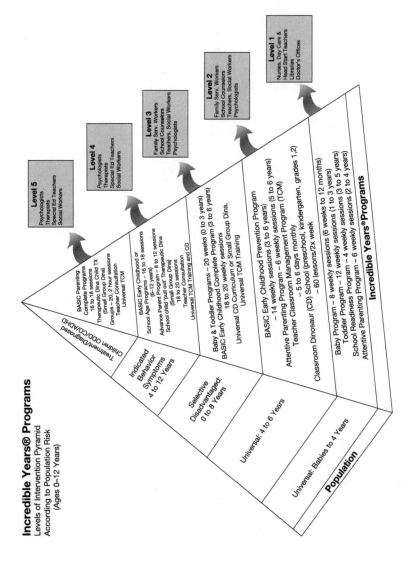

FIGURE 3.3 Incredible Years® Programs: Levels of Intervention Pyramid According to Popular Risk (Ages 0–12 Years). Source: www.incredibleyears.com

or elementary schools. The group format is a cost-efficient way of disseminating information to large numbers of people as a strategy to optimize positive parent–child interactions and to strengthen children's social and emotional competence and school readiness so that they are ready to start the next phase of their education.

Once children are in day care or preschool, providing universal supports for all children at this young age includes enhancing the capacity of day care, preschool, and Head Start teachers to provide structured, warm, and predictable environments. Thus, level 2 also involves training all early childhood teachers in effective classroom management strategies using the IY-TCM Program. After this training is completed, teachers also have the opportunity to receive training to deliver the child Dinosaur curriculum as a universal social skills intervention. This includes three different sets of lesson plans for preschool, kindergarten, and grades 1 and 2. Ideally, children receive this curriculum for three subsequent years, resulting in a strong emotional and social foundation by the time they are seven years old. This social and emotional competence is theorized to contribute to higher academic competence as children progress through school.

Level 3 is targeted at *"selective" or high-risk populations*. These are populations that are socioeconomically disadvantaged and highly stressed because of increased risk factors such as parental unemployment, low education, housing difficulties, single parenthood, poor nutrition, maternal depression, drug or alcohol addiction, child deprivation, new immigrant status, or lack of academic preparedness for school. These economically disadvantaged parents would benefit from the complete baby, toddler, and early childhood parent programs because of the ongoing support provided in the groups, the hope for change shown to them by group leaders, as well as their experiential learning that despite economic obstacles they can provide the best early years of emotional, social, and cognitive parenting possible for their children. In addition, the teachers and child care providers of these children could receive the IY-TCM program so that they are skilled at managing classroom behavior problems, which are exhibited at higher rates in this population. Lastly, children in these families aged 3–8 years would benefit from the child Dinosaur program at least twice a week year-round. This investment in building the social and emotional abilities in the first eight years of life for these vulnerable children can help to break the intergenerational transmission of disadvantage.

Level 4 on the pyramid is targeted at *"indicated populations"*, where children or parents are already showing symptoms of mental health problems. This could include, for example, parents referred to child protective services because of abuse or neglect, foster parents caring for children who have been neglected and removed from their homes, or children who are highly aggressive but not yet diagnosed as having ODD or CD. As can be seen on the pyramid, this level of intervention is offered to fewer people and offers a longer and more intensive

60 Carolyn Webster-Stratton

parenting program by a higher level of trained professionals. These parents or caregivers would complete the entire age appropriate BASIC parenting program followed by the ADVANCE program.

The teachers of these children should receive the IY-TCM program and offer the child Dinosaur program. In addition to this classroom curriculum, children with symptoms of externalizing or internalizing problems or ADHD are targeted to be pulled out of class twice a week for the small group therapeutic Dinosaur program delivered by school psychologists, counselors, specially trained social workers, or special education teachers. These children will meet in small groups (4–6 children) to get extra coaching and practice with social skills, emotional regulation, persistence coaching, literacy, and problem solving. This will reinforce the classroom learning of the program and will send these children back to a classroom where peers understand how to respond more positively to their special needs. In other words, the whole classroom community has learned solutions to how to respond to a peer who may be aggressive or one who is sad, withdrawn, or lonely.

Level 5 is the most comprehensive intervention, addressing multiple risk factors, and is usually offered in mental health clinics by therapists with graduate-level education in psychology, social work, or counseling. One of the goals of each of the prior levels is to maximize resources and minimize the number of children who will need these time- and cost-intensive interventions at level 5. At a minimum, the parents will receive the entire BASIC and ADVANCE curriculum for 24–28 weeks, while the children attend 2-hour weekly therapeutic Dinosaur groups at the same time. Therapists dovetail these two curricula and keep parents and teachers fully informed of the skills children are learning in their child groups so that they can reinforce these at home or in the classroom. Additionally, if parents need individual coaching in parent–child interactions, this can be provided in the clinic setting or in supplemental home visits using the home coaching protocols. Child and parent therapists work with parents to develop behavior problem plans and consult with teachers in partnerships to coordinate their plans, goals, and helpful strategies. Successful interventions at this level are marked by an integrated team approach with clear communication among all the providers and adult caregivers in the various settings where these children spend their time. Ideally mental health agencies would embody these services within schools, which allows for less stigmatization for parents, greater coordination with teachers regarding behavior plans, and more frequent pull-out groups for children.

Conclusion

Future directions for research on IY programs should include evaluating ways to promote the sustainability of results such as by targeting parents whose baseline or post-intervention parenting practices are particularly harsh or ineffective with additional resources such as offering a greater number of sessions, additional program adjuncts such as IY Advance Program, or IY Child Program and ongoing booster sessions. Similarly research concerning matching children to appropriate treatment combinations is needed. For example, children could be assigned to treatment program conditions according to their particular comorbidity combinations. Our research suggests that children with ODD are comorbid for other diagnoses such as ADHD, depression or anxiety, language delays, and Autism Spectrum Disorder. Our initial findings suggest that children scoring high on Attention Problems or with ADHD will fare better when IY-TCM or CT components are added to the PT program. Further research is needed for identification of children for whom the current interventions are inadequate. Finally, our three newest IY Programs (Baby Program, Attentive Parenting Program, and Autism Program) are in need of RCTs to determine their effectiveness.

At a time when the efficient management of human and economic resources is crucial, the availability of evidence-based programs to parents and teachers should form part of the public health mission. While the IY programs have been shown in dozens of studies to be transportable and effective across different contexts worldwide, barriers to fidelity of delivery impede the possibility for successful outcomes for parents, teachers, and children. The lack of sufficient funding has led to IY programs being delivered by group leaders without adequate training, sufficient support, coaching and consultation, and without agency monitoring or assessment of outcomes. Frequently, the programs have been sliced and diced and components dropped in order to offer the program in a dosage that can be funded. Few agencies support their group leaders to become accredited, and the program is often not sufficiently established to withstand staffing changes in an agency. Thus, the initial investment that an agency may make to purchase the program and train staff is often lost over time. If we think of disseminating evidence-based programs like constructing a house, it is as if the contractors hired electricians and plumbers who were not certified, disregarded the architectural plan and used poor-quality, cheaper materials. Under these conditions, the building will not be structurally sound. Just like building a stable house, it is important that the foundation and basic structure for delivering evidence-based programs be strong. This will include picking the right evidence-based program for the level of population risk and developmental status of the children, adequately training, supporting, and coaching group leaders so they become accredited, and providing quality control. In addition, providing adequate scaffolding through the use of trained and accredited coaches, mentors, and administrators who can champion quality delivery will make all the difference. With a supportive infrastructure surrounding the program, initial investments will pay off in terms of strong family outcomes and a sustainable intervention program that can withstand staffing and administrative changes.

62 Carolyn Webster-Stratton

References

Ainsworth, M. (1974). Infant–mother attachment and social development: Socialization as a product of reciprocal responsiveness to signals. In M. Richards (Ed.), *The integration of the child into the social world.* Cambridge: Cambridge University Press.

Bandura, A. (1977). Self-efficacy: Toward a unifying theory of behavioral change. *Psychological Review*, 84(2), 191–215.

Bandura, A. (1986). *Social foundations of thought and action.* Englewood Cliffs, NJ: Prentice-Hall.

Bandura, A. (1989). Regulation of cognitive processes through perceived self-efficacy. *Developmental Psychology*, 25, 729–735.

Beauchaine, T. P., Gatzke-Kopp, L., Neuhaus, E., Chipman, J., Reid, J., & Webster-Stratton, C. (2013). Sympathetic- and parasympathetic-linked cardiac function and prediction of externalizing behavior, emotion regulation, and prosocial behavior among preschoolers treated for ADHD. *Journal of Consulting and Clinical Psychology*, 81, 481–493.

Beauchaine, T. P., Webster-Stratton, C., & Reid, M. J. (2005). Mediators, moderators, and predictors of one-year outcomes among children treated for early-onset conduct problems: A latent growth curve analysis. *Journal of Consulting and Clinical Psychology*, 73(3), 371–388.

Beck, A. T. (1979). *Cognitive therapy and emotional disorders.* New York: New American Library.

Beck, J. S. (2005). *Cognitive therapy for challenging problems.* New York: The Guilford Press.

Bowlby, J. (1980). *Attachment and loss: Loss, sadness, and depression.* New York: Basic Books.

Collins, W. A., Maccoby, E. E., Steinberg, L., Hetherington, E. M., & Bornstein, M. H. (2000). Contemporary research on parenting: The case for nurture and nature. *American Psychologist*, 55, 218–232.

Costello, E. J., Foley, D. L., & Angold, A. (2006). 10-year research update review: The epidemiology of child and adolescent psychiatric disorders: II. *Journal of American Academy of Child and Adolescent Psychiatry*, 45(1), 8–25.

Dishion, T. J., & Piehler, T. F. (2007). Peer dynamics in the development and change of child and adolescent problem behavior. In A. S. Masten (Ed.), *Multilevel dynamics in development psychopathology: Pathways to the future* (pp. 151–180). Mahwah, NJ: Erlbaum.

Dodge, K. A. (1993). Social-cognitive mechanisms in the development of conduct disorder and depression. *Annual Review of Psychology*, 44, 559–584.

Drugli, M. B., & Larsson, B. (2006). Children aged 4–8 years treated with parent training and child therapy because of conduct problems: Generalisation effects to day-care and school settings. *European Child and Adolescent Psychiatry*, 15, 392–399.

D'Zurilla, T. J., & Nezu, A. (1982). Social problem-solving in adults. In P. C. Kendall (Ed.), *Advances in cognitive behavioral research and therapy* (Vol. 1). New York: Academic Press.

Eames, C., Daley, D., Hutchings, J., Whitaker, C. J., Bywater, T., Jones, K., & Hughes, J. C. (2010). The impact of group leaders' behaviour on parent acquisition of key parenting skills during parent training. *Behaviour Research and Therapy*, 48, 1221–1226.

Egger, H. L., & Angold, A. (2006). Common emotional and behavioral disorders in preschool children: Presentation, nosology, and epidemiology. *Journal of Child Psychology and Psychiatry*, 47, 313–337.

Furlong, M., McGilloway, S., Bywater, T., Hutchings, J., Donnelly, M. A., Smith, S. M., & O'Neill, C. (2010). Behavioural/cognitive-behavioural group-based parenting interventions for children age 3–12 with early onset conduct problems (Protocol). *Cochrane Database of Systematic Reviews 2010*(1), Art. No.: CD008225. doi: 008210.001002/14651858.CD14008225.

Gardner, F., Burton, J., & Klimes, I. (2006). Randomized controlled trial of a parenting intervention in the voluntary sector for reducing conduct problems in children: Outcomes and mechanisms of change. *Journal of Child Psychology and Psychiatry, 47*, 1123–1132.

Hartman, R. R., Stage, S., & Webster-Stratton, C. (2003). A growth curve analysis of parent training outcomes: Examining the influence of child factors (inattention, impulsivity, and hyperactivity problems), parental and family risk factors. *The Child Psychology and Psychiatry Journal, 44*(3), 388–398.

Hutchings, J., Gardner, F., Bywater, T., Daley, D., Whitaker, C., Jones, K., et al. (2007). Parenting intervention in Sure Start services for children at risk of developing conduct disorder: Pragmatic randomized controlled trial. *British Medical Journal, 334*(7595), 1–7.

Jacobson, N. S., & Margolin, G. (1979). *Marital therapy: Strategies based on social learning and behavior as exchange principles.* New York: Brunner/Mazel.

Jaffee, S. R., Caspi, A., Moffitt, T. E., & Taylor, A. (2004). Physical maltreatment victim to antisocial child: Evidence of environmentally mediated process. *Journal of Abnormal Psychology, 113*, 44–55.

Kazdin, A. E., & Weisz, J. R. (2010). *Evidence-based psychotherapies for children and adolescents, 2nd edition.* New York: Guilford Publications.

Knutson, J. F., DeGarmo, D., Koeppl, G., & Reid, J. B. (2005). Care neglect, supervisory neglect and harsh parenting in the development of children's aggression: A replication and extension. *Child Maltreatment, 10*, 92–107.

Larsson, B., Fossum, B., Clifford, G., Drugli, M., Handegard, B., & Morch, W. (2009). Treatment of oppositional defiant and conduct problems in young Norwegian children: Results of a randomized trial. *European Child Adolescent Psychiatry, 18*(1), 42–52.

Lavigne, J.V., LeBailly, S.A., Gouze, K. R., Cicchetti, C., Pochyly, J., et al. (2008). Treating oppositional defiant disorder in primary care: A comparison of three models. *Journal of Pediatric Psychology, 33*(5), 449–461.

Lynam, D. R., Caspi, A., Moffitt, T. E., Wikstrom, P. H., Loeber, R., & Novak, S. (2000). The interaction between impulsivity and neighborhood context on offending: The effects of impulsivity are stronger in poorer neighborhoods. *Journal of Abnormal Child Psychology, 109*, 563–574.

Menting, A. T. A., Orobio de Castro, B., & Matthys, W. (2013). Effectiveness of the Incredible Years® parent training to modify disruptive and prosocial child behavior: A meta-analytic review. *Clinical Psychology Review, 33*, 901–913.

Miller, W. R., & Rollnick, S. (2002). *Motivational interviewing.* New York: Guilford Press.

Moffitt, T. E. (1993). Adolescence-limited and life-course-persistent antisocial behavior: A developmental taxonomy. *Psychological Review, 100*, 674–701.

Offord, D. R., & Bennet, K. J. (1994). Conduct disorder: Long term outcomes and intervention effectiveness. *Journal of the American Academy of Child and Adolescent Psychiatry, 33*, 1069–1078.

Patterson, G. R., & Fisher, P. A. (2002). Recent developments in our understanding of parenting: Bidirectional effects, causal models, and search for parsimony. In M. H.

64 Carolyn Webster-Stratton

Bornstein (Ed.), *Handbook of parenting: Practical issues in parenting, vol. 5* (pp. 59–88). Mahwah, NJ: Erlbaum.

Patterson, G.R., Reid, J.B., & Dishion, T. (1992). *Antisocial boys: A social interactional approach* (Vol. 4). Eugene, OR: Castalia.

Patterson, G. R., Reid, J. B., Jones, R. R., & Conger, R. W. (1975). *A social learning approach to family intervention* (Vol. 1). Eugene, OR: Castalia.

Perrin, E. C., Sheldrick, R. C., McMenamy, J. M., Henson, B. S., & Carter, A. S. (2014). Improving parenting skills for families of young children in pediatric settings: A randomized clinical trial. *Journal of American Medical Association Pediatrics, 168*(1), 16–24.

Piaget, J., & Inhelder, B. (1962). *The psychology of the child.* New York: Basic Books.

Presnall, N., Webster-Stratton, C., & Constantino, J. (2014). Parent training: Equivalent improvement in externalizing behavior for children with and without familial risk. *Journal of American Academy of Child and Adolescent Psychiatry,* 53(8), 879–888.

Pye, K., Bywater, T., & Hutchings, J. (in preparation). Evaluation of the Incredible Years® School Readiness Programme.

Raaijmakers, M., Posthumus, J. A., Maassen, G. H., Van Hout, B., Van Engeland, H., & Matthys, W. (2008). *The evaluation of a preventive intervention for 4-year-old children at risk for disruptive behavior disorders: Effects on parenting practices and child behavior* Dissertation, University of Medical Center Utrecht, Utrecht.

Reedtz, C. (2010). *Promoting positive parenting practices in primary care: Outcomes in a randomized controlled risk reduction trial.* Dissertation for Doctor Philosophiae, University of Tromsø, Tromsø.

Reid, M. J., Webster-Stratton, C., & Beauchaine, T. P. (2001). Parent training in Head Start: A comparison of program response among African American, Asian American, Caucasian, and Hispanic mothers. *Prevention Science, 2*(4), 209–227.

Reid, M. J., Webster-Stratton, C., & Hammond, M. (2007). Enhancing a classroom social competence and problem-solving curriculum by offering parent training to families of moderate-to-high-risk elementary school children. *Journal of Clinical Child and Adolescent Psychology, 36*(5), 605–620.

Reinke, W. M., Stormont, M., Herman, K., Wang, Z., Newcomer, L., & King, K. (2014). Use of coaching and behavior support planning for students with disruptive behavior within a universal classroom management program. *Journal of Emotional and Behavioral Disorders, 22*(2), 74–82.

Reinke, W. M., Stormont, M., Webster-Stratton, C., Newcomer, L., & Herman, K. (2012). The Incredible Years® teacher training: Using coaching to support generalization to real world settings. *Psychology in Schools, 49*(2), 416–428.

Sawyer, M. G., Arney F. M., Baghurst, P. A., Clark, J. J., Graetz, B. W., Kosky, R. J., et al. (2000). *Child and adolescent component of the National Survey of Mental Health and Well Being: The mental health of young people in Australia.* Canberra, Australia: Mental Health and Special Programs Branch, Commonwealth Department of Health and Aged Care.

Scott, S., Briskman, J., & O'Connor, T. G. (2014). Early prevention of antisocial personality: Long-term follow-up of two randomized controlled trials comparing indicated and selective approaches. *American Journal of Psychiatry, 171*(6), 649–657.

Scott, S., Knapp, M., Henderson, J., & Maughan, B. (2001). Financial cost of social exclusion: Follow up study of antisocial children into adulthood. *British Medical Journal, 323*, 191–194.

Scott, S., Spender, Q., Doolan, M., Jacobs, B., & Aspland, H. (2001). Multicentre controlled trial of parenting groups for child antisocial behaviour in clinical practice. *British Medical Journal, 323*(28), 1–5.

Scott, S., Sylva, K., Doolan, M., Price, J., Jacobs, B., Crook, C., & Landau, S. (2010). Randomised controlled trial of parent groups for child antisocial behaviour targeting multiple risk factors: The SPOKES project. *The Journal of Child Psychology and Psychiatry, 51*, 48–57.

Snyder, H. (2001). Child delinquents. In R. Loeber & D. P. Farrington (Eds.), *Risk factors and successful interventions.* Thousand Oaks, CA: Sage.

Spaccarelli, S., Cotler, S., & Penman, D. (1992). Problem-solving skills training as a supplement to behavioral parent training. *Cognitive Therapy and Research, 16*, 1–18.

Stormont, M., Smith, S. C., & Lewis, T. J. (2007). Teacher implementation of precorrection and praise statements in Head Start classrooms as a component of a program-wide system of positive behavioral support. *Journal of Behavioral Education, 16*, 280–290.

Taylor, T. K., Schmidt, F., Pepler, D., & Hodgins, H. (1998). A comparison of eclectic treatment with Webster-Stratton's Parents and Children Series in a children's mental health center: A randomized controlled trial. *Behavior Therapy, 29*, 221–240.

Webster-Stratton, C. (1984a). The effects of father involvement in parent training for conduct problem children. *Child Psychology and Psychiatry, 26*, 801–810.

Webster-Stratton, C. (1984b). Randomized trial of two parent-training programs for families with conduct-disordered children. *Journal of Consulting and Clinical Psychology, 52*(4), 666–678.

Webster-Stratton, C. (1990). Long-term follow-up of families with young conduct problem children: From preschool to grade school. *Journal of Clinical Child Psychology, 19*(2), 144–149.

Webster-Stratton, C. (1992). Individually administered videotape parent training: "Who benefits?". *Cognitive Therapy and Research, 16*(1), 31–35.

Webster-Stratton, C. (1994). Advancing videotape parent training: A comparison study. *Journal of Consulting and Clinical Psychology, 62*(3), 583–593.

Webster-Stratton, C. (1996). Early onset conduct problems: Does gender make a difference? *Journal of Consulting and Clinical Psychology, 64*, 540–551.

Webster-Stratton, C. (1998). Preventing conduct problems in Head Start children: Strengthening parenting competencies. *Journal of Consulting and Clinical Psychology, 66*(5), 715–730.

Webster-Stratton, C. (2004). *Incredible Years® child group leader training: Therapist's guide for Dinosaur school treatment program.* Seattle, WA: Incredible Years®.

Webster-Stratton, C. (2005). *The Incredible Years®: A trouble-shooting guide for parents of children ages 2–8 years.* Seattle: Incredible Years® Press.

Webster-Stratton, C. (2012a). *Collaborating with parents to reduce children's behavior problems: A book for therapists using the Incredible Years® programs.* Seattle, WA: Incredible Years® Inc.

Webster-Stratton, C. (2012b). *Incredible teachers.* Seattle, WA: Incredible Years® Inc.

Webster-Stratton, C. (2012c). *The Incredible Years® parents, teachers, and children's training series: Program content, methods, research and dissemination 1980–2011.* Seattle, WA: Incredible Years®.

Webster-Stratton, C., & Hammond, M. (1990). Predictors of treatment outcome in parent training for families with conduct problem children. *Behavior Therapy, 21*, 319–337.

Webster-Stratton, C., & Hammond, M. (1997). Treating children with early-onset conduct problems: A comparison of child and parent training interventions. *Journal of Consulting and Clinical Psychology, 65*(1), 93–109.

Webster-Stratton, C., & Hammond, M. (1998). Conduct problems and level of social competence in Head Start children: Prevalence, pervasiveness and associated risk factors. *Clinical Child Psychology and Family Psychology Review, 1*(2), 101–124.

Webster-Stratton, C., & Herman, K. C. (2010). Disseminating Incredible Years® series early intervention programs: Integrating and sustaining services between school and home. *Psychology in Schools, 47*(1), 36–54.

Webster-Stratton, C., Hollinsworth, T., & Kolpacoff, M. (1989). The long-term effectiveness and clinical significance of three cost-effective training programs for families with conduct-problem children. *Journal of Consulting and Clinical Psychology, 57*(4), 550–553.

Webster-Stratton, C., Kolpacoff, M., & Hollinsworth, T. (1988). Self-administered videotape therapy for families with conduct-problem children: Comparison with two cost-effective treatments and a control group. *Journal of Consulting and Clinical Psychology, 56*(4), 558–566.

Webster-Stratton, C., & Reid, M. J. (2003). Treating conduct problems and strengthening social emotional competence in young children (ages 4–8 years): The Dina Dinosaur treatment program. *Journal of Emotional and Behavioral Disorders, 11*(3), 130–143.

Webster-Stratton, C., & Reid, M. J. (2004). Strengthening social and emotional competence in young children—The foundation for early school readiness and success: Incredible Years® classroom social skills and problem-solving curriculum. *Infants and Young Children, 17*, 96–113.

Webster-Stratton, C., & Reid, M. J. (2006). Treatment and prevention of conduct problems: Parent training interventions for young children (2–7 years old). In K. McCartney & D. A. Phillips (Eds.), *Blackwell handbook on early childhood development* (pp. 616–641). Malden, MA: Blackwell.

Webster-Stratton, C., & Reid, M. J. (2010). The Incredible Years® parents, teachers and children training series: A multifaceted treatment approach for young children with conduct problems. In A. E. Kazdin & J. R. Weisz (Eds.), *Evidence-based psychotherapies for children and adolescents, 2nd edition* (pp. 194–210). New York: Guilford.

Webster-Stratton, C., Reid, M. J., & Beauchaine, T. P. (2011). Combining parent and child training for young children with ADHD. *Journal of Clinical Child and Adolescent Psychology, 40*, 1–13.

Webster-Stratton, C., Reid, M. J., & Hammond, M. (2001a). Preventing conduct problems, promoting social competence: A parent and teacher training partnership in Head Start. *Journal of Clinical Child Psychology, 30*, 283–302.

Webster-Stratton, C., Reid, M. J., & Hammond, M. (2001b). Social skills and problem solving training for children with early-onset conduct problems: Who benefits? *Journal of Child Psychology and Psychiatry, 42*, 943–952.

Webster-Stratton, C., Reid, M. J., & Hammond, M. (2004). Treating children with early-onset conduct problems: Intervention outcomes for parent, child, and teacher training. *Journal of Clinical Child and Adolescent Psychology, 33*, 105–124.

Webster-Stratton, C., Reid, J. M., & Marsenich, L. (2014). Improving therapist fidelity during implementation of evidence-based practices: Incredible Years® program. *Psychiatric Services, 65*(6), 789–795.

Webster-Stratton, C., Reid, M. J., & Stoolmiller, M. (2008). Preventing conduct problems and improving school readiness: Evaluation of the Incredible Years® teacher and child training programs in high-risk schools. *Journal of Child Psychology and Psychiatry, 49*, 471–488.

Webster-Stratton, C., Rinaldi, J., & Reid, J. M. (2010). Long term outcomes of the Incredible Years® parenting program: Predictors of adolescent adjustment. *Child and Adolescent Mental Health, 16*, 38–46.

Weisz, J. R. (2004). *Psychotherapy for children and adolescents: Evidence-based treatments and case examples*. Cambridge: Cambridge University Press.

4

STRENGTHENING FAMILIES FOR MIDDLE/LATE CHILDHOOD

Karol L. Kumpfer, Catia Magalhães, Henry Whiteside, and Jing Xie

Adolescent behavioral health problems are on the rise worldwide. According to the SAMHSA's *Behavioral Health, United States, 2012* report, about 22% of adolescents (11 to 18 years) have been diagnosed with at least one mental or substance use disorder in the past year (SAMHSA, 2013), with the highest prevalence rates being 38% lifetime prevalence of an anxiety disorder in girls and 33% lifetime prevalence of impulse disorders in boys. Since only 0.4% of younger children aged 8 to 11 years have a diagnosed anxiety disorder and 1.5% have a conduct disorder, effective preventive interventions prior to adolescence are critical. One possible cause of this epidemic of adolescent mental and behavioral health problems is a more toxic and stressful family environment for children, which exacerbates the expression of inherited genetic risks for behavioral and emotional disorders. According to gene × environment interactions studies in epigenetics, the lack of nurturing and protective parents increases children's stress and cortisol levels and the expression of risky inherited genes (Jirtle, 2010). Some research even suggests parenting style can change genes structure for the next generation (Champagne & Meaney, 2007; Champagne, 2010).

Contributing to the issue of non-nurturing parenting is the high percentage of children growing up in homes with substance abusing and dysfunctional parents. About 12%, or over 8.3 million children in the United States, lived in 2007 with at least one alcohol or drug abusing parent (Kumpfer & Johnson, 2011). Children of parents with substance use disorders (SUDs) have two to nine times greater risk of becoming substance abusers as compared to children of parents without SUDs (Chassin, Carle, Nissim-Sabat, & Kumpfer, 2004). In the needs assessment for the *Strengthening Families Program* – the first family skills training program designed specifically for drug abusing parents – parents with SUDs were found to spend about half as much time with their children, lack positive parenting skills, and use excessive punishment as compared to matched and general population families (Kumpfer & DeMarsh, 1986), all of which can lead to increased risk for child neglect and child maltreatment. Unfortunately, even functional parents are spending less time with their children because of the worldwide economic crisis; working more hours, or multiple jobs, puts increasing demands on their time. If parents can't spend much time parenting their children, they need to get more efficient with the little parenting time they have available. Hence, disseminating effective parenting practices more widely could buffer against the current upswing in adolescent behavioral health problems and diagnoses (UNODC, 2009; Kumpfer, Xie, & Magalhães, 2012).

Developmental Needs of Elementary School Children

Children in the 6 to 11 year age range primarily need guidance and support from loving and nurturing parents and other family members to successfully achieve their developmental milestones, which include: 1) improved behavioral and emotional control; 2) early development of lasting friendships by improving their social skills; 3) academic success by learning impulse control and doing their homework; and 4) school bonding related to good behavior and relations with teachers and students in school, which can contribute to a more successful transition to middle school. The evidence-based family interventions for children in this age range (Biglan & Taylor, 2000; Bröning et al., 2012; Kumpfer & Alvarado, 2003; Kumpfer & Hansen, 2014) all include prevention components that can help elementary school children achieve these developmental milestones directly through children's skills training or indirectly by means of parents using skills taught in a parent training course.

The unique risk factors in this 6 to 11 year age range include: 1) individual child mental disorders such as early onset of conduct disorders, ADD/HD, impulse control disorders, autism spectrum disorders, and shyness mixed with aggression; 2) parent and family dysfunction such as parental behavioral health disorders (e.g., depression, anxiety, substance abuse, criminality, impulse disorders, etc.) and high family conflict and lack of communication and support; and 3) school and neighborhood problems (e.g., poverty, lack of opportunities for achievement and learning, lack of mentors, coaches, and role models). Family interventions can't address all of these risk factors, but they can help to reduce childhood behavioral and mental disorders through effective parenting, reduce family conflict and parental stress and depression, and help children to be more resilient in relation to poor family, school, and community environments, such as living with substance abusing parents (Kumpfer & Johnson, 2007; Kumpfer & Magalhães, in press).

70 Karol L. Kumpfer et al.

Evidence-based Family Programs for Elementary School Children

The most common evidence-based programs for high-risk elementary school age children are parenting and family skills training programs, including *Strengthening Families Program 6–11 Years and 10–14 Years*, *Preparing for the Drug-free Years*, *Families and Schools Together*, *Nurturing Program*, and the *Positive Parenting Program (Triple P)*. Although the family therapy programs, such as *Functional Family Therapy*, *Parenting Wisely*, *Multisystemic Family Therapy*, *Multidimensional Family Therapy*, and the *Adolescent Transitions Program* are generally reserved for *indicated* prevention with adolescents, sometimes they are used with mature 9-to-12 year olds. Also, home visitation and parent training programs such as the *Incredible Years* are used mostly for families of high-risk 2-to-8 year olds. The universal prevention programs for lower risk families such as *Preparing for the Drug-free Years (PDFY)* and *Strengthening Families Program 10–14 (SFP 10–14)* can be as short as 5 to 7 sessions and can be effective because the participating families have fewer problems; however, most selective and indicated prevention programs for higher risk families are longer (12 to 15 sessions). Many of these evidence-based parenting and family interventions are reviewed in their own chapters and will not be covered in this chapter, where the focus will be on the first author's *Strengthening Families Program (SFP) 6–11 Years*.

Core Components of Effective Family Interventions for 6–11 Year Olds

According to a recent review (Kaminski, Valle, Filene, & Boyle, 2008), the four most critical family intervention components found to be significant predictors of larger effect sizes included: emotional communication, practicing with own child and family coach, positive interactions with child, and consistent responding. All of these components are included in the SFP and many other evidence-based family interventions. In addition to changing parenting style, teaching elementary school children social and emotion regulation skills has been found to be critical in order to prevent later impulse control disorders (e.g., delinquency, substance abuse, obesity, and sexual acting out; Kumpfer, Alvarado, & Whiteside, 2003). These skills create self-reinforcing pro-social behaviors that allow the child to bond with positive peers, adults, authority figures, and role models. Through these positive relationships, they can have more school and community success, avoid delinquency, and have more positive life outcomes.

Other factors that increase family intervention success are those that can improve family enrollment and retention, such as having a strengths- and resilience-based focus (Kumpfer, 1999), involving fathers, adapting the program to target the needs and cultural sensitivities of the families, having the appropriate intervention dose, and removing attendance barriers by providing child care, attendance incentives, and transportation (Kumpfer & Alvarado, 2003; Kumpfer, 2014; Kumpfer & Hansen, 2014).

Strengthening Families Program

The *Strengthening Families Program (SFP) 6–11 Years*, developed by Dr. Karol Kumpfer at the University of Utah, is a highly structured family skills training program that is traditionally conducted in a 7-to-14 week multi-family group format involving three to four gender-balanced and culturally sensitive group leaders and a coordinator. Created in 1982, SFP was based on several existing evidence-based practices (e.g., Patterson's behavioral parent training, Spivack and Schure's *I Can Problem Solve* children's skills training, McMahon & Forehand's *Helping the Non-Compliant Child* parent/child training, and the Gurneys' *Family Relationship Enhancement Therapy*). The SFP was tested and found efficacious in a four-group NIDA randomized controlled trial aimed at promoting positive developmental outcomes and preventing later substance abuse among elementary school children of substance abusing parents (Kumpfer, 1998; Kumpfer & DeMarsh, 1986). Later age adaptations (*SFP 3–5, SFP 10–14*, and *SFP 12–16*) and cultural adaptations for all major ethnic groups were developed and found equally effective (Kumpfer, Alvarado, Smith, & Bellamy, 2002). Recently a new *SFP 7–17 Years Home Use DVD* and family group versions for 10–14 sessions (depending on risk levels) were developed and found effective (Kumpfer & Brown, 2012). A *SFP 0–3 Years* version is being tested on a federal ACF Children's Bureau grant in Delaware.

Etiological Theory and Mechanisms of Effectiveness

SFP is guided by its underlying etiological or SEM-tested causal theory, the *Social Ecology Model of Adolescent Substance Abuse* (Kumpfer et al., 2003), which found that the developmental pathway of family attachment, parenting skills and supervision, and communication of positive family values was the most powerful in terms of protecting youth from impulse control disorders (e.g., substance abuse, delinquency, teen pregnancy), particularly for girls (Kumpfer, Smith, & Summerhays, 2008; Kumpfer, 2014). This etiological theory, described in greater detail in our chapter on culture and gender, provided the content framework for SFP that focuses on increasing parent and child attachment, positive parental communication and time with the child, effective discipline, and clear communications about expectations.

Intervention Theories

The major theories guiding SFP's development are the family systems theories elaborated by Bowen (1991) and others clinicians who observed that children's problems were often rooted in the way parents dealt with them. Bandura's social learning and self-efficacy theories (Bandura, 2001) strongly influenced the cognitive behavioral skills training content of SFP and most evidence-based family interventions in this book. For instance, most are based on Patterson's highly effective clinical coaching and skills training methods developed at the University of Oregon in individual parent/child therapy sessions that taught parents to use positive reinforcement (attention, praise) for wanted behaviors and to ignore unwanted behaviors, in addition to avoiding inadvertent reinforcement of child coercive behavior through so-called coercion cycles (Patterson & Banks, 1989). His family techniques were designed originally for individual families in clinics, but later with Marion Forgatch, he developed a group-based version, called *Parent Management Training—Oregon Model* (Patterson, DeGarmo, & Forgatch, 2004).

The Resilience Framework (Kumpfer, 1999) also informed the SFP intervention content regarding how parents can increase resilience and positive outcomes in children living with adversity (Kumpfer, Xie, & Hu, 2011). This transactional Resilience Framework suggested that an important part of successful adaptation is learning techniques to deal effectively with stress, having goals and dreams to increase purpose in life, and relying on personal and social network strengths in recovering from major adversity. The SFP content has incorporated training in these important skills.

Program Long-term Goals and Intermediate and Immediate Objectives/Outcomes

The Logic Model for SFP is shown in Figure 4.1 and explained below starting with the right side or the Long-term Goals and moving to the intermediate and immediate objectives and outcomes measured. Finally, the Program Activities are listed, as well as the Resources needed.

The goal of SFP is to decrease or prevent adolescent substance abuse, mental health disorders, and child maltreatment by teaching positive parenting and family skills to raise healthy and happy children. To reach these long-term goals, the major short-term measurable objectives are to: 1) improve family relations (e.g., decrease family conflicts and improve family communication, family organization, and resilience); 2) improve parent and child attachment through increasing positive parent–child time together, parent's empathy with child, and positive parenting skills (e.g., positive attention and praise, effective discipline without physical punishment); 3) increase children's skills and resilience (e.g., dreams and goals, communication skills, peer refusal skills, recognition of feelings, and anger coping skills, which can increase child compliance and decrease overt and covert aggression, attention deficits, and depression); and 4) reduce parental and sibling substance use (Kumpfer, 1998; Kumpfer, Alvarado, Whiteside, & Tait, 2005).

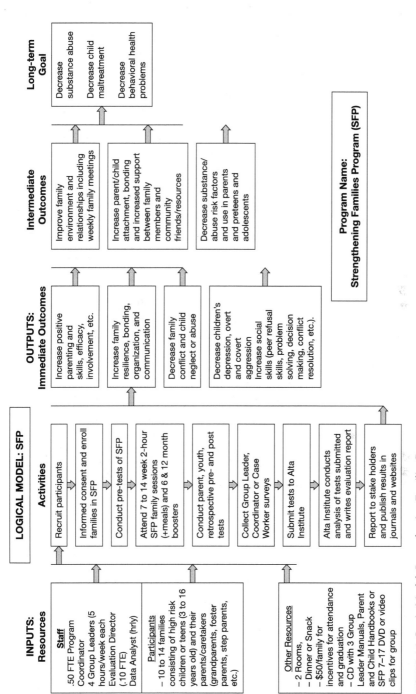

FIGURE 4.1 Logic Model: Strengthening Families Program

74 Karol L. Kumpfer et al.

Program Activities: Structure, Content, and Other Program Issues

Program activities include recruiting, consenting, enrolling, and pre-testing voluntary families often referred by schools or community services agencies. SFP's effectiveness is attributed to the fact that the whole family attends each week for 2.5 hours (starting with half an hour for a family meal), which can create change in the total family system. SFP has different dosage levels depending on family risk, with 14 weeks for high-risk families and 7 to 10 weeks for lower risk school-based families.

SFP includes three distinct program modules with separate curriculum manuals for implementers, including (1) behavioral parent training (PT) that targets discipline, supervision, limit setting, and family management skills, (2) children's skills training (CT) that targets social and life skills training, and (3) family skills training involving the whole family. In the first hour, the children and parents attend their own classes with two gender-balanced implementers. The content of the 7 to 14 week modules matches the program objectives listed above. In the second hour, the parents and children come together for training in (1) positive play (Child's Game) and togetherness time, (2) effective family communications, such as clear requests followed by appropriate consequences (Parent's Game), (3) family meetings to enhance conflict resolution, and (4) methods for ensuring behavioral compliance, such as creating chore and behavioral charts. The group leaders model effective parenting skills and reinforce behavior changes for both parents and children. These family sessions often include skills practice as role playing, which involve parents and children in problem-solving situations to encourage non-punitive interaction.

A very important component in SFP is teaching parents to implement special play, also called "Child's Game," with their children regularly. This technique, which is used to increase bonding and attachment, is a foundational basis of most behavioral skills training prevention and therapy programs (e.g., *FAST Track*, *Strengthening Families Program*, *Families and Schools Together*, *Parent Child Interactive Therapy*, and *Incredible Years* to name a few). This technique teaches parents to allow a child or teen to select an activity for them to do together to increase attachment. Parents are coached to use a non-judgmental running dialogue (like a sportscaster) of what the child is doing to show positive attention. They are not to take control by asking questions, teaching, criticizing, or suggesting new activities. This special play is different than play therapy where the therapist takes control by asking the child why they are doing certain types of play activities.

Recruitment and retention of hard-to-reach parents are enhanced by removing barriers to attendance by offering transportation, dinner, babysitting, incentives for homework completion, and graduation parties. SFP is also structured to minimize factors that impede widespread adoption and high-fidelity implementation; for example, SFP provides low-cost structured manuals, group leader training, and annual fidelity and outcome evaluations, and allows local and cultural adaptation (Kumpfer, 1991).

Target Audiences

SFP was first tested as a *selective* prevention program with high-risk children; however, later applications tested its effectiveness as a *universal* prevention program involving randomized rural elementary schools (Kumpfer, Alvarado, Tait, & Turner, 2002) and sixth graders (Spoth, Trudeau, Guyll, & Shin, 2012), as well as in urban schools (Gottfredson, Kumpfer, et al., 2006). Once the *indicated* adolescent version (*SFP 12–16 Years*) was developed, it was found effective with adolescents at risk of delinquency or already referred by juvenile corrections in Ireland and United States (Kumpfer, Xie, & O'Driscoll, 2012).

The program is appropriate for the prevention of a wide range of undesirable adolescent outcomes, including alcohol and drug use, depression/anxiety, violence and aggression, delinquency, early sexuality and HIV risk, and school and job failure. In addition, new SFP family physical activity modules (to be used prior to SFP sessions) and nutrition education during meals has been found to significantly increase physical activity and reduce weight in Pacific Islanders and American Indians (Kumpfer & Fenollar, 2011).

SFP has been tested in a wide variety of agencies and settings (e.g., schools, family services agencies, youth services agencies, mental health centers, churches, public housing complexes, homeless shelters, refugee centers, drug treatment agencies, jails, prisons, youth corrections, and hospitals) and found effective with similar results in each replication. In large-scale dissemination trials, SFP reduced children's behavioral and emotional disorders and substance abuse in New Jersey, Virginia, Washington D.C., and Canada, and reduced child maltreatment in Maine, North Carolina, Oklahoma, Iowa, and Kansas (Brook, McDonald, & Yan, 2012).

SFP 7–17 Years DVD

Recently, a 10 to 14 week video program on DVD was developed and tested for effectiveness in many different formats (e.g., home use, clinic or community use, multi-family skills training groups, and family discussion groups) and settings (e.g., elementary and middle schools, juvenile courts, child welfare, refugee services, etc.). The DVD video sessions are 20 to 30 minutes long, but parents have downloadable handouts and home practice sessions; hence, the home-use program is longer in practice. In a quasi-experimental school study, an 11-week multi-family group DVD version was found to be more effective that the regular 14-week SFP or the self-paced Home Use DVD (Kumpfer & Brown, 2012).

Evidence of Effectiveness

Efficacy Trials

The SFP has a long history of research demonstrating its efficacy in 12 randomized control trials, more than half by independent research teams including Drs. Spoth, Gottfredson, Coatsworth, Brody and Murry, Miller and Safyer, Orte, and Pinyuchon. The efficacy of SFP was first tested as *selective* drug prevention for elementary school children of drug abusers from 1982 to 1986. In a NIDA-funded, four-group randomized control trial (RCT), 288 families were randomly assigned over four years to 14 weeks of one of four experimental conditions—parent training only (PT), PT plus children's skills training (CT), family skills training plus PT and CT in the second hour, or treatment as usual. The outcomes revealed that the three component program (PT and CT plus family skills) improved more child and parenting substance use risk and protective factors and was the only experimental condition that reduced 30-day substance use in older teens and their parents (DeMarsh & Kumpfer, 1985; Kumpfer & DeMarsh, 1986).

A five-year RCT of *SFP 6–11 Years* in 12 elementary schools in two Utah rural school districts was compared to an 83-session teacher-delivered skills training program (*I Can Problem Solve*) with 688 families of first graders. Both programs produced positive results on the predictor variables, but the students that received both programs had results that were almost additive. By the end of the first year, the combined program significantly improved Parenting Skills ($d = .70$), School Bonding ($d = .44$), and Self-Regulation ($d = .45$); (Kumpfer, Alvarado, Tait, & Turner, 2002). School bonding improvements were even larger by the fourth year follow-up ($d = .70$). The *SFP 6–11 Years*-only condition improved outcomes over the five years, while the results for the youth-only program decreased over time, particularly by the second year (Kumpfer, Alvarado, Tait, & Turner, 2002). This suggests that improving the family environment can have a long-lasting positive impact on children's behaviors.

A shorter seven-session version for 10 to 14 year olds was developed on a NIDA grant to Iowa State University; the shorter version was designed for *universal* prevention for sixth graders and was tested in randomized schools in southern Iowa (Kumpfer, Molgaard, & Spoth, 1996). Two large-scale NIDA efficacy trials were conducted with this *SFP 10–14 Years* version in Iowa and Pennsylvania, comparing it to Hawkins and Catalano's family-based *Preparing for the Drug-free Years* (PFDY; now called *Guiding Good Choices*) and including Botvin's school-based *Life Skills Program*. In both of these longitudinal studies lasting up to 15 years, SFP was found to be more effective in reducing substance use initiation and levels of use than the comparison conditions (Spoth, Redmond, Shin, & Azevedo, 2004).

Spoth and associates (2006, 2012) reported in a 10-year follow-up study that drug and alcohol use was significantly reduced and that not a single sixth grader getting SFP in these Iowa schools reported methamphetamine use 10 years later, as compared to 3.2% in the randomly assigned no-treatment control group and 3.6% in the group that received PFDY. Relative reduction rates among young adults indicating problematic substance use ranged from 19% to 31% for the ISFP (i.e., the Iowa version of the SFP) and from 9% to 16% for PDFY (Spoth, Trudeau, Guyll, Shin, & Redmond, 2009). A review of school-based alcohol prevention by the Cochrane Systematic Review (Foxcroft, Ireland, Lister-Sharp, Lowe, & Breen, 2003) concluded that *SFP 10–14 Years* is twice as effective at preventing alcohol misuse as any program having at least two years of follow-up data. NIDA (1997) has also included SFP as one of a few evidence-based substance abuse prevention programs.

Effectiveness Trials in the USA

Based on the success of these efficacy studies, considerable Type 2 translational effectiveness research has been conducted, including hundreds of quasi-experimental studies in the US and about 35 countries. The overwhelming evidence from these studies is that SFP is very robust even when implemented independently and widely with many different populations and contexts. The first *SFP 6–11 Years* effectiveness trials were five SAMHSA-funded five-year phase-in studies (generic SFP for two years compared with culturally adapted SFP for two years), each with a different ethnic population (e.g., urban African American drug abusers in treatment in Detroit, rural African American drug abusing women, inner city Hispanic families in public housing, Hawaiian schools, and urban American Indian families). These independently evaluated studies produced outcomes similar to the original NIDA RCTs in terms of improving parenting, family, and child risk factors and reducing parental substance abuse. These studies are described in more detail in Kumpfer, Alvarado, Smith, and Bellamy (2002) and the chapter in this book on cultural and gender adaptations.

An independent quasi-experimental study of *SFP 6–11 Years* in Utah with 800 families and 5- and 10-year follow-ups found similar positive improvements in high-risk families (Harrison, Boyle, & Farley, 1999). A statewide dissemination study with 1,600 high-risk families in New Jersey of the four age versions of SFP (3–5, 6–11, 10–14, and 12–16 Years) in 75 different community agencies found *SFP 6–11 Years* produced the largest effect sizes compared to the three other age versions, with effect sizes larger than the prior RCTs. The authors were surprised not to find a watering down of effect sizes compared to clinical RCT outcomes and commented that possibly using seasoned clinicians and prevention specialists who are experienced with their type of families, plus high-quality training and online and phone supervision by program developers, can produce larger behavior changes than typically found in RCTs often implemented by graduate student interns (Kumpfer, Greene, Allen, & Miceli, 2010).

78 Karol L. Kumpfer et al.

Recently, *SFP 6–11 Years* was tested in a five-year federally funded child maltreatment prevention study in Kansas with substance abusing parents. Researchers at the University of Kansas (Brook et al., 2012) reported in a propensity analysis that SFP reduced the days to family reunification dramatically from 258 days to 125 days, thus saving considerable foster care costs. Replications of *SFP 3–5 Years* and *SFP 6–11 Years* are now getting excellent results in other statewide trials in Oklahoma, Iowa, North Carolina, and Maine. A new Birth-to-Three SFP (also called SFP 0–3) is being tested on a federal grant in Delaware and has excellent results in improving parenting outcomes.

SFP and Human Epigenetic Research

Epigenetic research with mice suggests that positive parenting and family functioning that reduces stress can reduce the manifestation of genetic problems. Researchers at McGill University suggested that maternal stress and fetal under-nutrition *in utero* leading to low birth weight can result in poorer health over the lifespan. Lack of a nurturing parent can program increased stress reactions in children, resulting in reduced exploratory behaviors, cognitive development, and oxytocin binding even in later generations (Champagne & Meaney, 2007; Champagne, 2010). According to these epigenetic researchers, nurturing parenting and family support that reduces cortisol levels appears to be a major protective mechanism in the phenotypic expression of genetic family history risks for substance abuse and other costly health conditions. Hence, the author (Kumpfer et al., 2011) hypothesized several years ago that evidence-based parenting and family interventions that increase nurturing parenting should also reduce the expression of risky genes (Kumpfer, 1987).

While there are likely many genes involved, researchers have found that genetically at-risk adolescents are those with one or two short alleles of the 5-HTTLPR serotonin transporter gene. Youth with short alleles are more likely to become substance abusers (Kaufman et al., 2007; Munafo, Lingford-Hughes, Johnstone, & Walton, 2005), depressed (Caspi et al., 2003), or delinquent with lower behavioral and emotional control (Propper & Moore, 2006; Kreek, Nielsen, & Laforge, 2004). As a high-risk group, these youth have received considerable attention from prevention researchers. For example, the Iowa SFP 10–14 Years was adapted for African American youth by Dr. Gene Brody and associates at University of Georgia. That program, called *Strong African American Families* (SAAF), was evaluated in randomized schools with 650 African American families of seventh graders in a retrospective five-year longitudinal epigenetic study. As discussed in Dr. Brody's chapter, SAAF reduced by about 50% diagnosed genetic diseases (e.g., substance abuse, depression, anxiety, thrill seeking, and HIV status) related to presence of risky short alleles of the 5-HTTLPR serotonin gene and the DRD4 7 repeat dopamine gene (Brody et al., 2012, 2013).

International Dissemination with Cultural Adaptations

Cultural adaptation is a required fidelity element in SFP; hence, age variants of SFP have been culturally adapted and replicated in 35 countries with dissemination funding from the United Nations Office of Drugs and Crime (UNODC), the Pan American World Health Association (PAHO), the International Rescue Committee (IRC), and various governments. Replications of SFP by independent evaluators have found SFP to be an effective prevention program in randomized control trials (RCTs) and quasi-experimental studies. These replications have been in different English language countries (United States, Canada, Australia, Ireland, England, and Northern Ireland) and non-English language countries requiring translation and more cultural adaptation in Europe (Sweden, Norway, Netherlands, Spain, Portugal, Azores, Italy, Greece, Poland, Germany, Austria, Slovenia, and France), the Balkans, Central Asia, Mexico, Central and South America, and Asia (Thailand and Myanmar). SFP outcomes in these different cultural contexts are consistent in reducing multiple risk factors for later alcohol and drug abuse, mental health problems and delinquency by increasing family strengths, children's social competencies, and improving parent's parenting skills (Kumpfer, Alvarado, Smith, & Bellamy, 2002). For a summary of the outcomes from foreign studies see Kumpfer, Pinyuchon, de Melo, and Whiteside (2008) and Kumpfer, Xie, and Magalhães (2012). For a more in-depth summary of these cultural replications and recommended steps to cultural adaptations of evidence-based family interventions, see the authors' chapter on Cultural and Gender Adaptations in this book.

Examples of SFP RCTs with Reduced Effectiveness

When not culturally adapted and implemented in high crime and disorganized communities, one RCT with 715 primarily high-risk African Americans in the Washington D.C. region found statistically significant positive results but reduced recruitment and retention rates (Gottfredson et al., 2006). The families were randomly assigned over five years in cohorts to either a full *SFP 6–11 Years*, the child skills training (CT) only, CT + family skills training (FT) or a minimal contact (MC) control. Preliminary results with the first 422 families found significant improvements with medium to large effect sizes ($d = .44$ to 1.09) for all 11 outcome variables by the post-test. Interestingly, the four-session minimal contact control families also reported improvements, particularly in reduced child hyperactivity, child antisocial behavior, consistency in discipline, and family cohesion; thus, when compared to the control condition, the intervention resulted in significant improvements in only the remaining 7 of 11 outcome variables (e.g., improved child school progress, social skills, child shyness, parenting confidence, parental depression, family organization, and family conflict).

80 Karol L. Kumpfer et al.

The results for all 715 families by the fifth year were not as good as the first few years due to modifications in the program format and length that reduced fidelity. The major issue with this implementation was staff demoralization when the funding agency decided that the promised cultural adaptation for African American families would compromise the study design and reduce statistical power by introducing a new experimental condition (e.g., the culturally adapted SFP vs. the standard SFP). The group leaders did implement the program with reasonable fidelity to the model, but with reduced enthusiasm that decreased the implementation quality in the opinion of the program developer.

There were also barriers to recruitment and retention as well as logistical issues that may have affected adherence to the program curriculum. For instance, parents in the minimal contact control condition were not supposed to receive any SFP skills training; they were limited to just some parent education topics. However, they did receive alternative services that contaminated the experimental assignment. In addition, there was inordinately high staff turnover throughout the duration of the five-year program. As the trial proceeded, the program developers noted impediments to staff training and challenges to the standardization of delivery that may have adversely influenced program outcomes. Gottfredson and associates (2006) at the University of Maryland, who conducted the evaluation, reported that the high community disorganization and situational factors influenced the poorer-than-usual outcomes (e.g., low perceived connection between participants and program delivery sites). Unlike most SFP trials, many of the families were not referred to SFP by implementing agencies or schools, but recruited from posters and newspaper ads.

Cost-Benefit Analyses

Cost-benefit studies (Miller & Hendrie, 2008; Spoth, Guyll, & Day, 2002) report a positive cost/benefit ratio of $9.60 to $11 for every dollar spent on SFP, which underestimated the total benefit to the family as they were based on benefits to just the student and not the whole family. In addition, the high cost of SFP at an average of $700 to $1,400 per family can be considerably reduced by using more efficient delivery systems to effectively engage more families; for example, costs can be reduced to $4 per family for the DVD and handbook and about $100 if adding a family coach.

Miller and Hendrie (2008) also reported that no other substance abuse prevention program was more successful at preventing substance use in adolescents. The tables in their Appendix show significant reductions in substance use in youth participating in SFP compared to no-treatment controls, including an 18% reduction in alcohol use, 15% for marijuana, 11% for other drugs and even 7% for tobacco. The next best prevention program was also a family-based program called *Adolescent Transitions Program*, which demonstrated a 14%

reduction in alcohol use and a 12% reduction in tobacco use. These reductions were higher than all other family-focused or youth-only prevention programs.

Selection and Training of SFP Group Leaders and Site Coordinators

Certified SFP group leaders are selected by community agencies from their own staff or hired specifically part-time to implement SFP with families. No professional degrees or preparation are required to be an SFP program implementer. The key requirement is good group and people skills (including warmth, commitment to helping families, and interpersonal competences), and some background in psychology and social work. Prior experience working in groups with children or adults is helpful. In the two-day training workshop for certification of SFP group leaders, the SFP trainers recommend the best staffing of the children's and parents' groups based on observation of experiential role plays by the trainees. Another important point is that a training team for the facilitators should be ethnically and linguistically matched to and culturally competent for the target population (Kumpfer, Pinyuchon, de Melo, & Whiteside, 2008; Kumpfer, Xie, & Magalhães, 2012; Kumpfer, Xie, & O'Driscoll, 2012). A strong implementation also requires good clinical supervisors, called SFP Site Coordinators, to meet with staff directly after each session and at least weekly to review the progress of each family and the program. The best qualities of effective group leaders include warm and welcoming characteristics (Truax & Carkhuff, 1967) but also "work 'em hard" factors (e.g., being on time, high degree of preparation and group skills, and communication of high expectations for behavior change and home practice completion including family meetings, chore charts, and Child's Games; Kumpfer, Park, Magalhães, Amer, & Orte, in preparation). Most important is that the facilitators believe in the effectiveness of SFP and convey this enthusiasm to the families. Basically, "true believers" make the best facilitators.

Summary and Conclusions

Because of the increased effectiveness of involving the total family, including the extended family, to change the family system, family interventions are very promising models for improving many social and health problems. Since one of the core ingredients in SFP is local adaptation, we expect SFP to grow and develop as future needs evolve. SFP and similar family skills programs are an excellent way to improve resilience and behavioral health outcomes for parents, children and adolescents (Kumpfer et al., 2011).

One area of future research with SFP is the use of the DVD video version or family group versions in primary care settings as recommended by the Institute of Medicine (2014). Currently none of the evidence-based family intervention programs mentioned in this book are approved for coverage in the Affordable Care Act because of a lack of RCTs in primary care. The US Preventive Task Force required existing studies of evidence-based programs in hospitals and outpatient clinics to approve them for government health care funding. Also, there is a need to get SFP on the web, YouTube, or in smart phone apps, which are currently being developed to speed up dissemination.

This article has reviewed the need for family interventions for high-risk children, the 30-year history of studies on SFP including mandated cultural adaptations, and the research results of the *Strengthening Families Program* in different contexts. The major goal of the developers is to improve the happiness and quality of life of families worldwide. As has been reported in this chapter, this can be achieved when using SFP as a tool for strengthening families. So far the research outcomes and family reports suggest this is true. Future dissemination of SFP and other family skills training programs in family groups or using digital technology could contribute greatly to improving behavioral and health outcomes for children and youth worldwide.

References

Bandura, A. (2001). Social cognitive theory: An agentic perspective. *Annual Review of Psychology, 52*(1), 1–26.

Biglan, A., & Taylor, T. K. (2000). Increasing the use of science to improve child-rearing. *Journal of Primary Prevention, 21*(2), 207–226.

Bowen, M. (1991). Alcoholism as viewed through family systems theory and family psychotherapy. *Family Dynamics Addiction Quarterly, 1*, 94–102.

Brody, G. H., Chen, Y.-f., Kogan, S. M., Yu, T., Molgaard, V. K., DiClemente, R. J., & Wingood, G. M. (2012). Family-centered program to prevent substance use, conduct problems, and depressive symptoms in Black adolescents. *Pediatrics, 129*(1), 108–115.

Brody, G. H., Chen, Y. F., Beach, S. R., Kogan, S. M., Yu, T., Diclemente, R. J. et al. (2013). Differential sensitivity to prevention programming: A dopaminergic polymorphism-enhanced prevention effect on protective parenting and adolescent substance use. *Health Psychology*, Feb. 4 (E publication ahead of print).

Bröning, S., Kumpfer, K. L., Kumpfer, K., Kruse, K., Sack, P. M., Schaunig-Busch, I. et al. (2012). Selective prevention programs for children from substance-affected families: A systematic review. *Substance Abuse Treatment, Prevention, and Policy, 7*, 23.

Brook, J., McDonald, T. P., & Yan, Y. (2012). An analysis of the impact of the Strengthening Families Program on family reunification in child welfare. *Children and Youth Services Review, 34*, 691–695.

Caspi, A., Sugden, K., Moffitt, T. E., Taylor, A., Craig, I. W., Harrington, H. et al. (2003). Influence of life stress on depression: Moderation by a polymorphism in the 5-HTT gene. *Science, 301*, 386–389.

Champagne, F. (2010). Epigenetic influences of social experiences across the lifespan. *Developmental Psychobiology, 52*, 299–311.

Champagne, F. A., & Meaney, M. J. (2007). Transgenerational effects of social environment on variations in maternal care and behavioral response to novelty. *Behavioral Neuroscience, 111*(6), 1353–1363.

Chassin, L., Carle, A., Nissim-Sabat, D., & Kumpfer, K. L. (2004). Fostering resilience in children of alcoholic parents. In Maton, K. I. (Ed.), *Investing in Children, Youth, Families, and Communities: Strengths-based Research and Policy.* Washington, DC: APA Books.

DeMarsh, J. P., & Kumpfer, K. L. (1985). Family-oriented interventions for the prevention of chemical dependency in children and adolescents. *Journal of Children in Contemporary Society: Advances in Theory and Applied Research, 18*(122), 117–151.

Foxcroft, D. R., Ireland, D., Lister-Sharp, D. J., Lowe, G., & Breen, R. (2003). Longer-term primary prevention for alcohol misuse in young people: A systematic review. *Addiction, 98*, 397–411.

Gottfredson, D., Kumpfer, K., Polizzi-Fox, D., Wilson, D., Puryear, V., Beatty, P., & Vilmenay, M. (2006). The Strengthening Washington D.C. Families Project: A randomized effectiveness trial of family-based prevention. *Prevention Science, 7*, 57–74.

Harrison, S., Boyle, S. W., & Farley, O. W. (1999). Evaluating the outcomes of a family-based intervention for troubled children: A pretest-posttest study. *Research on Social Work Practice, 9*(6), 640–655.

Institute of Medicine (2014). Strategies for scaling tested and effective family-focused preventive interventions to promote children's cognitive, affective, and behavioral health: A workshop. April 1–2, 2014, National Academy of Sciences, Washington, DC.

Jirtle, R. (2010). Epigenetic mechanisms on gene expression. Plenary Session I, Annual Conference of the Society for Prevention Research. Denver, Colorado, June 2.

Kaminski, J. W., Valle, L. A., Filene, J. H., & Boyle, C. L. (2008). A meta-analytic review of components associated with parent training program effectiveness. *Journal of Abnormal Psychology, 36*, 567–589.

Kaufman, J., Yang, B.-Z., Douglas-Palumber, H., Crouse-Artus, M., Lipschitz, D., Krystal, J., & Gelernter, J. (2007). Genetic and environmental predictors of early alcohol use. *Biological Psychiatry, 61*, 1228–1234.

Kreek, M. J., Nielsen, D. A., & Laforge, K. S. (2004). Genes associated with addiction: Alcoholism, opiate, and cocaine addiction. *Neuromolecular Medicine, 5*(1), 85–108.

Kumpfer, K. L. (1987). Special populations: Etiology and prevention of vulnerability to chemical dependency in children of substance abusers. In Brown, B. S. & Mills, A. R. (Eds.), *Youths at High Risk for Substance Abuse* (pp. 1–71). Rockville, MD: NIDA.

Kumpfer, K. L. (1991). How to get hard-to-reach parents involved in parenting programs. In Pines, D., Crute, D., & Rogers, E. (Eds.), *Parenting as Prevention* (pp. 87–95). Rockville, MD: OSAP.

Kumpfer, K. L. (1998). Selective prevention interventions: The Strengthening Families Program. In Ashery, R., Robertson, E., & Kumpfer, K. L. (Eds.), *Drug Abuse Prevention through Family Intervention.* NIDA Research Monograph Series #177: DHHS Pub. No. 99-4135.

Kumpfer, K. L. (1999). Factors and processes contributing to resilience: The resilience framework. In Glantz, M. D. & Johnson, J. L. (Eds.), *Resilience and Development: Positive Life Adaptations.* New York: Kluwer Academic/Plenum.

Kumpfer, K. L. (2014). Family-based interventions for the prevention of substance abuse and other impulse control disorders in girls. Invited Spotlight Article, *ISRN Addiction,* Hindawi Publishing.

Kumpfer, K. L., & Alvarado, R. (2003). Family-strengthening approaches for the prevention of youth problem behaviors. *American Psychologist, 58*, 6–7.

Kumpfer, K. L., Alvarado, R., Smith, P., & Bellamy, N. (2002). Cultural sensitivity in universal family-based prevention interventions. *Prevention Science, 3*(3), 241–244.

Kumpfer, K. L., Alvarado, R., Tait, C., & Turner, C. (2002). Effectiveness of school-based family and children's skills training of substance abuse prevention among 6–8 year old rural children. *Psychology of Addictive Behaviors, 16*(4 Suppl): S65–71.

Kumpfer, K. L., Alvarado, R., & Whiteside, H. O. (2003). Family-based interventions for substance abuse prevention. *Substance Use and Misuse, 38*(11–13): 1759–1789.

Kumpfer, K. L., Alvarado, R., Whiteside, H. O., & Tait, C. (2005). The Strengthening Families Program (SFP): An evidence-based, multi-cultural family skills training program. In Szapocznik, J., Tolan, P., & Sambrano, S. (Eds.), *Preventing Substance Abuse* (pp. 3–14). Washington, DC: American Psychological Association.

Kumpfer, K. L., & Brown, J. (2012). New way to reach parents: A SFP DVD. Western States Substance Abuse Annual ATOD conference, Boise, ID. Sept. 22, 2012.

Kumpfer, K. L., & DeMarsh, J. P. (1986). Family environmental and genetic influences on children's future chemical dependency. In Ezekoye, S., Kumpfer, K. L., & Bukoski, W. (Eds.), *Childhood and Chemical Abuse: Prevention and Intervention*. New York: Haworth.

Kumpfer, K. L., & Fenollar, J. (2011). Evaluation of the Strengthening Families Health Program with Pacific Islanders. Unpublished report to the Utah State Department of Health, Salt Lake City, Utah.

Kumpfer, K. L., Greene J. A., Allen, K. C., & Miceli, F. (2010). Effectiveness outcomes of four age versions of the Strengthening Families Program in statewide field sites. *Group Dynamics: Theory, Research, and Practice, 14*(3), 211–229.

Kumpfer, K. L., & Hansen, W. (2014). Family based prevention programs. In Scheier, L. & Hansen, W. (Eds.), *Parenting and Teen Drug Use* (pp. 166–192). Oxford: Oxford University Press.

Kumpfer, K. L., & Johnson, J. (2007). Strengthening family interventions for the prevention of substance abuse in children of addicted parents. *Addicciones, 11*(1), 1–13.

Kumpfer, K. L., & Johnson, J. L. (2011). Enhancing positive outcomes for children of substance-abusing parents, In Johnson, B. A. (Ed.), *Addiction Medicine: Science and Practice* (pp. 30–50). New York: Springer.

Kumpfer, K. L., & Magalhães, C. (in press). Prevention as treatment: Enhancing resilience in high-risk children. In Maltzman, S. (Ed.), *The Oxford Handbook of Treatment Processes and Outcomes in Counseling Psychology*. Oxford: Oxford University Press.

Kumpfer, K. L., Molgaard, V., & Spoth, R. (1996). The Strengthening Families Program for the prevention of delinquency and drug use. In Peters, R. D. & McMahon, R. J. (Eds.), *Preventing Childhood Disorders, Substance Abuse, and Delinquency* (pp. 241–267). Thousand Oaks, CA: Sage Publications.

Kumpfer, K. L., Park, M., Magalhães, C., Amer, J., & Orte, C. (in preparation). The impact of client satisfaction and quality of the facilitator on family intervention outcomes. *Journal of Health Education Research*.

Kumpfer, K. L., Pinyuchon, M., de Melo, A., & Whiteside, H. (2008). Cultural adaptation process for international dissemination of the Strengthening Families Program (SFP). *Evaluation and Health Professions, 33*(2), 226–239.

Kumpfer, K. L., Smith, P., & Summerhays, J. F. (2008). A wake-up call to the prevention field: Are prevention programs for substance use effective for girls? *Substance Use and Misuse, 43*(8), 978–1001.

Kumpfer, K. L., Xie, J., & Hu, Q. (2011). Engendering resilience in families facing chronic adversity through family strengthening programs. In Gow, K. & Celinski, M. (Eds.), *Wayfinding through Life's Challenges: Coping and Survival* (pp. 461–483). New York: Nova Science.

Kumpfer, K. L., Xie, J., & Magalhães, C. (2012). Cultural adaptations of evidence-based family interventions to strengthen families and improve children's outcomes. *European Journal of Developmental Psychology, 9*(1), 104–116.

Kumpfer, K. L., Xie, J., & O'Driscoll, R. (2012). Effectiveness of a culturally adapted Strengthening Families Program 12–16 Years for high risk Irish families. *Child and Youth Care Forum, 41,* 173–195.

Miller, T. A., & Hendrie, D. (2008). *Substance Abuse Prevention: Dollars and Cents: A Cost-Benefit Analysis.* DHHS Pub. No. 07-4298. Rockville, MD: Center for Substance Abuse Prevention (CSAP), SAMHSA.

Munafo, M., Lingford-Hughes, A., Johnstone, E., & Walton, R. (2005). Association between serotonin transporter gene and alcohol consumption in social drinkers. *American Journal of Medical Genetics, Part B: Neuropsychiatric Genetics,* 135B, 10–14.

NIDA (1997). *Drug Prevention for At-risk Groups.* National Institute on Drug Abuse. Rockville, MD: Government Printing Office.

Patterson, G. R., & Banks, C. L. (1989). Some amplifying mechanisms for pathologic processes in families. In Gunnar, M. & Thelen, E. (Eds.), *Systems and Development: Symposia on Child Psychology* (pp. 167–210). Hillsdale, NJ: Erlbaum.

Patterson, G. R., DeGarmo, D., & Forgatch, M. (2004). Systematic changes in families following prevention trials. *Journal of Abnormal Child Psychology, 32,* 621–633.

Propper, C., & Moore, G. A. (2006). The influence of parenting on infant emotionality: A multi-level psychobiological perspective. *Developmental Review, 26,* 427–460.

SAMHSA (2013). *Behavioral Health, United States, 2012.* Rockville, MD: Substance Abuse and Mental Health Services Administration.

Spoth, R., Clair, S., Shin, C., & Redmond, C. (2006). Long-term effects of universal preventive interventions on methamphetamine use among adolescents. *Archives of Pediatrics & Adolescent Medicine, 160,* 876–882.

Spoth, R. L., Guyll, M., & Day, S. (2002). Universal family-focused interventions in alcohol-use disorder prevention: Cost-effectiveness and cost-benefit analyses of two interventions. *Journal of Studies on Alcohol, 63*(2), 219–228.

Spoth, R., Redmond, C., Shin, C., & Azevedo, K. (2004). Brief family intervention effects on adolescent substance initiation: School-level growth curve analysis 6 years following baseline. *Journal of Consulting and Clinical Psychology, 72,* 535–542.

Spoth, R. L., Trudeau, L. S., Guyll, M., & Shin, C. (2012). Benefits of universal intervention effects on a youth protective shield 10 years after baseline. *Journal of Adolescent Health, 50*(4), 414–417.

Spoth, R., Trudeau, L., Guyll, M., Shin, C., & Redmond, C. (2009). Universal intervention effects on substance use among young adults mediated by delayed adolescent substance initiation. *Journal of Consulting and Clinical Psychology, 77*(4), 620–632.

Truax, C. B., & Carkhuff, R. R. (1967). *Towards Effective Counseling and Psychotherapy.* Chicago, IL: Aldine.

United Nations Office on Drugs and Crime (UNODC, 2009). *Guide to Implementing Family Skills Training Programs for Drug Abuse Prevention.* Geneva: UN Publications.

5

THE FAMILY CHECK-UP MODEL AS PREVENTION AND TREATMENT OF ADOLESCENT DRUG (AB)USE

The Intervention Strategy, Outcomes, and Implementation Model

Thomas J. Dishion and Anne Marie Mauricio

Introduction

During the past 20 years of research, our understanding of the contribution of the family to the etiology of adolescent drug use has evolved tremendously in terms of the sophistication of measurement, research design, and experimental rigor. Several recent randomized prevention trials targeting parenting practices have revealed benefits for reducing problem behavior and drug use in adolescence and young adulthood (e.g., Gonzales et al., 2012; Liddle, 2010; Sandler, Schoenfelder, Wolchik, & MacKinnon, 2011; Szapocznik & Williams, 2000; Waldron & Brody, 2010; Wolchik et al., 2013). In this chapter, we provide an overview of the empirical literature that reports about the contribution of the family in general and parenting in particular to adolescent drug use. We then review recent iterations in the design of the Family Check-Up model (FCU; Dishion & Kavanagh, 2003b; Dishion & Stormshak, 2007) based on these findings. The FCU is an integrated brief, tailored prevention and treatment strategy that focuses on support of family management strategies.

Before the 1970s, longitudinal studies about the contribution of the family to adolescent problem behavior focused primarily on delinquency (Loeber & Dishion, 1983). These studies, conducted largely by criminologists, strongly implicated disorganized, harsh, or lenient parenting as among the strongest predictors of delinquent behavior in adolescence. Another powerful predictor, as might be suspected, was antisocial behavior in childhood, consisting of unconventional rules-transgressing behaviors rated by teachers or parents (Loeber & Dishion, 1983). McCord's (1981) important longitudinal study of male preadolescents residing in the Boston area revealed that problem drinking and criminal behavior in adulthood were associated with early aggression, harsh

The Family Check-Up Model **87**

and punitive parenting, conflict in the family, and poor supervision after school. Alternatively, the childrearing histories for adults with problem drinking but no history of criminal behavior were similar to those of adults with moderate or little alcohol use. Together, these findings suggest that family dynamics contribute to the etiology of problem drinking and criminal behavior. A notable feature of the McCord study was the use of home visitors' observations to measure parenting practices. A methodological weakness of early studies of adolescent drug use was reporting bias, in that only the youths described their problem behavior and their perceptions of parent and peer influences.

The McCord study (1981) is also a good example of scientific progress in the etiological studies of problematic substance use. In fact, it was not until the 1970s that an empirically supported connection was made between the etiology of adolescent problem behavior and multiple forms of substance use (e.g., Smith & Fogg, 1979). Carefully conducted longitudinal research with epidemiologically defined samples of youths confirmed that problem behavior (e.g., aggression) and emotional adjustment (e.g., shyness) preceded both tobacco and marijuana use in adolescence (Kellam, Brown, Rubin, & Ensminger, 1983). Findings from longitudinal research also suggested that aggression and parenting practices both preceded adult alcohol abuse (McCord, 1988). Findings such as these were a beacon to an emerging field of drug prevention research that targeted aggression and family management practices.

The shared developmental pathway of problem behavior and substance use suggests shared genetic and environmental etiologies (Cadoret, 1992; Cloninger & Gottesman, 1987; McCord, 1988). Genetic and environmental models of influence posit that parental drug use is a principal antecedent to adolescent substance use and abuse. One of the barriers to identifying a significant relation between parental behaviors and adolescent outcome was the weak measurement of parental drug use, which often relied on single-item measures. Studies that more intensively measured parental substance use have found more robust connections between parent and adolescent use (Chassin, Presson, Sherman, Corty, & Olshansky, 1984). However, as longitudinal studies progressed to include a wider array of risk factors, including peer influences (Kandel, 1973), it was generally found that a shift occurred in early adolescence toward peer influences exceeding those of parents in predicting adolescent substance use (Chassin, Presson, Sherman, Montello, & McGrew, 1986; Kandel, 1973; Patterson, 1993). Moreover, when parental influence was separated into parental substance use and parental monitoring practices, evidence strongly favored the weight of parental monitoring over parental substance use as a more direct influence on adolescent drug use (Baumrind, 1985; Dishion & Loeber, 1985). Longitudinal models became more sophisticated over time and revealed that parental substance use effects on adolescent drug use were mediated by factors such as parental monitoring (Chassin, Pillow, Curran, Molina, & Barrera, 1993a, 1993b).

Developmental Cascades

The converging perspective of shared environmental etiology of problem behavior and the role of parenting and peer environments naturally led to a broader ecological view of adolescent drug use etiology (Bronfenbrenner, 1989). Dishion, Capaldi, and Yoerger (1999) studied the impact of 200 boys' behavior patterns and ecology on the initiation of tobacco, alcohol, and marijuana use. As expected, the onset of alcohol and marijuana use was predicted by the boys' antisocial behavior, parents' poor discipline practices, and parental substance use. The onset of tobacco use was predicted not only by antisocial behavior but also by family low socioeconomic status and the boys' low social preference according to peer nominations. In this longitudinal study, parental monitoring and involvement with drug-using peers did not emerge as strong predictors of adolescent substance use until age 13–14 (Dishion, Capaldi, Spracklen, & Li, 1995).

A developmental perspective on the emergence of adolescent drug use suggests that a series of behavioral stages begins in early childhood that can result in increasingly serious forms of adolescent problem behavior and substance use (see Figure 5.1). In early childhood, behaviors such as defiance and poor self-regulation are prognostic of antisocial behavior in elementary school (Shaw, Gilliom, Ingoldsby, & Nagin, 2003). As described earlier, antisocial behavior in childhood is a strong predictor of more serious forms of problem behavior

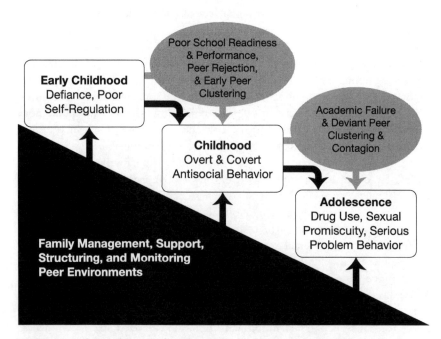

FIGURE 5.1 Behavioral Stages of Adolescent Problem Behavior and Substance Use

in adolescence, including substance use. In this cascade of outcomes, each stage of development leads to a series of adaptations, each of which forms the foundation for behavior that follows (Patterson, Reid, & Dishion, 1992). In this model, the downward direction of youth adjustment involves engagement in behaviors that are increasingly self-destructive and antisocial.

Figure 5.1 illustrates two important features of the developmental cascade perspective. First, each stage of development is accompanied by amplifying mechanisms (e.g., Patterson & Bank, 1989). In childhood, poor performance (i.e., lack of school readiness) and rejection by peers because of significant antisocial behavior at school entry are particularly problematic and are the two strongest predictors of early deviant peer involvement (Dishion, Patterson, Stoolmiller, & Skinner, 1991). As such, the dynamics of peer rejection and peer clustering begin much earlier than in early adolescence. Snyder et al. (2005) found that children in kindergarten were beginning the process of deviancy training by supporting one another in enacting deviant behavior in the school setting, including mimicking adult behaviors, such as cigarette smoking. Cairns and colleagues (Cairns, Cairns, Neckerman, Gest, & Gariepy, 1988) also found that early aggression was associated with peer clustering in elementary school, and these groups often formed the core social network of the school. School contexts that have a high prevalence of problem behavior are also those that confer high social status to children who are antisocial (Stormshak et al., 1999).

The early shift from aggressive behavior to other forms of problem behavior has been given various labels, including *covert antisocial behavior* and *overt antisocial behavior* (Loeber & Schmaling, 1985; Patterson et al., 1992). The terms *proactive antisocial behavior* and *reactive antisocial behavior* may be more accurate because in this definitional framework the first term suggests a modicum of planning and masking, whereas the latter term suggests behavior that is emotionally driven and impulsive. The two types of antisocial behaviors are obviously correlated, but the key is that proactive antisocial behavior is highly embedded within a deviant peer environment, and it is often furtive and avoidant of detection (Poulin & Boivin, 2000).

The movement from antisocial behavior in childhood to more serious forms of problem behavior is amplified by the increasing tendency for youths to self-organize into groups that directly support, model, reinforce, and provide resources to engage in drug use and other forms of antisocial behavior. In one longitudinal study, daily telephone interviews were conducted with adolescents and their parent, during which time they were asked to recall their experiences in the family and the peer group in the previous 24 hours. "Number of unsupervised hours with peers" was the best predictor of growth in substance use in early adolescence and was stronger than youth and parent report of exchanges of affection, talking about the day's activities, and having meals together (Dishion, Bullock, & Kiesner, 2008).

The central role of parenting from early childhood through adolescence is the second important feature of the developmental cascade in preventing or reducing progression of the high-risk trajectory (see Figure 5.1). In early childhood, direct socialization of children requires more intense daily teaching and positive behavior support (Shaw et al., 2003), whereas in adolescence, monitoring and structuring of peer environments comes increasingly into play (Dishion, Nelson, & Bullock, 2004). Several studies have suggested the importance of family management and parental monitoring, particularly with respect to adolescent drug use, and their pivotal role holds across cultural groups (Barrera, Castro, & Biglan, 1999; Catalano et al., 1992).

Most of the links in the developmental cascade model from early childhood through adolescence have been investigated in unique research studies. Dodge et al. (2009) tested much of the model depicted in Figure 5.1 by using a sample of 585 youths first assessed in early childhood and followed through adolescence. As expected, early childhood behavior difficulties led to later behavior problems at school age, which in turn predicted peer relationship difficulties. Peer relationship difficulties and deviant peer involvement were prognostic of adolescent drug use. Early parenting in this study was assessed primarily by conducting interviews with youths and parents. Laird and colleagues (Laird, Criss, Pettit, Dodge, & Bates, 2008) examined the same sample and found that youths whose parents maintained their monitoring practices were less influenced by deviant peer involvement in adolescence. Thus, the consequential role of parenting through adolescence was confirmed longitudinally after a person-centered approach was used to analyze the youths' developmental trajectories. Later, Dick et al. (2009) analyzed the European American subset of this sample and found evidence that parental monitoring moderates the impact of genetic susceptibility (GABRA2 polymorphism) on the emergence and course of a high-risk trajectory for problem behavior and substance use. This finding fits the general perspective that genetic risk for problem behavior is most likely a tendency for some children to be more susceptible than others to risky environments (Belsky, Bakermans-Kranenburg, & van Izendoorn, 2007).

Although the developmental progression of substance use to adolescence and young adulthood has been well studied, there are two major limitations to the existent science. First, the vast majority of research about adolescent substance use is based on youth self-reports at long temporal intervals, often occurring once a year. Only a handful of studies have examined adolescent substance use in shorter time intervals, which could potentially identify different predictors. For example, the Dishion and Medici Skaggs (2000) study of monthly "bursts" of adolescent substance use involved a combination of monthly parent and youth report. The maximum score of each reporting agent was used, and then monthly covariates were identified using generalized estimation equations. It was found that variation in amount of unsupervised time with peers predicted monthly bursts in substance use. In general, the development of ecological momentary assessments will lend itself to a renewed appreciation of the covariates of substance use (e.g., Stone & Shiffman, 1994). The second major limitation is that models that incorporate molecular genetic effects are limited with respect to the amount of variation accounted for by genetic factors. Although these pioneering studies suggest interesting and potentially important gene by environment interactions, there is less evidence that such findings will inform future intervention research. One of the key scientific benchmarks in family-based research about substance use is to also identify the endophenotype or temperament factor that accurately describes the mediation of genetic effects on adolescent drug use (Rutter, 2006; Wills & Dishion, 2004). It is likely that the application of diverse methodological strategies for studying substance use will define new directions for the study of family contributions to adolescent substance use.

Translational Research: Design of the Family Check-Up Model

Intervention experiments and developmental research are mutually informative, and randomized studies that are designed to intervene on developmental mediators can be thought of as tests of causal hypotheses (Cook & Campbell, 1979; MacKinnon & Fairchild, 2009). When developmental hypotheses are translated into prevention experiments, we can test the extent to which manipulation of a developmental dynamic confers reduced risk on participating children (Dishion & Patterson, 1999; McCord & Tremblay, 1992; Sandler et al., 2011). To date, several longitudinal intervention experiments have provided empirical support for interventions that target parenting and result in reductions in adolescent substance use (e.g., Gonzales et al., 2012; Kosterman, Hawkins, Guo, Catalano, & Abbott, 2000; Liddle, 2010; Spoth, Redmond, & Shin, 2001; Spoth, Reyes, Redmond, & Shin, 1999; Waldron & Brody, 2010).

In the late 1980s, Dishion and colleagues embarked on a first effort to apply the developmental model shown in Figure 5.1 to prevent the emergence of substance use among high-risk adolescents (Dishion, Reid, & Patterson, 1988). This NIDA-funded study tested two model-driven intervention paradigms to formulate the core components of what became the Adolescent Transitions Program (ATP; Dishion & Kavanagh, 2003a). A randomized trial of the ATP model tested the unique and combined efficacy of a cognitive-behavioral approach to supporting high-risk adolescents' self-regulation with an intervention focusing on parents' family management strategies. Both the youth and parent interventions were administered in a group format during a 12-week period, with manualized curricula. In short, our findings strongly suggested that the family management groups reduced risk for substance use (Dishion & Andrews, 1995), but unfortunately, we also found that aggregating youths into groups increased early-onset substance use (Poulin, Dishion, & Burraston, 2001).

This early intervention experiment suggested three revisions to the intervention program for young adolescents. First, because aggregating youths into groups for preventive curricula might actually increase risk in some circumstances, an outcome later revealed in a more comprehensive review, we eliminated the intervention component that involved aggregating youths into groups to minimize potential harm (Dodge, Dishion & Lansford, 2006; Poulin et al., 2001). Second, to reach parents of high-risk youths, family-based services were embedded in the public school venue, a critical step for addressing the developmental trajectory of youths (Dishion, Andrews, Kavanagh, & Soberman, 1996). Third, a brief, motivational approach to engaging parents was essential so that families could be linked into more intensive supports as needed. This approach defines the integration of prevention and treatment. The early-starting and late-starting framework (Moffitt, 1993; Patterson, 1993) lends a developmental perspective on the intervention needs of adolescents and families at risk. *Early starting* refers to a general pattern of youths engaging in problem behavior during the childhood phase of development. In contrast, *late starting* refers to adolescent onset of problem behavior. Families of late-starting adolescents would likely require less support than those of early-starting adolescents. Thus, we created an adaptive and tailored approach to family intervention, the Family Check-Up, which uses assessments to identify the level and type of intervention that are optimal for each family (Dishion, Kavanagh, & Keisner, 1999). The overall intervention strategy defined universal, selected, and indicated components that would increase reach and effectiveness and featured repeated opportunities for families to engage (Dishion & Kavanagh, 2003b). In this chapter, we focus on the selected and indicated levels of the intervention model (shown in Figure 5.2).

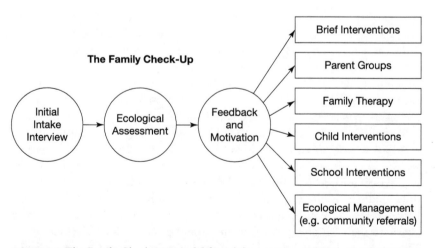

FIGURE 5.2 The Family Check-Up Model for Adolescent Drug (Ab)Use. Source: Dishion, T. J., & Stormshak, E. A. (2007). *Intervening in children's lives: An ecological, family-centered approach to mental health care.* American Psychological Association.

The Family Check-Up (FCU) model is a brief, three-session intervention based on motivational interviewing and modeled on the Drinker's Check-Up (Miller & Rollnick, 2002). The three FCU sessions include (a) an initial interview (20–30 minutes), (b) an assessment session (60 minutes), and (c) a feedback session involving the consultant and the parents (usually 60 minutes). In the initial interview, a parent consultant explores parent concerns and stage of change and encourages the parents to engage in a family assessment. In the assessment session, family members are videotaped while they engage in discussions about eight topics that are meant to help evaluate parent–child interactions. Topics include planning a family fun activity, discussing a family problem identified by the parent, and discussing how parents could help their adolescent improve in an area of personal growth identified by the youth. During the feedback session with the parent, the parent consultant summarizes the results of the assessment while using motivational interviewing strategies to support the parents' reflection on their own parenting practices. The approach is strengths based, in that parents are encouraged to reflect on those parenting practices that help reduce risk and promote the competence of their youth, as well as those parenting practices that may require attention. An essential objective of the feedback session is to explore potential evidence-based intervention services to support family management practices or potentially support the youth (as shown in Figure 5.2).

The major focus of the FCU is for the parent and parent consultant to reach a collaborative decision about the indicated services most appropriate for the family. Services include a tailored approach to parent management training based on the Everyday Parenting Curriculum (EPC; Dishion, Stormshak, & Kavanagh, 2011). The EPC is grounded in the Adolescent Transitions Program parenting group intervention (Dishion & Andrews, 1995) and the Parent Management Training–Oregon group parent training (Forgatch & Patterson, 2010). Although family management is the primary target in families that require indicated services, it is often recommended that youths engage in evidence-based interventions that support youth self-regulation with regard to depression, anxiety, or problem behaviors.

Figure 5.3 provides an overview of how interventions are tailored and adapted to meet youths' and families' specific needs. The specific intervention menu tailored to each family is based on findings from the ecological assessment of the child and family (Dishion & Stormshak, 2007). As shown in Figure 5.3, four broad domains of the youth and family environment are assessed for strengths and weaknesses: family context, family management, peer environment and youth behavior, and emotional adjustment. Following are three prototypical family profiles and the recommended approach to tailoring intervention support to address specific strengths and vulnerabilities as revealed in the child and family assessment.

- *Late-starting male with disrupted parenting and family stress*: This two-parent family included a stepfather and biological mother. The stepfather had been in the family since the youth's early childhood. The youth had a well-documented developmental history of attention deficit with hyperactivity that had largely been addressed by long-term motivated parenting and no use of medication. In recent years, the youth's otherwise average academic performance had dropped to failing. The parents' families of origin had recently had significant physical and mental health problems. The family's stress was linked to marital strains, maternal depression, and changes in parenting. The family's strengths were the parents' monitoring and limit-setting skills. Potential areas of vulnerability included the parents' need to work as a team and provide support for the youth to meet the challenge of increasing demands of school. The youth generally had not been involved with drug-using peers until recently. The tailored intervention focused on improving the parents' teamwork toward supporting positive behavior, increasing their awareness of the impact of stress on the marriage, and structuring positive activities for the youth that avoided unsupervised time with peers. A total of four post-FCU sessions focused on involving the youth and family in specific positive behavior support strategies (incentive system for meeting goals) and relationship building (negotiation of conflict).
- *Thirteen-year-old early-maturing female*: This single-mom, single-child family had substantial extended family involvement, and the mother had a strong, positive relationship with her daughter. The daughter was interpersonally competent and presented well socially. Her strengths included good grades, low levels of antisocial behavior, and her pleasant appearance. The family's vulnerability was the girl's increasing contact with an older male and his substance-using peer group. Following the feedback session, parental monitoring and limit setting were identified as the intervention target. The post-FCU intervention included two sessions about monitoring and limit setting.
- *Early-starting, early-maturing 12-year-old male with potential*: In this single-parent family with three children, the middle child was the intervention target. The older adolescent had had repeated contact with police and drug-use involvement, and was no longer living at home. The target child had shown problem behavior through elementary school. However, middle school constituted a period of improvement because the youth had strong athletic skills. As such, he had strong ties to older, gang-oriented peers as well as to prosocial peers. Although the mother was highly motivated and involved, she would escalate in her coercive exchanges with the youth when he became defiant, and her efforts to influence his behavior were limited. This family's six post-FCU sessions emphasized positive behavior support, monitoring and limit setting, and relationship building. Two family–school consultations focused on improving communication and cooperation between the family and school.

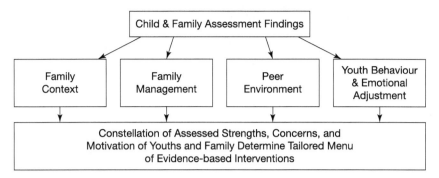

FIGURE 5.3 Tailoring Interventions to Meet Youths' and Families' Needs

These three profiles are common examples of families with early- to middle-adolescence youths who are showing problem behaviors and early involvement with drugs and alcohol. Although not exhaustive, these types of cases provide a sense of the assessment-driven tailoring strategies that follow the FCU. A critical foundation for tailoring is a collaborative set between the parent consultant and the engaged parent. Thus, strategies that fall within motivational interviewing and a generally respectful exchange of information and potential solutions frequently result in moving forward with future sessions. It has been found that following the FCU, 70% of the families of adolescents engaged in at least one parent training session using the EPC (Connell, Dishion, Yasui, & Kavanagh, 2007; Véronneau, Dishion, Connell, & Kavanagh, under review).

The principles that define the adapted and tailored approach to service delivery of the FCU model are summarized in Figure 5.4. For many families deemed as at risk, the key focus is on reducing the youth's risk by promoting family management practices. Three domains of family management skills are addressed in the EPC. The first is positive behavior support, which involves the use of tracking and positive reinforcement for promoting positive youth behavior. The second is monitoring the youth outside the home and using

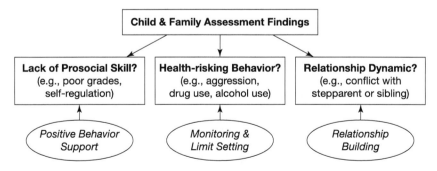

FIGURE 5.4 Three Domains of Family Management Skills

skillful limit setting that emphasizes planful and sane reactions to youth behaviors that are potentially hurtful to others (e.g., social or physical aggression) or to themselves (e.g., drug use). The third is relationship-building skills, which focuses on increasing the number of pleasant activities that involve each family member and the family as a whole and the use of well-developed problem-solving skills, which can include negotiating conflicts and disagreements between adolescents and their parents (Forgatch & Patterson, 1989).

When possible, it is preferable to begin with positive behavior support, move to monitoring and limit setting, and then to relationship building, as has been demonstrated in the parent management training developed at the Oregon Social Learning Center (see Forgatch & Patterson, 2010). If the parent possesses strong positive support strategies but circumstances outside the family (e.g., peers, romantic relationships) pull the youth toward health-risking behaviors, we begin with limit setting and monitoring. Relationship-building skills are typically not the beginning point when problem behaviors require resolution, in that unresolved adolescent problem behavior is one of the major disruptors of family relationships.

Intervention Outcomes from Randomized Trials

During the past 15 years since the original ATP trials, three randomized trials of the FCU were completed in the school setting, two randomized trials in early childhood were completed through the Women, Infants and Children (WIC) service delivery setting, and one randomized effectiveness trial was completed in community mental health settings. The WIC trials began with a study reported by Shaw et al. (Shaw, Dishion, Supplee, Gardner, & Arnds, 2006) during which child problem behavior between ages 2 and 4 improved, as did ratings of parents' involvement at home. The second WIC multi-site trial generated several outcomes studies. Of interest was the impact of the FCU on reducing maternal depression (Shaw, Connell, Dishion, Wilson, & Gardner, 2009). When the FCU was offered to high-risk WIC families during early childhood, school readiness improved and problem behavior decreased in the child by age 7.5 (Dishion et al., 2014). Consistent with the health maintenance approach of this intervention (offering the FCU annually), the effect sizes on parent- and teacher-reported problem behavior increased as a function of the number of FCU engagements at ages 2, 3, 4, and 5 years. As suggested by the developmental cascade model shown in Figure 5.1, early family support improved outcomes and reduced the risk that the child would progress to substance use.

Most relevant to this chapter are the FCU studies that focused on young adolescents. The two randomized trials in the public middle school settings, called Project Alliance 1 and Project Alliance 2, involved sixth-grade students in three multiethnic public middle schools. In both trials, the students were randomly assigned at the individual level to the FCU model or to public middle school as usual. A parent consultant was assigned to each school to engage parents of youths who had been identified as at risk by teachers. Services were provided primarily in the seventh and eighth grades. We also conducted an effectiveness trial, the Next Generation Project, which was based on the same intervention model.

In Project Alliance 1, we actively engaged 25% of the families assigned to the treatment group in the FCU during the 2 years of service. We had contact with an additional 25% of the families who did not receive the FCU. Largely, we found that the families at highest risk were the most likely to participate in the FCU (Connell, Dishion, & Deater-Deckard, 2006). They included single-parent families, those with students involved in a deviant peer group, and those rated by teachers as at high risk. Families at highest risk had an average of 6 hours of parent consultant contact. As one would expect, amount of contact time correlated with the student's risk level. Families with students at moderate risk engaged in approximately 3.5 hours of contact, and families at low risk averaged less than 1 hour of contact. Contact included telephone calls and personal communication and was recorded by the parent consultants by the minute (Dishion, Kavanagh, Schneiger, Nelson, & Kaufman, 2002).

The covariation between level of engagement and risk suggested that a response to intervention framework was appropriate for family interventions in school. The lowest risk families received minimal, universal support, which included a homeroom curriculum designed to promote success, health, and nonviolence and access to school-based family resource center services, which included brief consultations with parents and access to videotapes and books relevant to parents' concerns. Moderate-risk families more commonly used these general services, and high-risk families tended to engage in more intensive services, including the FCU. Consistent with an adaptive and tailored approach to intervention, the parent consultant was flexible in terms of the time of day, place (home vs. school), and type (individual or group). In addition, community referrals were used to address other aspects of the family ecology, such as parent depression, substance use, and/or need for psychiatric mediation. This flexibility and menu approach to intervention ensures that family ecology is recognized and addressed.

Intervention effects on parent engagement were also examined in the Next Generation project, which was conducted in another set of four public middle schools. In this study, we also carefully counted the minutes of contact with parents of students. Parent consultants often used creative means to engage parents. In one middle school, the parent consultant established a coffee cart for parents and would meet parents as they dropped their child off at school and picked up coffee. We found that the number of parent contacts in sixth, seventh, and eighth grades was associated with reductions in the growth of teacher-rated risk (Stormshak, Dishion, Light, & Yasui, 2005).

Several reports from these trials have been published regarding intervention effects on substance use. The first revealed that randomization to the family resource center in sixth grade was associated with reductions in substance use (Dishion, Kavanagh, et al., 2002) and in deviant peer involvement (Dishion, Bullock, & Granic, 2002) during a 4-year period. For youths at highest risk, reductions in drug use were mediated by changes in parental monitoring practices rated by independent observers (Dishion, Nelson, & Kavanagh, 2003). Key to this research was the proportion of the population who engaged in the intervention at the community level. One of the strengths of the intervention trials was that 90% of the identified population were included in the study, with 80% retention throughout a 10-year period. Thus, a 25% engagement rate with the highest risk participants suggests that the FCU intervention strategy is a viable component of a public health approach to reduce the prevalence of substance abuse.

In the past 10 years our research group augmented the analysis of family intervention effects by using complier average causal effect (CACE; Jo, 2002) modeling to systematically study how engagement in the FCU improves prevention outcomes for youths. This particular application of mixture modeling estimates engagement and nonengagement in the randomized control group, in that it defines a group of participants from the control group that resembles the nonengagers in the intervention group. In mixture modeling, estimates of engagers and nonengagers in the control group provide a latent variable of engagement for all participants. In the CACE framework, engagement status is modeled as a moderator of growth and change in problem behavior.

Using CACE modeling, we found that engagement in the FCU predicted long-term reductions in several indices of adolescent problem behavior. Moreover, the most dramatic effects of the FCU model were with sixth-grade students who were most severely problematic and whose families were most in need of services (Connell et al., 2007). When we used an intention-to-treat (ITT) design in which participants' outcomes were analyzed and reported based on initial placement in the control or intervention group regardless of whether or not they actually engaged in the offered treatment, the effects on outcomes were modest. However, when we compared the outcomes of families who were actively engaged in the intervention to those of control families who would have likely engaged in the FCU, the positive effects of the family intervention at age 19 were in the moderate to large range for several outcomes, including alcohol abuse and dependence ($OR = 0.09$), marijuana use ($OR = 0.22$), and arrest ($OR = 0.39$).

In our analysis of problem behavior, we found a marked reduction in the percentage of youths arrested among participants from the engager group who actually received the FCU (15% arrested), compared with those who would have engaged (based on their high-risk profile) but who were assigned to the control group (100% arrested). Thus, sixth-grade students at high risk whose parents were in need of support were 6 times as likely to be arrested within the next 5 years if they were not offered the FCU. Similarly, these youths used marijuana 5 times more frequently during a 1-month period than did the intervention group. These findings were extended to marijuana and to tobacco dependence by age 18 as well. In another study, CACE analyses revealed that random assignment to the intervention resulted in a 50% reduction in days absent from school from sixth through eleventh grade. Engagers in the control group missed an average of 32 days during the school year, and engagers in the intervention group missed only 13 (Stormshak, Connell, & Dishion, 2009).

The different sets of findings we attained from an ITT design and a CACE model point out the challenge for many randomized prevention trials: Many participants do not actually engage in the intervention, especially when it is offered on a voluntary basis. As mentioned earlier, when we tested the efficacy of the Family Check-Up intervention in public middle schools, 25% of all families in the randomized intervention group engaged in the FCU. In the context of CACE modeling, analyses revealed that single-parent families whose sixth-grade student reported deviant peer involvement and family conflict at baseline were the most likely to eventually engage in the intervention condition (Connell et al., 2007).

A new set of CACE analyses was performed to verify if the beneficial effects of the intervention on at-risk participants' substance use were maintained into early adulthood, that is, more than 10 years after the beginning of the study (Véronneau et al., under review). Results confirmed that engagers assigned to the control group used more alcohol throughout adolescence until age 21, and they presented more symptoms of alcohol abuse and dependence at age 23–24 than did at-risk students from the treatment group who engaged in the intervention. The same pattern of results emerged for tobacco use. Even though engagers who were assigned to the control group started to reduce their use of tobacco in late adolescence/early adulthood, their tobacco use was still estimated to be almost 2 times as much as that of engagers in the treatment group who benefited from the FCU, and they presented more symptoms of tobacco dependence at age 23–24.

Regarding marijuana use, engager participants assigned to the control group were marginally more likely to report symptoms of marijuana abuse or dependence at age 23–24 than were engagers who benefited from the treatment. Even more compelling, engagers assigned to the control group increased their marijuana use throughout adolescence at a much faster pace than did their counterparts who received the intervention, such that by age 21, the estimated use of this substance for engagers in the control group was 3 times greater than it was for their counterparts whose families had engaged in the FCU (Véronneau et al., under review).

Another trend is particularly important to consider in these three CACE analyses. Although it is often said that families who are at low or no risk are most likely to engage in family-based services offered in the school, we did not find this to be the case. Our proactive approach to offering the FCU suggested that, in fact, the families who declined participation were those who were at lowest risk. In other words, those parents accurately assessed their young adolescents' risk status and did not feel the need to receive information or support regarding behavior management strategies. This is an optimistic finding indeed, because it suggests that if the appropriate outreach and engagement strategies are in place for caregivers of the highest risk students, we are likely to reduce their long-term risk by motivating parental monitoring and positive behavior support. Because the highest risk parents engaged in the FCU services, collaboration between parents and schools seems possible and advisable. Overall, this study suggests the public health utility of the FCU model offered in a public school environment.

In a second randomized trial, Project Alliance 2, we randomly assigned 593 youths at the beginning of sixth grade to either the FCU model or middle school as usual. We examined the efficacy of the FCU regarding a number of outcomes related to successful youth development. Using CACE modeling, we found that participation in the FCU intervention substantially reduced the increase of substance use and problem behavior during the middle school years (Stormshak et al., 2011) and across the transition to high school (Van Ryzin, Stormshak, & Dishion, 2012). ITT analyses revealed that the intervention improved self-regulation skills, which in turn predicted decreased depression and increased school engagement (Stormshak, Fosco, & Dishion, 2010; Fosco, Frank, Stormshak, & Dishion, 2013). One of our goals was to engage a high percentage of families in the treatment model, and in meeting that goal, we also successfully recruited a robust number of families of ethnic minority status (64%). The percentage of families receiving the FCU or other intervention support was similar across ethnic groups, and the intervention was equally successful with all ethnic minority groups and with both males and females (Stormshak et al., 2010; Van Ryzin et al., 2012). Furthermore, the rate of engagement in the FCU was nearly double that of Project Alliance 1, with 42% of families in the intervention group receiving the entire FCU intervention, compared with 25% in the earlier project (Connell et al., 2007). We speculate that the increased level of engagement in Project Alliance 2 compared with that of Project Alliance 1 was the result of parent consultants' efforts to actively engage families and to match ethnicity of the parent consultant to that of each family. We also worked closely with schools to attend behavior support meetings and coordinate our services with those provided in the middle school setting.

We carefully examined the role of parenting in the development of problem behavior and maintenance of problem behavior over time in this sample. Several studies have revealed that parental monitoring and positive family relationships reduce the risk of depression (Margolis, Fosco, & Stormshak, 2014) and lead to positive changes in self-regulation and reductions in problem behavior (Fosco et al., 2013), whereas poor parental monitoring and negative family relationships predict declines in self-regulation and are associated with poor outcomes, such as substance use and affiliation with deviant peers (Fosco, Stormshak, Dishion, & Winter, 2012). Results from this series of studies underscore the importance of the parent–child relationship during the adolescent years, both as a risk factor and as a protective factor.

Because of the effectiveness of the FCU in remediating risk for adolescent substance use, problem behavior, and emotional distress, a true effectiveness study was conducted in community mental health settings. Smith, Stormshak, and Kavanagh (2014) randomly assigned indigenous therapists to training in the FCU model and tracked the outcomes of youths for 6 months afterward using parent report. The training in the FCU model, described in the following sections of this chapter, involved didactic workshop instruction and coaching and supervision of therapists by Dr. Kate Kavanagh. Study findings revealed that the therapists trained in the FCU model had improved outcomes with respect to parent reports of conduct problems. Because the average age of the youths was late childhood, the incidence of drug use was too low for analysis. This study suggests that the FCU model is potentially useful when the providers are trained mental health professionals.

Implementation Model

With strong empirical support across multiple service delivery contexts and the subsequent identification of the FCU as a model program (e.g., http://www. blueprintsprograms.com), scale-up of the FCU is underway. The FCU implementation model is based on the EPIS framework and has four phases: exploration, preparation, implementation, and sustainability (Novins, Green, Legha, & Aarons, 2013a, 2013b). Paralleling the "collaborative set" that is key to the success of the FCU model with families (Dishion & Stormshak, 2007), progression through each of the four phases is a collaborative process between the potential implementation site and the external FCU implementation team (ImpT). In collaboration with a leadership team that comprises the site's lead administrators and decision makers, model-specific benchmarks that are tailored to a site's context and capacity are identified for each phase. The FCU ImpT works with the leadership team to self-assess progress on and motivate achievement of benchmarks. If necessary, benchmarks are adapted during implementation in response to changes in the organization (e.g., unexpectedly high provider turnover) or external contextual factors (e.g., greater access to healthcare increases or decreases potential reach of the FCU). An at-least-once monthly meeting between the site's leadership team and the FCU ImpT to identify and resolve any potential barriers to implementation is common to all four phases.

Exploration Phase

The exploration phase involves information transfer about the FCU to the site's lead administrators/decision makers and an individualized multilevel assessment of the target site's readiness and capacity to implement the FCU with sustainability. At the organizational level, the aim of the readiness assessment is to discern that the personnel, fiscal, space, and technological resources required to implement the FCU with integrity are available. The extent to which the FCU is a fit with the organization's mission, has buy-in from lead administrators with decision-making power, and can be integrated into the organization's service delivery systems is also assessed as key indicators of readiness. Because excessively high caseloads with limited supervisory support are commonplace in public service sectors (Aarons & Sawitzky, 2006), a priority during the exploration phase is to ensure lead administrators' commitment to clinical supervision time. At the provider level, data are collected to assess provider and client perspectives about feasibility and acceptability of the FCU (Proctor et al., 2011). These data are used to inform selection of providers to be trained in the model and to highlight potential client-related implementation barriers (e.g., client resistance to videotaping). If the site does not meet the required benchmarks to implement the FCU with integrity and does not demonstrate the capacity for sustainability, the FCU ImpT outlines a readiness plan tailored to a site's strengths (e.g., providers highly motivated to implement the FCU) and challenges (e.g., inadequate fiscal capacity) that includes detailed actions the organization could take to attain benchmarks.

Preparation Phase

In the preparation phase, a team is assembled that is responsible for implementing the FCU at the site. The team includes an implementation coordinator and expert consultant from the FCU ImpT and lead administrators, supervisory staff, and providers from the implementation site; one of the team members from the implementation site, usually a supervisor, is the liaison between the external FCU ImpT and the implementation site. The site acquires (if necessary) and allocates required fiscal, space, and technology (e.g., video equipment) resources. Implementation benchmarks and a corresponding timeline are established; benchmarks include training dates and goals, and numbers of providers trained and certified in the model with specified target dates (i.e., rate of adoption). The training is a 4-day workshop and involves both didactic content presentation, which is effective for transferring knowledge, and enactive training methods, such as behavioral rehearsal, role-play, and modeling for skills acquisition (Lyon, Stirman, Kerns, & Bruns, 2011). A component of the training focuses on the transfer of technological skills and knowledge required to use the FCU systems that support implementation, monitoring, and quality assurance.

Implementation Phase

In the implementation phase, trained staff begin using the FCU with families and participate in weekly or biweekly group and individual consultation with the FCU consultant expert. Individual consultation focuses on assessing providers' adherence to the core FCU components and competence in delivering the FCU by using an empirically validated, observational implementation fidelity coding system, the COACH (Smith, Dishion, Shaw, & Wilson, 2013). The multidimensional COACH uses a 9-point scale (*needs work*, 1–3; *acceptable work*, 4–6; *good work*, 7–9) to assess the provider on five FCU-prescribed skills: (a) conceptual accuracy: provider understands the FCU model; (b) observant and responsive: provider shows clinical responsiveness to the client's immediate concerns and contextual factors; (c) actively structures sessions: provider skillfully structures the change process using assessment-driven case conceptualization; (d) careful and appropriate teaching: provider is able to skillfully give feedback and guidance to increase client motivation to change; and (e) hope and motivation: provider skillfully integrates therapeutic techniques that promote client hope, motivation, and change. The COACH's 9-point scale also is used to rate the client's level of engagement in the FCU session. Consistent with the FCU's theoretical model (Dishion & Stormshak, 2007), variations in fidelity link to change in child problem behaviors through improved parenting (Smith et al., 2013). Provider certification requires competent (i.e., 4–6 range) delivery of the FCU, and providers targeted to be on-site FCU trainers and supervisors begin the supervisor certification process immediately after achieving provider certification. Web-based assessment tools and feedback report functions help monitor providers' implementation and families' clinical outcomes, and FCU consultant experts use these data as quality assurance feedback loops (Bickman, 2008).

Sustainability Phase

The sustainability phase is defined by site capacity to maintain implementation of the FCU and its benefits over time (Schell et al., 2013). Benchmarks for the sustainability phase include significant reach and penetration of the FCU (e.g., 90% of all families serviced receive the FCU), which indicates that the FCU has been institutionalized at the site as usual care (Proctor et al., 2011). Indicators of institutionalization also include adoption of the FCU model and its processes into the site's operations and service delivery systems such that resources (e.g., space) and infrastructure (e.g., adequate number of trained/certified providers) required for implementation are inherent to the site. A supervisory structure that includes a fixed ratio of certified FCU trainers/supervisors per FCU providers and the capacity to train, supervise, and certify providers independent of the FCU ImpT is also required. A critical benchmark of the sustainability phase is an annually renewable funding source allocated specifically for FCU implementation. The site has also successfully adapted FCU monitoring systems and feedback loops to optimize implementation and outcomes and support practitioner efficacy in the model. In addition to within-organization political support among lead administrators, in the outer political context there is also explicit support for the program among political leaders with the power to shape policies that can have an impact on funding (Schell et al., 2013).

Conclusion

Research unequivocally supports the influential role of the family environment and parenting on the initiation and escalation of substance use in adolescence, which may lead to substance abuse and dependence in adulthood. Intervention researchers have translated the results of this science to develop family-centered interventions that efficaciously modify family environments and parenting practices, with subsequent reductions in substance use and other problem behaviors in adolescence and young adulthood. The FCU is one such intervention that has robust research support for effects on substance use and dependence, with the strongest effects emerging for families with youths at greatest risk for substance use and dependence (e.g., Véronneau et al., under review). The FCU's robust effects with regard to reduced substance use in conjunction with its success in engaging families, particularly those that are at high risk, and an empirically-informed, well-defined implementation model that successfully bolsters scalability suggests that the FCU has the potential for a significant public health impact.

References

Aarons, G. A., & Sawitzky, A. C. (2006). Organizational climate partially mediates the effect of culture on work attitudes and staff turnover in mental health services. *Administration and Policy in Mental Health and Mental Health Services Research, 33*(3), 289–301.

Barrera, M., Castro, F. G., & Biglan, A. (1999). Ethnicity, substance use and development: Exemplars for exploring group differences and similarities. *Development and Psychopathology, 11,* 805–822.

Baumrind, D. (1985). Familial antecedents of adolescent drug use: A developmental perspective. In C. L. Jones & R. J. Battjes (Eds.), *Etiology of drug abuse: Implication for prevention* (Research Monograph No. 56, pp. 14–44). Washington, DC: Government Printing Office.

Belsky, J., Bakermans-Kranenburg, M. J., & van Izendoorn, M. H. (2007). For better and for worse: Differential susceptibility to environmental influences. *Current Directions in Psychological Science, 16,* 300–304.

Bickman, L. (2008). A measurement feedback system (MFS) is necessary to improve mental health outcomes. *Journal of the American Academy of Child and Adolescent Psychiatry, 47*(10), 1114.

Bronfenbrenner, U. (1989). Ecological systems theory. In R. Vasta (Ed.), *Annals of child development: Vol. 6. Six theories of child development: Revised formulations and current issues* (pp. 187–249). London: Jai.

Cadoret, R. J. (1992). Genetic and environmental factors in initiation of drug use and the transition to abuse. In M. D. Glantz & R. W. Pickens (Eds.), *Vulnerability to drug abuse* (pp. 99–113). Washington, DC: American Psychological Association.

Cairns, R. B., Cairns, B. D., Neckerman, H. J., Gest, S. D., & Gariepy, J. (1988). Social networks and aggressive behavior: Peer support or peer rejection. *Developmental Psychology, 24,* 815–823.

Catalano, R. F., Morrison, D. M., Wells, E. A., Gilmore, M. R., Irritani, B., & Hawkins, J. D. (1992). Ethnic differences and family factors related to early drug initiation. *Journal of Studies on Alcohol, 53,* 208–217.

Chassin, L., Pillow, D. R., Curran, P. J., Molina, B. S., & Barrera, M. (1993a). Relation of parental alcoholism to early adolescent substance use: A test of three mediating mechanisms. *Journal of Abnormal Psychology, 102,* 3–19.

Chassin, L., Pillow, D. R., Curran, P. J., Molina, B. S., & Barrera, M. (1993b). Relation of parental alcoholism to early adolescent substance use: A test of three mediating mechanisms: Correction. *Journal of Abnormal Psychology, 102,* 558.

Chassin, L., Presson, C., Sherman, S., Corty, E., & Olshansky, R. (1984). Predicting the onset of cigarette smoking in adolescents: A longitudinal study. *Journal of Applied Social Psychology, 14,* 224–243.

Chassin, L., Presson, C. C., Sherman, S. J., Montello, D., & McGrew, J. (1986). Changes in peer and parent influence during adolescence: Longitudinal versus cross-sectional perspectives on smoking initiation. *Developmental Psychology, 22,* 327–334.

Cloninger, C. R., & Gottesman, I. I. (1987). Genetic and environmental factors in antisocial behavior disorders. In S. A. Mednick, T. E. Moffitt, & S. A. Stack (Eds.), *The causes of crime: New biological approaches* (pp. 92–109). Cambridge, UK: Cambridge University Press.

Connell, A. M., Dishion, T. J., & Deater-Deckard, K. (2006). Variable- and person-centered approaches to the analysis of early adolescent substance use: Linking peer, family, and intervention effects with developmental trajectories [Special Issue]. *Merrill-Palmer Quarterly, 52,* 421–448.

Connell, A. M., Dishion, T. J., Yasui, M., & Kavanagh, K. (2007). An adaptive approach to family intervention: Linking engagement in family-centered intervention to reductions in adolescent problem behavior. *Journal of Consulting and Clinical Psychology, 75,* 568–579.

Cook, T. D., & Campbell, D. T. (1979). *Quasi-experimentation design and analysis issues for field settings.* Boston, MA: Houghton Mifflin.

Dick, D. M., Latendresse, S. J., Lansford, J. E., Budde, J. P., Goate, A., Dodge, K. A., et al. (2009). Role of GABRA2 in trajectories of externalizing behavior across development and evidence of moderation by parental monitoring. *Archives of General Psychiatry, 66,* 649–657.

Dishion, T. J., & Andrews, D. (1995). Preventing escalations in problem behaviors with high-risk young adolescents: Immediate and 1-year outcomes. *Journal of Consulting and Clinical Psychology, 63,* 538–548.

Dishion, T. J., Andrews, D. W., Kavanagh, K., & Soberman, L. H. (1996). Preventive interventions for high-risk youth: The Adolescent Transitions Program. In B. McMahon & R. D. Peters (Eds.), *Conduct disorders, substance abuse and delinquency: Prevention and early intervention approaches* (pp. 184–214). Newbury Park, CA: Sage.

Dishion, T. J., Brennan, L. M., Shaw, D. S., McEachern, A. D., Wilson, M. N., & Jo. B. (2014). Prevention of problem behavior through annual Family Check-Ups in early childhood: Intervention effects from the home to early elementary school. *Journal of Abnormal Child Psychology, 42*(3), 343–354.

Dishion, T. J., Bullock, B. M., & Granic, I. (2002). Pragmatism in modeling peer influence: Dynamics, outcomes, and change processes. *Development and Psychopathology, 14*, 969–981.

Dishion, T. J., Bullock, B. M., & Kiesner, J. (2008). Vicissitudes of parenting adolescents: Daily variations in parental monitoring and the early emergence of drug use. In M. Kerr, H. Stattin, & R. C. M. E. Engels (Eds.), *What can parents do? New insights into the role of parents in adolescent problem behavior* (pp. 113–133). Chichester, UK: John Wiley & Sons.

Dishion, T. J., Capaldi, D., Spracklen, K. M., & Li, F. (1995). Peer ecology of male adolescent drug use. *Development and Psychopathology, 7*, 803–824.

Dishion, T. J., Capaldi, D. M., & Yoerger, K. (1999). Middle childhood antecedents to progression in male adolescent substance use: An ecological analysis of risk and protection. *Journal of Adolescent Research, 14*(2), 175–206.

Dishion, T. J., & Kavanagh, K. (2003a). The Adolescent Transitions Program: A family-centered prevention strategy for schools. In J. B. Reid, J. J. Snyder, & G. R. Patterson (Eds.), *Antisocial behavior in children and adolescents: A developmental analysis and the Oregon model for intervention* (pp. 257–272). Washington, DC: American Psychological Association.

Dishion, T. J., & Kavanagh, K. (2003b). *Intervening with adolescent problem behavior: A family-centered approach.* New York: Guilford.

Dishion, T. J., Kavanagh, K., & Kiesner, J. (1999). Prevention of early adolescent substance use among high-risk youth: A multiple gating approach to parent intervention. Drug abuse prevention through family interventions. In R. S. Ashery (Ed.), *Research meeting on drug abuse prevention through family interventions* (NIDA Research Monograph No. 177, pp. 208–228). Washington, DC: U.S. Government Printing Office.

Dishion, T. J., Kavanagh, K., Schneiger, A., Nelson, S. E., & Kaufman, N. (2002). Preventing early adolescent substance use: A family-centered strategy for the public middle-school ecology. In R. L. Spoth, K. Kavanagh, & T. J. Dishion (Eds.), Universal family-centered prevention strategies: Current findings and critical issues for public health impact [Special Issue]. *Prevention Science, 3*, 191–201.

Dishion, T. J., & Loeber, R. (1985). Adolescent marijuana and alcohol use: The role of parents and peers revisited. *American Journal of Drug and Alcohol Abuse, 11*, 11–25.

Dishion, T. J., & Medici Skaggs, N. (2000). An ecological analysis of monthly "bursts" in early adolescent substance use. *Applied Developmental Science, 4*, 89–97.

Dishion, T. J., Nelson, S. E., & Bullock, B. M. (2004). Premature adolescent autonomy: Parent disengagement and deviant peer process in the amplification of problem behavior [Special Issue]. *Journal of Adolescence, 27*, 515–530.

Dishion, T. J., Nelson, S. E., & Kavanagh, K. (2003). The Family Check-Up for high-risk adolescents: Preventing early-onset substance use by parent monitoring. In J. E. Lochman & R. Salekin (Eds.), Behavior-oriented interventions for children with aggressive behavior and/or conduct problems [Special Issue]. *Behavior Therapy*, 553–571.

Dishion, T. J., & Patterson, G. R. (1999). Model-building in developmental psychopathology: A pragmatic approach to understanding and intervention. *Journal of Clinical Child Psychology, 28*, 502–512.

Dishion, T. J., Patterson, G. R., Stoolmiller, M., & Skinner, M. (1991). Family, school, and behavioral antecedents to early adolescent involvement with antisocial peers. *Developmental Psychology, 27*, 172–180.

Dishion, T. J., Reid, J. B., & Patterson, G. R. (1988). Empirical guidelines for the development of a treatment for early adolescent substance use. In R. E. Coombs (Ed.), *The family context of adolescent drug use* (pp. 189–224). New York: Haworth.

Dishion, T. J., & Stormshak, E. A. (2007). *Intervening in children's lives: An ecological, family-centered approach to mental health care.* Washington, DC: APA Books.

Dishion, T. J., Stormshak, E. A., & Kavanagh, K. A. (2011). *Everyday parenting: A professional's guide to building family management skills*: Champaign, IL: Research Press.

Dodge, K. A., Dishion, T. J., & Lansford, J. E. (Eds.). (2006). *Deviant peer influences in programs for youth: Problems and solutions.* New York: Guilford.

Dodge, K. A., Malone, P. S., Lansford, J. E., Miller, S., Pettit, G. S., & Bates, J. E. (2009). A dynamic cascade model of the development of substance-use onset: Early peer relations problem factors. *Monographs of the Society for Research in Child Development, 74*, 51–54.

Forgatch, M. S., & Patterson, G. R. (1989). *Parents and adolescents living together: Part 2. Family problem-solving.* Eugene, OR: Castalia.

Forgatch, M. S., & Patterson, G. R. (2010). Parent management training—Oregon model: An intervention for antisocial behavior in children and adolescents. In J. R. Weisz & A. E. Kazdin (Eds.), *Evidence-based psychotherapies for children and adolescents* (pp. 159–178). New York: Guilford Press.

Fosco, G. M., Frank, J. L., Stormshak, E. A., & Dishion, T. J. (2013). Opening the "black box": Family Check-Up intervention effects on self-regulation that prevents growth in problem behavior and substance use. *Journal of School Psychology, 51*(4), 455–468.

Fosco, G. M., Stormshak, E. A., Dishion, T. J., & Winter, C. (2012). Family relationships and parental monitoring during middle school as predictors of early adolescent problem behavior. *Journal of Clinical Child and Adolescent Psychology, 41*(2), 202–213.

Gonzales, N. A., Dumka, L. E., Millsap, R. E., Gottschall, A., McClain, D. B., Wong, J. J., et al. (2012). Randomized trial of a broad preventive intervention for Mexican American adolescents. *Journal of Consulting and Clinical Psychology, 80*(1), 1–16.

Jo, B. (2002). Model misspecification sensitivity analysis in estimating causal effects of interventions with noncompliance. *Statistics in Medicine, 21*, 3161–3181.

Kandel, D. (1973). Adolescent marijuana use: Role of parents and peers. *Science, 181*, 1067–1081.

Kellam, S. G., Brown, C. H., Rubin, B. R., & Ensminger, M. E. (1983). Paths leading to teenage psychiatric symptoms and substance use: Developmental epidemiological studies in Woodlawn. In S. R. Guze, F. J. Earns, & J. E. Barrett (Eds.), *Childhood psychopathology and development* (pp. 17–51). New York: Raven.

Kosterman, R., Hawkins, J. D., Guo, J., Catalano, R. F., & Abbott, R. D. (2000). The dynamics of alcohol and marijuana initiation: Patterns and predictors of first use in adolescence. *American Journal of Public Health, 90*, 360–366.

Laird, R. D., Criss, M. M., Pettit, G. S., Dodge, K. A., & Bates, J. E. (2008). Parents' monitoring knowledge attenuates the link between antisocial friends and adolescent delinquent behavior. *Journal of Abnormal Child Psychology, 36*, 299–310.

Liddle, H. A. (2010). Treating adolescent substance abuse using multidimensional family therapy. In J. R. Weisz & A. E. Kazdin (Eds.), *Evidence-based psychotherapies for children and adolescents* (2nd ed.). New York: Guilford Press.

Loeber, R., & Dishion, T. J. (1983). Early predictors of male delinquency: A review. *Psychological Bulletin, 94*(1), 68–99.

Loeber, R., & Schmaling, K. B. (1985). Empirical evidence for overt and covert patterns of antisocial conduct problems: A meta-analysis. *Journal of Abnormal Child Psychology, 13,* 337–352.

Lyon, A. R., Stirman, S. W., Kerns, S. E., & Bruns, E. J. (2011). Developing the mental health workforce: Review and application of training approaches from multiple disciplines. *Administration and Policy in Mental Health and Mental Health Services Research, 38*(4), 238–253.

MacKinnon, D. P., & Fairchild, A. J. (2009). Current directions in mediation analysis. *Current Directions in Psychological Science, 18*(1), 16.

Margolis, K. L., Fosco, G. M., & Stormshak, E. A. (2014). Circle of care: Extending beyond primary caregivers to examine collaborative caretaking in adolescent development. *Journal of Family Issues,* OnlineFirst May 29, doi:10.1177/0192513X14536565.

McCord, J. (1981). Consideration of some effects of a counseling program. In S. E. Martin, L. B. Sechrest, & R. Redner (Eds.), *New directions in the rehabilitation of criminal offenders* (pp. 394–405). Washington, DC: The National Academy of Sciences.

McCord, J. (1988). Identifying developmental paradigms leading to alcoholism. *Journal of Studies on Alcohol, 49,* 357–362.

McCord, J., & Tremblay, R. E. (Eds.). (1992). *Preventing antisocial behavior: Interventions from birth through adolescence.* New York: Guilford Press.

Miller, W. R., & Rollnick, S. (2002). *Motivational interviewing: Preparing people for change* (2nd ed.). New York: Guilford.

Moffitt, T. E. (1993). Adolescence-limited and life course persistent antisocial behavior: Developmental taxonomy. *Psychological Review, 100,* 674–701.

Novins, D. K., Green, A. E., Legha, R. K., & Aarons, G. A. (2013a). Dissemination and implementation of evidence-based practices for child and adolescent mental health: A systematic review. *Journal of the American Academy of Child & Adolescent Psychiatry, 52*(10), 1009–1025.

Novins, D. K., Green, A. E., Legha, R. K., & Aarons, G. A. (2013b). Dissemination and implementation of evidence-based practices for child and adolescent mental health: A systematic review. Correction. *Journal of the American Academy of Child & Adolescent Psychiatry, 53*(3), 382.

Patterson, G. R. (1993). Orderly change in a stable world: The antisocial trait as a chimera. *Journal of Consulting and Clinical Psychology, 61,* 911–919.

Patterson, G. R., & Bank, L. (1989). Some amplifying mechanisms for pathologic processes in families. In M. R. Gunnar & E. Thalen (Eds.), *Systems and development: The Minnesota symposia on child psychology* (Vol. 22, pp.167–209). Hillsdale, NJ: Lawrence Erlbaum.

Patterson, G. R., Reid, J. B., & Dishion, T. J. (1992). *Antisocial boys.* Eugene, OR: Castalia.

Poulin, F., & Boivin, M. (2000). The role of proactive and reactive aggression: The formation and development of friendships in boys. *Developmental Psychology, 36,* 1–8.

Poulin, F., Dishion, T. J., & Burraston, B. (2001). 3-year iatrogenic effects associated with aggregating high-risk adolescents in cognitive–behavioral preventive interventions. *Applied Developmental Science, 5,* 214–224.

Proctor, E., Silmere, H., Raghavan, R., Hovmand, P., Aarons, G., Bunger, A., et al. (2011). Outcomes for implementation research: Conceptual distinctions, measurement challenges, and research agenda. *Administration and Policy in Mental Health and Mental Health Services Research, 38*(2), 65–76.

Rutter, M. (2006). *Genes and behavior: Nature–nurture interplay explained.* Malden, MA: Blackwell.

Sandler, I. N., Schoenfelder, E. N., Wolchik, S. A., & MacKinnon, D. P. (2011). Long-term impact of prevention programs to promote effective parenting: Lasting effects but uncertain processes. *Annual Review of Psychology, 62,* 299–329.

Schell, S. F., Luke, D. A., Schooley, M. W., Elliott, M. B., Herbers, S. H., Mueller, N. B., & Bunger, A. C. (2013). Public health program capacity for sustainability: A new framework. *Implementation Science, 8*(1), 15.

Shaw, D. S., Connell, A. M., Dishion, T. J., Wilson, M. N., & Gardner, F. (2009). Improvements in maternal depression as a mediator of intervention effects on early childhood problem behavior. *Development and Psychopathology, 21,* 417–439.

Shaw, D. S., Dishion, T. J., Supplee, L., Gardner, F., & Arnds, K. (2006). Randomized trial of a family-centered approach to the prevention of early conduct problems: Two-year effects of the Family Check-Up in early childhood. *Journal of Consulting and Clinical Psychology, 74,* 1–9.

Shaw, D. S., Gilliom, M., Ingoldsby, E. M., & Nagin, D. (2003). Trajectories leading to school-age conduct problems. *Developmental Psychology, 39,* 189–200.

Smith, G. M., & Fogg, C. P. (1979). Psychological antecedents of teen-age drug use. In R. G. Simmons (Ed.), *Research in community and mental health* (Vol. 1, pp. 87–102). Greenwich, CT: JAI Press.

Smith, J. D., Dishion, T. J., Shaw, D. S., & Wilson, M. N. (2013). Indirect effects of fidelity to the Family Check-Up on changes in parenting and early childhood problem behaviors. *Journal of Consulting and Clinical Psychology, 81*(6), 962–974.

Smith, J. D., Stormshak, E. A., & Kavanagh, K. (2014). Results of a pragmatic effectiveness– implementation hybrid trial of the Family Check-Up in community mental health agencies. *Administration and Policy in Mental Health and Mental Health Services Research.* Advance online publication.

Snyder, J., Schrepferman, L., Oeser, J., Patterson, G., Stoolmiller, M., Johnson, K., & Snyder, A. (2005). Deviancy training and association with deviant peers in young children: Occurrence and contribution to early-onset conduct problems. *Development & Psychopathology, 17,* 397–413.

Spoth, R. L., Redmond, C., & Shin, C. (2001). Randomized trial of brief family interventions for general populations: Adolescent substance use outcomes 4 years following baseline. *Journal of Consulting and Clinical Psychology, 69,* 627–642.

Spoth, R. L., Reyes, M. L., Redmond, C., & Shin, C. (1999). Assessing a public health approach to delay onset and progression of adolescent substance use: Latent transition and log-linear analyses of longitudinal family preventive intervention outcomes. *Journal of Consulting and Clinical Psychology, 67,* 619–630.

Stone, A. A., & Shiffman, S. (1994). Ecological momentary assessment (EMA) in behavioral medicine. *Annals of Behavioral Medicine, 16,* 199–202.

Stormshak, E. A., Bierman, K. L., Bruschi, C. J., Dodge, K. A., Coie, J. D., & Conduct Problems Prevention Research Group. (1999). The relation between behavior problems and peer preference in different classroom contexts. *Child Development, 70,* 169–182.

Stormshak, E. A., Connell, A. M., & Dishion, T. J. (2009). An adaptive approach to family-centered intervention in schools: Linking intervention engagement to academic outcomes in middle and high school. *Prevention Science, 10,* 221–235.

Stormshak, E. A., Connell, A. M., Véronneau, M.-H., Myers, M. W., Dishion, T. J., Kavanagh, K., & Caruthers, A. S. (2011). An ecological approach to promoting early adolescent mental health and social adaptation: Family-centered intervention in public middle schools. *Child Development, 82*, 209–225.

Stormshak, E. A., Dishion, T. J., Light, J., & Yasui, M. (2005). Implementing family-centered interventions within the public middle school: Linking service delivery change to change in problem behavior. *Journal of Abnormal Child Psychology, 33*, 723–733.

Stormshak, E. A., Fosco, G. M., & Dishion, T. J. (2010). Implementing interventions with families in schools to increase youth school engagement: The Family Check-Up model. *School Mental Health, 2*, 82–92.

Szapocznik, J. F., & Williams, R. A. (2000). Brief strategic family therapy: Twenty-five years of interplay among theory, research and practice in adolescent behavior problems and drug abuse. *Clinical Child and Family Psychology Review, 3*, 117–134.

Van Ryzin, M. J., Stormshak, E. A., & Dishion, T. J. (2012). Engaging parents in the Family Check-Up in middle school: Longitudinal effects on family conflict and problem behavior through the transition to high school. *Journal of Adolescent Health, 50*(6), 627–633.

Véronneau, M.-H., Dishion, T. J., Connell, A. M., & Kavanagh, K. (under review). A randomized, controlled trial of the Family Check-Up model in public secondary schools: Linking parent engagement to substance use progressions from early adolescence to adulthood. *Journal of Consulting and Clinical Psychology.*

Waldron, H. B., & Brody, J. L. (2010). Functional family therapy for adolescent substance use disorders. In J. R. Weisz & A. E. Kazdin (Eds.), *Evidence-based psychotherapies for children and adolescents* (pp. 401–415). New York: Guilford Press.

Wills, T. A., & Dishion, T. J. (2004). Temperament and adolescent substance use: A transactional analysis of emerging self-control [Special Issue]. *Journal of Clinical Child and Adolescent Psychology, 33*(1), 69–81.

Wolchik, S. A., Sandler, I. N., Tein, J.-Y., Mahrer, N. E., Milsap, R. E., Winslow, E., et al. (2013). Fifteen-year follow-up of a randomized trial of a preventive intervention for divorced families: Effects on mental health and substance use outcomes in young adulthood. *Journal of Consulting & Clinical Psychology, 81*(4), 660–673.

PART II

Large-Scale Dissemination of Family-Based Programs

6

EARLY RESULTS FROM IMPLEMENTING PMTO

Full Transfer on a Grand Scale

Marion S. Forgatch, Laura A. Rains, and Margrét Sigmarsdóttir

Introduction

As the landscape of health care changes dramatically in the United States, systems of care are responding to the need to make evidence-based resources available to improve family functioning for at-risk populations. Implementation research must become standard practice to improve the link between dissemination efforts, community collaboration, and healthy outcomes for families. Parent Management Training—Oregon Model (PMTO®) is an evidence-based practice (EBP) with programs ranging from prevention through treatment that have been implemented with sustained fidelity in communities in the United States and internationally. The model's core principles and practices are designed to promote healthy development and to prevent as well as reduce behavior problems.

PMTO is based on decades of an integrated approach to theory, research, and intervention development led by Gerald Patterson and his group of colleagues at the Oregon Social Learning Center (OSLC; e.g., Forgatch & Patterson, 2010; Patterson, 1982, 2005; Patterson, Reid, & Dishion, 1992; Reid, Patterson, & Snyder, 2002). PMTO provides parent training programs in group or individual family format and has been implemented in a number of wide-scale applications in the United States and several other countries. The model has had to adjust to meet the requirements of each implementation site in terms of targeted populations, delivery format and intervention length, family circumstances, age of children, service provider, insurance, and access criteria related to billing. When applied in prevention programs (i.e., Tier 2, targeting at-risk populations), parent groups meet for 6 to 14 weeks and are conducted at agencies, in schools, faith centers, and community sites. In clinical programs

114 Marion S. Forgatch et al.

(i.e., Tier 3, targeting high-risk populations), individual families receive treatment in their homes, agencies, or community settings for 20 to 40 sessions. Session structure varies: group sessions last 1.5 to 2 hours and follow a highly structured agenda; individual sessions generally last 50 to 60 minutes and are more flexible in the amount of time spent on specific content areas. In all PMTO formats, practitioners maintain a balance between following a structured agenda and being responsive to family needs (Rains, Forgatch, & Knutson, 2010). Because the theoretical model specifies parents as the agents of change, parents are the focus of the intervention, although children often participate in family sessions. A description of session content and processes is provided later.

Adaptation of PMTO

Studies have evaluated the PMTO program with prevention and clinical samples with youngsters between ages 2 and 18 and have reported benefits to problems that include noncompliance, internalizing and externalizing behaviors, delinquency, substance abuse, and poor academic performance. A review describing 25 studies conducted between 1979 and 2009 provides details regarding samples and outcomes (see Forgatch & Patterson, 2010). In this chapter, we review findings from more recent work and emphasize issues related to implementation, particularly with reference to the challenge of adapting the program for contextual and cultural needs while sustaining model fidelity and positive outcomes.

PMTO programs have been shaped and evaluated for several contexts. For example, stressful contexts such as family structure transitions and living in high crime neighborhoods are known risk factors for youngsters' adjustment (Patterson et al., 1992). We have used such contexts for testing selective (i.e., Tier 2) prevention programs. In a randomized controlled trial (RCT) delivered to families in schools in high crime neighborhoods, findings revealed reduced aggression observed on playgrounds immediately following intervention and reduced tobacco and illicit drug use based on youth report with seven-year follow-up data (DeGarmo, Eddy, Reid, & Fetrow, 2009; Reid, Eddy, Fetrow, & Stoolmiller, 1999). That program combined parent training in parent groups, classroom problem-solving training for students, and improved monitoring on playgrounds by school staff. In a Tier 2 RCT in which the risk was recent marital separation, mothers attended 14 parent group sessions; children were not involved in the intervention. Benefits to parenting practices based on observations of parent–child interactions showed moderate effect sizes at 12-month follow-up. These benefits mediated nine-year follow-up effects on reductions in teacher-reported delinquency and child-reported deviant peer association, as well as fewer police arrests for boys and their mothers based on records data, and increased education, occupation, and income for mothers based on maternal report (Forgatch & DeGarmo, 1999; Forgatch, Patterson, DeGarmo, & Beldavs,

2009; Patterson, Forgatch, & DeGarmo, 2010). Other benefits included reduced child noncompliance and maternal depression at 30 months (DeGarmo, Patterson, & Forgatch, 2004; Martinez & Forgatch, 2001). In all the distal outcomes, effect sizes were small but significant. In another preventive RCT with newly reconstituted stepfamilies, improvements in observed parenting practices at six months yielded moderate effect sizes, which in turn produced small but significant indirect effects on observed child noncompliance and parent ratings of behavior at home at 12 months, and teacher ratings of school behavior at two-year follow-up. Marital interactions observed as the couples discussed their parenting and personal issues improved at two years, and this led to improved ratings of their marital satisfaction (Bullard et al., 2010; Forgatch, DeGarmo, & Beldavs, 2005). All of these prevention programs employed no-treatment control groups and intent-to-treat analysis.

When evidence-based programs are implemented in community service agencies, they must be tailored to address the unique needs of the contexts in which they are delivered (Domenech Rodríguez & Bernal, 2012). PMTO programs have been adapted for populations in the US and other countries; leader manuals and parent materials are available in English, Norwegian, Dutch, Icelandic, Spanish, and Danish. In the US, adaptations have largely focused on Latino families using the parent group format (Domenech Rodríguez, Franceschi-Rivera, Sella-Nieves, & Félix-Fermín, 2013; Parra-Cardona et al., 2012). The US Latino manual (Domenech Rodríguez, 2008) was tailored slightly for use in Mexico City. An RCT with a prevention sample using a wait-list control design showed significant modest reductions in parent reports of child behavior problems, parental depression, and stress (Castillo et al., 2015).

Nationwide implementations of PMTO using the individual family format in Norway (Amlund Hagen, Ogden, & Bjørnebekk, 2011) and Iceland (Sigmarsdóttir, Thorlacius, Guðmundsdóttir, & DeGarmo, 2014) have produced small but significant effects on children's behavior problems using a multiple method assessment. In Norway, the parent group approach showed significant modest reductions in parent-reported conduct problems when provided to ethnically Norwegian families (Kjøbli, Hukkelberg, & Ogden, 2013). The group program was adapted slightly and tested with immigrant Pakistani and Somali mothers in Norway using a wait-list control design, with small but significant effects (Bjørknes, Kjøbli, Manger, & Jakobsen, 2012). The Norwegians also adapted and tested a PMTO program for brief intervention (3–6 sessions) provided in primary care settings, again with modest significant reductions in conduct problems and increases in social competence (Kjøbli & Ogden, 2012).

Theoretical Foundation of PMTO

Social interaction learning (SIL), the theoretical foundation of the PMTO program, fuses social interaction, social learning, and behavioral perspectives

(Patterson et al., 2010). The SIL model takes into account the effect of contexts on families, specifying that adverse family circumstances have the most proximal impact on parenting practices, which in turn mediate the effect of contexts on children. Several longitudinal and cross-sectional studies have tested this model. Specifically, adverse conditions such as low socioeconomic status, divorce and repartnering, and parental psychopathology have been found to impact children's behavior problems as mediated by disrupted parenting practices (e.g., DeGarmo, Forgatch, & Martinez, 1999; Forgatch, 1991; Patterson et al., 1992).

Given the centrality of parenting practices to the SIL model, we have paid particular attention to parenting assessment. Most of the basic and applied research related to PMTO is based on direct observations of parenting practices, assessed from parent–child interactions videotaped during a set of structured interaction tasks, which are scored by reliable coders (Patterson et al., 1992). Two main types of parenting are specified: coercion and positive parenting. Coercion takes place during sequential interactions in which two people exchange negative behaviors until one person "wins" the conflict bout by using aversive (often high intensity) behaviors to get the other person to give in or back down. These conflicts yield a "reinforcement trap" with two short-term outcomes: The "winner" is positively reinforced for using intense negative behavior and the "loser" is negatively reinforced by escaping the hostile interchange. The longer-term outcome is an increased likelihood that the winner will resort to similar tactics in future interchanges and the loser will withdraw quickly to escape the escalating conflict. Coercive behavior is measured with rates of aversive behavior, negative reciprocity, and negative reinforcement. The positive parenting practices deemed central to PMTO interventions are skill encouragement, effective limit setting, monitoring, problem solving, and positive involvement. Some analyses examine coercion and positive parenting as separate constructs and some combine them in a construct of "effective parenting", with the scores for coercion reversed (e.g., Forgatch & DeGarmo, 2002). Additional skills that support and strengthen these core parenting dimensions are also integral to the intervention. Supporting skills include emotion identification and regulation, use of clear directions, and effective communication skills (Forgatch, 1994; Forgatch & DeGarmo, 2002).

Delivery of PMTO: Content and Format

PMTO sessions are designed to teach parents the core and supporting parenting practices pertinent to the SIL model (Forgatch & Patterson, 2010). Understanding the principles of the theoretical model enables certified practitioners at the level of service delivery to adjust program details to tailor the intervention for children's age, family contexts (rural/urban), family structure (single parent/blended/grandparent), and financial resources. For example, tailoring can involve the reinforcers parents use with their children: rewards relevant for 6-year-old children are seldom appropriate for teenagers. Negative sanctions are also adjusted according to age: Time Out is recommended for younger children and work chores for older youth. The amount of monitoring required for a 4-year-old is considerably more extensive than what is needed for a responsible 12-year-old; an unreliable 12-year-old requires closer supervision than one who is dependable. In all such cases, the underlying principles and core components remain the same; only the details are adjusted. Adapting the program for different ethnic and cultural groups is described later in the implementation section.

The intervention proceeds step by step, with each skill serving as a foundation for subsequent skills. Sessions begin with a warm-up phase followed by review of the home practice assignment that incorporates troubleshooting as necessary; introduction of new content, tailoring new material to the family's specific milieu and practice; and closing with a summary, prediction of challenges ahead, and a new home practice assignment. Sessions include the following content: (1) initial session identifying strengths, setting goals, and noting relevant contextual issues; (2) encouraging cooperation through clear directions; (3) promoting skill development with contingent encouragement; (4) identifying and regulating emotions; (5) setting limits with effective, non-corporal discipline strategies; (6) monitoring children's activities at home and away; (7) communication and interpersonal problem solving; (8) managing conflict within and outside of the family and strengthening the parenting team; (9) promoting school success; and (10) balancing work, love, and play.

Large-Scale Implementation

PMTO programs have been implemented domestically and in several other countries, including Norway, Iceland, the Netherlands, Denmark, Mexico, and Uganda. Within some countries, adaptations have been made for immigrant populations, including Somali and Pakistani families in the US and Norway, non-native Dutch in the Netherlands, and Arabic and Latino communities in the US. To address relevant cultural and contextual factors, the purveyor[1] of the implementation collaborates with on-site cultural brokers to tailor materials and language and address other concerns. PMTO has been adapted for families in the child welfare system by highlighting emotion regulation, adult/adult and adult/child communication, and conflict management strategies (Rains & Forgatch, 2013). An adaptation has been made for military personnel returning from the wars in Afghanistan and Iraq by strengthening the focus on emotion regulation and adding a mindfulness component, thereby yielding a trauma-informed version of PMTO (Gewirtz, Pinna, Hanson, & Brockberg, 2014). Other innovations include web-enhancements for the military adaptation (Gewirtz et al., 2014) and a recently funded study that will evaluate the relative efficacy of group, web-based, and web-based with telephone support formats of delivery (Gewirtz, 2014–2019). A pilot program is being conducted in Northern Uganda with war-displaced mothers (Wieling et al., in press).

118 Marion S. Forgatch et al.

In summary, PMTO programs have been tested with families with children, from toddlerhood through adolescence, and adapted and tested with families from several contexts, cultures, and countries.

PMTO Emphasizes Teaching and Process Skills

A unique feature of the PMTO method is the strong emphasis on the manner in which content is delivered and teaching is conducted. Interventionists practice supportive process skills to establish a collaborative relationship with families and promote growth and satisfaction, and they employ an active rather than didactic teaching approach. This focus on clinical process and teaching style grew out of a series of "resistance" studies conducted in the 1980s and early 1990s (e.g., Patterson & Chamberlain, 1988; Patterson & Forgatch, 1985; Stoolmiller, Duncan, Bank, & Patterson, 1993). These studies examined the extent to which interactions between practitioners and clients influence cooperation within and across sessions and ultimately contribute to positive intervention outcomes. A key finding was that when practitioners pair confrontation with teaching, the likelihood that the next client behavior will be resistant increases sevenfold over baseline rates (Patterson & Forgatch, 1985). This tendency for practitioners to combine confrontation and teaching tends to occur in high rates in community practice, as it was in early PMTO practice. This view of resistance as a transactional process removes the stigma of refusal from the client and replaces it with a degree of practitioner responsibility (Forgatch & Domenech Rodríguez, in press).

Assessing Fidelity

Two dimensions of assessing method fidelity have been identified as critical: *adherence* to the core components of a program as specified in manuals as well as delivery of the program with *competence* (Dumas, Lynch, Laughlin, Smith, & Prinz, 2001; Perepletchikova & Kazdin, 2005). Raters score video recordings of practitioner–client interactions during intervention sessions using the Fidelity of Implementation Rating System (FIMP; Knutson, Forgatch, Rains, & Sigmarsdóttir, 2009). Competent adherence of PMTO practice is scored in terms of five theoretically relevant dimensions (i.e., PMTO knowledge, session structure, teaching skills, process skills, and overall development). We assess adherence in the dimensions of knowledge and session structure and evaluate competence in the dimensions of teaching, process, and overall development. Raters are certified PMTO practitioners who maintain rigorous reliability standards. Ratings are based on a 9-point Likert scale: the 1–3 range indicates needs work; 4–6 reflects acceptable work; and 7–9 indicates good work. To become certified, PMTO practitioners must achieve a mean of 6.0 on the five theoretical dimensions based on four sessions showing work with at least two different families.

Four separate studies have evaluated the predictive validity of the FIMP measure. FIMP scores rated during the intervention predicted improvements in parenting practices observed during parent–child interactions assessed before and after the intervention (Forgatch & DeGarmo, 2011; Forgatch et al., 2005; Ogden & Amlund Hagen, 2008). Another study found FIMP ratings to predict change in parent ratings of child behavior before and after the intervention in Norway (Hukkelberg & Ogden, 2013).

Scoring fidelity from observations of intervention sessions ensures that tailoring programs for specific contexts, cultures, and populations has not led to drift from the principles that make PMTO programs efficacious. All PMTO implementation sites are required to assess their practitioners' fidelity using the FIMP measure. Each site establishes a FIMP team leader or leadership team who conducts training, retraining, and regular reliability checks of their raters through monthly recalibration and retraining sessions. FIMP team leaders participate in annual reliability tests with the FIMP team from Implementation Sciences International, Inc. (ISII) to ensure continuing reliability. The ISII FIMP team also maintains reliability through monthly checks. Scores evaluated within and across sites prevent drift in PMTO practice. For detailed information about fidelity, see Forgatch, Patterson, & Gewirtz, 2013.

Testing PMTO and its Theoretical Model

Over the course of 50 years, more than 30 tests of the intervention have been conducted. A review of 25 studies is provided in Forgatch and Patterson (2010). Of course, the early tests in the 1960s and 1970s would not meet the standards of rigor demanded today. They involved case examples or small sample tests with outcomes evaluated before and after intervention. Eventually follow-up data and replication designs were added. The first RCT was completed in the early 1980s with a clinical sample with community treatment as usual as the control condition (Patterson, Chamberlain, & Reid, 1982). Assessment also improved over the years, advancing from self-report to the use of multi-method and multi-agent assessments, and analytic strategies made it possible to evaluate longitudinal change and mediational models that test for mechanisms of change. In prevention and clinical samples, positive outcomes have been reported for families in RCTs contrasting PMTO with control conditions. In prevention studies, control conditions have included no-treatment controls (e.g., Forgatch & DeGarmo, 1999; Forgatch et al., 2005) or wait-list controls (e.g., Bjørknes et al., 2012). In clinical samples, control conditions were treatment as usually offered in the community (Amlund Hagen et al., 2011; Bank et al., 1991; Patterson et al., 1982; Sigmarsdóttir et al., 2014).

Outcomes for youth include: improvements in children's social skills and externalizing behavior according to observations and parent and teacher ratings (e.g., Castillo et al., 2015; DeGarmo & Forgatch, 2005; Ogden & Amlund

120 Marion S. Forgatch et al.

Hagen, 2008; Sigmarsdóttir et al., 2014); standardized tests of reading and math performance (Forgatch & DeGarmo, 2002); youth report of deviant peer association (Forgatch et al., 2009), internalizing problems (DeGarmo et al., 2004), and substance use/abuse (Beldavs, Forgatch, Patterson, & DeGarmo, 2006); records data regarding police arrests (Forgatch et al., 2009) and out-of-home placement (Patterson & Forgatch, 1995); and observations of non-compliance (Forgatch et al., 2005; Martinez & Forgatch, 2001). Intervention benefits for parents include observations of reduced coercive parenting and increased positive parenting (Forgatch et al., 2005, 2009); self-report of standard of living (i.e., income, occupation, education, financial stress, and rise out of poverty; Forgatch & DeGarmo, 2007; Patterson et al., 2010); maternal depression (DeGarmo et al., 2004) and marital satisfaction (Bullard et al., 2010); and records reports of police arrests (Patterson et al., 2010). Most of the studies were conducted by members of the OSLC group. Independent investigations were completed by Castillo et al. (2015), Amlund Hagen et al. (2011), Bjørknes et al. (2012), Kjøbli et al. (2013), Kjøbli and Ogden (2012), and Sigmarsdóttir et al. (2014). A chapter describing the development of PMTO over its 50-year history is found in Forgatch and Domenech Rodríguez (in press).

A criticism leveled at evidence-based parenting programs is that few studies have evaluated the putative mechanisms of change (Weersing & Weisz, 2002). PMTO programs have used preventive intervention to conduct experimental tests using mediational modeling. Mediational modeling tests the relationship among an independent variable (group assignment), dependent variable (child outcome) and the mechanisms presumed to produce change (e.g., parenting practices; Baron & Kenny, 1986; MacKinnon, Krull, & Lockwood, 2000). The SIL model underlying interventions for children specifies parents as the primary socializing influence. As children reach adolescence and spend more time with peers, their social environment changes; peer influence increases. Thus, a delinquency model for adolescents must add the socializing influence of peers to that of parents (Dishion & Patterson, 2006).

A test of the SIL model for delinquency was conducted in a nine-year follow-up study in the Oregon Divorce Study with 238 recently separated single mothers with sons in grades 1–3 at baseline. Mothers received the intervention through a course of 14 weekly parent group sessions; there was no direct intervention with children (Forgatch, et al., 2009). This test of the model specified parenting practices as well as deviant peer association as mediators of delinquency (Patterson, 2002). Parenting was assessed from observation of parent/child interactions, deviant peer association (DPA) was reported by the youngsters, and delinquency was rated by teachers annually over the course of nine years.

As expected, the intent-to-treat analysis showed a significant direct effect of the intervention on growth and average rates of delinquency, with less delinquency over nine years for boys in the PMTO group compared to their counterparts in the control condition. These direct effects on delinquency were

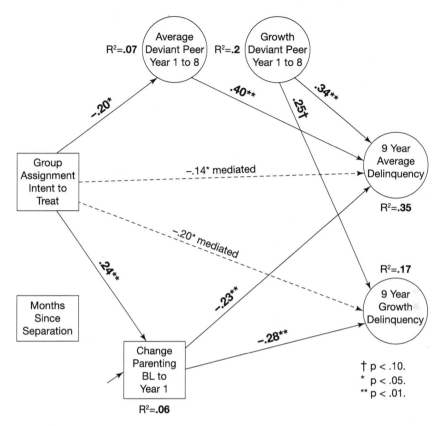

FIGURE 6.1 An Experimental Test of the SIL Delinquency Model: A Latent Growth Model for the Test of Mediation on 9-Year Teacher-Rated Delinquency

mediated by the intervention effects on both putative mediators (parenting and deviant peer association). Relative to mothers in the control group, mothers assigned to PMTO showed significant benefits to parenting practices observed from parent–child interactions at baseline and 12 months. Similarly, relative to boys in the control group, the sons of the PMTO mothers showed significantly less boy-reported deviant peer association from baseline through eight years.

Benefits to parenting and to deviant peer association proved to be significant predictors of growth and average levels of teacher-rated delinquency. Adding the two mediating variables to the equation explained the relationship between group assignment and the intervention effect on delinquency, making the path from group to delinquency growth nonsignificant. Thus, support was provided for the expanded theoretical position underlying the PMTO intervention for delinquency (Forgatch et al., 2009). One surprise in the findings was that changes in parenting practices as observed during parent–child interactions were not associated with changes in deviant peer association (DPA). How was

122   Marion S. Forgatch et al.

this change effected since youth did not participate in the intervention? Was the problem related to measurement issues? Or, was there another variable not assessed that could explain the effect? Clearly, the failure to identify the mechanism of change in DPA leaves room for exploration in future studies.

Implementation

Relative to other parent training programs (e.g., Triple P, Incredible Years, the Strengthening Families Program), PMTO was a late entry into the implementation field. Decades had been spent developing the program and testing it with a variety of clinical and prevention populations before the nationwide PMTO implementation in Norway (see Forgatch & DeGarmo 2011; Forgatch & Patterson, 2010; Forgatch et al., 2013; Ogden et al., 2012; Ogden, Forgatch, Askeland, Patterson, & Bullock, 2005). The approach established by ISII, the purveyor of PMTO programs, has been applied since then in several wide-scale applications. The strategy is to fully transfer the program from purveyor to the adopting community (Forgatch & DeGarmo, 2011; Forgatch et al., 2013). This full transfer approach has been carried out in four nationwide programs (i.e., Norway, Iceland, the Netherlands, and Denmark); two statewide programs (i.e., Michigan and Kansas); and city/countywide in Detroit/Wayne County, which was conducted in tandem with the Michigan statewide program. Full transfer implementation takes place in four major stages as the program purveyor gradually passes the reins of leadership into the hands of the adopting community (Forgatch et al., 2013). Each of these stages is discussed below.

In **Stage 1,** *Preparation*, activities are conducted separately by purveyor and community. For example, the community must establish a governing authority to be responsible for the project and its activities, such as making a plan, gathering resources, engaging point people, and selecting a program. The purveyor has already developed its program with supporting materials and technology, evaluated efficacy/effectiveness, established generalizability, and formulated Readiness Checklists at leadership, agency, and practitioner levels.

Stage 2, *Early Adoption*, involves developing a collaborative relationship between purveyor and community to manage logistics and adapt materials needed for the training activities. So far, all PMTO implementations in foreign countries have been conducted in English with English materials. As the training program progresses, local experts assigned by the community translate and adjust materials for language, artwork, and metaphor usage, and these changes are negotiated with the purveyor. Such adaptations are considered surface rather than deep (Resnicow, Soler, Braithwaite, Ahluwalia, & Butler, 2000). The key outcome of this stage is certification of Generation 1 (G1), a progenitor group of community practitioners. Trainees are selected by the community from participating agencies and range from highly seasoned clinicians with graduate degrees to providers with bachelors' degrees new to the field. From this group of practitioners who become certified, leaders are selected to fill pivotal roles: trainers to conduct workshops, coaches to guide new and experienced PMTO practitioners, and fidelity raters to evaluate competent adherence to the method and certify and recertify practitioners, coaches, and trainers during the *Implementation* phase. A brief description of the training process is described below in "Training the Progenitor Generation".

By **Stage 3, *Implementation*,** families are served by the certified practitioners in community agencies, and the purveyor focuses on mentoring and supporting leaders in developing the infrastructure. A well-articulated infrastructure plan is formulated. The purveyor supports the adopting community through consultation and targeted booster workshops, and further adaptations are made to strengthen the fit between the method and local needs. Consultations are conducted via videoconferencing (e.g., Skype or GoToMeeting), through written feedback, and on-site.

Stage 4, *Sustainability*, focuses on supporting the program within and across systems and levels. Fidelity and outcomes are assessed, and reach is extended to new and underserved populations. From this stage forward, the purveyor provides consultation and support upon request and assesses method fidelity on an annual basis (see "Sustaining Method Fidelity", below). Adopting communities employ their systems for recruiting and enrolling families, scheduling appointments, and delivering the intervention as part of their service delivery plan. The purveyor supports these efforts by sharing successful recruitment, engagement, and retention strategies used in their years of family research.

Training the Progenitor Generation (G1)

The PMTO training program is extensive and employs best-practice adult-learning methods supplemented with detailed practitioner manuals and parent materials (Rains et al., 2010), active workshops, abundant practice, and observation-based coaching. Bringing practitioners to certification (approximately 12 to 24 months) requires perseverance and collaboration between purveyor and adopting community; the payoff is long-term sustainability with fidelity (Forgatch & DeGarmo, 2011; Forgatch et al., 2013). Workshops are provided in five sets (4, 4, 3, 3, and 3 days) for a total of 17 days spread across the initial training period (10–12 months). Workshop trainers create a secure learning environment by embedding core content and process skills in activities that promote mastery. Trainers introduce teaching strategies using role plays of ineffective and effective examples in which a practice is demonstrated, debriefed, and differentiated. Practitioners learn to use problem-solving strategies to help parents address family issues and troubleshoot problems as they apply the procedures at home. Rapport-building activities enable practitioners to support parents in the process of identifying their parenting, family, and children's strengths. In PMTO, trainers and coaches practice active teaching strategies to educate

124 Marion S. Forgatch et al.

practitioners in parenting tools that will be taught to parents who will practice with their children.

PMTO's active "show rather than tell" training program elicits high marks from practitioners, and workshops have been called both a sprint and a marathon. Initially, however, trainees can be less than enthusiastic to meet one of the requirements of the PMTO method—use of role play. Some practitioners comment that they have role played before, but the approach used in PMTO activates their teaching with joy. "I've learned it's important to have fun while you do therapy," a Norwegian practitioner commented at a PMTO certification ceremony in Oregon. "I've never had so much fun as I have now!" (Forgatch, Knutson, & Rains, 2001).

Following the second workshop, trainees begin working with families referred to their agency and receive written and verbal coaching based on video recordings of their practice, a procedure that strengthens the transfer of learning from training to application (Salas & Cannon-Bowers, 2001). Observation-based coaching has evolved from the early days when videotapes were shipped across the North Pole from Norway to Oregon. Currently, communities use a web-based, HIPAA-compliant portal system that tracks progress and enhances communication, allowing coaches to view sessions from anywhere in the world where Internet access is available. During basic training, practitioners work with a minimum of three families until achieving a standard of proficiency that leads to invitation to work with two new "certification" families. Candidates are certified when they attain a specified passing FIMP score on each of four sessions on core PMTO topics.

The purveyor's training team consists of mentors who themselves have achieved certification as PMTO specialists, coaches, and trainers. Mentors are also reliable fidelity raters who can score family and group sessions to certify trainees. The majority of the current training team reside in Oregon, although mentors also live in Michigan, Minnesota, Utah, Norway, Iceland, the Netherlands, and Mexico. In each case, mentors achieved their status by becoming certified PMTO practitioners within their local community and subsequently attaining certification at additional levels (trainer, coach, fidelity rater). Mentors from the various implementation sites maintain a collaborative relationship with the ISII group through shared training activities. Languages spoken include English, Norwegian, Danish, Icelandic, Spanish, and Dutch.

When the majority of G1 trainees near certification, the next phase of full transfer begins as the purveyor team assists the community in selecting leaders to build a self-sustaining infrastructure that includes workshop trainers, coaches, and fidelity raters. Workshops tailored to provide training for these key infrastructure roles are complemented by on-site and distance mentoring and coaching. A document defining the roles and responsibilities for leadership and practitioners at all levels within the PMTO system is drawn up by each implementation site. An excellent example of such a document was collaboratively developed for the Michigan statewide program for children in the Community Mental Health System (Gray, Rains, & Forgatch, 2009). Training during the final move toward full transfer includes booster workshops, strengthening the community FIMP team to become the guardians of model fidelity, support for leadership, and confirmation of a governing authority. Each implementation site collects its own outcome data. For example, child welfare tends to evaluate reunification rates and time to reunification; child mental health tends to evaluate levels of child functioning.

Sustaining Method Fidelity

Once full transfer has taken place, adopting communities have one requirement to enable them to continue using the PMTO trademarked name and materials: Their fidelity team must pass an annual reliability test. The test is taken by accessing *FIMP Central*, a portal maintained by the purveyor. Available on this confidential portal are a supply of video-recorded intervention sessions that have been provided by each implementation site. Families and practitioners have given consent for this material to be viewed for this purpose. These sessions are scored by ISII's team of raters, which comprises a culturally diverse group of mentors who are reliable FIMP raters. This team meets monthly by video conference to assess their reliability and establish consensus scores. Each month a session from a different implementation site is rated and the leader(s) of that site's FIMP team participate. In this manner, the coding system is applied across cultures and sites to sustain fidelity without method drift.

The full transfer approach to implementation raises an important question: Does method fidelity deteriorate with each successive generation? Two studies have tested this question with data based on certification scores from different generations of trainees. One study was with three generations of Norwegians and one with four generations of Icelanders (Forgatch & DeGarmo, 2011; Sigmarsdóttir, DeGarmo, Forgatch, & Guðmundsdóttir, 2013). In each site, there was a small but significant drop in fidelity scores from G1 to G2. However, the G3 practitioners at each site achieved scores significantly equivalent with those attained by G1. In Iceland, the test carried out to the fourth generation showed that fidelity continued to be sustained at the level of G1. These findings indicate that communities can sustain high levels of fidelity following transfer of the program with minimal involvement by the program purveyor.

A second critical question asks whether positive outcomes are maintained following transfer. In Norway and Iceland, nationwide RCTs were conducted to evaluate PMTO effectiveness following implementation. These studies were conducted independent of the purveyor. In Norway, one-year follow-up data using a multiple agent construct (parent, teacher, and observation data) showed positive outcomes with a small effect size (Amlund Hagen et al., 2011; Ogden

126 Marion S. Forgatch et al.

& Amlund Hagen, 2008). In Iceland, pre/post outcomes based on parent, teacher, and child ratings showed a small-effect improvement in the child outcome construct (Sigmarsdóttir et al., 2014). A study in Norway evaluated the extent to which outcome effect sizes changed following the PMTO implementation 15 years earlier. With a sample of 323 families referred for treatment of child behavior problems, they found no attenuation of program effect sizes, contrary to their expectations (Tømmeraas, & Ogden, 2014).

Outcomes of PMTO Implementation

An implementation cannot be sustained unless the community practitioners achieve certification and subsequently conduct community practice with method fidelity (Durlak & DuPre, 2008; Proctor et al., 2011). We use data from two early implementations to address this issue (Forgatch et al., 2013). In Norway, 83% of the 36 G1 practitioners who began training in 1999 achieved certification; in Michigan, 89% of the 19 who began in 2006 achieved certification. To sustain an implementation, the practitioners must retain their credentials and continue practicing with fidelity. In Norway, eight years after certification, 91% of the G1 Norwegians had maintained certification and continued providing PMTO treatment to families. In Michigan, 16 of the 17 (94%) completers were still certified seven years later and providing community service.

The full transfer implementation approach provides a cost-efficient way to extend reach throughout the system as certified practitioners become trainers, coaches, and fidelity raters for subsequent generations without paying a purveyor for these services. In 2014 in Norway, the 30 therapists certified by the purveyor in G1 have expanded their group to 290 certified PMTO specialists trained by Norwegian leaders (Askeland & Christiansen, 2014). In Michigan, the pool of 17 G1 certified practitioners has grown to 180 (Gray, Lawson, Burrows, & Rains, 2014).

In Norway, a shift from a focus on treatment to prevention with a variety of at-risk samples has resulted in the addition of five approaches informed by PMTO: parent group for immigrant mothers, parent group for Norwegian families, brief parent training, child social skills training, and teacher consultations. Each of these approaches has been tested with RCTs. Findings supported individual family and parent groups for Norwegians and immigrants as well as the brief parent training programs (Bjørknes et al., 2012; Kjøbli et al., 2013; Kjøbli & Ogden, 2012). Findings did not support the stand-alone child social skills training (Askeland & Christiansen, 2014). Research on the teacher consultation approach is still under way. To increase their pool of service providers, the Norwegians shortened the training programs for prevention services. To date they have nearly 1179 practitioners operating from 333 registered work places in 113 municipalities providing brief parent training (Askeland & Christiansen, 2014).

The PMTO program has become thoroughly embedded in the Michigan Department of Community Health. Over the course of 10 years of implementation, this solid infrastructure has enabled the program to expand so that 76% of the agencies serving severely emotionally disturbed children have certified PMTO practitioners. The state has 20 trainers, 30 coaches, and 13 reliable fidelity raters. Michigan offers individual and parent group options for treatment and delivers integrated key principles of the model across community systems partners such as mental health, school, judicial, juvenile justice, transportation, and respite care (Gray & Lawson, 2014).

Financing

Funding for implementation is provided by the adopting sites and can emerge from a call to replace services as usual with evidence-based practice. The process must be led by a cohesive group that has social/political capital, leadership skills, access to resources, and a commitment to establish change (Forgatch et al., 2013). These initiating groups develop strategies to fund and conduct the multiple stages of implementation. In Norway, the Ministries of Child and Family Affairs and Social and Health Affairs established a center tasked with implementing and evaluating evidence-based family treatment programs on a nationwide basis. The ministries provided funding for infrastructure development, training, and supervision through the center (Ogden et al., 2005). In Michigan, in spite of being a state that has suffered more than most from economic downturn, the statewide director of community programs for severely emotionally disturbed children competed for and won funds from the National Institute of Mental Health to begin the implementation process with PMTO (Wotring, Hodges, Xue, & Forgatch, 2005). In Kansas, a program was initiated through a five-year grant (Children's Bureau Express, 2011) provided to the University of Kansas by the US Department of Health and Human Services, Administration for Children and Families (Bryson, Akin, Blase, McDonald, & Walker, 2014). Thus, in each of these examples, the initiation of wide-scale implementation of PMTO was fully or partially supported with government funds designed to increase the availability of evidence-based interventions for youngsters with behavior problems.

Conclusions

The PMTO program meets EBP standards (Chambless & Hollon, 1998; Flay et al., 2005). It builds on a strong theoretical basis that has been well supported across youngsters' developmental phases from toddlerhood through adolescence in prevention and treatment work by RCT and mediational studies. The method has been implemented and tested in several countries with positive outcomes. A well-validated, observation-based fidelity measure is applied across implementation sites, making the dissemination of PMTO in community

128 Marion S. Forgatch et al.

practice possible while respecting other critical stages of implementation (Fixsen et al., 2005). It will be of great interest in the future to see how sophisticated implementation methods help EBPs travel safely from the scientific community to clinical practice in different settings.

The full transfer approach to implementing evidence-based practice in diverse contexts, cultures, and countries is an adventure filled with challenges and gifts. Because full transfer requires working within large systems, adopting communities must have strong leadership with significant socio-political resources to carry the program through to completion. Because it is expensive to train the progenitor generation, leaders must recognize the long-term benefits of this approach. A return on the initial investment occurs when systems have the capacity to conduct PMTO replacement trainings using their own certified team to address inevitably high levels of staff turnover in community health practice. Practitioners choose careers in mental health and child welfare because they want to help others; yet in the face of extremely harsh contexts, even the most dedicated can become discouraged. PMTO practitioners report that providing parents with effective parenting tools restores belief in themselves as instruments of change, which helps prevent burnout. One Norwegian practitioner said it best at the conclusion of PMTO training: "I was about to leave. I've done therapy for many years and have wanted to help these families. But it's difficult and you get burned out. Actually, I was thinking of retiring as a therapist, and I'm very glad I didn't. There's the saying you can't teach an old dog new tricks, and I've proven you can." (Forgatch et al., 2001).

Implementation has the power to create change at many levels: practitioners can change the way they interact with co-workers, client families, and their own families; agency culture can improve; and dissemination can influence change at the policy level. In Norway, researchers note an increased commitment to evidence-based practice among policy makers and greater willingness among practitioners to be more accountable and concerned with outcomes (Ogden, Kärki, & Teigen, 2010). While it must be acknowledged that the full-transfer approach comes with many upfront demands and challenges, the Norwegian and Michigan examples indicate that systems can sustain a wide-scale implementation with fidelity. Greater reach can be achieved when the adopting community establishes an infrastructure that supports training, coaching, and fidelity rating, and the purveyor simply supports their efforts. The long-term role of the purveyor in this approach is to evaluate fidelity to prevent against drift and offer consultation when invited to do so.

Note

1 We use this term to describe the group with the authority and skill required to implement an EBP or specified practice at a particular location with model fidelity and positive effects (see Fixsen, Naoom, Blase, Friedman, & Wallace, 2005).

References

Amlund Hagen, K., Ogden, T., & Bjørnebekk, G. (2011). Treatment outcomes and mediators of parent management training: A one-year follow-up of children with conduct problems. *Journal of Clinical Child & Adolescent Psychology*, *40*, 165–178.

Askeland, E., & Christiansen, T. (2014, June). *Latest findings from the Norwegian PMTO implementation.* Paper presented at the Norwegian visit to Implementation Sciences International, Inc., Eugene, OR.

Bank, L., Marlowe, J. H., Reid, J. B., Patterson, G. R., & Weinrott, M. R. (1991). A comparative evaluation of parent-training interventions of families of chronic delinquents. *Journal of Abnormal Child Psychology, 19*, 15–33. doi:10.1007/BF00910562.

Baron, R. M., & Kenny, D. A. (1986). The moderator-mediator variable distinction in social psychological research: Conceptual, strategic, and statistical considerations. *Journal of Personality and Social Psychology*, *51*, 1173–1182.

Beldavs, Z. G., Forgatch, M. S., Patterson, G. R., & DeGarmo, D. S. (2006). Reducing the detrimental effects of divorce: Enhancing the parental competence of single mothers. In N. Heinrichs, K. Haalweg, & M. Döpfner (Eds.), *Strengthening families: Evidence-based approaches to support child mental health* (pp. 143–185). Münster: Verlag für Psychotherapie.

Bjørknes, R., Kjøbli, J., Manger, T., & Jakobsen, R. (2012). Parent training among ethnic minorities: Parenting practices as mediators of change in child conduct problems. *Family Relations: An Interdisciplinary Journal of Applied Family Studies*, *61*, 101–114.

Bryson, S. A., Akin, B. A., Blase, K. A., McDonald, T., & Walker, S. (2014). Selecting an EBP to reduce long-term foster care: Lessons from a university-child welfare agency partnership. *Journal of Evidence-Based Social Work, 11*, 208–221.

Bullard, L., Wachlarowicz, M., DeLeeuw, J., Snyder, J., Low, S., Forgatch, M. S., & DeGarmo, D. S. (2010). Effects of the Oregon Model of Parent Management Training (PMTO) on marital adjustment in new stepfamilies: A randomized trial. *Journal of Family Psychology*, *24*, 485–496.

Castillo, C., Amador Buenabad, N. G., Domenech Rodríguez, M. M., Baumann, A. A., Villatoro, J., & Moreno, D. (2015). Direct benefits to parents: Improvements to parenting stress and depression from participating in an evidence-based parenting intervention. Manuscript under review.

Chambless, D. L., & Hollon, S. D. (1998). Defining empirically supported therapies, *Journal of Consulting and Clinical Psychology*, *66*, 7–18.

Children's Bureau Express. (2011). Kick-off for the Permanency Innovations Initiative. *Online Digest*, February, 12. Retrieved from https://cbexpress.acf.hhs.gov/index.cfm?event=website.viewArticles&issueid=123&articleid=3087

DeGarmo, D. S., Eddy, J. M., Reid, J. B., & Fetrow, R. A. (2009). Evaluating mediators of the impact of the Linking the Interests of Families and Teachers (LIFT) multimodal preventive intervention on substance use initiation and growth across adolescence. *Prevention Science, 10*, 208–220.

DeGarmo, D. S., & Forgatch, M. S. (2005). Early development of delinquency within divorced families: Evaluating a randomized preventive intervention trial. *Developmental Science, 8*, 229–239.

DeGarmo, D. S., Forgatch, M. S., & Martinez, C. R., Jr. (1999). Parenting of divorced mothers as a link between social status and boys' academic outcomes: Unpacking the effects of SES. *Child Development, 70*, 1231–1245.

DeGarmo, D. S., Patterson, G. R., & Forgatch, M. S. (2004). How do outcomes in a specified parent training intervention maintain or wane over time? *Prevention Science, 5,* 73–89.

Dishion, T. J., & Patterson, G. R. (2006). The development and ecology of antisocial behavior in children and adolescents. In D. Cicchetti & D. Cohen (Eds.), *Developmental psychopathology. Vol. 3: Risk, disorder, and adaptation* (Revised ed., pp. 503–541). New York: Wiley.

Domenech Rodríguez, M. M. (2008). *Criando con Amor: Promoviendo Armonía y Superación [PMTO parent group manual].* Logan, UT: Utah State University.

Domenech Rodríguez, M. M., & Bernal, G. (2012). Translating models of research in empirically based practice. In G. Bernal & M. M. Domenech Rodríguez (Eds.), *Cultural adaptations: Tools for evidence-based practice with diverse populations* (pp. 265–289). Washington, DC: American Psychological Association.

Domenech Rodríguez, M., Franceschi-Rivera, N., Sella-Nieves, Z., & Félix-Fermín, J. (2013). Parenting in Puerto Rican families: Mothers and father's self-reported practices. *Interamerican Journal of Psychology, 47,* 229–312.

Dumas, J. E., Lynch, A. M., Laughlin, J. E., Smith, E. P., & Prinz, R. J. (2001). Promoting intervention fidelity: Conceptual issues, methods, and preliminary results from the EARLY ALLIANCE prevention trial. *American Journal of Preventive Medicine, 20*(Suppl 1), 38–47.

Durlak, J. A., & DuPre, E. P. (2008). Implementation matters: A review of research on the influence of implementation on program outcomes and the factors affecting implementation. *American Journal of Community Psychology, 41,* 327–350.

Fixsen, D. L., Naoom, S. F., Blase, K. A., Friedman, R. M., & Wallace, F. (2005). *Implementation research: A synthesis of the literature.* Tampa, FL: University of South Florida, Louis de la Parte Florida Mental Health Institute, National Implementation Research Network.

Flay, B. R., Biglan, A., Boruch, R. F., Gonzalez Castro, F., Gottfredson, D., Kellam, S. G., et al. (2005). Standards of evidence: Criteria for efficacy, effectiveness and dissemination. *Prevention Science, 6,* 151–175.

Forgatch, M. S. (1991). The clinical science vortex: A developing theory of antisocial behavior. In D. Pepler & K. H. Rubin (Eds.), *The development and treatment of childhood aggression* (pp. 291–315). Hillsdale, NJ: Erlbaum.

Forgatch, M. S. (1994). *Parenting through change: A programmed intervention curriculum for groups of single mothers [training manual].* Eugene, OR: Oregon Social Learning Center.

Forgatch, M. S., & DeGarmo, D. S. (1999). Parenting through change: An effective prevention program for single mothers. *Journal of Consulting and Clinical Psychology, 67,* 711–724.

Forgatch, M. S., & DeGarmo, D. S. (2002). Extending and testing the social interaction learning model with divorce samples. In J. B. Reid, G. R. Patterson, & J. Snyder (Eds.), *Antisocial behavior in children and adolescents: A developmental analysis and model for intervention* (pp. 235–256). Washington, DC: American Psychological Association.

Forgatch, M. S., & DeGarmo, D. S. (2007). Accelerating recovery from poverty: Prevention effects for recently separated mothers. *Journal of Early and Intensive Behavioral Intervention, 4,* 681–702.

Forgatch, M. S., & DeGarmo, D. S. (2011). Sustaining fidelity following the nationwide PMTO implementation in Norway. *Prevention Science, 12,* 235–246.

Forgatch, M. S., DeGarmo, D. S., & Beldavs, Z. (2005). An efficacious theory-based intervention for stepfamilies. *Behavior Therapy, 36,* 357–365.

Forgatch, M. S., & Domenech Rodríguez, M. M. (in press). Addressing coercion in intervention: Balancing content and process. In T. J. Dishion & J. J. Snyder (Eds.), *Oxford handbook of coercive relationship dynamics*. New York: Oxford University Press.

Forgatch, M. S., Knutson, N. M., & Rains, L. A. (2001, May). Transcript of Norwegian PMTO Ceremony, Oregon Social Learning Center, Eugene.

Forgatch, M. S., & Patterson, G. R. (2010). Parent Management Training—Oregon Model: An intervention for antisocial behavior in children and adolescents. In J. R. Weisz & A. E. Kazdin (Eds.), *Evidence-based psychotherapies for children and adolescents* (2nd ed., pp. 159–178). New York: Guilford.

Forgatch, M. S., Patterson, G. R., DeGarmo, D. S., & Beldavs, Z. G. (2009). Testing the Oregon delinquency model with 9-year follow-up of the Oregon Divorce Study. *Development and Psychopathology, 21*, 637–660.

Forgatch, M. S., Patterson, G. R., & Gewirtz, A. H. (2013). Looking forward: The promise of widespread implementation of parent training programs. *Perspectives on Psychological Science, 8*, 682–694.

Gewirtz, A. H., Principal Investigator. (2014–2019). Comparing web, group, and telehealth formats of a military parenting program (W81XWH-14-1-0143). Washington, DC: Department of Defense.

Gewirtz, A. H., Pinna, K. L. M., Hanson, S. K., & Brockberg, D. (2014). Promoting parenting to support reintegrating military families: After deployment, adaptive parenting tools. *Psychological Services, 11*, 31–40.

Gray, L. J., & Lawson, N. (2014, April). *Ten years and counting: Latest findings for PMTO in Michigan.* Paper presented at the Michigan PMTO leaders' visit to ISII, Eugene, OR.

Gray, L. J., Lawson, N., Burrows, K., & Rains, L. A. (2014, July). Embedding and sustaining evidence-based practices in systems of care. Paper presented at the Georgetown University Center for Child and Human Development 2014 Training Institutes, Washington, DC.

Gray, L. J., Rains, L. A., & Forgatch, M. S. (2009). *PMTO requirements to ensure sustainable fidelity and quality [training manual].* Lansing, MI: Michigan Department of Community Health.

Hukkelberg, S., & Ogden, T. (2013). Working alliance and treatment fidelity as predictors of externalizing problem behaviors in Parent Management Training. *Journal of Consulting and Clinical Psychology, 81*, 1010–1020.

Kjøbli, J., Hukkelberg, S., & Ogden, T. (2013). A randomized trial of group parent training: Reducing child conduct problems in real-world settings. *Behaviour Research and Therapy, 51*, 113–121.

Kjøbli, J., & Ogden, T. (2012). A randomized effectiveness trial of brief parent training in primary care settings. *Prevention Science, 13*, 616–626.

Knutson, N. M., Forgatch, M. S., Rains, L. A., & Sigmarsdóttir, M. (2009). *Fidelity of Implementation Rating System (FIMP): The manual for PMTO™.* Eugene, OR: Implementation Sciences International, Inc.

MacKinnon, D. P., Krull, J. L., & Lockwood, C. M. (2000). Equivalence of the mediation, confounding and suppression effect. *Prevention Science, 1*, 173–181.

Martinez, C. R., Jr., & Forgatch, M. S. (2001). Preventing problems with boys' noncompliance: Effects of a parent training intervention for divorcing mothers. *Journal of Consulting and Clinical Psychology, 69*, 416–428.

Ogden, T., & Amlund Hagen, K. (2008). Treatment effectiveness of Parent Management Training in Norway: A randomized controlled trial of children with conduct problems. *Journal of Consulting and Clinical Psychology, 76*, 607–621.

Ogden, T., Bjørnebekk, G., Kjøbli, J., Patras, J., Christiansen, T., Taraldsen, K., & Tollefsen, N. (2012). Measurement of implementation components ten years after a nationwide introduction of empirically supported programs—a pilot study. *Implementation Science*, 7(49).

Ogden, T., Forgatch, M. S., Askeland, E., Patterson, G. R., & Bullock, B. M. (2005). Implementation of parent management training at the national level: The case of Norway. *Journal of Social Work Practice*, *19*, 317–329.

Ogden, T., Kärki, F. U., & Teigen, K. S. (2010). Linking research, policy and practice in welfare services and education in Norway. *Evidence & Policy: A Journal of Research, Debate and Practice*, *6*, 161–177.

Parra-Cardona, J. R., Domenech Rodríguez, M. M., Forgatch, M. S., Sullivan, C., Bybee, D., Holtrop, K., et al. (2012). Culturally adapting an evidence-based parenting intervention for Latino immigrants: The need to integrate fidelity and cultural relevance. *Family Process*, *51*, 56–72.

Patterson, G. R. (1982). *A social learning approach: Coercive family process*. Eugene, OR: Castalia.

Patterson, G. R. (2002). Etiology and treatment of child and adolescent antisocial behavior. *The Behavior Analyst Today*, *3*, 133–145.

Patterson, G. R. (2005). The next generation of PMTO models. *Behavior Therapist*, *28*, 25–32.

Patterson, G. R., & Chamberlain, P. (1988). Treatment process: A problem at three levels. In L. C. Wynne (Ed.), *The state of the art in family therapy research: Controversies and recommendations* (pp. 189–223). New York: Family Process Press.

Patterson, G. R., Chamberlain, P., & Reid, J. B. (1982). A comparative evaluation of a parent-training program. *Behavior Therapy*, *13*, 638–650.

Patterson, G. R., & Forgatch, M. S. (1985). Therapist behavior as a determinant for client noncompliance: A paradox for the behavior modifier. *Journal of Consulting and Clinical Psychology*, *53*, 846–851.

Patterson, G. R., & Forgatch, M. S. (1995). Predicting future clinical adjustment from treatment outcome and process variables. *Psychological Assessment*, *7*, 275–285.

Patterson, G. R., Forgatch, M. S., & DeGarmo, D. S. (2010). Cascading effects following intervention. *Development & Psychopathology*, *22*, 949–970

Patterson, G. R., Reid, J. B., & Dishion, T. J. (1992). *Antisocial boys* (Vol. 4). Eugene, OR: Castalia.

Perepletchikova, F., & Kazdin, A. E. (2005). Treatment integrity and therapeutic change: Issues and research recommendations. *Clinical Psychology: Science and Practice*, *12*, 365–383.

Proctor, E. K., Silmere, H., Raghavan, R., Hovmand, P., Aarons, G., Bunger, A., et al. (2011). Outcomes for implementation research: Conceptual distinctions, measurement challenges, and research agenda. *Administration and Policy in Mental Health and Mental Health Services Research*, *38*, 65–76.

Rains, L. A., & Forgatch, M. S. (2013). Trauma-informed PMTO: An adaptation of the Oregon Model of Parent Management Training. *Trauma-Informed Child Welfare Practice*, *24*, 38–42.

Rains, L. A., Forgatch, M. S., & Knutson, N. M. (2010). *A course in the basic PMTO model, vols. 1–5* [training manuals]. Implementation Sciences International, Inc. Eugene, OR.

Reid, J. B., Eddy, J. M., Fetrow, R. A., & Stoolmiller, M. (1999). Description and immediate impacts of a preventive intervention for conduct problems. *American Journal of Community Psychology*, *27*, 483–517.

Reid, J. B., Patterson, G. R., & Snyder, J. (2002). *Antisocial behavior in children and adolescents: A developmental analysis and model for intervention.* Washington, DC: American Psychological Association.

Resnicow, K., Soler, R., Braithwaite, R. L., Ahluwalia, J. S., & Butler, J. (2000). Cultural sensitivity in substance use prevention. *Journal of Community Psychology, 28,* 271–290.

Salas, E., & Cannon-Bowers, J. A. (2001). The science of training: A decade of progress. *Annual Review of Psychology, 52,* 471–499.

Sigmarsdóttir, M., DeGarmo, D. S., Forgatch, M. S., & Guðmundsdóttir, E. V. (2013). Treatment effectiveness of PMTO for children's behavior problems in Iceland: Assessing parenting practices in a randomized controlled trial. *Scandinavian Journal of Psychology, 54,* 468–476.

Sigmarsdóttir, M., Thorlacius, Ö., Guðmundsdóttir, E. V., & DeGarmo, D. S. (2014). Treatment effectiveness of PMTO™ for children's behavior problems in Iceland: Child outcomes in a nationwide randomized controlled trial. *Family Process,* Online first, November 19. doi:10.1111/famp.12109.

Stoolmiller, M., Duncan, T. E., Bank, L., & Patterson, G. R. (1993). Some problems and solutions in the study of change: Significant patterns of client resistance. *Journal of Consulting and Clinical Psychology, 61,* 920–928.

Tømmeraas, T., & Ogden, T. (2014, May). *Is there a scale up penalty? Attenuation of program effects in large scale implementation of the Oregon model of Parent Management Training (PMTO).* Paper presented at the 22nd Annual Meeting of the Society for Prevention Research, Washington, DC.

Weersing, V. R., & Weisz, J. R. (2002). Mechanisms of action in youth psychotherapy. *Journal of Child Psychology and Psychiatry, 43,* 3–29.

Wieling, E., Mehus, C., Mollerherm, J., Neuner, F., Achan, L., & Catani, C. (in press). Assessing the feasability of providing a parenting intervention for war affected families in Northern Uganda. *Family and Community Health.*

Wotring, J., Hodges, K., Xue, Y., & Forgatch, M. S. (2005). Critical ingredients for improving mental health services: Use of outcome data, stakeholder involvement, and evidence-based practices. *Behavior Therapist, 28,* 150–158.

7

THE TRIPLE P – POSITIVE PARENTING PROGRAM

A Community-Wide Approach to Parenting and Family Support

Matthew R. Sanders, Karen M. T. Turner, and Jenna McWilliam

> **Author Note**
> The Triple P – Positive Parenting Program is owned by The University of Queensland. The university, through its main technology transfer company, UniQuest Pty Ltd, has licensed Triple P International Pty Ltd to publish and disseminate the program worldwide. Royalties stemming from published Triple P resources are distributed in accordance with the University's intellectual property policy and flow to the Parenting and Family Support Centre, School of Psychology, Faculty of Health and Behavioural Sciences, and contributory authors. No author has any share or ownership in Triple P International Pty Ltd. Drs Sanders and Turner are authors of various Triple P programs and are members of the Triple P Research Network. Jenna McWilliam is an employee of Triple P International Pty Ltd.

Brief Overview of the Program

The Triple P – Positive Parenting Program is a preventively oriented multi-level system of family intervention which aims to promote positive, caring relationships between parents and their children, and to help parents develop effective management strategies for dealing with a variety of childhood behavioral and emotional problems, and common developmental issues (Sanders, 2012). The Triple P system draws on social learning theory (Bandura, 1977; Patterson, 1982), applied behavior analysis (Baer, Wolf, & Risley, 1968), research on child development and developmental psychopathology (Hart & Risley, 1995; Rutter, 1985a, 1985b), social information processing models (e.g., Dodge, 1986), and public health principles (e.g., Farquhar et al., 1985). It has many distinguishing features in its flexibility, varied delivery modalities, multi–disciplinary approach, and focus on self-regulation and generalization of parenting skills.

The Triple P – Positive Parenting Program   **135**

Triple P teaches parents strategies to encourage their child's social and language skills, emotional self-regulation, independence, and problem-solving ability. Attainment of these skills promotes family harmony, reduces parent–child conflict and risk of child maltreatment, fosters successful peer relationships, and prepares children for successful experiences at school and later in life. This reduces the risk for a developmental trajectory leading to poor outcomes such as school failure, substance abuse, juvenile offending, and risk taking, including sexually risky behavior (Guajardo, Snyder, & Petersen, 2009; Moffitt et al., 2011; Stack, Serbin, Enns, Ruttle, & Barrieau, 2010).

Target Populations

Triple P incorporates five levels of intervention of increasing strength for parents of children from birth to age 16. The interventions encompass universal, selective, and indicated prevention as well as treatment programs, and include variants for specific populations such as children with a developmental disability and families at risk for child maltreatment. While positive parenting methods are relevant to all parents, parents of children who are demanding, disobedient, defiant, aggressive, or generally disruptive are particularly likely to benefit from more intensive Triple P interventions (Sanders, Markie-Dadds, Tully, & Bor, 2000). Although the Triple P system has been designed as an early intervention strategy within a prevention framework, many of the principles and techniques have been successfully used in intervention programs for clinically diagnosed children with severe behavior problems (particularly children with oppositional defiant disorder, conduct disorder, or attention-deficit/hyperactivity disorder).

The Triple P Multi-level System

Table 7.1 summarizes the multi-level Triple P approach, which aims to provide the "minimally sufficient" effective intervention to meet a family's needs in order to maximize efficiency and ensure that support becomes widely available to all parents.

Level 1: Universal Triple P aims to use health promotion and social marketing strategies to deter the onset of child behavior problems by: promoting the use of positive parenting practices and decreasing dysfunctional parenting in the community; increasing parents' receptivity towards participating in a parenting program; increasing favorable community attitudes towards parenting programs and parenting in general; de-stigmatizing and normalizing the process of seeking help for parenting issues; increasing the visibility and reach of effective programs; and countering alarmist, sensational, or parent-blaming messages in the media.

Level 2: Selected Triple P/Brief Primary Care Triple P is delivered through primary care or community services as brief 10–20 minute individual sessions on a specific concern (e.g., disobedience, bedtime problems) or a 90-minute

TABLE 7.1 The Triple P Multi-level System

Level of intervention	Target population	Intervention methods	Facilitators
Level 1 Media and communications strategy (very low intensity) • *Universal Triple P* • *Stay Positive*	All parents interested in information about parenting and promoting their child's development.	Coordinated communications strategy raising awareness of parent issues and encouraging participation in parenting programs. May involve electronic and print media (e.g., brochures, posters, websites, television, talk-back radio, newspaper and magazine editorials).	Typically coordinated by communications, health or welfare staff.
Level 2 Health promotion strategy/ brief selective intervention (low intensity) • *Selected Triple P* • *Selected Teen Triple P* • *Selected Stepping Stones Triple P*	Parents interested in parenting education or with specific concerns about their child's development or behavior.	Health promotion information or specific advice for a discrete developmental issue or minor child-behavior problem. May involve a 90-minute group seminar format or brief (up to 20 minutes) telephone or face-to-face clinician contact.	Practitioners who provide parent support during routine well-child health care (e.g., health, education, allied health, and childcare staff).
Level 3 Narrow focus parent training (low–moderate intensity) • *Primary Care Triple P* • *Triple P Discussion Groups* • *Primary Care Teen Triple P* • *Teen Triple P Discussion Groups*	Parents with specific concerns as above who require consultations or active-skills training.	Brief program (about 80 minutes over four sessions, or 2-hour discussion groups) combining advice, rehearsal and self-evaluation to teach parents to manage a discrete child problem behavior. May involve telephone contact.	Same as for Level 2.
• *Primary Care Stepping Stones Triple P*	Parents of children with disabilities, with concerns as above.	A parallel program with a focus on disabilities.	Same as above.

Level 4	Parents wanting intensive training in positive parenting skills. Typically parents of children with behavior problems such as aggressive or oppositional behavior.	Broad focus program (about 10 hours over 8–10 sessions) focusing on parent–child interaction and the application of parenting skills to a broad range of target behaviors. Includes generalization-enhancement strategies. May be self-directed, online, involve telephone or face-to-face clinician contact, group sessions.	Intensive parenting intervention workers (e.g., mental health and welfare staff, and other allied health and education professionals who regularly consult with parents about child behavior).
Broad focus parent training (moderate–high intensity) • *Standard Triple P* • *Group Triple P* • *Self-Directed Triple P* • *Triple P Online Standard* • *Standard Teen Triple P* • *Group Teen Triple P* • *Self-Directed Teen Triple P*			
• *Standard Stepping Stones Triple P* • *Group Stepping Stones Triple P* • *Self-Directed Stepping Stones Triple P*	Parents of children with disabilities who have or are at risk of developing behavioral or emotional disorders.	A parallel series of tailored programs with a focus on disabilities.	Same as above.
Level 5 Intensive family intervention (high intensity) • *Enhanced Triple P*	Parents of children with behavior problems and concurrent family dysfunction such as parental depression or stress, or conflict between partners.	Intensive individually tailored program with modules (60–90 minute sessions) including practice sessions to enhance parenting skills, mood management and stress coping skills, and partner support skills.	Intensive family intervention workers (e.g., mental health and welfare staff).
• *Pathways Triple P*	Parents at risk of child maltreatment. Targets anger-management problems and other factors associated with abuse.	Intensive individually tailored or group program with modules (60–120 minute sessions depending on delivery model) including attribution retraining and anger management.	Same as above.
• *Lifestyle Triple P*	Parents of overweight or obese children. Targets healthy eating and increasing activity levels as well as general child behavior.	Intensive 14-session group program (including telephone consultations) focusing on nutrition, healthy lifestyle and general parenting strategies. Includes generalization enhancement strategies.	As above plus dieticians/ nutritionists with experience in delivering parenting interventions.
• *Family Transitions Triple P*	Parents going through separation or divorce.	Intensive 12-session group program (including telephone consultations) focusing on coping skills, conflict management, general parenting strategies and developing a healthy co-parenting relationship.	Intensive family intervention workers (e.g., counselors, mental health, and welfare staff).

138 Matthew R. Sanders et al.

group seminar series. The seminar program is particularly useful as a universal transition program for parents enrolling their children in child care, kindergarten, or preschool, although it can also be used as a booster program or refresher course for parents who have completed a higher level of intervention such as Group Triple P.

Level 3: Primary Care Triple P/Triple P Discussion Groups comprise a more intensive (e.g., 3–4 half-hour individual sessions or 2-hour discussion groups), selective prevention strategy targeting parents who have mild and relatively discrete concerns about their child's behavior or development. This intervention level incorporates active skills training and the selective use of parenting tip sheets or workbooks covering common developmental and behavioral problems. It also builds in generalization enhancement strategies for teaching parents how to apply knowledge and skills gained to non-targeted behaviors and other siblings.

Level 4: Standard Triple P/Group Triple P/Self-Directed Triple P/Triple P Online Standard are indicated prevention/early intervention programs (e.g., 10 individual 60-minute sessions or eight interactive online modules) targeting families of higher risk children identified as having detectable sub-clinical problems, or who meet diagnostic criteria, with the aim of preventing the progression of problem behavior. Group (e.g., five 2-hour groups plus three brief telephone consultations) and self-directed (a 10-session workbook) variants at this level of intervention can also be offered to an entire population to improve parenting capacity and identify individual children at risk. Parents are taught a variety of child management skills including: monitoring problem behavior; building relationships through spending quality time, talking, and affection; providing brief contingent praise and attention for desirable behavior; arranging engaging activities in high-risk situations; establishing limits and rules; using directed discussion and planned ignoring for minor problem behavior; giving clear, calm instructions; and backing up instructions with logical consequences, quiet time (non-exclusionary time-out), and time-out. Parents learn to apply these skills both at home and in the community, and to generalize and maintain parenting skills across settings and over time. While all principles and strategies are introduced, content is individually tailored as families develop their own goals and select strategies to form their own personalized parenting plans.

Level 5: Enhanced Triple P is an indicated level of intervention for families with additional risk factors that have not changed as a result of participation in a lower level of intervention. It extends the intervention to include up to five modules (three 60–90 minute sessions each) that focus on areas such as partner support and communication, mood management and stress coping skills, and anger management skills for parents. Usually, at this level of intervention, children have behavior problems that are complicated by additional family adversity factors. Families typically complete a Level 3 or 4 intervention prior to Level 5, but practitioners may run Level 5 sessions concurrently with, or even prior to, parenting sessions based on their case formulation and family need.

Tailoring to Individual Needs

Within each level of intervention, considerable tailoring of the program to parents' particular circumstances is possible to enable specific risk and protective factors to be addressed. Indeed, even though the interventions are manualized, considerable practitioner ingenuity is required to adapt a program to parents' unique goals and family circumstances. With the exception of Level 1 media and communications strategies and Level 2 seminars, families commencing a face-to-face Triple P program complete a comprehensive intake interview and assessment process to determine the nature and history of the presenting problem, develop goals for change, determine the best approach to meet their needs and their capacity to complete program sessions and practice tasks, and negotiate an intervention plan. Families may also choose a self-directed program such as a self-help workbook or online program which may or may not be couched within a therapeutic relationship.

Program resources are designed to minimize potential barriers, such as targeting an average 6th grade reading level in parent resources to avoid difficulties with literacy, using video and live practitioner modeling to demonstrate parenting strategies, and including families from diverse ethnic and cultural backgrounds in video demonstration resources. It is our view that positive parenting principles and strategies can cross cultures. What may vary according to culture are the goals and target behaviors, practical implementation of strategies, and ways of sharing information. Triple P resources have to date had 22 language translations and have been disseminated in 25 countries, with surprisingly little need for adaptation (Morawska et al., 2011). Programs have been deployed in many different cultural contexts, including ethnically diverse populations in Australasia (e.g., Australia, New Zealand), the UK (e.g., England, Scotland), North America (e.g., Canada, the USA), Western Europe (e.g., Ireland, Sweden, Germany, Belgium, the Netherlands, Switzerland), the Middle East (e.g., Iran, Turkey), South America (e.g., Chile), Asia (e.g., Japan, Hong Kong, Singapore), and with Indigenous parents in Australia, Canada, New Zealand, and the USA.

The one major cultural adaptation of Triple P has been for Australian Indigenous families when the mainstream program was sought by Indigenous workers, but potential barriers for families were identified. Community consultation with elders, professionals, and parents resulted in the development of culturally adapted resources and minor program delivery variation, such as adding a preliminary session to the group program to discuss current and historical issues in the community and share stories about parents' experiences and attitudes relating to parenting (Turner, Richards, & Sanders, 2007). This adaptation has been adopted by other First Nations communities in Canada, New Zealand, and the USA.

140 Matthew R. Sanders et al.

Evidence for Triple P

Triple P research has incorporated a range of qualitative and quantitative methodologies to evaluate interventions, from single case experiments using interrupted time series designs (e.g., Sanders & Glynn, 1981) to randomized controlled efficacy trials (e.g., Sanders et al., 2000) to large-scale population-level effectiveness evaluations of Triple P as a multi-level system in communities (e.g., Prinz, Sanders, Shapiro, Whitaker, & Lutzker, 2009). A recent meta-analysis (Sanders, Kirby, Tellegen, & Day, 2013) reviewed research from 1970 to 2013 and quantitatively analyzed 101 Triple P evaluation studies (comprising 16,099 families). Statistically and clinically significant (Cohen's d) effects were found for all delivery formats and program variants, even with small sample sizes. Overall, across all intervention levels, significant short-term effects were found for: children's social, emotional, and behavioral outcomes ($d = 0.473$); parenting practices ($d = 0.578$); parenting satisfaction and efficacy ($d = 0.519$); parental adjustment ($d = 0.340$); parental couple relationship ($d = 0.225$); and observed child behavior ($d = 0.501$). Significant effects were found for all outcomes at longer-term follow-up, including observed parent behavior ($d = 0.249$). The positive family outcomes demonstrated for each of the five Triple P levels of intervention provide support for a multi-level, multi-disciplinary system of parenting programs, including prevention and treatment options, to increase timely access to cost-effective services promoting child, parent, and family wellbeing.

These findings are consistent with previous Triple P meta-analyses. Nowak and Heinrichs (2008) investigated 55 studies and found effect sizes for child problem behavior and parenting to range between 0.35 and 0.48 for between-groups and 0.45 and 0.57 for within-groups post-intervention comparisons. Thomas and Zimmer-Gembeck (2007) found effect sizes for 11 studies ranged from 0.31 to 0.73 for child behavior and 0.38 to 0.70 for parenting. In another series of meta-analyses, 15 studies resulted in an overall effect size of 0.42 for child behavior problems (de Graaf et al., 2008a), and 19 studies found an overall effect size of 0.54 for dysfunctional parenting (de Graaf et al., 2008b). Wilson et al. (2012) found an effect size of 0.61 for maternal-reported child behavior problems based on 23 RCTs.

Dissemination and Implementation Approach

The dissemination of Triple P is managed through an exclusive license agreement between The University of Queensland (the copyright holders) and Triple P International (TPI: a proprietary company established to disseminate Triple P). In recent years, TPI has developed a Triple P Implementation Framework (the Framework), drawing on best practice from the field of implementation science (e.g., The Active Implementation Frameworks: Fixsen, Naoom, Blase, Friedman,

& Wallace, 2005; the RE-AIM Framework: Glasgow, Vogt, & Boles, 1999) and 15 years of experience supporting organizations to adopt and implement Triple P.

The five phases of the Framework (see Figure 7.1) focus on the core elements of implementation, including: choosing the right practices and program; articulating desired outcomes; preparing the organization or community for effective implementation; ensuring practitioners and supervisors are prepared for training and service delivery; providing the training; and supporting the development of an evaluation and monitoring process to support maintenance and sustainability. Each phase contains a set of critical activities to be addressed by an organization or community. For each set of activities, guiding questions, discussion areas, tools, and resources are available. TPI Implementation Consultants (ICs) provide support to ensure that the implementation process is smooth, timely, and responds to the needs and constraints of the implementing organization and community.

Most community-wide roll outs of Triple P involve a number of organizations and sectors within a community. TPI uses the Framework to support communities to establish a collaborative approach and implementation systems that develop the capacity for effective, sustainable program implementation. Taking a systematic approach, the Framework addresses implementation considerations at each layer of a community system roll out, with a focus on self-regulation and minimal sufficiency, to scale up at a pace that allows for maximum

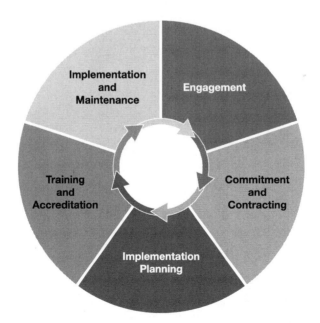

FIGURE 7.1 Triple P Implementation Framework. Source: www.triplep.net

142 Matthew R. Sanders et al.

community benefit. Promoting self-regulation at the systems level aims to build capacity for the system to self-sustain once full implementation has been achieved. Taking a minimally sufficient approach at the systems level involves ensuring that processes and implementation activities are context-specific and recognizing the existing capacity within the system. The five phases of the Framework and their application for a community-wide approach are described below in more detail.

Engagement

It is critical that the right programs and practices are chosen (the "fit") by implementing organizations. This requires a sound knowledge of the community and the organization as well as a good understanding of the Triple P system. Through dialogue and guided questions, organizations are assisted by an IC to assess which programs are the best fit for the outcomes they hope to achieve. During the engagement phase, the organization and TPI begin to develop an understanding of how the Triple P system may best suit the needs of their community and what may need to be considered for effective implementation and sustainability. Considerations include whether there are gaps within the existing services of the community, which Triple P services are the best fit for these gaps, how organizations could work collaboratively, and how referrals between services could happen. During this initial phase, organizations also consider the cultural acceptability of the program. When introduced into new countries, cultural acceptability research is encouraged to ensure programs are delivered in a culturally sensitive way.

Commitment and Contracting

Organizations that plan to deliver Triple P must clearly articulate who they would like to see served and what they would like to see achieved by providing Triple P. Given the breadth of interventions available in the Triple P system and the program's multi-disciplinary approach, there is no one right way to configure a community-wide roll out of the program. Organizations and ICs work together to develop a shared understanding of the scope of the implementation and the local capacity to implement and sustain the program. Key activities include determining the target population, how the proposed programs will fit within the community, and calculating the capacity needed to meet the initiative's intended reach and goals. TPI has developed a tool to assist this process for community-wide roll outs – the Capacity Calculator. This is an epidemiological planning tool designed to assist policy makers, funders, and organizations to plan the implementation of Triple P as a population approach, based on desired outcomes.

Organizations looking to adopt Triple P as a community-wide roll out are encouraged to establish partnerships with other organizations committed to the

The Triple P – Positive Parenting Program **143**

approach, goals, and methods used in the intervention. Establishing these partnerships helps to support the implementation of Triple P throughout a community by increasing the reach of the program to the populations served by different organizations. Through these partnerships and shared planning, the mix of programs is aligned with each organization's mandate, workforce, and service delivery methods, providing for broad and balanced availability of services throughout the community.

Implementation Planning

There are many examples of the successful implementation of Triple P in regular services following foundational efficacy trials; however, agencies have varying degrees of preparedness to adopt and maintain a new program or intervention system, and a thorough planning process is critical. Frequently, organizations move directly from training practitioners to expecting them to deliver the service within the unchanged context of the organization. This approach does not support long-term sustainability. For practitioners to successfully achieve the proven outcomes from Triple P, an organization must have the appropriate supports and infrastructure to sustain the program (e.g., providing time for practitioners to adequately prepare, engage in peer support, and establish effective data collection systems).

An organization or group of partner organizations (collaborative) must examine the match between their practices and the requirements of the levels of Triple P to be implemented. ICs support an organization or collaborative to assess their existing capacity and resources through five key activities: considering organization readiness; preparing to plan; organizational assessment; developing an implementation plan; and developing an evaluation plan. These activities are designed to ensure that an organization or collaborative develops awareness for their capacity to implement Triple P and puts in place the planning and implementation structures and processes required. They are encouraged to identify how existing functions operate within their organization and the changes needed to support effective implementation by considering the Active Implementation Drivers (see Fixsen et al., 2005). An organization or collaborative is then supported through the implementation planning process to identify the sequence of activities needed to support effective implementation and to develop an evaluation plan.

As part of this planning process, the practitioners who will deliver Triple P are carefully selected (e.g., considering their capacity to engage with families in different ways, such as groups versus individual programs) and prepared by their organization prior to undertaking any training. The organization's implementation planning process should also attend to logistical issues, such as planning to ensure that sufficient time is allocated in practitioners' work duties to deliver programs and anticipating potential barriers to the accessibility of programs (e.g., child care, transportation, location, hours). Other factors to consider include resource costs, future training support to allow for staff attrition, and administrative implications, which need to be considered at the outset to promote sustainability.

Romney and colleagues (Romney, Israel, & Zlatevski, 2014) found significantly better client completion rates and cost-effectiveness for those agencies that completed a site readiness process intended to prepare them for the implementation demands of successfully delivering Group Triple P (e.g., desire for and belief in the "fit" of the program, commitment to train at least three practitioners and commence delivering within 30 days of training completion, administrative support, and regular supervision). For agencies where administrators and staff completed the readiness process, the odds of parents completing the first Triple P group were 12.2 times greater than for those in groups run by sites that had not completed the readiness process. This meant the average cost-per-client was over seven times higher for the agencies that had not completed the readiness process.

Training and Accreditation

Practitioner training may be contracted by a commissioning agency seeking to have its staff trained, or may involve attendance of individual practitioners in open enrollment training courses conducted by TPI in different countries.

Training process

A standardized professional training program is available for all levels of the Triple P system (with the exception of Level 1). Triple P Provider Training Courses use an active skills training approach that involves a combination of didactic input by an accredited trainer, video and live demonstration of core consultation skills, small group exercises to practice skills, problem-solving exercises, course readings, and competency-based assessment. This assessment includes a written quiz and live or videotaped demonstration by participants to show mastery of core competencies specific to the level of training undertaken. Triple P training is designed to be relatively brief to minimize disruption to staff schedules and to reduce the need for relief workers while staff undertake training. The training experience comprises attendance at a 1–5 day training course (based on the level of intervention), a pre-accreditation day, and an accreditation.

A range of professionals deliver Triple P interventions to parents. To be eligible to undertake the training, participants are recommended to have professional training in psychology, medicine, nursing, social work, counseling, or other related fields so that they have some prior exposure to principles of child development, and experience working with families. However, there are

The Triple P – Positive Parenting Program **145**

some instances where Level 2 and 3 programs are delivered by paraprofessionals working in a family support role. Only practitioners who complete accreditation requirements can be considered properly trained to deliver the intervention. Follow-up studies of participants in Triple P training show that about 85% of practitioners who start training become accredited and, of those, about 90% implement Triple P (Seng, Prinz, & Sanders, 2006). While different professional groups have varying qualifications, from certificate to postgraduate training (Sethi, Kerns, Sanders, & Ralph, 2014) and number of years of previous experience (Turner, Nicholson, & Sanders, 2011), these have not been found to be significant predictors of program use.

Central training team

All Triple P Provider Training Courses are facilitated by Triple P trainers, who are Masters or PhD level professionals (mainly clinical or educational psychologists). Professionals invited to become trainers undergo an intensive 6-day Triple P Trainer Course that prepares them to conduct provider training and accreditation. The course involves simulated training sessions and ongoing peer review and feedback to develop trainer skills. After initial induction, trainers are awarded provisional status and can begin conducting Triple P Provider Training Courses under supervision from TPI (i.e., co-facilitating with another trainer). In order to receive full accreditation status they are required to receive satisfactory evaluations for at least two Triple P Provider Training Courses and complete the required Triple P Trainer Accreditation Quiz.

Although many agencies favor a train-the-trainer model, such an approach can lead to substantial program drift and poorer client outcomes. Program disseminators can quickly lose control of the training process and, as a result, find it harder to efficiently incorporate revisions that are required when ongoing research indicates changes need to be included in the program. Maintaining control over the initial training of providers, although not without its challenges, is achievable and helps to promote quality standards. Triple P trainers do not work independently; they are contracted by TPI and use standardized training materials which serve to ensure that program integrity is protected. While the majority of Triple P Provider Training occurs in English, training resources have been translated into eight additional languages to date.

Tailoring training methods to target groups

Triple P training is delivered to a broad range of service providers. The delivery of courses has to be customized to a certain extent to cater for the special characteristics of the service providers undergoing training. This can be accomplished by ensuring trainers are familiar with the local context, including where providers work, their role in providing parenting support, their professional backgrounds,

146 Matthew R. Sanders et al.

and levels of experience. Quality training is flexible enough that the experience and learning styles of the group can be addressed while ensuring that essential content is properly covered. This tailoring can involve selection of relevant (to the audience) case examples and illustrations, drawing upon the knowledge, experience, and expertise of the group, being sensitive to the cultural background and values of the group, and by drawing the attention of the group to the variant and invariant (i.e. core content and process) features of the program.

Maintaining training quality

Maintaining the quality of the training process itself needs to be carefully managed by TPI to minimize program drift at source. To prevent drift, all trainers use standardized materials (including participant notes, training exercises, and training DVDs demonstrating core consultation skills), become part of a trainer network, and adhere to a quality assurance process as part of the maintenance of their ongoing accreditation. In order to maintain their fully accredited status, for each successive 2-year quality assurance period, Triple P trainers are required to: 1) complete at least one training or accreditation course per year; 2) maintain satisfactory course ratings; 3) participate in at least 10 hours of approved peer support groups using the Peer-Assisted Supervision and Support Model (PASS; Sanders & Murphy-Brennan, 2010); and 4) complete a minimum of 10 hours of relevant professional development (e.g., attendance at an annual Trainer's Day, other training update sessions, training observation and feedback, delivery of Triple P to parents, review of research papers, conference presentations).

TPI also directly manages all aspects of the professional training programs, including the initial practitioner training courses, pre- and post-training support for practitioners, an online provider network, and follow-up technical assistance.

Technical support

Positive child and parent outcomes are expected when practitioners deliver programs with fidelity (Little et al., 2012). This fidelity is often associated with practitioners receiving adequate supervision and implementation support, particularly during initial implementation. TPI encourages capacity building within organizations and has a range of support options available (e.g., a Triple P Workshop Series, with topics such as engaging hard to reach families, assessment, managing group processes).

An online provider network has also been established for accredited practitioners to make ongoing technical support available to Triple P practitioners (www.triplep-parenting.net/provider). This network provides practitioners with practice tips and suggestions as well as downloadable clinical tools and resources (e.g., monitoring forms, public domain questionnaires, session checklists), and keeps practitioners up to date with the latest research findings and new programs being released.

Implementation and Maintenance

Following training, practitioners begin to offer Triple P in their community. Sustaining the changes put in place during implementation planning requires support through all implementing organizations in a community. These changes occur at multiple levels within the organization, including with practitioners (e.g., delivering Triple P with fidelity, attending peer support sessions, accessing support as required), managers (e.g., encouraging service delivery, clarifying performance expectations and outcomes), organizations (e.g., reflecting on challenges and variances, implementing processes for peer support, coaching and supervision, funding), and at the systems level (e.g., using data to review support processes, service delivery, administrative support, and leadership structures).

It is essential that organizations and communities actively evaluate the impact of the implementation (e.g., Plan, Do, Study, Act Cycle; Deming, 1986). As a practice takes hold, an organization enters into an implementation evaluation stage for approximately 6–12 months to accumulate enough service delivery data for analyses. Ideally, the resulting performance evaluations demonstrate which systems can effectively sustain the successful delivery of Triple P. The data also show areas that need refinement, revision, or expansion for effective service delivery to continue over time.

Supporting implementation fidelity

Evidence-based programs achieve the best results when delivered with fidelity and competence (Beidas & Kendall, 2010), while incompetently delivered evidence-based programs may even be harmful (Henggeler, 2011). Fidelity of implementation of Triple P is promoted through the Framework and through standardized parent and practitioner resources. During the implementation planning phase, organizations consider how program fidelity checks will be embedded in core service delivery. In addition to the standardized professional training process described above, providers receive detailed written and video resources. Practitioner resources specific to each level of the intervention (levels 2–5) and program variants (e.g., Stepping Stones Triple P, Teen Triple P) include comprehensive manuals that detail each session's activities, PowerPoint presentations, DVDs demonstrating the parenting skills being introduced to parents, and self-report session fidelity checklists (e.g., Sanders, Markie-Dadds, & Turner, 2013). In addition, there are parent resources that include tip sheets and workbooks for specific program variants. Implementation fidelity can also be enhanced through the use of supervision and peer coaching (see supervision of providers section below).

148 Matthew R. Sanders et al.

Promoting flexible tailoring and responsive program delivery

Many manualized evidence-based programs have been criticized as being rigid and inflexible. Mazzucchelli and Sanders (2010) argued that delivering a program with fidelity does not mean inflexible delivery, and that there are high- and low-risk variations in content and process that can influence clinical outcomes. The training process encourages practitioners to work collaboratively with parents and to be responsive to client need and situational context while preserving the key or essential elements of the program. Core content, such as the positive parenting principles and strategies, must be presented to parents. However, adapting examples used to illustrate key teaching points, using customized homework tasks, and varying session length and number can be used to respond to the needs and goals of specific clients. Through this type of tailoring, core concepts and procedures are preserved but the idiosyncratic needs of particular parent groups are also addressed (e.g., parents of twins or triplets, parents of children with special needs).

Assessing program outcomes

Program outcome assessment for the Triple P system occurs at two different levels: program effects for individual families and changes at a whole population level. Each program level and program variant has a set of recommended outcome measures to assess child-, parent-, and family-level outcomes. As an example, recommended measures for Level 4 Standard Triple P are outlined in Table 7.2.

Organizations are encouraged to establish an evaluation plan and develop processes for how pre- and post-intervention data will be collected by practitioners in the context of their broader evaluation framework. A data scoring application is available to help practitioners score and track the most commonly used questionnaires. While a comprehensive assessment battery may not be possible for population-level evaluations, some population evaluations have the capacity to use a single standardized measure such as the Eyberg Child Behavior Inventory delivered universally to a target population (e.g., Sarkadi, Sampaio, Kelly, & Feldman, 2014), or a number of standardized measures (e.g., Salari et al., 2013). To assess population outcomes, various evaluation projects have conducted random population surveys, via telephone or face-to-face, using brief demographic and program awareness items as well as standardized measures such as The Strengths and Difficulties Questionnaire (e.g., Sanders et al., 2008; Fives et al., 2014). Other measures include independent community prevalence data such as substantiated child maltreatment cases recorded by child protective services, child out-of-home placements recorded through the foster care system, and child hospitalizations and emergency-room visits due to child maltreatment injuries (e.g., Prinz et al., 2009).

The Triple P – Positive Parenting Program **149**

TABLE 7.2 Assessment Measures Commonly Used in Standard Triple P (Level 4)

Domain	Measure
Child adjustment	• Eyberg Child Behavior Inventory (Eyberg & Pincus, 1999). • Sutter-Eyberg Student Behavior Inventory – Revised (Eyberg & Pincus, 1999). • The Strengths and Difficulties Questionnaire (Goodman, 1997, 1999). • Child Adjustment and Parent Efficacy Scale (Morawska, Sanders, Haslam, Filus, & Fletcher, 2014).
Parenting and family adjustment	• Parenting Scale (Arnold, O'Leary, Wolff, & Acker, 1993). • Parenting Tasks Checklist (Sanders & Woolley, 2005). • Parent Problem Checklist (Dadds & Powell, 1991). • Parenting and Family Adjustment Scales (Sanders, Morawska, Haslam, Filus, & Fletcher, 2014).
Parent adjustment	• Depression-Anxiety-Stress Scales (Lovibond & Lovibond, 1995). • Relationship Quality Index, also known as the Quality Marriage Index (Norton, 1983).
Behavior monitoring (selected based on the nature of the target behavior)	• Behavior diary (episodic record) of the problem behavior, when and where it occurred, what happened before (triggers) and what happened afterwards (maintaining factors). • Frequency tally (event record) noting each occurrence of the target behavior. • Permanent product tally of the specific outcome of a behavior or series of behaviors. • Duration record tracking how long a behavior lasts in hours, minutes or seconds. • Partial interval time sample recording the presence or absence of a behavior in a specified time interval (e.g., 10-minute blocks). • Momentary time sample recording the behavior occurring at the moment a given time interval ends.
Direct observation	• Family Observation Schedule (Sanders, 2000). • Functional analysis: Competing behaviors (behaviors to increase and decrease).
Consumer satisfaction	• Consumer Satisfaction Questionnaire (Sanders, Markie-Dadds, & Turner, 2013).

Supervision of providers

Practitioners who have access to supervision and workplace support post-training are more likely to implement Triple P (Turner, Sanders, & Hodge, 2014). The PASS model (Sanders & Murphy-Brennan, 2010) was developed to provide practitioners with implementation support following training. The model is introduced during training so that practitioners can establish a supervision network in their workplace, with initial consultation support or facilitation by a TPI trainer if required. PASS involves practitioners meeting in small groups to review their sessions with parents. As different organizations have varying capacity for clinical supervision, this process is largely self-directed and applies a self-regulatory framework to promote reflective practice and to encourage practitioners to deliver sessions according to the standardized protocols in the manuals. Sessions are recommended to occur every two weeks for the first six sessions and then monthly thereafter. A manual and video demonstrating core skills for practitioners, peer mentors, and supervisors were created to aid training in the PASS model.

The self-regulation approach to supervision is an alternative to more traditional, hierarchically based clinical supervision with an experienced expert supervisor who provides feedback and advice to a supervisee. The self-regulation model utilizes the power and influence of the peer group to promote reciprocal learning outcomes for all participants in supervision groups, which means that peers become attuned to not only assessing their own clinical skills and those of fellow practitioners, but also to providing a motivational context to enable peer colleagues to change their own behaviors, cognitions, and emotions so they become proficient in delivering interventions.

Maintenance supports

Maintaining the implementation of Triple P requires intentional feedback loops to ensure that the practice, organizational, and systems changes put in place are achieving the desired outcomes. Organizations should use available data to revise support processes or service delivery, and to confirm that leadership structures and administrative support are operating effectively. Ongoing procedures should be established to maintain workforce staffing levels, support program fidelity, and promote a shared understanding of the overall initiative aims. An organization or collaborative implementing Triple P in a community-wide approach can work with an IC to estimate their impact to date in the community using the Triple P Capacity Calculator. This process can then help to inform goals to maintain, adjust, or expand service delivery.

Effectiveness of Dissemination and Implementation Efforts

Practitioners have been trained in 25 countries with large-scale roll outs (if not country-wide roll outs), including Australia, Canada, the UK, Ireland, the Netherlands, Belgium, Hong Kong, and the USA. At time of writing, 90,000 training attendances have involved over 60,000 unique practitioners (i.e., many practitioners attend training in more than one program variant).

Population Outcomes

Research evaluating the impact of Triple P on population-level indicators is in its infancy. To date, five population-level studies have been published documenting

The effects of the multi-level system. These studies have occurred in Australia, the USA, Germany, Sweden, and Ireland. For example, the US Triple P Systems Trial conducted in 18 counties in South Carolina showed that the implementation of the Triple P system reduced several population-level indicators of child maltreatment including 16% fewer children in out-of-home placements, 17% fewer hospitalizations due to child maltreatment related injuries, and the growth of confirmed cases of child abuse slowed (22% lower; Prinz et al., 2009).

Another example of a large-scale implementation of the Triple P system was in two central Ireland counties and assessed the population level impact via 6000 random household surveys (3000 before and 3000 after the implementation) in the intervention and matched comparison counties. A significant population impact was demonstrated, with a 30% reduction in the population prevalence of "caseness" (i.e., clinical-level severity) for behavioral and emotional problems in children, and also reductions in parental psychological distress and stress. A number of other significant, small-to-medium population effects were found, including improvements in reporting a good relationship with one's child, appropriate parenting strategies, satisfaction with parenting information and services available, and likelihood of participation in future parenting programs (Fives et al., 2014).

Cost-effectiveness

Independent economic analyses of the Triple P system have shown the intervention to be very cost-effective. For example, for the US Triple P Systems Trial, the Washington State Institute for Public Policy has found that implementation of the Triple P system resulted in a $6 return per $1 invested based on child maltreatment costs alone (2011 data; Lee et al., 2012), and an $8.80 return based on child maltreatment, education, crime, property, and health care (major depression) costs (2012 data; Washington State Institute for Public Policy, 2014).

Policy Implications

Lessons for Policy Makers

The traditional approach, to concentrate parenting support only for those families in dire need or when there are well-established problems, is highly unlikely to reduce the prevalence rates of these problems at a population level. In contrast, the adoption of a population approach, in which services are more widely available, does not require all families to receive in-person services in order for a prevalence rate reduction to occur in child abuse and social and emotional problems in a community (Prinz et al., 2009).

In general, policy changes are needed so that agencies delivering family and mental health services to children can be reimbursed for delivering universal, selective, and targeted prevention programs to a wider range of parents. Typically, funding is dependent on clinical diagnosis and tertiary (treatment) service provision rather than prevention and early intervention programs. To ensure adequate reach of evidence-based programs and access for all families, funding models need to be altered to include prevention and early intervention services. Policy and funding models should also prioritize effective implementation practices to ensure that evidence-based programs can be funded and implemented effectively and in a sustained way.

While there are increasing policy imperatives for accountability, which can be assessed at an individual family level and aggregated for agencies, the movement towards universal population-level program roll outs requires better evaluation mechanisms, such as population surveys linking funding to outcome deliverables. Such evaluations can assure policy makers and funders of the practical benefit and dollar value of such approaches.

Influencing Policy

We have taken a multi-pronged approach to influence policy makers, including: conducting briefings for senior bureaucrats, policy makers, and politicians; making formal in-person and written submissions to various National and State Royal Commissions of Inquiry (e.g., Commission into Child Abuse; Carmody, 2013); joining advocacy groups seeking to change the law relating to use of corporal punishment by parents; making television programs and radio broadcasts to promote positive parenting messages in the community (e.g., Driving Mum and Dad Mad, UK); establishing a research blog documenting the latest research findings (triplepblog.net); and hosting an annual international conference for researchers, policy makers, and practitioners (www.helpingfamilieschange.org).

Influencing policy is a challenging and ongoing process. In many ways, having others not connected with a program advocate for the program is the most powerful form of policy influence. In our experience, support from service-based champions and independent expert committees who review available evidence (e.g., NICE, 2013; Blueprints for Healthy Youth Development, 2014) brings the approach to the attention of key decision makers. Ultimately, these decision makers need to be convinced that adoption of a program or system can be sold to their own parliamentary colleagues in treasury or cabinet and ultimately to the public, and that the adoption can be defended in the media.

Challenges and Barriers to Sustained Implementation

Capacity to Go to Scale

The capacity of an evidence-based program to be scaled up is crucial in a public health context. "Going to scale" means that program developers and disseminators

The Triple P – Positive Parenting Program **153**

(purveyors) have the relevant knowledge, experience and resources to roll out programs on a large scale, and the ability to respond to workforce training demands. When efforts to disseminate Triple P began in earnest in 1996, we could find no well-established exemplars of how to undertake the task. As noted earlier, to enable The program to go to scale, a purveyor organization, TPI, was licensed by The University of Queensland to disseminate the program worldwide. This has also required significant university investment and involvement in the development of intellectual property protocols, licenses, and contracts.

The breadth of Triple P dissemination would not have been achieved without a dedicated dissemination organization with the resources and expertise to manage the process internationally. Large-scale roll outs require the capacity to go to scale rapidly. This has involved responding quickly by having a training team ready to travel internationally to conduct training according to demand, as well as building a local workforce of trainers in countries where training demand warrants this. The development of the Implementation Framework and creation of a team of implementation consultants further enables TPI to respond quickly to support organizations and communities to take their implementation of Triple P to scale, no matter the size of the initiative. The team of ICs regularly communicates via peer networks, allowing for knowledge and experience from a wide range of implementations to be shared. This knowledge exchange allows organizations to benefit from learnings from other roll outs around the world.

Achieving Adequate Population Reach

Despite good intentions and formal written agreements between funders and delivery agencies, not all practitioners or agencies reach the number of families they intend to serve. Failure to achieve implementation targets adds to the cost of the intervention and reduces the return on investment in training. Several strategies have been developed to assist agencies to reach their intended number of families. These include providing templates for promotional material such as posters and brochures, and using a strong communications strategy known as "Stay Positive" that aims to normalize and de-stigmatize participation in parenting support services. Encouragement of "peer-to-peer" advocacy creates "pull demand" for Triple P. For example, Fives and colleagues (2014) showed that parents who had participated in Triple P commonly speak to people they know (friends, neighbors, and relatives) about their experiences. This peer-to-peer advocacy helps mobilize a social contagion which, in turn, attracts other parents to the program. This social network effect may be an important by-product of community-level implementation.

Future Directions

Triple P has evolved considerably over the past three decades, from a program for parents of disruptive preschoolers delivered individually through clinic-based

154 Matthew R. Sanders et al.

and home coaching, to a multi-level system of intervention with varied delivery modalities and formats that is used around the world. This is due to an ongoing commitment to research and innovation, and a successful and evolving dissemination and implementation support mechanism.

Triple P continues to evolve in four directions concurrently: 1) ongoing research and development work to improve the existing intervention system, so that population-level change can be achieved; 2) the development, testing, and dissemination of additional targeted interventions for vulnerable populations (e.g., parents of children with fetal alcohol problems, parents of pre-term babies); 3) the development, testing, and dissemination of programs through new technology platforms such as responsive online programs (e.g., creating parallel online versions of varying levels of Triple P, evaluating an online triaging system into online programs of varying intensity); and 4) strategic initiatives to further strengthen the scientific basis of all aspects of the program (e.g., developing and testing a public health model of Triple P for deployment in low- and middle-income countries [LMICs]).

There is a complementary role of both developer-led and independent evaluations of Triple P (Sanders & Kirby, 2014). We have taken several quality assurance steps to promote high-quality research training in our doctoral program so that empirical findings on Triple P continue to be nourished by ongoing research and development. This feeds into other processes such as a robust scientific forum for researchers through an annual scientific retreat and international conference, a searchable evidence base of published studies on Triple P, a research blog for rapid dissemination on new findings, and an ongoing commitment to consumer and end-user input into the development of Triple P.

A commitment to provide parenting support for all families requires a major effort to ensure that programs are suitable and effective with a very diverse range of parent and family situations. With that goal in mind, to date, we have developed and tested programs for children from infancy to adolescents, for parents of children with a range of mental health and developmental problems (e.g., conduct problems, ADHD, anxiety disorders, feeding disorders, pain syndromes, autism spectrum disorders, traumatic brain injury, cerebral palsy), parents with a variety of adjustment difficulties (e.g., parents with a depressive disorder, intellectual impairment, anger management problems, marital distress), and families in a number of living circumstances (e.g., parents who are separated and divorced, single parents, grandparents, working parents suffering from occupational stress and burnout).

Although the growing reach of the program and associated research being conducted in multiple countries is encouraging, there is still much to do. Evidence-based parenting programs are under-developed and not accessible to the vast majority of the world population, particularly in low-resource environments. Recently the World Health Organization (2009) and United Nations Office on Drugs and Crime (2009) have called for evidence-based parenting programs to be implemented in LMICs. We are developing and testing Triple P in several of these countries, including sub-Saharan countries of Kenya and South Africa, and Latin American countries (e.g., Panama). This work involves a coalition of non-governmental and philanthropic organizations, and work has been done in some of the most challenging communities, such as urban ghettos. Current work also focuses on parenting programs with Indigenous populations including Aboriginal and Torres Strait Island populations in Australia, Maori and Pacific Island people in New Zealand, and First Nations populations in North America. Current large-scale implementation trials are also under way, testing the multi-level Stepping Stones Triple P intervention for parents of children with a disability. Other RCTs are under way with parents with bipolar disorder, parents of young children who are offenders, vulnerable first-time pregnant parents, and parents of children with chronic illnesses including diabetes, asthma, and eczema.

The goal is to develop the minimally sufficient number of additional program variants to ensure all parents can access a culturally and contextually relevant program suited to their needs. It is also important that Triple P programs continue to evolve for new generations of parents with very different circumstances and histories as compared to the generation who participated in the original trials. For example, many time-poor modern families and practitioners raised in a digital world may wish to access parenting programs advice and training through the Internet. This has the potential to increase reach, reduce costs, and enhance public health impact. However, this represents a major challenge and potential threat for developers and purveyor organizations and, indeed, practitioners who have relied on face-to-face intervention delivery and in-person training programs. The next generation of parenting programs will need to develop creative ways of preserving features of interventions that are highly valued, or seen as crucial mechanisms for change, while integrating technology-assisted ways of mobilizing the same mechanisms (e.g., peer support via closed social communities linked to online programs).

Finally, we are embarking on some new synergies between different disciplines to create new opportunities for prevention using population-based approaches. We have recently teamed with the field of Engineering and Global Change Scientists interested in energy poverty and promoting the sustainable use of natural resources to test whether the combination of engineering solutions (e.g., using cooking devices that burn gas instead of traditional methods using animal manure as a fuel source) and parenting and family-based population health interventions can concurrently produce healthier and more sustainable environments to raise children.

References

Arnold, D. S., O'Leary, S. G., Wolff, L. S., & Acker, M. M. (1993). The Parenting Scale: A measure of dysfunctional parenting in discipline situations. *Psychological Assessment*, *5*, 137–144.

156 Matthew R. Sanders et al.

Baer, D. M., Wolf, M. M., & Risley, T. R. (1968). Some current dimensions of applied behavior analysis. *Journal of Applied Behavior Analysis, 1*(1), 91–97.

Bandura, A. (1977). *Social learning theory.* Englewood Cliffs, NJ: Prentice-Hall.

Beidas R. S., & Kendall, P. C. (2010). Training therapists in evidence-based practice: A critical review of studies from a systems-contextual perspective. *Clinical Psychology: Science and Practice, 17,* 1–30.

Blueprints for Healthy Youth Development (2014). *Triple P System fact sheet.* Boulder, CO: Institute of Behavioral Science, University of Colorado Boulder.

Carmody, T. (2013). *Taking responsibility: A roadmap for Queensland child protection.* Brisbane, Australia: State of Queensland (Queensland Child Protection Commission of Inquiry).

Dadds, M. R., & Powell, M. B. (1991). The relationship of interparental conflict and global marital adjustment to aggression, anxiety, and immaturity in aggressive nonclinic children. *Journal of Abnormal Child Psychology, 19,* 553–567.

de Graaf, I., Speetins, P., Smit, F., de Wolff, M., & Tavecchio, L. (2008a). Effectiveness of the Triple P Positive Parenting Program on parenting: A meta-analysis. *Journal of Family Relations, 57,* 553–566.

de Graaf, I., Speetjens, P., Smit, F., de Wolff, M., & Tavecchio, L. (2008b). Effectiveness of the Triple P-Positive Parenting Program on behavioral problems in children: A meta-analysis. *Behavior Modification, 32,* 714–735.

Deming, W. E. (1986). *Out of the crisis.* Cambridge, MA: Massachusetts Institute of Technology, Center for Advanced Engineering Study.

Dodge, K. (1986). A social information processing model of social competence in children. In M. Perlmutter (Ed.), *Minnesota Symposia on Child Psychology: Vol. 18. Cognitive perspectives on children's social and behavioral development* (pp. 77–125). Hillsdale, NJ: Lawrence Erlbaum.

Eyberg, S. M., & Pincus, D. (1999). *Eyberg Child Behavior Inventory and Sutter-Eyberg Student Behavior Inventory—Revised: Professional manual.* Odessa, FL: Psychological Assessment Resources.

Farquhar, J. W., Fortmann, S. P., Maccoby, N., Haskell, W. L., Williams, P. T., Flora, J. A., et al. (1985). The Stanford Five-City Project: Design and methods. *American Journal of Epidemiology, 122*(2), 323–334.

Fives, A., Pursell, L., Heary, C., Nic Gabhainn, S., & Canavan, J. (2014). *Parenting support for every parent: A population-level evaluation of Triple P in Longford Westmeath. Final report.* Athlone: Longford Westmeath Parenting Partnership (LWPP).

Fixsen, D. L., Naoom, S. F., Blase, K. A., Friedman, R. M., & Wallace, F. (2005). *Implementation research: A synthesis of the literature.* Tampa, FL: University of South Florida, Louis de la Parte Florida Mental Health Institute, The National Implementation Research Network.

Glasgow, R. E., Vogt, T. M., & Boles, S. M. (1999). Evaluating the public health impact of health promotion interventions: The RE-AIM framework. *American Journal of Public Health, 89*(9), 1322–1327.

Goodman, R. (1997). The Strengths and Difficulties Questionnaire: A research note. *Journal of Child Psychology and Psychiatry, 38,* 581–586.

Goodman, R. (1999). The extended version of the Strengths and Difficulties Questionnaire as a guide to child psychiatric caseness and consequent burden. *Journal of Child Psychology and Psychiatry, 40*(5), 791–799.

Guajardo, N. R., Snyder, G., & Petersen, R. (2009). Relationships among parenting practices, parental stress, child behaviour, and children's social-cognitive development. *Infant and Child Development, 18,* 37–60.

The Triple P – Positive Parenting Program **157**

Hart, B. M., & Risley, T. R. (1995). *Meaningful differences in the everyday experience of young American children*. Baltimore, MD: Paul. H. Brooks.

Henggeler, S. W. (2011). Efficacy studies to large-scale transport: The development and validation of multisystemic therapy programs. *Annual Review of Clinical Psychology, 7*, 351–81.

Lee, S., Aos, S., Drake, E., Pennucci, A., Miller, M., & Anderson, L. (2012) *Return on investment: Evidence-based options to improve statewide outcome, April 2012*. (Document No. 12—4-12-1). Olympica: Washington State Institute for Public Policy.

Little, M., Berry, V., Morpeth, L., Blower, S., Axford, N., Taylor, R., Bywater, T., Lehtonen, M., & Tobin, K. (2012). The impact of three evidence-based programmes delivered in public systems in Birmingham, UK. *International Journal of Conflict and Violence, 6*, 260–272.

Lovibond, S. H., & Lovibond, P. F. (1995). *Manual for the Depression Anxiety Stress Scales (2nd Ed.)*. Sydney, NSW: Psychology Foundation of Australia.

Mazzucchelli, T. G., & Sanders, M. R. (2010). Facilitating practitioner flexibility within an empirically supported intervention: Lessons from a system of parenting support. *Clinical Psychology: Science and Practice, 17*(3), 238–252.

Moffitt, T. E., Arseneault, L., Belsky, D., Dickson, N., Hancox, R. J., Harrington, H., et al. (2011). A gradient of childhood self-control predicts health, wealth, and public safety. *Proceedings of the National Academy of Sciences of the USA, 108*, 2693–2698.

Morawska, A., Sanders, M., Goadby, E., Headley, C., Hodge, L., McAuliffe, C., et al. (2011). Is the Triple P-Positive Parenting Program acceptable to parents from culturally diverse backgrounds? *Journal of Child and Family Studies, 20*(5), 614–622.

Morawska, A., Sanders, M. R., Haslam, D., Filus, A., & Fletcher, R. (2014). Child Adjustment and Parent Efficacy Scale: Development and initial validation of a parent report measure. *Australian Psychologist, 49*(4), 241–252.

National Institute for Health and Care Excellence [NICE]. (2013). *Antisocial behaviour and conduct disorders in children and young people: The NICE guideline on recognition, intervention and management* (National Clinical Guideline Number 158). London: The British Psychological Society and The Royal College of Psychiatrists.

Norton, R. (1983). Measuring marital quality: A critical look at the dependent variable. *Journal of Marriage and the Family, 45*, 141–151.

Nowak, C., & Heinrichs, N. (2008). A comprehensive meta-analysis of Triple P-Positive Parenting Program using hierarchical linear modeling: Effectiveness and moderating variables. *Clinical Child Family Psychology Review, 11*, 114–144.

Patterson, G. R. (1982). *A social learning approach to family intervention: III. Coercive family process*. Eugene, OR: Castalia.

Prinz, R. J., Sanders, M. R., Shapiro, C. J., Whitaker, D. J., & Lutzker, J. R. (2009). Population-based prevention of child maltreatment: The U.S. Triple P system population trial. *Prevention Science, 10*, 1–12.

Romney, S., Israel, N., & Zlatevski, D. (2014). Exploration-stage implementation variation: Its effect on the cost-effectiveness of an evidence-based parenting program. *Zeitschrift für Psychologie, 222*(1), 37–48.

Rutter, M. (1985a). Family and school influences on cognitive development. *Journal of Child Psychology and Psychiatry and Allied Disciplines, 26*(5), 683–704.

Rutter, M. (1985b). Resilience in the face of adversity: Protective factors and resistance to psychiatric disorder. *British Journal of Psychiatry, 147*, 598–611.

Salari, R., Fabian, H., Prinz, R., Lucas, S., Feldman, I., Fairchild, A., & Sarkadi, A. (2013). The Children and Parents in Focus project: A population-based cluster-randomised controlled trial to prevent behavioural and emotional problems in children. *BMC Public Health, 13*, 961.

Sanders, M. R. (2000). *Family observation schedule*. Brisbane, Australia: Parenting and Family Support Centre, The University of Queensland.

Sanders, M. R. (2012). Development, evaluation, and multinational dissemination of the Triple P – Positive Parenting Program. *Annual Review of Clinical Psychology, 8*, 1–35.

Sanders, M. R., & Glynn, T. (1981). Training parents in behavioral self-management: An analysis of generalization and maintenance. *Journal of Applied Behavior Analysis, 14*, 223–237.

Sanders, M. R., & Kirby, J. N. (2014). Surviving or thriving: Quality assurance mechanisms to promote innovation in the development of evidence-based parenting interventions. *Prevention Science*, published online March 2014.

Sanders, M. R., Kirby, J. N., Tellegen, C. L., & Day, J. J. (2013). Towards a public health approach to parenting support: A systematic review and meta-analysis of the Triple P-Positive Parenting Program. *Clinical Psychology Review, 34*(4), 337–357.

Sanders, M. R., Markie-Dadds, C., Tully, L. A., & Bor, W. (2000). The Triple P-Positive Parenting Program: A comparison of enhanced, standard, and self-directed behavioral family intervention for parents of children with early onset conduct problems. *Journal of Consulting and Clinical Psychology, 68*, 624–640.

Sanders, M. R., Markie-Dadds, C., & Turner, K. M. T. (2013). *Practitioner's manual for Standard Triple P* (2nd ed.). Brisbane, Australia: Triple P International Pty Ltd.

Sanders, M. R., Morawska, A., Haslam, D. M., Filus, A., & Fletcher, R. (2014). Parenting and Family Adjustment Scales (PAFAS): Validation of a brief parent-report measure for use in assessment of parenting skills and family relationships. *Child Psychiatry and Human Development, 45*(3), 255–272.

Sanders, M. R., & Murphy-Brennan, M. (2010). Creating conditions for success beyond the professional training environment. *Clinical Psychology: Science and Practice, 17*, 31–35.

Sanders, M. R., Ralph, A., Sofronoff, K., Gardiner, P., Thompson, R., Dwyer, S., & Bidwell, K. (2008). Every Family: A population approach to reducing behavioral and emotional problems in children making the transition to school. *Journal of Primary Prevention, 29*, 197–222.

Sanders, M. R., & Woolley, M. L. (2005). The relationship between maternal self-efficacy and parenting practices: Implications for parent training. *Child: Care, Health and Development, 31*(1), 65–73.

Sarkadi, A., Sampaio, F., Kelly, M. P., & Feldman, I. (2014). A novel approach used outcome distribution curves to estimate the population-level impact of a public health intervention. *Journal of Clinical Epidemiology, 67*(7), 785–792.

Seng, A. C., Prinz, R. J., & Sanders, M. R. (2006). The role of training variables in effective dissemination of evidence-based parenting interventions. *International Journal of Mental Health Promotion, 8*(4), 20–28.

Sethi, S., Kerns, S. E. U., Sanders, M. R., & Ralph, A. (2014). The international dissemination of evidence-based parenting interventions: Impact on practitioner content and process self-efficacy. *International Journal of Mental Health Promotion, 16*(2), 126–137.

Stack, D. M., Serbin, L. A., Enns, L., Ruttle, P., & Barrieau, L. (2010). Parental effects on children's emotional development over time and across generations. *Infants and Young Children, 23*, 52–69.

Thomas, R., & Zimmer-Gembeck, M. J. (2007). Behavioral outcomes of parent–child interaction therapy and Triple P-Positive Parenting Program: A review and meta-analysis. *Journal of Abnormal Child Psychology, 35*, 475–495.

Turner, K. M. T., Nicholson, J. M., & Sanders, M. R. (2011). The role of practitioner self-efficacy, training, program and workplace factors on the implementation of an evidence-based parenting intervention in primary care. *Journal of Primary Prevention*, *32*(2), 95–112.

Turner, K. M. T., Richards, M., & Sanders, M. R. (2007). Randomised clinical trial of a group parent education programme for Australian Indigenous families. *Journal of Paediatrics and Child Health*, *43*(6), 429–437.

Turner, K. M. T., Sanders, M. R., & Hodge, L. (2014). Issues in professional training to implement evidence-based parenting programs: The needs of Indigenous practitioners. *Australian Psychologist*. Accepted 28 August, 2014.

United Nations Office on Drugs and Crime [UNODC] (2009). *Guide to implementing family skills training programmes for drug abuse prevention*. New York: United Nations.

Washington State Institute for Public Policy. (2014). *Child welfare benefit-cost results* (Document No. 11-07-1201). Olympia: Washington State Institute for Public Policy.

Wilson, P., Rush, R., Hussey, S., Puckering, C., Sim, F., Allely, C. S., et al. (2012). How evidence-based is an 'evidence-based parenting program'? A PRISMA systematic review and meta-analysis of Triple P. *BMC Medicine*, *10*, 130.

World Health Organization [WHO] (2009). *Preventing violence through the development of safe, stable and nurturing relationships between children and their parents and caregivers. Series of briefings on violence prevention: The evidence*. Geneva, Switzerland: WHO.

8

THE PROSPER DELIVERY SYSTEM AND IMPLEMENTATION OF THE STRENGTHENING FAMILIES PROGRAM: FOR PARENTS AND YOUTH 10–14

Cleve Redmond, Richard L. Spoth, Lisa M. Schainker, and Mark E. Feinberg

Despite their potential for substantially enhancing public health, evidence-based family and school interventions remain underutilized, failing to reach enough of the U.S. population to have their intended impact. The need to address this problem is underscored by the 2009 National Research Council and Institute of Medicine report *Preventing Mental, Emotional, and Behavioral Disorders Among Young People*, with its urgent call for research on the integration of prevention programming into service systems "which routinely involves the formation of partnerships and the development of an infrastructure" (p. 325). One approach strongly recommended in the NRC and IOM report is for the dissemination of evidence-based interventions through programming implemented by community-based partnerships (Butterfoss, Goodman, & Wandersman, 1996; Kumpfer, Turner, Hopkins, & Librett, 1993; Minkler & Wallerstein, 2002). Salient literature provides a compelling case for the role of coalitions in prevention-related activities, suggesting that they can enhance the capacity of collaborating organizations by sharing information, pooling resources and skills, and minimizing the duplication of efforts (e.g., Butterfoss, Goodman, & Wandersman, 1993; Spoth, Rohrbach et al., 2013; Wandersman & Florin, 2003). Moreover, community coalitions have demonstrated effectiveness in addressing behavioral health issues such as the prevention of substance misuse, delinquency, and violence (e.g., Chou et al., 1998; Hawkins et al., 2009; Miller & Hendrie, 2008; Spoth & Greenberg, 2011).

Despite their key role in advancing the field, school-community partnerships and primary care-community partnerships remain relatively rare (NRC & IOM, 2009), and there are major barriers to surmount in conducting them effectively. For example, as highlighted by Hallfors and colleagues (2002), prevention programming delivered by local coalitions is not always effective. Community-based partnerships, coalitions, or teams may have competing agendas, become diffuse in focus, and may be unable to sustain programming efforts, or be unsustainable themselves due to time-limited funding and a tendency to not plan for sustainability after the funding period ends. Community-based intervention effectiveness may also be diminished by limited program reach or program adaptations that reduce intensity or otherwise threaten fidelity.

The PROSPER Delivery System (PROSPER, for short) is a partnership developed to surmount the barriers articulated in the literature. Toward this end, it was designed to support the dissemination and sustained, high-quality delivery of evidence-based programs (EBPs) by community teams in order to maximize their potential for the prevention of adolescent substance misuse and related problem behaviors (Spoth, Greenberg, Bierman, & Redmond, 2004). Evidence from studies of PROSPER have been reviewed and recognized by the USDA (Program of Distinction), Blueprints for Healthy Youth Development (Promising Program), the Coalition on Evidence-Based Policy (Near Top Tier), and the Social Impact Exchange (S & I Top 100 Nonprofits for Social Impact).

This chapter will provide: (1) an introduction to the partnership-based PROSPER Delivery System; (2) an overview of the Strengthening Families Program: For Parents and Youth 10–14 (SFP 10–14—previously called the Iowa Strengthening Families Program, as described below), the primary family program disseminated through PROSPER; (3) a detailed description of how PROSPER serves to address challenges in achieving broad dissemination of EBPs and public health impact; (4) a summary of PROSPER research findings to date; and (5) what is now needed to promote future dissemination of family-focused preventive interventions. The content in this chapter complements a chapter by Spoth and colleagues (Spoth, Redmond, Mason, Schainker, & Borduin, 2015) which focuses on the SFP 10–14, its effectiveness as a partnership-supported, community-based prevention program, and its delivery through PROSPER.

Overview of the PROSPER Program Delivery System Approach

As the name implies, PROSPER (PROmoting School-community-university Partnerships to Enhance Resiliency) is based in partnerships among key stakeholders at multiple levels dedicated to supporting the sustained, high-quality delivery of EBPs. Briefly, PROSPER is based on a multi-tiered structure, consisting of (a) community teams, (b) a state-level management team, (c) a prevention coordinating team, and (d) a national-level tier, the PROSPER Network Team, composed of prevention scientists, faculty, and professionals involved in the development and original implementation of PROSPER in Iowa and Pennsylvania (see Figure 8.1).

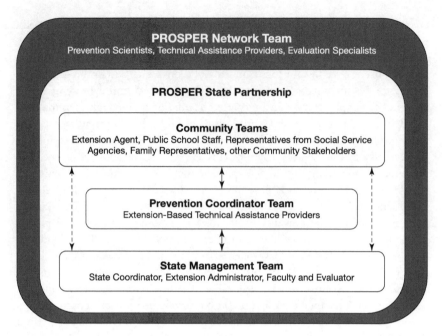

FIGURE 8.1 The PROSPER Four-Tiered Delivery System

A unique aspect of PROSPER is the involvement of the land grant university Cooperative Extension System (CES). CES staff have key roles in PROSPER implementation, including serving as Community Team Leaders. Serving on the community teams are representatives from public schools, community human service agencies, and other local stakeholders. Informing this approach is Rogers' 1995 Diffusion of Innovation Theory work describing "change agent linking functions" that connect resource and client systems (Rogers, 2003). Salient in this regard for PROSPER is how linking capacity-building agents (i.e., the CES and public school systems) can support sustained, high-quality delivery of EBPs (Spoth et al., 2004). PROSPER training, technical assistance (TA), and other supports facilitate the linking of these systems and other program providers to promote the sharing of expertise and resources to support local EBP delivery.

Because they reach every community in the nation, the CES and public school systems have immense potential for scaling up EBPs for public health impact. Unfortunately, there are significant barriers concerning infrastructure and capacity that limit that potential. CES staff often lack training in key areas related to EBP implementation, rigorous evaluation, and sustainability, and schools typically lack personnel and expertise needed to integrate school-based and family-focused prevention efforts. As a solution to these limitations, PROSPER is designed to build capacity through a partnership infrastructure providing the training and TA to support the delivery of EBPs through community teams (Spoth et al., 2004).

Although the PROSPER structure could be adapted to support the delivery of programs targeting a wide range of public health-related issues (e.g., obesity/healthy lifestyle, youth violence, bullying), to date, it has focused on the delivery of universal EBPs for middle school-aged youth and their parents designed to prevent adolescent substance misuse and related problem behaviors. Because of the large number of relevant adolescent risk and protective factors that originate in the family and school environments (e.g., Dishion, Patterson, Stoolmiller, & Skinner, 1991; Hawkins, Catalano, & Miller, 1992; Romer, 2003), PROSPER was designed to support multicomponent intervention delivery that includes both school and family interventions.

Community teams select a family and school program from a menu of PROSPER-supported evidence-based interventions and manage the delivery of those programs.

Programs Disseminated Through the PROSPER Delivery System

A key aspect of PROSPER is its focus on evidence-based interventions. At the time the original PROSPER randomized controlled trial (RCT) was planned, selection of programs for its menu was guided by the evidentiary standards of the U.S. Department of Education Expert Review Panel for the Safe and Drug Free Schools program. The original menu offered to community teams consisted of three family and three school programs. Five of the six programs had been previously evaluated, shown to be effective, and were classified as "Exemplary" or "Promising" programs, based on the USDE standards; one program on the menu qualified on the basis of findings made available after the initial USDE list was published. School-based programs on the menu were Life Skills Training (Botvin, 2000), All Stars (Hansen, 1996), and Project Alert (Ellickson, Bell, Thomas, Robyn, & Zellman, 1988). Ongoing monitoring of the developing evidence-base is one of the functions of the PROSPER Network Team; based on later published research findings, Project Alert was replaced on the PROSPER menu by Lions Quest *Skills for Adolescence* (Quest International, 1992).

School programs on the menu target a range of skills and knowledge relevant to key risk and protective factors, such as substance resistance skills, and correcting misperceptions about peer substance-related norms and attitudes. The school-based programs consist of 11 to 15 lessons and are taught as part of the 7th grade curriculum in PROSPER community schools, generally by a regular classroom teacher. Each of the school-based programs on the menu has been selected by one or more of the 14 PROSPER community teams in the original PROSPER RCT (involving 28 communities randomly assigned to intervention or control conditions).

164 Cleve Redmond et al.

Family-focused programs on the original PROSPER menu were Guiding Good Choices (Haggerty, Kosterman, Catalano, & Hawkins, 1999), the Strengthening Families Program: For Parents and Youth 10–14 (SFP 10–14; Kumpfer, Molgaard, & Spoth, 1996; Molgaard, Kumpfer, & Fleming, 1997; Molgaard & Spoth, 2001) and the Adolescent Transitions Program (Dishion, Andrews, Kavanagh, & Soberman, 1996). All sites selected the SFP 10–14. As such, PROSPER has become closely associated with the SFP 10–14 and has become an important avenue for its dissemination in states that have adopted PROSPER.

The Strengthening Families Program: For Parents and Youth 10–14

The SFP 10–14 is a group-based, seven-session universal intervention that employs a skill-building approach to preventing adolescent substance use and other problem behaviors. Program content includes both parent- and youth-specific topics and activities that are addressed independently, as well as activities that are done together as a family. The current SFP 10–14 curriculum is a slightly revised version of its predecessor, the Iowa Strengthening Families Program (ISFP). ISFP was a seven-session universal preventive intervention which was adapted from the 14-session selective Strengthening Families Program for high-risk families (Kumpfer, DeMarsh, & Child, 1989), described in greater detail in Chapter 4 of this book (by Kumpfer, Magalhães, Whiteside, & Xie). In addition to the core set of seven sessions, there are four optional booster sessions that can be delivered three months to a year after conclusion of the core program to reinforce key program content.

SFP 10–14 sessions are two hours long, work optimally with groups of seven to 12 families, and are divided into parent, youth, and family segments. Parents and youth participate in separate segments during the first hour and then meet together during the family segment in the second hour. Parent segment content focuses on effectively dealing with youth in everyday situations, providing nurturance while setting appropriate limits, and clearly communicating their beliefs and expectations related to alcohol and drug use. Material in the parent segments is presented via DVD instruction and facilitated discussion. Youth segment content focuses on goals and dreams for the future, appreciating parents, dealing with stress and emotions, and building skills to deal with peer pressure. These topics are covered by activities (games and projects) and discussions that address session objectives and highlight key messages. Family segments include games and projects that allow parents and youth to practice communicating and problem solving (see https://www.ncjrs.gov/pdffiles1/ojjdp/182208.pdf for further detail).

Evidence of SFP 10–14 effectiveness was provided by two earlier RCTs. The first RCT, Project Family, evaluated the ISFP as a stand-alone intervention compared to a reading materials-only control condition. In the second RCT, CaFaY, the SFP 10–14 was evaluated in combination with an evidence-based school program (Life Skills Training—LST). Findings from both RCTs demonstrated a range of program effects on substance use outcomes across adolescence and into young adulthood, with reported relative reductions in use (how much lower the intervention group rate is than the control group rate, expressed as a percentage of the control group rate) for significant effects ranging from approximately 20% to 65% across the two studies. Project Family ISFP findings included: significantly improved parenting skills and improved adolescent alcohol refusal skills; reduced gateway and illicit substance initiation, and reduced substance use in young adulthood; and reduced health-risking sexual behaviors. CaFaY SFP 10–14+LST findings included: reduced initiation of drunkenness, marijuana, and cigarettes; reduced frequency of alcohol, cigarette, and marijuana use, and drunkenness; and reduced monthly poly-substance use, past year and lifetime methamphetamine use, and prescription drug misuse. Intervention effects were frequently stronger for higher risk students. A comprehensive discussion of SFP 10–14 studies and findings can be found in Spoth et al. (2015).

Importantly, the Project Family and CaFaY studies were intervention effectiveness trials; although there was some involvement of University Extension and local stakeholders in those studies, program recruitment and implementation was directly managed by university researchers and supported by research grant funds in a manner that was not sustainable following the end of the grants. In contrast, the primary goal of PROSPER is locally sustainable program delivery that will yield positive youth and family outcomes similar to those found in prior evaluations of SFP 10–14 and the other programs on the PROSPER menu.

PROSPER Delivery System Structure

As illustrated in Figure 8.1, the PROSPER Delivery System involves a four-tiered partnership structure to support community-based EBP delivery. Three of these tiers, Community Teams, the Prevention Coordinator Team, and the State Management Team comprise the State Partnership; linking and supporting PROSPER State Partnerships is the PROSPER Network Team. These implementation tiers are described below:

Community Teams

The first PROSPER tier consists of small (typically 10–15 members), strategic (focused on specific EBP implementation goals) community teams. Community teams are led by local CES staff who typically specialize in youth or family programming and have experience in community leadership development. Community Team Leaders are supported by a local school district co-leader,

166 Cleve Redmond et al.

typically a principal or other school administrator. The school co-leaders are the primary liaison between the community team and the school district. School co-leaders help to maintain school involvement in the local PROSPER effort, ensure proper implementation of the selected school program, and help secure necessary resources (e.g., locations for family program group sessions, family contact information for family program recruitment). Rounding out the community teams are local community service providers and other stakeholders, such as representatives of the juvenile court system, members of faith-based organizations, parents, and youth.

Community teams are responsible for prevention program selection and implementation, as well as the long-term sustainability of intervention delivery. Key program implementation responsibilities include family program logistics, hiring and monitoring of family program facilitators, and the recruitment of families. Key sustainability tasks include fund raising and grant writing to support program delivery.

Prevention Coordinator and State Management Teams

Prevention Coordinators function as the most direct technical assistance providers to community teams (see Figure 8.2). They attend community team meetings and maintain regular contact with the Community Team Leaders, placing an emphasis on proactive technical assistance (see Mihalic, Fagan, Irwin, Ballard, & Elliot, 2002) around a range of issues, including local program selection and implementation (e.g., recruitment strategies, fidelity monitoring), team processes (e.g., meeting facilitation, new member orientation), and team and program sustainability (e.g., the development of fund raising strategies, grant writing).

The *State Management Team* comprises the final tier of the State Partnership. This state-level team is comprised of university researchers, CES faculty/ program specialists, and CES administrators. The State Management Team provides guidance and administrative oversight for the PROSPER effort across the state. Specific roles on this team include a State Evaluator who is responsible for ensuring that monitoring activities are conducted as recommended and a State Coordinator responsible for overseeing implementation in the state and providing support to and coordination of the team of Prevention Coordinators.

PROSPER Network Team

Each state's three-tiered structure becomes part of the network of states that are supported by the national PROSPER Network Team. The Network Team is comprised of prevention scientists and specialists involved in the original PROSPER project in Iowa and Pennsylvania. Proactive technical support from the PROSPER Network Team is part of an annual contractual agreement with each participating state's CES. Each state in the network has an

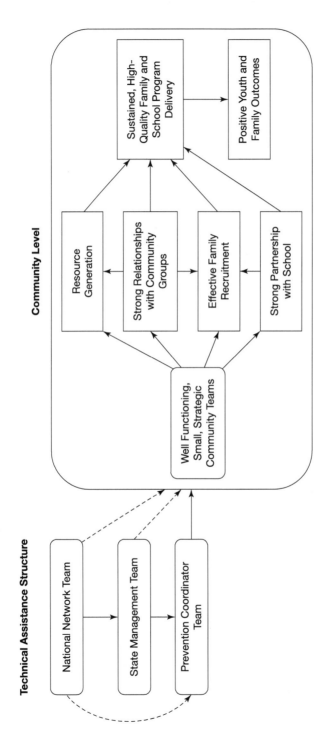

FIGURE 8.2 Technical Assistance to Community-Level Impact Model

168 Cleve Redmond et al.

assigned PROSPER Network Team coach who communicates with the State Coordinator to facilitate ongoing collaboration with the Network Team (Spoth & Greenberg, 2011).

Implementation Quality Maintenance and Monitoring

PROSPER includes a range of strategies and tools to ensure that teams are functioning effectively and that programming is conducted with quality and fidelity. All team members receive training and are provided with standardized materials and ongoing technical assistance from PROSPER Network staff on how to use them, as well as access to a variety of web-based applications to assist with PROSPER and EBP implementation, including a Prevention Coordinator reporting center to track community team progress, a resource tracker for Team Leaders to keep track of funds and in-kind resources they have generated, and a program implementation application that helps teams monitor program reach and dosage.

Standardized Materials and Training

There are three multi-day trainings for PROSPER State Management Team members, Prevention Coordinators, and Team Leaders. All PROSPER trainings are conducted by a certified PROSPER Network trainer from Iowa State University. Trainings are scheduled as community teams meet task-focused benchmarks (e.g., completion of seven team meetings for the second training, one implementation year of the family program for the third training). The initial training focuses on the basics of prevention science, such as the importance of addressing risk and protective factors, the value of using programs that have evidence to show that they work, and team development. The second training focuses on the selection of the family program, and recruitment and program delivery strategies. The third training addresses school program selection, advanced team development issues, and sustainability strategies such as securing funding and other resources for the future. In addition, Community Team Leaders and Prevention Coordinators receive manuals that provide guidance and outline their respective recommended action steps for PROSPER implementation. Team Leaders and Prevention Coordinators also receive access to a range of web-based materials, such as standardized presentations, worksheets, and other resources to be used during team meetings.

Structured Communication

To help ensure that technical support is both timely and ongoing, key relevant interactions are structured and documented. Most central among these are (1) bi-weekly phone contacts between PROSPER Network State Coaches and each state's State Coordinator, and (2) monthly in-person meetings and bi-weekly phone contacts between Prevention Coordinators and Community Team Leaders within the State Partnership. Regular communication also occurs between the State Coordinator and the Prevention Coordinators, and among members of the State Management Team. Two other examples of structured activities are quarterly learning community meetings and annual statewide meetings. These meetings are used to share data, provide professional development opportunities for Team Leaders and team members, and to address implementation challenges using a group problem-solving approach.

Implementation Fidelity Monitoring

To address overall fidelity to core PROSPER implementation elements, a benchmark scoring guide was developed. At the end of each implementation year, Prevention Coordinators rate each community team on each aspect of PROSPER implementation at the local level (e.g., leader effectiveness, team functioning, family/school program delivery) to inform TA needs for the next year. If mandatory benchmarked activities (i.e., delivery of family or school programs) do not occur for more than one year and TA cannot resolve the issue, the PROSPER effort in that community may be suspended until requirements can be met. Fidelity of family and school program implementation is monitored with on-site observers who attend selected sessions. Observers complete standardized fidelity assessment forms that are available for each program on the PROSPER menu, as well as rate participant engagement and facilitator/teacher effectiveness.

System Financing

Financing for the PROSPER Delivery System to date has been derived from a range of sources and has varied both across implementation phases and tiers of the partnership. The general financing approach in all PROSPER states (eight, to date) has included initial support provided to community teams to cover Team Leader salaries, program facilitator pay, and other direct costs associated with program delivery during the initial program implementation period. Then, consistent with PROSPER's developmental phase design, support for community teams is reduced across the next few years until community teams become responsible for all direct local program delivery costs, as well as the Team Leader's salary. As support is reduced, community team activities and related TA increasingly focus on local resource generation. Financing for PROSPER occurs differently at each level (community, state, and network) and has presented challenges at each of those levels. For this reason, and in consideration of space constraints, the specific challenges and relevant findings or illustrative strategies for addressing them will be summarized in the Challenges section below.

170 Cleve Redmond et al.

PROSPER Delivery System Evaluation and Impacts

PROSPER process and programming outcomes have been examined in an RCT conducted in Iowa and Pennsylvania involving 28 rural town and small city school districts. Community populations ranged from 6,975 to 44,510 (2000 U.S. Census). Community recruitment procedures are described comprehensively elsewhere (Spoth, Clair, Greenberg, Redmond, & Shin, 2007). Fourteen of the communities (seven in each state) were randomly assigned to the PROSPER intervention condition; the remaining 14 communities served as no-treatment controls. Community teams were formed in each intervention community to manage preventive intervention delivery supported by PROSPER. Control communities received no project support for prevention programming, but were free to continue implementing whatever programming their communities and school districts normally provided.

PROSPER Delivery System Implementation

Once formed, community teams selected a universal family program from a menu of three evidence-based interventions. To assist them in their decision, teams were provided with materials describing each program and its evidence base. Each of the 14 community teams chose SFP 10–14, often citing the involvement of youth in all program sessions (in contrast to other family programs on the PROSPER menu) as a motivation for their selection. Following program selection, community teams progressed to hiring program facilitators (who subsequently received standard SFP 10–14 facilitator training), making arrangements for program meetings, recruiting families, and delivering the program to a first cohort of 6th grade students and their families during the spring semester. A few of the PROSPER communities also delivered the four SFP 10–14 booster sessions the following year. The SFP 10–14 was delivered to a new cohort of 6th grade students and their families each successive year.

Following delivery of the SFP 10–14 to the first cohort of students and their families, community teams selected a school intervention from among the three on the program menu with input from the middle-school teaching staff. Project ALERT and Life Skills Training were each selected by four teams and All Stars was selected by six. Beginning in the school year following the initial SFP 10–14 implementation, school programs were implemented yearly in 7th grade classrooms. The school programs were generally taught by regular classroom teachers who attended standard program trainings.

PROSPER Delivery System Assessments

Overall, evaluation results, as described below, indicate that PROSPER is an effective mechanism for supporting the high-quality delivery of evidence-based interventions by community teams, based on comparisons of findings from other empirical research on implementation quality (e.g., Fixsen, Naoom, Blase, Friedman, & Wallace, 2005), as reported in Spoth, Guyll, Redmond, Greenberg, and Feinberg (2011). Various aspects of PROSPER implementation-related assessments were intended to evaluate common challenges to successful community-based EBP implementation, including family recruitment, maintaining program fidelity, and promoting team and EPB sustainability. For this reason, the primary results from the implementation assessments bearing on those challenges will be presented in the Challenges section.

Preventive Intervention Outcomes

Primary PROSPER-supported programming outcomes were evaluated with two cohorts of middle school students in the 28 Iowa and Pennsylvania project school districts. Across the two cohorts, a total of 10,849 students (90% of those eligible) completed in-school pretest surveys in the fall of their 6th grade year. In-school follow-up surveys were conducted annually during the spring semesters of the 7th to 12th grades (additional sample detail is provided elsewhere, e.g., Spoth, Redmond et al., 2013).

PROSPER-supported programming effects on a range of youth and family outcomes have been examined, including youth and family skills, youth substance use, and youth conduct problems. All analyses were conducted via multi-level models (intervention effects were tested at the community/school-district level) using an intent-to-treat approach.

Protective factor outcomes

Analyses of data collected from youth participating in the in-school survey showed significant intervention effects on a range of youth, parent, and family protective factor outcomes from the 7th through 9th grades (Redmond et al., 2009). For example, relative to control condition youth, PROSPER condition youth reported less association with antisocial peers, less positive substance use expectancies, lower perceived peer substance use norms, better problem-solving skills, and higher levels of assertiveness at the 7th, 8th, and 9th grade assessments. PROSPER condition youth also reported better child management practices by their parents and more frequent activities with their parents at each assessment point, as well as higher levels of parent–child affective quality at most assessment points. Individual-level effect sizes for significant effects ranged from .05 to .24; community/school district-level effect sizes for significant effects ranged from .10 to .91.

Substance use outcomes

Adolescent substance use outcomes were evaluated at the 7th, 10th, and 12th grade assessments. At the 7th grade assessment, analyses showed significant intervention effects on a range of substance initiation outcomes (Spoth, Redmond et al., 2007), including lower new-user rates among the intervention group versus controls for drunkenness, cigarette use, marijuana use, inhalant use, methamphetamine use, and ecstasy use. Additional effects found at the 7th grade assessment included lower rates of past-month cigarette use and past-year drunkenness, marijuana use, and inhalant use among intervention group students versus controls. Effects sizes for significant effects ranged from .10 to .63 at the individual-level and from .37 to .74 at the community/school-district level. Subsequent analysis of those outcomes at the 10th grade showed generally stronger results; individual-level effect sizes ranged from .11 to .91, while community/school district-level effect sizes ranged from .32 to .74 (Spoth et al., 2011). Corresponding relative reductions ranged from 5% to 52%. In addition, growth curve results showed significant intervention main effects (lower rates of use for the intervention group) for all assessed outcomes except new-user rates of alcohol use, as well as significant intervention × time effects for all outcomes except past-year inhalant use, demonstrating slower rates of growth in use for the intervention group from the 6th to 10th grades.

More recently, substance use outcomes were examined at the 11th and 12th grade assessment points (Spoth, Redmond et al., 2013). Outcomes included past-month or past-year use of a range of substance use behaviors (use of cigarettes, marijuana, inhalants, and methamphetamines), lifetime use of illicit substances (assessed by an index addressing five illicit substances), and the frequency of drunkenness and driving after drinking. Significantly lower prevalence rates or behavior frequencies were found for the intervention group for the majority of outcomes at both assessment points, and for all outcomes except those addressing driving after drinking, for at least one of the two assessment points. Relative reduction rates ranged from 3% for frequency of drunkenness to 31% for lifetime use of methamphetamine. Growth trajectory analyses confirmed slower growth in substance use behaviors between the 6th and 12th grades for most outcomes, while risk moderation analyses showed a pattern of stronger intervention effects for higher risk adolescents. Prescription drug misuse at the 12th grade has also been examined (Spoth, Trudeau et al., 2013) and results showed significantly lower initiation rates of opiate misuse and overall prescription drug misuse for students in the PROSPER intervention condition relative to controls; 22.1% of the intervention condition participants versus 27.8% of the control condition participants reported lifetime misuse of prescription opiates (a relative reduction of 21%) and 23.1% of intervention condition participants versus 29.0% of control condition participants reported lifetime prescription drug misuse (a relative reduction of 20%).

Conduct problem outcomes

In addition to examining intervention effects on substance use, "cross-over" effects on conduct problems were also examined. Although not directly targeted by PROSPER menu programs, adolescent conduct problems and substance misuse share a number of risk and protective factors addressed by the programs. Analyses were conducted to assess intervention effects on a 12-item measure of conduct problems at grades 8 through 12 (Spoth et al., under review). Intervention effects (lower conduct problem rates among the intervention group versus controls) were significant at each grade. Individual-level effect sizes ranged from .10 to .13. Risk-moderation analyses indicated stronger intervention effects for students who had initiated gateway substance use by the fall of 6th grade.

Costs, Cost-Efficiency, and Cost-Effectiveness

PROSPER implementation costs have been evaluated both in the context of the original PROSPER RCT and in subsequent PROSPER dissemination efforts in other states. Recent post-RCT cost estimates show that PROSPER costs per participant vary depending on a number of factors (e.g., timing of trainings, size of community, and implementation groups). However, on average, excluding direct program costs, PROSPER has an estimated average annual unit cost of $123 per participant in a community with a population of 50,000 and an expectation that approximately 1,130 middle school students and their parents would be reached. This is the number that would be expected following completion of initial implementation of programs on the menu, requiring up to three years of time. This unit cost decreases in larger communities and increases in smaller ones (see www.blueprintsprograms.com).

The additional costs of implementing the specific family- and school-based programs also will vary, depending on the programs selected. A conservative cost analysis showed that, within PROSPER, the costs of delivering SFP 10–14 are $278–$348 per family, 59% less than delivery costs outside of PROSPER. Costs per student for the school programs on the PROSPER menu are $9–$27 (see Crowley, Jones, Greenberg, Feinberg, & Spoth, 2012).

In the PROSPER trial, cost-effectiveness concerning individual substance use initiation outcomes ranged from a low of $9,929 for each youth prevented from initiating marijuana use by the 10th grade, to a high of $17,884 for each youth prevented from initiating ecstasy use, with relatively better cost-effectiveness estimates for more commonly used substances (Guyll et al., in preparation). The pattern of cost-effectiveness outcomes in the trial supports the conclusion that a universal intervention is more likely to be economically viable for reducing problem behaviors that are both costly and prevalent (Offord, Kraemer, Kazdin, Jensen, & Harrington, 1998; Spoth, Guyll, & Day, 2002). Because reduction of gateway substance misuse has been shown to reduce subsequent misuse of other substances such as methamphetamine in late adolescence and young adulthood (e.g., Spoth, Trudeau, Guyll, & Shin, 2012), the economic viability is likely to be stronger over time.

174 Cleve Redmond et al.

Challenges to PROSPER Delivery System Implementation and Dissemination at Multiple Levels: Findings and Lessons Learned

Key challenges in the achievement of community-level impact, related "grand" challenges in large-scale translation of EBPs like the SFP 10–14, and how PROSPER addresses those challenges have been summarized in an earlier article (Spoth & Greenberg, 2011). As indicated in that article, there are multiple challenges at each level at which PROSPER operates.

Community-Level Challenges

At the community level, important challenges are similar to those for many community-based coalitions or teams implementing universal EBPs, including family-focused ones. Three primary areas of challenge are: family recruitment, program fidelity, and sustainability (particularly financing). Illustrative findings and successful strategies in each of these areas are described below.

Family Recruitment

One of the key challenges that PROSPER was designed to address is the low recruitment rate that is often experienced using traditional community programming approaches. During the PROSPER RCT in Iowa and Pennsylvania, PROSPER Community Teams were able to successfully recruit 17% of all eligible 6th grade families into the SFP 10–14 during the first two years of implementation (Spoth, Clair et al., 2007)—a rate that greatly exceeds the 1–6% rates that are typical for community-based preventive interventions (Jensen, 2003; Saunders, Greaney, Lees, & Clark, 2003). Community team functioning (e.g., production of quality team promotional materials) and TA variables (e.g., effective collaboration with TA, frequency of TA requests) were associated with higher recruitment rates, even after controlling for community and school district contextual influences (Spoth, Clair et al., 2007). Importantly, recruitment rates in the original Iowa and Pennsylvania communities, as well as in newer sites, have remained considerably higher than typical rates for community-based interventions.

Teams have achieved these rates through a variety of strategies, but one of the primary mechanisms is asking team members to utilize their existing networks and personal connections for family recruitment. Examples of strategies have included school administrators conducting a "call-a-thon," personally calling and inviting all of the parents of the 6th graders in their school to participate. Other examples include having families that participated in previous years conduct outreach activities to share their positive experiences with the program. And, as social media has become more widely used and accessible, teams have begun to use Facebook and Twitter to reach families.

Program Fidelity

Trained observers attending family and school program sessions reported average rates of implementation adherence that exceeded 90% for both the family and school programs. Ratings were also high on other indicators of implementation quality, such as group participation and facilitation quality for the SFP 10–14. A long-term examination of implementation showed SFP 10–14 implementation adherence ratings remained near 90% across all 14 PROSPER community sites through six years of program delivery (Spoth et al., 2011).

Sustainability

An emerging literature underscores the many interrelated barriers to both sustainability of community-based teams and EBPs (Scheirer & Dearing, 2011). Among these barriers, achieving stable funding and sufficient human resources to support long-term EBP implementation are central. For this reason, a key question addressed by the PROSPER RCT was whether community teams could be sustained and maintain high-quality delivery of their family and school programs over time. One indicator of PROSPER's success is that all 14 of the original PROSPER community teams in Iowa and Pennsylvania continued to deliver their selected EBPs for five years following their formation. And now, 12 years after formation, most of those teams continue to deliver both the family and school programs.

In this regard, data collected from the original trial demonstrated that community teams were successful in garnering resources for sustained implementation, raising an average of approximately $20,000 in funds and in-kind services per year by their fourth year of operation (Greenberg et al., 2014). Teams have utilized a variety of strategies for resource generation, and all community teams have been able to secure local support to cover some or all of their programming and team activities. Moreover, most "mature" community teams (stable teams > 4–5 years old) have routinized their sustainability efforts, raising funds on an annual basis from sources such as state agencies, foundations, and school districts (Greenberg et al., 2014), as well as garnering substantial in-kind support from multiple community groups and businesses. Much of the in-kind support comes in the form of volunteerism, donations of meals, child care, incentives for families to participate in the program, and publicity for family program recruitment.

Adoption and Integration within the Extension System

A central goal of PROSPER is to catalyze transformation of Extension Systems at the state level in order to facilitate successful adoption and implementation of PROSPER. However, many Extension Systems, particularly during recent years, have been experiencing significant changes, including downsizing and restructuring at the state- and county-levels, along with associated shifts in priority programming areas. Changes such as these can have a major impact on the PROSPER State Partnership structure and related TA provision. Iowa and Pennsylvania are both cases in point. Due to staff cuts and CES reorganization in Pennsylvania, a number of community teams no longer have an assigned Prevention Coordinator. Instead, the State Coordinator works directly with the Team Leaders to provide TA as needed. In Iowa, CES staffing cutbacks and restructuring led to a change in the oversight of county Extension Offices and staff from university administrators to local county-based Extension Councils who are elected officials. PROSPER Team Leaders in Iowa now report to their county councils, weakening the administrative connections between the university-based State Management and Prevention Coordinator Teams and the county-based Team Leaders.

A related challenge, exacerbated by state CES staffing cuts and funding-driven reorganization, concerns turnover in key implementation roles, notably Community Team Leaders. This is especially salient given the importance of having competent leaders who have developed relevant skills and gained experience (Butterfoss et al., 1996), and is consistent with previous findings concerning challenges associated with turnover of key community-level staff (Phillips & Springer, 1997). Although PROSPER is designed to accommodate the training and integration of new Team Leaders (and other team members), depending on the length of time and the effectiveness of the transition plan between the old and new leaders, team functioning and programming-related activities may be less efficient or interrupted until the new leader becomes acclimated to the role.

Another challenge to PROSPER integration within Extension concerns its relatively narrow current focus on the delivery of family and school EBPs targeting substance misuse prevention. Conversely, Extension Systems are tasked with a broader mission, to provide programs and services addressing multiple-program priorities to all populations within their state, including ethnic or cultural minorities that may require tailored programming. While PROSPER could be used to deliver these types of programs to different cultural groups or high-risk populations, appropriate EBPs for those populations may be lacking, and PROSPER Network staff may lack sufficient expertise to adequately support a given program or program area. In cases where CES priorities do not align with the currently available menu of programs, Extension administrators have not viewed PROSPER as a viable option for their state.

Reductions in federal and state funding for state Extension Systems also create challenges related to the dissemination of PROSPER. Decreases in funding during recent years have diminished the willingness and capacity of many states to adopt new initiatives requiring significant investments of either money or staff time. Moreover, in many instances, the budgets of other state agencies were reduced along with CES budgets, reducing their ability to partner with CES in support of programming efforts. As a result, finding funds to pay for the Network-delivered trainings, technical assistance, and evaluation support is often not feasible for many Extension Systems given current funding conditions.

State- and Network-Level Financing

State-level financing

The PROSPER Network Team works with the State Management Teams in Network states to develop financing strategies to initiate and sustain PROSPER implementation. State Management Team members have worked directly with their university development officers and other financing experts to identify potential funding opportunities from state-based foundations and agencies. Another mechanism that has successfully supported PROSPER State Partnerships is the Children, Youth, and Families at Risk (CYFAR) grant program through the USDA. In two states, CES directly provided funding to start PROSPER. In Pennsylvania, where the state infrastructure already existed from the original project, funding was secured from the Pennsylvania Commission on Crime and Delinquency to support new community teams. Nonetheless, state-level financing, like Network-level financing (see below) remains a challenge.

Network Team financing

Research grants supporting dissemination and evaluation of PROSPER have also included support for developing funding strategies to support the Network's training, TA provision, and evaluation services, as these costs are currently passed on to state Extension Systems through a fee-for-service arrangement. Members of the Network Team are in the process of seeking support from a variety of philanthropic sources (e.g., Social Impact Exchange, Iowa State University Foundation, micro philanthropic website) with the goal of being able to offset the cost of its services to states. Unfortunately, the range of approaches used highlights the lack of significant, stable funding streams to support EBP dissemination infrastructures and related TA provision, despite their demonstrated capacity for ensuring high-quality, impactful program delivery.

Related Policy Issues and Needed Changes

Funding challenges across all levels of PROSPER are indicative of the existential challenge facing EBP dissemination systems more generally. That is, funding for

178 Cleve Redmond et al.

the infrastructures needed to ensure the high-quality EBP implementation necessary to maximize public health impact remains both limited and unstable. The following section addresses the policy changes needed to meet this challenge.

Braided Funding

As noted in the impact challenges article by Spoth and Greenberg (2011), accomplishing effective EBP dissemination across U.S. communities will necessitate changes in policies (both state and national) and operating procedures. An especially important set of policies and procedures are those necessary to support braided funding. Effective preventive interventions to reduce youth problem behaviors do not fall solely in the domain of any single federal or state agency. For example, a range of youth-related outcomes can be affected positively by EBPs targeting shared risk and protective factors. Broad-based, empirically driven prevention efforts will require braiding service and research funding to increase the capacity to broadly disseminate EBPs, implement those EBPs in a sustained, effective way, and to integrate their evaluation.

A recent article by the Society for Prevention Research Task Force on Translation Research also addresses the widespread dissemination of community EBPs, focusing on core challenges in interrelated aspects of translation research and practice (Spoth, Rohrbach et al., 2013). In addition to further emphasizing the need for braided funding, it delineates other federal or state policy, operating procedure, and funding mechanism recommendations, along with advocating for germane policy-related research. Especially important is research that could guide the development of relevant federal funding policies that includes addressing how community- or county-level policies (e.g., mandated set-aside funds from local taxes) can be aligned with federal-level policies and funding streams to support a wide range of EBP dissemination activities (e.g., purchase of EBP materials, program delivery, implementer training, and evaluation support) at the local level (see Pentz, 2007).

Needed Policy Changes and Action Steps for Governmental Agencies

The article by Spoth, Rohrbach, and colleagues (2013) discusses a number of action steps that could serve to enhance effective coordination and collaboration among federal and state agencies, toward the end of designing, developing, and testing effective and sustainable infrastructures for prevention practice and research, as strongly recommended by the NRC and IOM (2009). Basically, there are two types of action steps to be taken, both of which could facilitate the dissemination of delivery systems like PROSPER.

Steps concerning coordination of prevention dissemination efforts

In June 2011, the National Prevention, Health Promotion, and Public Health Council (National Prevention Council), created by the Affordable Care Act, released a comprehensive strategy for disease prevention and health promotion called the National Prevention Strategy (National Prevention, Health Promotion, and Public Health Council, 2011). Each of four strategic directions and seven priority areas articulated by the strategy includes recommended actions, including the organization of representative, multi-sector community partnerships and associated collaborations between researchers and the advocacy community. Implementing these recommendations would greatly facilitate broader implementation of PROSPER, particularly given the aforementioned issues with obtaining support for partnership infrastructure.

The type of federal agency coordination illustrated by the National Prevention Council suggests one way to move toward the common conceptual framework for prevention across federal agencies. As noted, a key aspect of a common framework concerns the risk and protective factors shared by the diverse problems addressed by various agencies, given the clear evidence indicating that the same EBPs can positively affect seemingly disparate health-related behaviors and outcomes (NRC and IOM, 2009). Essentially, federal and state agencies must give greater attention to building frameworks for health outcomes that are important across stakeholder groups, including how risk and protective factors cluster and cross over their interest areas and how to measure and increase the impact of interventions targeting youth across outcomes of interest.

Support innovative funding mechanisms

In addition to braided funding models that could support the combined services and evaluation components of PROSPER, it is critical to develop other innovative federal and state funding models. Given the magnitude of the dissemination and scale-up work to be accomplished, such funding models will likely require resource contributions from multiple agencies. Funding models could include consideration of collaboration between federal and state agencies, through which state agencies fund grants to community-based organizations for program implementation and the federal agencies fund partnership grants to universities for collaboration on community-based dissemination research in the same communities. Ideally, this approach would be integrated with private–public partnerships that channel additional foundation and corporate funding streams into the mix to scale up EBPs (e.g., The Social Impact Exchange Scaling Marketplace).

One of the most difficult barriers to surmount in optimizing funding mechanisms for delivery systems like PROSPER is limited funding and financing strategies and structures, as previously noted. Spoth, Rohrbach, and colleagues (2013) recommended that each state organize "Prevention Translation Financing Teams" to support priority prevention goals through state EBP-delivery systems. The purpose of these teams would be to develop a strategic plan for financing population-impact oriented EBPs within each state. The teams' composition could follow guidelines used by successful initiatives in states such as Maryland, as illustrated by Langford, Flynn-Khan, English, Grimm, and Taylor (2012), to assure inclusion of all appropriate stakeholders for broad EBP implementation in state delivery systems.

Central to action steps recommended in the relevant literatures are strategies to address the spectrum of developing, testing, and better coordinating scalable delivery systems as recommended by the newest IOM and NRC forum workshop report (IOM & NRC, 2014). Among the points of emphasis in the literature is the need to improve existing service delivery systems, such as those supporting community teams or coalitions like PROSPER. Basically, the goal is to develop strategies to better realize systems' potential, synergize collective efforts, and build on lessons learned through PROSPER and other trials (e.g., Communities That Care [CTC], www.communitiesthatcare.net).

While the SAMHSA National Registry of Effective Programs and Policies (NREPP) and other national lists of EBPs (e.g., NIDA, Blueprints) have facilitated access to EBP information to help with selection, more could be done, such as listing comparative effectiveness with effect sizes and better matching of interventions to local needs. One exemplary effort is being led by The Coalition for Evidence-Based Policy (CEBP). The CEBP has fostered legislative and policy change that supports broader dissemination of effective programs, particularly through its tiered initiatives that fund evidence-based social programs (see Baron & Haskins, 2011; www.coalition4evidence.org). Such efforts to support widespread dissemination of EBPs have great potential to increase the prevalence of healthy, nurturing environments (Biglan, Flay, Embry, & Sandler, 2012).

Future Directions

Streamlined Delivery System

In response to challenges concerning available supports for the broad dissemination of family and other EBPs, in general, and support for delivery system infrastructure, in particular, we plan to implement and evaluate less resource-intensive adaptations of PROSPER. For example, given the reduced staffing capacity often faced by state Extension Systems, one way is to create a direct link from community teams to a Network-based coach, reducing or eliminating the state-based Prevention Coordinator Team. Developing a streamlined TA structure would reduce Extension staff commitments within the State Partnership, potentially reducing a key barrier to System implementation.

Another strategy for reducing costs to the State Partnership is the increased use of virtual technologies (e.g., web or DVD-based) for Network-provided trainings and proactive technical assistance. Reactive technical support/problem-solving would still be provided through direct contact between Network Coaches and members of the State Partnership.

Integration with Primary Care Services

The NRC and IOM (2009) report emphasized the need for improved integration of evidence-based behavioral health interventions with primary care services. In addition, the Substance Abuse and Mental Health Services Administration has recommended that individual states develop infrastructures and systems to support the improved integration of evidence-based behavioral health services and primary care services (F. Harding, personal communication, June 17, 2014). PROSPER could be well-integrated with primary care facilities in underserved areas to better serve youth and families. Universal EBPs supported by PROSPER could function as gateways to indicated, evidence-based behavioral health services for at-risk youth and families.

At the local level, primary care liaisons could serve on PROSPER community teams, facilitating referrals to EBPs on the PROSPER menu from primary care facilities. This adaptation of PROSPER would also emphasize linkages with school-based and Community Health Centers, which have become an essential primary care medical home for underserved rural and other populations, particularly for preventive and behavioral health care.

Delivery of EBPs to Sub-populations

Finally, future research will involve adapting PROSPER to meet the needs of specific sub-populations, such as military-connected youth and families. A study has recently been initiated in North Carolina to adapt PROSPER for the delivery of evidence-based family programming to military families. Planned adaptations include involving military stakeholders in each tier of the State Partnership to ensure that programming offered meets the needs of this population, and finding organizations and businesses willing to provide funding and in-kind services specifically for programs that support military-connected families.

References

American Academy of Pediatrics. (2008). *Bright Futures: Guidelines for health supervision of infants, children, and adolescents* (3rd edition). Elk Grove Village, IL: American Academy of Pediatrics.

Baron, J., & Haskins, R. (2011, October). Building the connection between policy and evidence: The Obama evidence-based initiatives [paper commissioned by the U.K. National Endowment for Science, Technology and the Arts]. Retrieved from http://coalition4evidence.org/468-2/publications/

Biglan, A., Flay, B. R., Embry, D. D., & Sandler, I. (2012). The critical role of nurturing environments for promoting human wellbeing, *American Psychologist, 67,* 257–271.

Botvin, G. J. (2000). *Life Skills Training: Promoting health and personal development.* Princeton, NJ: Princeton Health Press.

Butterfoss, F. D., Goodman, R. M., & Wandersman, A. (1993). Community coalitions for prevention and health promotion. *Health Education Research, 8,* 315–330.

Butterfoss, F. D., Goodman, R. M., & Wandersman, A. (1996). Community coalitions for prevention and health promotion: Factors predicting satisfaction, participation, and planning. *Health Education Quarterly, 23,* 65–79.

Chou, C. P., Montgomery, S., Pentz, M. A., Rohrbach, L. A., Johnson, C. A., Flay, B. R., & MacKinnon, D. P. (1998). Effects of a community-based prevention program on decreasing drug use in high-risk adolescents. *American Journal of Public Health, 88,* 944–948.

Crowley, D. M., Jones, D. E., Greenberg, M. T., Feinberg, M. E., & Spoth, R. L. (2012). Resource consumption of a dissemination model for prevention programs: The PROSPER delivery system. *Journal of Adolescent Health, 50,* 256–263.

Dishion, T. J., Andrews, D. W., Kavanagh, K., & Soberman, L. H. (1996). Preventive interventions for high-risk youth: The Adolescent Transitions Program. In R. D. Peters & R. J. McMahon (Eds.), *Preventing childhood disorders, substance abuse, and delinquency* (pp. 184–214). Thousand Oaks, CA: Sage.

Dishion, T. J., Patterson, G. R., Stoolmiller, M., & Skinner, M. L. (1991). Family, school, and behavioral antecedents to early adolescent involvement with antisocial peers. *Developmental Psychology, 27,* 172–180.

Ellickson, P. L., Bell, R. M., Thomas, M. A., Robyn, A., & Zellman, G. L. (1988). *Designing and implementing project ALERT.* Santa Monica, CA: Rand Corporation.

Fixsen, D. L., Naoom, S. F., Blase, K. A., Friedman, R. M., & Wallace, F. (2005). *Implementation research: A synthesis of the literature.* Tampa, FL: University of South Florida, Louis de la Parte Florida Mental Health Institute, The National Implementation Researcher Network (FMHI Publication #231).

Greenberg, M. T., Feinberg, M. E., Johnson, L. E., Perkins, D. F., Welsh, J., & Spoth, R. L. (Epub April 2014). Factors that predict financial sustainability of community coalitions: Five years of findings from the PROSPER partnership project. *Prevention Science.*

Guyll, M., Crowley, D. M., Jones, D. E., Spoth, R., & Ralston, E. (in preparation). Cost-effectiveness of substance use prevention by community teams with PROSPER supports.

Haggerty, K. P., Kosterman, R., Catalano, R. F., & Hawkins, J. D. (1999). Parenting for prevention of adolescent problem behaviors with Preparing for the Drug Free Years. *OJJDP (Office of Juvenile Justice and Delinquency Prevention): Juvenile Justice Bulletin.*

Hallfors, D., Cho, D., Livert, D., & Kadushin, C. (2002). Fighting back against substance abuse: Are community coalitions winning? *American Journal of Preventive Medicine, 23,* 237–245.

Hansen, W. B. (1996). Pilot test results comparing the All Stars program with seventh grade D.A.R.E. program integrity and mediating variable analysis. *Substance Use and Misuse, 31,* 1359–1377.

Hawkins, J. D., Catalano, R. F., & Miller, J. Y. (1992). Risk and protective factors for alcohol and other drug problems in adolescence and early adulthood: Implications for substance abuse prevention. *Psychological Bulletin, 112*, 64–105.

Hawkins, J. D., Oesterle, S., Brown, E. C., Arthur, M. W., Abbott, R. D., Fagan, A. A., & Catalano, R. F. (2009). Results of a Type 2 translation research trial to prevent adolescent drug use and delinquency: A test of Communities That Care. *Archives of Pediatrics & Adolescent Medicine, 163*, 790–798.

Institute of Medicine and National Research Council (2014). *Strategies for scaling effective family-focused preventive interventions to promote children's cognitive, affective, and behavioral health: Workshop summary.* Washington, DC: The National Academies Press.

Jensen, P. S. (2003). Commentary: The next generation is overdue. *Journal of the American Academy of Child & Adolescent Psychiatry, 42*, 527–530.

Kumpfer, K. L., DeMarsh, J. P., & Child, W. (1989). Strengthening Families Program: Children's skills training curriculum manual, parenting training manual, children's skill training manual, and family skills training manual (Prevention Services to Children of Substance-abusing Parents). Salt Lake City, UT: University of Utah, Social Research Institute, Graduate School of Social Work.

Kumpfer, K. L., Molgaard, V., & Spoth, R. (1996). The Strengthening Families Program for the prevention of delinquency and drug use. In R. D. Peters & R. J. McMahon (Eds.), *Preventing childhood disorders, substance abuse, and delinquency* (pp. 241–267). Thousand Oaks, CA: Sage.

Kumpfer, K. L., Turner, C., Hopkins, R., & Librett, J. (1993). Leadership and team effectiveness in community coalitions for the prevention of alcohol and other drug abuse. *Health Education Research: Theory and Practice, 8*(3), 359–374.

Langford, B. H., Flynn-Khan, M., English, K., Grimm, G., & Taylor, K. (2012). *Evidence2Success, making wise investments in children's futures: Financing strategies and structures.* Baltimore: The Annie E. Casey Foundation.

Mihalic, S., Fagan, A., Irwin, K., Ballard, D., & Elliott, D. (2002). *Blueprints for violence prevention replications: Factors for implementation success.* Boulder, CO: University of Colorado, Center for the Study and Prevention of Violence, Institute of Behavioral Science.

Miller, T., & Hendrie, D. (2008). Substance abuse prevention dollars and cents: A cost–benefit analysis, DHHS Pub. No. (SMA) 07-4298. Rockville, MD: Center for Substance Abuse Prevention, Substance Abuse and Mental Health Services Administration.

Minkler, M., & Wallerstein, N. (2002). Improving health through community organizing and community building. In K. Glanz, F. M. Lewis, & B. K. Rimer (Eds.), *Health behavior and health education: Theory, research and practice* (3rd edition) (pp. 241–269). San Francisco, CA: Jossey-Bass.

Molgaard, V. M., Kumpfer, K. L., & Fleming, E. (1997). *Strengthening Families Program for parents and youth 10–14: A video-based curriculum.* Ames, IA: Institute for Social and Behavioral Research.

Molgaard, V., & Spoth, R. (2001). Strengthening Families Program for young adolescents: Overview and outcomes. In S. I. Pfeiffer & L. A. Reddy (Eds.), *Innovative mental health programs for children: Programs that work* (pp. 15–29). Binghamton, NY: Haworth Press.

National Prevention, Health Promotion, and Public Health Council (2011). *National Prevention Strategy.* Washington, DC: National Prevention, Health Promotion, and Public Health Council.

National Research Council and Institute of Medicine (2009). *Preventing mental, emotional, and behavioral disorders among young people: Progress and possibilities*. Committee on the Prevention of Mental Disorders and Substance Abuse Among Children, Youth, and Young Adults: Research Advances and Promising Interventions. M. E. O'Connell, T. Boat, & K. E. Warner (Eds). Washington, DC: The National Academies Press.

Offord, D. R., Kraemer, H. C., Kazdin, A. E., Jensen, P. S., & Harrington, R. (1998). Lowering the burden of suffering from child psychiatric disorder: Trade-offs among clinical, targeted, and universal interventions. *Journal of the American Academy of Child and Adolescent Psychiatry, 37*, 686–694.

Pentz, M. A. (2007). Disseminating effective approaches to drug use prevention. In M. K. Welch-Ross & L. G. Fasig (Eds.), *Handbook on communicating and disseminating behavioral science* (pp. 341–364). Thousand Oaks, CA: Sage.

Phillips, J. L., & Springer, J. F. (1997). *Implementation of community partnerships: Lessons learned*. Folsom, CA: EMT Associates.

Quest International (1992). *Quest International Lions–Quest Skills for Adolescence* (3rd edition). Newark, OH: Quest International.

Redmond, C., Spoth, R. L., Shin, C., Schainker, L. M., Greenberg, M. T., & Feinberg, M. E. (2009). Long-term protective factor outcomes of evidence-based interventions implemented by community teams through a community-university partnership. *Journal of Primary Prevention, 30*, 513–530.

Rogers, E. (2003). *Diffusion of innovations*. New York: Free Press.

Romer, D. (2003). Prospects for an integrated approach to adolescent risk reduction. In D. Romer (Ed.). *Reducing adolescent risk: Toward an integrated approach* (pp. 1–8). Thousand Oaks, CA: Sage Publications.

Saunders, S. D., Greaney, M. L., Lees, F. D., & Clark, P. G. (2003). Achieving recruitment goals through community partnerships: The SENIOR project. *Family and Community Health, 26*, 194–202.

Scheirer, M. A., & Dearing, J. W. (2011). An agenda for research on the sustainability of public health programs. *American Journal of Public Health, 101*, 2059–2067.

Spoth, R., Clair, S., Greenberg, M., Redmond, C., & Shin, C. (2007). Toward dissemination of evidence-based family interventions: Maintenance of community-based partnership recruitment results and associated factors. *Journal of Family Psychology, 21*, 137–146.

Spoth, R., & Greenberg, M. (2011). Impact challenges in community science-with-practice: Lessons from PROSPER on transformative practitioner-scientist partnerships and prevention infrastructure development. *American Journal of Community Psychology, 48*, 106–119.

Spoth, R., Greenberg, M., Bierman, K., & Redmond, C. (2004). PROSPER community-university partnership model for public education systems: Capacity-building for evidence-based, competence-building prevention. *Prevention Science, 5*, 31–39.

Spoth, R., Guyll, M., & Day, S. X. (2002). Universal family-focused interventions in alcohol-use disorder prevention: Cost-effectiveness and cost-benefit analyses of two interventions. *Journal of Studies on Alcohol, 63*, 219–228.

Spoth, R., Guyll, M., Redmond, C., Greenberg, M., & Feinberg, M. (2011). Six-year sustainability of evidence-based intervention implementation quality by community-university partnerships: The PROSPER study. *American Journal of Community Psychology, 48*, 412–425.

Spoth, R., Redmond, C., Mason, W. A., Schainker, L., & Borduin, L. (2015). Research on the Strengthening Families Program for Parents and Youth 10–14: Long-term effects, mechanisms, translation to public health, PROSPER partnership scale up. In L. M. Scheier (Ed.), *Handbook of adolescent drug use prevention: Research, intervention strategies, and practice* (pp. 267–292). Washington, DC. American Psychological Association.

Spoth, R., Redmond, C., Shin, C., Greenberg, M., Clair, S., & Feinberg, M. (2007). Substance use outcomes at 18 months past baseline: The PROSPER community-university partnership trial. *American Journal of Preventive Medicine, 32*, 395–402.

Spoth, R., Redmond, C., Shin, C., Greenberg, M., Feinberg, M., & Schainker, L. (2013). PROSPER community-university partnership delivery system effects on substance misuse through 6½ years past baseline from a cluster randomized controlled intervention trial. *Preventive Medicine, 56*, 190–196.

Spoth, R., Rohrbach, L. A., Greenberg, M., Leaf, P., Brown, C. H., Fagan, A., et al. (Society for Prevention Research Type 2 Translational Task Force Members and Contributing Authors) (2013). Addressing core challenges for the next generation of type 2 translation research and systems: The Translation Science to Population Impact (TSci Impact) framework. *Prevention Science, 14*, 319–351.

Spoth, R., Trudeau, L., Guyll, M., & Shin, C. (2012). Benefits of universal intervention effects on a youth protective shield 10 years after baseline. *Journal of Adolescent Health, 50*, 414–417.

Spoth, R., Trudeau, L., Redmond, C., Shin, C., Greenberg, M., Feinberg, M., & Hyun, G. (under review). PROSPER partnership delivery system: Effects on conduct problem behavior outcomes through 6.5 years past baseline.

Spoth, R., Trudeau, L., Shin, C., Ralston, E., Redmond, C., Greenberg, M., & Feinberg, M. (2013). Longitudinal effects of universal preventive intervention on prescription drug misuse: Three RCTs with late adolescents and young adults. *American Journal of Public Health, 103*, 665–672.

Wandersman, A., & Florin, P. (2003). Community intervention and effective prevention. *American Psychologist, 58*, 441–448.

9

SCALING UP TREATMENT FOSTER CARE OREGON

A Randomized Trial of Two Implementation Strategies

Patricia Chamberlain and Lisa Saldana

Overview

There is much to be learned about "what it takes" to scale-up evidence-based practices in real-world community settings. Although increasing attention has focused on factors that influence the adoption, implementation, and sustainability of evidence-based practices (EBPs) in child and family service sectors, controlled studies that directly examine these factors empirically in real-world settings are limited. This chapter describes the need for scale-up of EBPs and provides a description of a large-scale randomized implementation trial of an evidence-based mental health intervention delivered through county social service systems. In this trial, 51 counties in California and Ohio were randomly assigned to one of two implementation conditions for one of the few evidence-based training programs for foster parents, called Treatment Foster Care Oregon (TFCO; formerly Multidimensional Treatment Foster Care; MTFC). TFCO is a community-based alternative to placement in residential or group care settings for children and adolescents with severe behavioral and/or emotional problems (www.mtfc.com). The two study conditions were: 1) the experimental condition called the Community Development Teams (CDT), an implementation strategy that brings together cohorts of 5–8 counties that use peer-to-peer learning to facilitate successful implementation and outcomes, or 2) the no-treatment control condition called the "business as usual" model of individualized single site/agency implementation (IND). As will be described, TFCO is a top-tier evidence-based mental health intervention for high-needs youth in the juvenile justice and child welfare systems. In this chapter we describe the need for the scale-up of practices such as TFCO, the background of the TFCO model, the implementation trial design, a comparison of implementation outcomes for

What is Scale-up and Why is it Important?

In recent years, there has been increased attention on moving evidence-based practices (EBPs) into real-world community settings (Horwitz et al., 2010). When treatments that have been shown through research to provide positive clinically and cost-effective outcomes are not utilized by the general populations for which they were designed, the potential public health impacts are not realized. When existing successful treatments are not available to the families who most need them, resources utilized to develop those treatments are wasted, and vulnerable populations are left without the most effective treatments. As more and more EBPs are developed with support by funders such as the National Institutes of Health (NIMH), there is increased recognition that many behavioral and medical advances are under-utilized by real-world community populations. According to recent estimates, EBPs are implemented in only 10% of agencies within child public service systems such as child welfare, juvenile justice, and mental health (Hoagwood & Olin, 2002). This implementation failure has become the focus of a specialized field in health research called Implementation Science. The goals of implementation science include understanding the contextual facilitators and barriers to successfully move more EBPs into common practice. The notion of "scaling up" an intervention is implementing the EBP on a large enough scale to have a significant public health impact and result in system reformation. Reducing behavioral health care costs are also a major goal through provision of effective interventions.

One of the greatest challenges of implementation science is to move EBPs into systems that do not typically consider adopting EBPs. Progressive agencies that implement one or more EBPs are the exception rather than the rule. Further, the agencies with an openness to adopt an EBP once are more likely to do so again (Aarons, Hurlburt, & Horwitz, 2011; Rogers, 1995), creating a "needs-innovation paradox." While those agencies who appreciate EBPs utilize them when appropriate, those agencies with the highest need for innovative intervention methods (i.e., those serving the most high-risk populations) are the least likely to adopt an EBP, leaving a gap that could have negative implications for public health outcomes and child public service systems. Resource-poor agencies may be less likely to adopt evidence-based family programs because, in general, evidence-based family interventions require more than one day of training, and family programs are not yet approved for Affordable Care Act (ACA) funding.

As has been noted in several recent papers on implementation science and in public forums on scaling up EBPs (Institute of Medicine and National Research Council, 2013), there are numerous factors that affect the quality of EBP implementation that have little to do with the effectiveness of the individual program. These involve what Aarons and colleagues (2011) describe as "inner and outer context factors." Examples of inner context factors include the quality and commitment of the system or site/agency leadership, readiness of the site/agency to receive the EBP, how well the components of the EBP fit in to current agency practice, how intervention fidelity will be measured, monitored, and used to continually improve intervention quality, and the establishment of an exit plan for the intervention developers that allows the site/agency to sustain the EBP with fidelity over time. Examples of outer context factors include the funding environment and the sustainability of that funding for the EBP, the political environment in which the agency/site resides, and changes to that environment over time. Each of these inner and outer context variables can have a significant impact on the scale-up of EBPs and can have an influence along the continuum of the implementation process ranging from the decision to adopt a program to the decision of whether or not to continue an already certified program.

Opportunity to Study Scale-Up

In 2002, the California Institute for Mental Health (CIMH) obtained foundation funding to promote the implementation of EBPs in the child welfare and juvenile justice systems across the state of California. CIMH intended to address a problem that had been highlighted in a recent state report, which criticized the use of group care placements to meet the needs of high-risk children and adolescents. The report (Marsenich, 2002) discussed California's increasing reliance on group care placements for the most needy youth, the lack of evidence on the effectiveness of group care, and the escalating expenses associated with congregate care. Although TFCO, an evidence-based practice that addressed the needs of high-risk adolescents and children, was implemented in 10 counties, only those counties that were well resourced had volunteered to adopt TFCO. Subsequently, one of the first implementation science studies funded by the National Institute of Health (Primary Investigator: Chamberlain) was to examine two implementation strategies for scaling up TFCO in the remaining non-early adopting counties. This study is the focus of this chapter.

Brief Overview of TFCO

The Treatment Foster Care Oregon (TFCO) model involves placing youth individually in well-trained and supervised foster homes. Close consultation, training, and support of the foster parents form the cornerstone of the TFCO model. Foster parents receive state certification after a 20-hour pre-service orientation. Program Supervisors with small caseloads (10 families each) maintain daily contact with TFCO parents to collect data on youth adjustment and to provide ongoing consultation, support, and crisis intervention. The basic components of TFCO include the following: (a) daily (M–F) telephone contact with TFCO parents using the Parent Daily Report checklist (PDR; Chamberlain & Reid, 1987); (b) weekly foster parent group meetings led by the Program Supervisor focused on supervision, training in parenting practices, and support; (c) an individualized behavior management program implemented daily in the home by the foster parents; (d) individual therapy for the youth; (e) individual skills training/coaching for the youth; (f) family therapy (for biological/adoptive/ relative family of the youth) focused on parent management strategies; (g) close monitoring of school attendance, performance, and homework completion; (h) case management to coordinate the TFCO, family, peer, and school settings; (i) 24-hour on-call staff availability to TFCO and biological parents; and (j) psychiatric consultation as needed. The TFCO intervention embodies a strong focus on strength-building and positive reinforcement, and specific intervention components are tailored to the child's age and developmental level. The TFCO team consists of a Program Supervisor (who is the clinical lead), the treatment foster parents, family and individual therapists, a skills trainer, and a foster parent recruiter/trainer. Additional information on the basic TFCO model is described in detail elsewhere (Chamberlain, 2003).

The TFCO model has received national attention as a cost-effective alternative to residential care (Aos et al., 2011). Findings from multiple RCTs have led TFCO to be selected as 1 of 10 evidence-based National Model Programs (The Blueprints Programs; Elliott, 1998) by the Office of Juvenile Justice and Delinquency Prevention and as 1 of 9 National Exemplary Safe, Disciplined, and Drug Free Schools model programs. The TFCO model also was highlighted in two recent U.S. Surgeon's General reports (U.S. Department of Health and Human Services, 2000a, 2000b) and was selected by the Center for Substance Abuse Prevention and the Office of Juvenile Justice and Delinquency Prevention as an Exemplary I program for Strengthening America's Families (Chamberlain, 1998). In addition, it was selected in 2009 by the Coalition for Evidence-Based Policy as meeting "top tier" evidence of effectiveness (www.toptierevidence.org). Since 1998, TFCO has been implemented in over 150 sites. Current implementations efforts are occurring in 40 sites in the U.S. and over 50 sites internationally including in the UK, Denmark, Norway, Sweden, Scotland, New Zealand, and Ireland (www.tfco.com).

Dissemination Approach

Implementation Research

We started implementing TFCO in California in 2000 in partnership with Lynne Marsenich and Todd Sosna from the California Institute for Mental

Health (CIMH). As noted previously, the goal was to decrease the group home population in California. Group home placements were both expensive and resulted in poor outcomes (Marsenich, 2002). CIMH obtained foundation funding to pay for 10 counties to receive training in TFCO as an alternative to placing youth in group homes. The counties who stepped forward had experience innovating, sufficient resources, and solid leadership. This is not surprising given the "needs–intervention paradox" identified by Rogers (1995). Our experiences working with these counties, which effectively blazed the trail for TFCO implementation in California, encouraged us to think about how we could engage and motivate non-early adopting counties to implement. That is, how could we provide the intervention to the counties who were most in need, yet failed to adopt TFCO? At the same time, CIMH was looking for ways to provide technical assistance and support to counties implementing EBPs with the goal of increasing the reach, fidelity, and sustainability of EBPs in California. To do this, they developed a peer-to-peer learning model called the Community Development Team (CDT).

With the dual goal of conducting the first test of the effectiveness of CDT as an implementation strategy and also engaging non-early adopting counties to implement TFCO, we submitted a proposal to the National Institute of Mental Health. We proposed to compare the use of CDT with an implementation "as usual" condition. The proposal was submitted after an extensive period of planning and input from Marsenich and Sosna (the partners at CIMH) and leaders from child welfare, juvenile justice, and mental health systems in California. To our knowledge, this was not only the first evaluation of the CDT implementation strategy, but the first head-to-head trial comparing two implementation strategies.

The Community Development Team Model

The CDT model was first developed by CIMH and used to help implement TFCO in California in 2000. As noted, CDT was then utilized across California for the TFCO initiative being described in this chapter. However, since the TFCO effort was initiated, CDT has been used to implement a number of additional EBPs including Functional Family Therapy, Trauma-Focused Cognitive Behavioral Therapy, and Aggression Replacement Training.

The CDT model has four goals: (a) to improve outcomes for children and families participating in public service systems; (b) to promote the delivery of evidence-based services in communities; (c) to continually evaluate the effectiveness of methods and services to improve subsequent efforts; and (d) to build on and build up positive relationships, collaborations, and partnerships among consumers, system and political leaders, agencies, and practitioners.

The CDT operates through multi-county development team meetings that are augmented by individualized technical assistance to counties. Key stakeholders in each county are drawn from multiple levels (consumers, system leaders, organizations/agencies, practitioners) to participate in the CDT intervention (Sosna & Marsenich, 2006). The intervention is implemented in three phases: (a) *pre-implementation*: designed to engage, prepare, and train sites to implement an evidence-based practice; (b) *implementation*: designed to assist sites to run model-adherent programs staffed by competent practitioners and administrators; and (c) *sustainability*: designed to promote autonomous model-adherent programs. Each CDT is staffed by two CIMH consultants who have been selected based on previous training and experience related to the local child service system and their ability to establish credible relationships with key stakeholders. A key feature of the CDT model is peer-to-peer exchange and support where a number of sites (usually 6–7) implementing the same EBP share experiences and challenges in a series of 6–8 meetings that occur throughout the three implementation phases described above. Depending on the phase, the meetings are attended by leaders and staff in a variety of roles. For example, in pre-implementation, typically decision makers such as child welfare or other agency directors participate. In the implementation phase, although decision makers are invited to participate, it is critical that program champions and managers in charge of implementation activities are involved. In addition to peer-to-peer meetings, CDT consultants provide routine technical assistance on topics such as financing and adaptations of local regulations and rules that are indicated by the EBP (i.e., having "on-call" staff available 24 hours). Monthly conference calls with key leaders and staff are held throughout the implementation and sustainability phases. Leaders are encouraged to share challenges they experience in the implementation process, and the CDT facilitators assist the leaders and staff to problem-solve these challenges. Moreover, the CDT facilitators serve as liaisons between the leaders and the EBP developer. For example, when rural counties expressed ongoing barriers with TFCO recruitment, the census requirements were renegotiated with the TFCO developer (i.e., the first author) for these counties. All meeting notes were logged into an electronic record-keeping database designed for this study.

Design of the Randomized Implementation Trial

Research questions

In collaboration with Drs. John Reid and C. Hendricks Brown and the partners from CIMH, Chamberlain and her research team designed a study to address the question of whether implementation success in non-early adopting counties was enhanced by participation in the CDT. To address this question, we decided to compare participation in CDT to implementation "as usual" where entities (agencies or county systems) decide to implement and work individually (IND)

192 Patricia Chamberlain and Lisa Saldana

with the EBP developer. In the implementation trial we asked the following research questions:

1. Were counties with no prior experience with TFCO (non-early adopters) that participated in CDT more successful in implementing than similar counties assigned to the IND condition?
2. Did CDT counties begin delivering TFCO program services more quickly (e.g., start-up), more successfully (e.g., number of youth served), and more completely (e.g., reach full credentialing) compared to those in IND?

The trial began in California in 2006, and in 2008 the study was expanded to include counties from Ohio to increase the sample size.

Experimental design and randomization

The study design required randomization at two levels: study condition (CDT or IND) and time-frame (three yearly cohorts). Eligible counties were matched on demographic variables including size, number of children in poverty, number of minority children, use of Medicaid, and per capita group home placement rate. A total of six equivalent groups of counties in California, each with six to eight counties, were constructed using simulation calculations so as to minimize between-group differences on all county demographic variables among thousands of possible groups of the same size. These six groups were then assigned randomly to implementation condition (CDT or IND) and to three sequential cohorts with start-up timelines staggered at yearly intervals. In Ohio there was only one cohort (Year 3) so randomization only occurred at one level: implementation condition (CDT or IND). As described elsewhere, randomization was successful (Chamberlain et al., 2008) and a network analysis of advice relationships among agency leadership (Palinkas et al., 2013) found that there was minimal contamination across conditions.

Participants

A total of 51 counties participated in this study: 40 in California and 11 in Ohio. Two exclusion criteria were used in selecting counties across the two states: (1) Counties could not have been early adopters of TFCO such that they had prior experience implementing the model; therefore, all participants were from non-early adopting counties; (2) The county's placement of foster youth eligible for TFCO could not be of insufficient size to preclude the adoption of TFCO in that county (i.e., six or fewer youth in care on snapshot days during the prior year). Los Angeles County also was excluded from randomization due to a class action lawsuit which resulted in a State decision to provide TFCO/CDT to this county. In addition, eight other counties were excluded that had a low "need" for TFCO (six or fewer youth in care on snapshot days). The remaining 40 eligible California counties were targeted for recruitment and were randomized in 2006. System leaders from child welfare, juvenile justice, and mental health from each county were invited to consent to participate using the same procedures across implementation conditions and states. Consent from only one of the three systems was necessary for the county to be included in the participant pool.

Two years into the project, recruitment was extended to Ohio. Due to study resource limitations, only 12 Ohio counties were sought for recruitment. Using virtually identical inclusion/exclusion criteria as applied to the California counties, 38 of 88 total Ohio counties were deemed eligible. These counties were randomly ordered and recruited for participation in the trial based on this ordering. Eleven counties agreed to participate. Therefore, a total of 51 counties were recruited for participation.

Measuring Implementation Outcomes: The Stages of Implementation Completion™

In order to measure progress (or lack thereof) in the implementation process, the Stages of Implementation Completion (SIC; Chamberlain, Brown, & Saldana, 2011; Saldana & Chamberlain, 2012; Saldana et al., 2012) measure was developed to evaluate outcomes in both the CDT and IND conditions. Because implementation requires interactions between a variety of stakeholders during various phases of the process, the SIC is designed to capture interactions between the intervention developers (TFCO in this case), system leaders, agency directors, front-line practitioners, families, and youth. For example, measuring implementation progress in the first three stages included the involvement of system leaders in activities such as agreement to consider implementation of TFCO (Stage 1), assessments of the feasibility of implementing in their systems (Stage 2), and development and review of a funding plan (Stage 3). In this study, the system leader completed these activities through interactions with the EBP purveyor in the IND condition or the CDT facilitator depending on their randomization condition. Counties in the CDT condition completed the activities as part of a multi-county team and received hands-on support from their CDT consultant, whereas those in the IND condition completed the activities with the EBP purveyor (TFCO) on their own. The SIC measure includes eight stages of implementation as detailed in Table 9.1.

As shown in Table 9.1, the measure incorporates the actions of a diverse group of stakeholders whose involvement is relevant at different stages. For example, for SIC Stage 1 (engagement), decision makers/system leaders often play a key role in initial decisions to adopt an EBP, but by the time the practice is delivered to clients (SIC Stage 6), the key agent of implementation shifts to the service provider. As such, the SIC can be used to measure the involvement

194 Patricia Chamberlain and Lisa Saldana

TABLE 9.1 TFCO Activities Within the Eight SIC™ Stages and Agents Involved

Stage	Activity	Agent Involved
Stage 1: Engagement	Date site is informed services/program available (not scored) Date of interest indicated Date agreed to consider implementation	System Leader
Stage 2: Consideration of Feasibility	Date of first county response to first planning contact Date of first CDT meeting/IND Feasibility Assessment Date feasibility questionnaire completed	System Leader, Agency
Stage 3: Readiness Planning	Date of cost/funding plan review Date of staff sequence, timeline, hire plan review Date of Foster Parent recruitment review Date of referral criteria review Date of communication plan review Date of CDT Meeting #2/IND Stakeholder meeting Date written implementation plan complete Date TFCO Service Provider selected	System Leader, Agency
Stage 4: Staff Hired & Trained	Date agency checklist completed Date 1st staff hired Date Program Supervisor trained Date clinical training held Date Foster Parent training held Date Expert Consultant assigned to site	Agency, Practitioner
Stage 5: Adherence Monitoring Processes in Place	Date Parent Daily Report training held (fidelity measure) Date of 1st program admin. call	Practitioner, Child/Family
Stage 6: Services and Consultation Begin	Date of first placement Date of first consult call Date of first clinical meeting video received Date of first foster parent meeting video received	Practitioner, Child/Family
Stage 7: Ongoing Services, Consultation, Fidelity Monitoring and Feedback	Dates of site visits (3) Date of implementation review (3) Date of final program assessment	Practitioner, Child/Family
Stage 8: Competency	Date of certification application Date certified	System Leader, Agency, Practitioner

of diverse stakeholders in the implementation process. As described next, there is evidence from data collected using the SIC that system leaders have influence over the ultimate success of program start-up (Saldana et al., 2012), suggesting that each of these stages and the associated key players are significant to the successful implementation of programs.

The eight SIC stages were designed so that they could potentially be applied to other EBPs and currently this is being investigated (Saldana: R01 MH097748) with adaptations of the SIC for Multisystemic Therapy (MST; Henggeler et al., 2009), Multidimensional Family Therapy (MDFT; Liddle, 2002), and Coping Cat (Kendall & Khanna, 2008). In each stage, it is expected that there will be some activities that are universal to all EBPs (e.g., staff are trained), while other activities within each stage are intended to be flexible in order to reflect the unique components of the specific EBP practice being studied. For the current study, the SIC included steps that were identified as essential to the successful adoption, implementation, and initial sustainability of TFCO. Like most EBPs, TFCO follows a manualized protocol that includes numerous organizational and planning tasks and specific intervention strategies. The activities for implementing TFCO within each of the eight SIC stages are shown in Table 9.1. Detailed data analysis procedures for the study are outlined in Brown and associates (2014).

Results

Primary Outcomes

The primary study questions revolved around the utility of the CDT model to promote successful implementation. No differences were found between CDT and IND counties on key implementation outcomes such as speed of start-up and the number of counties that reached Stage 6 (when service to youth and families begins). That is, an equivalent number of sites failed to successfully serve TFCO families across both conditions. However, for those programs that did become operational, significant differences were found with regard to achieving key implementation milestones favoring the CDT condition. Additionally, of the counties that successfully achieved program start-up, those in the CDT condition completed the implementation process more thoroughly as indicated by more of the CDT counties achieving Competency, the final SIC stage (Wang et al., 2010).

Results from the trial showed that participation in CDT increased the number of placements referred to the TFCO program and increased the quality of implementation once the decision to implement had been made. In contrast to these positive findings on quantity and quality of implementation, there were no significant differences across implementation conditions regarding the speed in passing through stages, the time to first placement, or on the highest implementation stage attained during the trial. Neither did participation in the CDT condition significantly affect the initial decision to implement. However, CDT appeared to result in more robust programs as indicated by having significantly more children placed in TFCO during the study period and completing more implementation activities throughout each of the implementation stages. This more thorough completion of the implementation process resulted in more viably sustainable programs, with programs randomized to CDT serving more than twice the number of clients (Brown et al., 2014).

The CDT implementation strategy, which uses trained consultants with knowledge of local policies and conditions to guide problem-solving in teams of counties facing similar implementation challenges, is thought to be particularly important in implementing complex interventions, such as TFCO, especially in non-early adopting counties. In extending Rogers' research, which indicates that innovations that can be implemented relatively simply have high potential for rapid diffusion, we hypothesize that a more intensive implementation strategy such as CDT may be helpful when implementing complex interventions to less innovation-seeking organizations. The notion that routine face-to-face and telephone conference call peer-to-peer exchanges with consultants who are knowledgeable about state and county conditions, regulations, policies, and politics can boost implementation prospects seems intuitively obvious but our trial was the first to definitively show such an effect. To our knowledge, this is the largest county-level randomized trial to compare two implementation strategies against each other to examine implementation effectiveness.

CDT costs

A major potential caveat is the cost of using the CDT approach, because the cost of all CDT activities must be added to the business-as-usual costs enacted in the IND condition. However, we found that although these direct costs were higher for CDT than IND (cost difference $14,000 per county), the CDT counties invested fewer additional leadership and staff hours to complete implementation (Saldana et al., 2014).

Within the context of this study, the development of the SIC allowed us to measure implementation processes across multiple stages and milestones, and across multiple levels of participants, from system leaders in county government to foster parents on the TFCO team. Assessing the timing, quality, and quantity of implementation allowed for the ability to accurately pinpoint what changes in implementation processes occurred including progress or lack thereof. This methodological approach can potentially be applied to other EBPs. Currently, the second author (Saldana: R01 MH097748) is adapting the SIC for other child and family EBPs in diverse service sectors including schools, juvenile justice, child welfare, and substance abuse treatment. The goal is to evaluate the common or universal implementation activities that are utilized across EBPs in their implementation strategies and to determine if these universal items are equally important in achieving implementation success across EBPs. Similarly, the Saldana study examines whether the SIC stages are stable across EBPs even when the within-stage activities differ. These adapted SIC tools then will be evaluated for adequate psychometric properties, including predictive ability, in order to further examine the value of implementation process and milestones in achieving successful program implementation.

The SIC scale may also be relevant to the field of translational research, which has focused primarily on milestone attainment and less on quality and quantity (Trochim et al., 2011). The analytic methods described here could be used to monitor the entire translational process from bench to bedside to community.

Qualitative Research

Palinkas and colleagues examined the social networks of directors and senior administrators of child welfare agencies, probation departments, and mental health departments participating in the study (Palinkas et al., 2011). They found that these networks cut across the organizational and jurisdictional boundaries used to define the unit of randomization (i.e., the county). Therefore, they concluded that while the county organizations were responsible for the implementation of TFCO, the influence networks of the county leaders of these organizations represented relevant units to consider, and possibly to randomize, in future implementation research.

In a second analysis examining the degree of connectedness among county leaders, Palinkas and colleagues (2013) further evaluated these influence networks to determine whether they cut across implementation strategy conditions, thus posing a threat to the study's internal validity. The objective was to identify the network characteristics of the CDT and the IND (control) conditions and to determine the number of direct and indirect influence linkages across the two study arms. Semi-structured interviews were conducted with 38 county directors, assistant directors, and program managers of probation, mental health, and child welfare departments. Network analyses were conducted to determine whether participants in the CDT condition had more ties to others implementing TFCO than those counties who were randomized to individualized implementation, as was hypothesized from the peer-to-peer nature of CDT. A second analysis was conducted to determine whether network ties spanned across conditions.

Results showed that the CDT networks were more interconnected than the networks in the IND (control) condition, which were fragmented into several disconnected components. This is consistent with the peer-to-peer approach utilized by CDT. Fortunately, there were very few direct ties in this study across condition and only a modest number of second degree ties. The authors concluded that the integrity of the RCT was not compromised by the existence of overlapping influence networks in this study. However, in this randomized trial as in others, the potential for contamination through cross-condition network ties was a clear concern. That is, when groups of contrasting conditions occur within contexts that are in close social proximity of each other (e.g., in classrooms within the same schools, therapists in the same mental health clinics, professional relationships in social service settings), there is a threat for those randomized to the control condition to be exposed to aspects of the experimental condition. Such threats to internal validity are real and should be considered and measured as part of future implementation trials (Palinkas et al., 2013).

Considerations for Conducting Large-Scale Implementations

As noted at the beginning of this chapter, successful scale-up of EBPs is influenced by both outer and inner context variables. This implementation study is no exception, and multiple factors should be considered when interpreting findings.

Outer Context Factors

In the TFCO implementation study described here, there were significant shifts in the outer context during the course of the study that directly affected the ability and desire of the counties to participate in implementing TFCO under both implementation conditions. These factors created two significant barriers to enrolling counties in the study and, once enrolled, limited and slowed their participation in implementation activities. From a design perspective, these barriers limited the potential power to detect hypothesized differences between the two implementation conditions. The barriers affected the two conditions equally so did not jeopardize the randomization design.

Funding instability

The first barrier was related to funding instability for mental health services stemming from the 1991 legislation in California that realigned funding for mental and public health services to be the fiscal responsibility of the individual counties rather than of the state. Under this realignment arrangement, the California State Department of Mental Health (DMH) essentially subcontracted with counties to manage care using a combination of state and federal Medicaid funds. These funds were used to pay for services within the TFCO model. Due largely to an accounting error between the Departments of Health Services and Mental Health, the DMH ended the 2005 fiscal year with many unpaid claims from counties. The situation created severe cash-flow problems for several counties, which threatened their ability to provide mandated mental health services, let alone new service models such as TFCO.

DMH subsequently assured counties that all claims would be paid but the reimbursement rates were slow and this jeopardized the counties' ability to move forward as planned to implement TFCO within the original study time-line. Many counties expressed a strong desire to implement but simply did not have the ability to move forward on a new initiative at the time due to being owed money from the state. There were several proposed remedies, including legislation (SB 1349) that required reimbursement for claims within 90 days and interest on late payments. Furthermore, the state reassured counties in writing that they would be paid all funds owed. However, this outer context situation effectively slowed the momentum of study enrollment among California counties.

Budget cuts

The second and perhaps more critical problem area was instability due to significant and sustained budget cuts to mental health, public health, and educational services by Governor Schwarzenegger during the recession in 2007 that also impacted service delivery nationwide. These cuts stemmed from challenging economic times that hit California especially hard, particularly in the housing sector. This situation fed into a picture of uncertainty for California counties that caused them to proceed cautiously on new initiatives, including the decision to implement TFCO.

Solutions and adaptations

At the end of study year 2, in consultation with our NIMH Program Officer, we began to consider extending the study to another state in order to restore the original level of power that we had calculated when we submitted the application for funding. Ohio quickly became the most likely state for the following reasons: (1) the Center for Innovative Practices (CIP) at the Institute for the Study and Prevention of Violence (ISPV) at Kent State University is parallel in function and experience to the California Institute for Mental Health; (2) CIP had been interested in implementing the Community Development Team approach for several years and had been in ongoing discussions with CIMH about looking for an opportunity to do so; and (3) Ohio had numerous counties that were non-early adopters of TFCO. We entered into a formal collaboration with CIP to take a parallel role to CIMH in recruiting Ohio counties and overseeing the TFCO planning process for counties in the CDT condition. As previously described, using the same randomization and recruitment methods as we did in California, we successfully recruited an additional 11 counties in Ohio to participate in the study.

Inner Context Factors

In addition, we found that key inner context factors had a major effect on the implementation effort, including our ability as developers and implementers of TFCO to successfully support sites/agencies to deliver high-quality services. Among these were (1) our ability to monitor the fidelity of the delivery of key components of the TFCO model, (2) provision of supportive and instructive feedback to front-line personnel delivering the model, (3) development of our own infrastructure to train and support expert TFCO consultants, and (4) strategies for helping sites/agencies to build their infrastructure to sustain TFCO with fidelity once the study and the involvement of our developer group ended. These factors are discussed in more detail below.

Monitoring fidelity of the intervention delivery

Fidelity is typically described as the demonstration that an intervention is conducted as planned (Dumas et al., 2001), and incorporates the concepts of *adherence* to the intervention's core content components and *competent* execution using proven clinical teaching practices (Forgatch, Patterson, & DeGarmo, 2005). Provision of in-depth training in the intervention model and goals, curriculum content, and training procedures are necessary for intervention fidelity, as is a properly supervised staff. However, neither training nor supervision alone is sufficient in ensuring that the intervention is conducted as planned (Dumas et al., 2001). Therefore, we included a dual focus on facilitator adherence to the TFCO core content components and to the process-oriented delivery of the intervention. As is typical for the TFCO model, all program supervisors record their weekly foster parent group sessions and their weekly clinical team supervision meetings (teams quickly adapt to being recorded when it occurs every session). Videotaped recordings of both TFCO meeting were rated for: (a) coverage of key session components, and (b) effective communication processes. The study sites demonstrated varying abilities to accomplish the needed session recordings and required different levels of support and technical assistance to implement this. A major barrier was encountered when attempting to use the recordings to provide timely feedback to sites; tapes had to be sent to/received by the developers and coded within 7 days prior to the next scheduled weekly meeting to have the feedback be meaningful. This observation-based fidelity system is part of the typical consultation package delivered with the TFCO model. Since the time of the study, we have developed a HIPAA-compliant video recording system that uses a laptop camera. Developers and sites can access video for only their sites, review the weekly session videos, and complete the fidelity scoring on the website. This advance in technology has improved our ability to provide timely, observation-based feedback to sites. All recordings are reviewed by the site consultant weekly (i.e., each site consultant views two videos per site per week).

Providing continuous feedback to improve intervention quality

Weekly between-session meetings with feedback to on-site staff are critical to maintaining intervention fidelity. In fact, weekly clinical meetings are usually an essential part of the development and testing of EBPs. What is less understood are effective ways to deliver that feedback. We have developed a model called R^3 that draws on the core theoretical components of social learning-based interventions. The model's three primary principles include: (1) reinforcing the clinicians' efforts to engage, support, and provide skills; (2) reinforcing the relationship between the clinician and the family; and (3) reinforcing the identification and execution of a small step to move the client's progress forward. In TFCO, R^3 has direct parallels to the clinician's work with the family; the clinical supervisors reinforce caregivers' effort, their relationship with their child, and weekly small steps to improve parenting skills. R^3 also applies to the on-site supervisor's relationship with the clinician using the same strength-based principles. We are currently examining the R^3 method as a stand-alone intervention in child welfare systems with casework supervisors, case workers, and families involved in the child welfare system.

Development of an adequate infrastructure to deliver the implementation

The resources and skills needed to widely implement an intervention differ from those required to develop and test it in RCTs. In addition, the workforce needs for implementation overlap, but are more complex for supporting widespread implementations at multiple sites. A major barrier for us has been the lack of a large enough workforce of well-trained clinical personnel to provide expert consultation to the implementation sites. Several factors contribute to this problem. First, there is no apparent funding source that can be dedicated to recruiting and training the developer/clinical expert workforce who will provide training workshops and ongoing fidelity support and feedback to sites. There are obvious funding sources to develop and test interventions and for funding implementation efforts; however, those efforts assume the availability of an expert developer workforce. It is obviously best to have staff with direct experience delivering the EBP (preferably in the RCT) as part of the developer team of experts who are supporting sites to implement the EBP. However, as the demand for implementation increases, the need for these individuals trumps their availability. Additionally, we lack effective models for training new expert-level staff to assure high-quality support for implementing sites. Therefore, strategies for the development and maintenance of an adequate cadre of well-trained EBP experts are needed, including cost models that provide a return on training investments and clinical models that allow for development of expertise.

Development of on-site infrastructure to sustain the intervention

The sustainment of EBPs is an understudied area; however, whether a site/agency can continue to implement EBPs with fidelity is perhaps *the* key outcome that predicts large-scale improvement in public health (Scheirer & Dearing, 2011). The identification of strategies that facilitate and barriers that impede the sustainability of EBPs in community settings is of critical importance. Of equal importance is the development of valid and reliable methods for objectively measuring sustainability.

In TFCO, we use a strategy whereby programs are certified to provide services without continued developer involvement once they meet fidelity criteria. The program certification protocol provides standardized measurement of all key model components and sets consistent standards that must be met for programs to be certified. For detailed certification criteria, see www.tfco.com. As part of the process, detailed feedback is provided to applicants regarding program strengths and areas in need of improvement. Applications can be submitted by any organization that believes their TFCO program meets certification criteria, regardless of whether they received previous training or technical assistance from the developer team.

Program staff can use a self-assessment form to estimate the degree to which they think their program meets certification standards. The certification process involves a thorough evaluation of several components of the site/agency program, including coding videotapes of foster parent and clinical staff meetings. The certification model, in tandem with the availability of consultation and technical assistance tailored to the specific needs of each applicant, is intended to provide a cost-effective, individualized mechanism for ongoing assurance of model fidelity and outcomes. Once a program is certified, the certification is valid for two years, and re-certifications are valid for three years.

Although it is clear that establishing independence from developers and continuing to implement EBPs sustainably is a high priority for agency/sites, optimal models for accomplishing these goals have not been studied. Clearly, this is an area for future research if EBPs are to have long-term public health-level impacts.

Closing Comments

Implementation science is a relatively new field and as such, it is not surprising that there are many more questions and theories about what it takes to successfully implement and sustain EBPs than there are empirical studies that test well-specified predictors, moderators, and mediators of implementation and sustainability. A major barrier to advancing the field of implementation science is the development and verification of measures of key variables and processes

Treatment Foster Care Oregon **203**

that can be used across studies. The Stages of Implementation Completion (SIC) described in this chapter is one such developing measure. As standardized measures become more commonplace in implementation science, we will be able to examine an array of future questions. Importantly, we will begin to learn if there is consistency in what it takes for scale-up to be attained across different EBPs and within different service sectors. As more outcomes are found to be generalizable, we will be able to hone in on strategies that increase successful adoption. Similarly, we will be able to better understand and articulate implementation theory.

In addition, more research on what promotes and predicts sustainability is needed, as are coherent, well-conceptualized theoretical paradigms that include key factors that facilitate or impede long-term sustainability. Methods of measuring activities needed to sustain programs, environments, and contexts that are potentially generalizable across diverse topical areas would help to promote the conceptualization of what it takes to facilitate long-term sustainability in challenging situations such as shifts in outer contexts.

Although there is still much to be learned, the TFCO implementation trial was a significant step forward for implementation science. Since its commencement, multiple implementation studies have been funded and are underway. As the implementation literature expands, we hope to ultimately increase the number of individuals who have access to high-quality health care.

Acknowledgements

The development of this chapter was supported by NIDA P50 DA035763 Translational Drug Abuse Prevention Center NIMH R01 MH097748, The Stages of Implementation Completion for Evidence-Based Practice, and NIMH R01 MH076158, Community Development Teams to Scale-Up MTFC in California. Chamberlain is a partner in TFCC Inc., the company that implements TFCO in community settings.

References

Aarons, G. A., Hurlburt, M., & Horwitz, S. (2011). Advancing a conceptual model of evidence-based practice implementation in public service sectors. *Administration and Policy in Mental Health and Mental Health Services Research*, *38*, 4–23.

Aos, S., Lee, S., Drake, E., Pennucci, A., Klima, T., Miller, M., Anderson, L., Mayfield, J., & Burley, M. (2011). *Return on investment: Evidence-based options to improve statewide outcomes* (Document No. 11-07-1201). Olympia: Washington State Institute for Public Policy.

Brown, C. H., Chamberlain, P., Saldana, L., Padgett, C., Wang, W., & Cruden, G. (2014). Evaluation of two implementation strategies in fifty-one child county public service systems in two states: Results of a cluster randomized head-to-head implementation trail. *Implementation Science*, *9*, 134.

204 Patricia Chamberlain and Lisa Saldana

Chamberlain, P. (1998). Treatment foster care. *Family Strengthening Series.* Washington, DC: U.S. Department of Justice. (OJJDP Bulletin NCJ l734211).

Chamberlain, P. (2003). *Treating chronic juvenile offenders: Advances made through the Oregon multidimensional treatment foster care model.* Washington, DC: American Psychological Association.

Chamberlain, P., Brown, C. H., & Saldana, L. (2011). Observational measure of implementation progress: The Stages of Implementation Completion (SIC). *Implementation Science, 6,* 116.

Chamberlain, P., Price, J., Leve, L. D., Laurent, H., Landsverk, J. A., & Reid, J. B. (2008). Prevention of behavior problems for children in foster care: Outcomes and mediation effects. *Prevention Science, 9*(1), 17–27.

Chamberlain, P., & Reid, J. B. (1987). Parent observation and report of child symptoms. *Behavioral Assessment, 9,* 97–109.

Dumas, J. E., Lynch, A. M., Laughlin, J. E., Smith, E. P., & Prinz, R. J. (2001). Promoting intervention fidelity: Conceptual issues, methods, and preliminary results from the EARLY ALLIANCE prevention trial. *American Journal of Preventive Medicine, 20*(1 Suppl), 38–47.

Elliott, D. S. (1998). *Prevention programs that work for youth: Violence prevention.* Boulder, CO: Center for the Study & Prevention of Violence, University of Colorado.

Forgatch, M. S., Patterson, G. R., & DeGarmo, D. S. (2005). Evaluating fidelity: Predictive validity for a measure of competent adherence to the Oregon Model of Parent Management Training. *Behavior Therapy, 36,* 3–13.

Henggeler, S. W., Schoenwald, S. K., Borduin, C. M., Rowland, M. D., & Cunningham, P. B. (2009). *Multisystemic therapy for antisocial behavior in children and adolescents* (2nd ed.). New York: Guilford Press.

Hoagwood, K., & Olin, S. S. (2002). The NIMH blueprint for change report: Research priorities in child and adolescent mental health. *Journal of the American Academy of Child and Adolescent Psychiatry, 41,* 760–767.

Horwitz, S. M., Chamberlain, P., Landsverk, J., & Mullican, C. (2010). Improving the mental health of children in child welfare through the implementation of evidence-based parenting interventions. *Administration Policy in Mental Health, 37,* 27–39.

Institute of Medicine and National Research Council. (2013). *New directions in child abuse and neglect research.* Washington, DC: The National Academies Press.

Kendall, P. C., & Khanna, M. (2008). *Coach's manual for Camp Cope-A-Lot: The Coping Cat CD-ROM.* Ardmore, PA: Workbook Publishing.

Liddle, H. A. (2002). Multidimensional Family Therapy for adolescent cannabis users. *Cannabis Youth Treatment (CYT) Series, Volume 5.* Rockville, MD: Center for Substance Abuse Treatment, Substance Abuse and Mental Health Services Administration.

Marsenich, L. (2002, March). *Evidence-based practices in mental health services for foster youth.* Sacramento, CA: California Institute for Mental Health.

Palinkas, L. A., Holloway, I .W., Rice, R., Fuentes, D., Wu, Q., & Chamberlain, P. (2011). Social networks and implementation of evidence-based practices in public youth-serving systems: A mixed methods study. *Implementation Science, 6,* 113.

Palinkas, L. A., Holloway, I. W., Rice, E., Brown, C. H., Valente, T., & Chamberlain, P. (2013). Influence network linkages across implementation strategy conditions in a randomized controlled trial of two strategies for scaling up evidence-based practices in public youth-serving systems. *Implementation Science, 8,* 113.

Rogers, E. M. (1995). *Diffusion of innovations* (4th ed.). New York: Free Press.

Saldana, L., & Chamberlain, P. (2012). Supporting implementation: The role of community development teams to build infrastructure. *American Journal of Community Psychology, 50*, 334–346.

Saldana, L., Chamberlain, P., Bradford, W. D., Campbell, M., & Landsverk, J. (2014). The cost of implementing new strategies (COINS): A method for mapping implementation resources using the Stages of Implementation Completion. *Children and Youth Services Review, 39*, 177–182.

Saldana, L., Chamberlain, P., Wang, W., & Brown, H. (2012). Predicting program start-up using the stages of implementation measure. *Administration and Policy in Mental Health Research, 39*, 419–425.

Scheirer, M. A., & Dearing, J. W. (2011). An agenda for research on the sustainability of public health programs. *American Journal of Public Health, 101*, 2059–2067.

Sosna, T., & Marsenich, L. (2006). *Community development team model: Supporting the model adherent implementation of programs and practices.* Sacramento: California Institute for Mental Health.

Trochim, W., Kane, C., Graham, M. J., & Pincus, H. A. (2011). Evaluating translational research: A process marker model. *Clinical Translational Science, 4*, 153–162.

U.S. Department of Health and Human Services. (2000a). Children and mental health. In *Mental health: A report of the Surgeon General* (DHHS Publication No. DSL 2000–0134–P). Washington, DC: U.S. Government Printing Office.

U.S. Department of Health and Human Services. (2000b). Prevention of violence. In *Mental health: A report of the Surgeon General* (DHHS Publication No. DSL 2000–0134–P). Washington, DC: U.S. Government Printing Office.

Wang, W., Saldana, L., Brown, C. H., & Chamberlain, P. (2010). Factors that influenced county system leaders to implement an evidence-based program: A baseline survey within a randomized controlled trial. *Implementation Science, 5*, 72.

PART III

Innovations and Adaptations of Family-Based Programs

10

STAYING CONNECTED WITH YOUR TEEN® AND THE PROMISE OF SELF-DIRECTED PREVENTION PROGRAMS

Kevin P. Haggerty, Tali Klima, Martie L. Skinner,
Richard F. Catalano, and Susan Barkan

Introduction

Problem behaviors in adolescence and young adulthood, such as substance use, violence, and risky sexual practices, carry heavy social, economic, and health consequences for individuals and entire communities (Catalano et al., 2012; Rehm et al., 2009). Research in developmental and prevention sciences (Hawkins, Catalano, & Miller, 1992) has identified key antecedents, or risk factors, for these behaviors. For instance, favorable parental attitudes towards antisocial behavior, lack of clear guidelines for behavior, poor monitoring, harsh or inconsistent discipline, and high levels of family conflict are predictive of more adolescent problem behavior. In adolescence, more proximal risk factors include peer norms that problem behavior is acceptable, perceptions of little harm as a result of engaging in these behaviors, and association with deviant peers (Catalano, Haggerty, Hawkins, & Elgin, 2011; Hawkins et al., 1992; Herrenkohl, Lee, & Hawkins, 2012). Research has also identified protective factors that lead youth toward prosocial paths and away from problem behaviors. Examples of protective factors include strong parent–child and school bonding, opportunities for active involvement in the family and other institutions (e.g., school), and recognition for positive behaviors (Herrenkohl et al., 2012).

The prevention science literature identifies parenting behaviors and family dynamics as key points of intervention for various types of problem behavior (for review, see Haggerty, McGlynn-Wright, & Klima, 2013). Furthermore, this literature has shown that by intervening with families early, proximal risk factors that develop in adolescence may be avoided (Haggerty & Kosterman, 2012; Skinner, Haggerty, & Catalano, 2009). In response, many successful family-based prevention programs have been developed (Biglan & Metzler, 1998; Farrington

210 Kevin P. Haggerty et al.

& Welsh, 2002; Foxcroft, Ireland, Lister-Sharp, Lowe, & Breen, 2003; Kumpfer & Alvarado, 2003). Although these programs have demonstrated efficacy in research settings, large-scale dissemination of these programs faces significant barriers, including cost, difficulty with recruitment and retention, and decreased effectiveness for certain groups of participants. Notably, minorities, low-income/SES families, and single-parent households suffer most from these barriers to participation in group interventions (Bauman, Ennett, Foshee, Pemberton, & Hicks, 2001; Fleming, Marchesini, Haggerty, Hill, & Catalano, 2012; Gorman-Smith, Tolan, Henry, & Leventhal, 2002; Haggerty et al., 2002; Heinrichs, Bertram, Kuschel, & Hahlweg, 2005), perhaps due to logistic difficulties (e.g., making time, driving to meeting places, finding childcare for siblings) and the stigma of participating in such programs (Offord, 2000; Spoth, Redmond, Hockaday, & Shin, 1996).

Self-directed or self-administered programs, which can be conducted at home with various program materials but minimal professional contact, seek to address such challenges. For example, completion of a program at home avoids the stigma associated with service delivery through traditional mental health systems. It also removes logistic barriers, such as the need to drive to a specified location, coordination of multiple family members, and allocating large amounts of time for sessions (Haggerty, MacKenzie, Skinner, Roberson et al., 2006). Prevention scientists are only recently beginning to devise and test family-based programs that can be self-administered. In this chapter we describe one such program, review the theory, logic model, structure, and content of the program, present the evidence for its success (as compared to no intervention and to a traditional group format), and discuss dissemination efforts in the community.

Staying Connected with Your Teen®

Previously known as "Parents Who Care," Staying Connected with Your Teen® (SCT) is a universal prevention program for adolescents ages 12 to 17 developed by Drs. J. David Hawkins and Richard F. Catalano. The program is designed to increase protective factors and reduce risk factors for problem behavior through family psychoeducation, skill-building exercises, and generalization to the home setting.

Foundations of SCT

The theoretical foundation of SCT lies in the social development model (SDM), which specifies the mechanisms and causal pathways by which risk and protective factors contribute to healthy as well as maladaptive development (Catalano & Hawkins, 1996). The SDM posits that children are socialized through four key processes: (a) *opportunities* for involvement in activities and interactions with family, (b) *skills* (such as communication, conflict management,

Staying Connected With Your Teen® **211**

problem solving) to participate in such involvement and interaction, and (c) perceived *rewards* or recognition from their involvement and interactions. These processes enhance (d) *bonding*—a strong sense of attachment and commitment to others. When children bond to socializing units such as family, school, or peers, they are more likely to follow the *beliefs and standards* and values of these units. Thus, strong family bonds inhibit deviant behavior, while bonds to antisocial socializing units promote it.

Staying Connected with Your Teen® was developed to help parents of teens put the social development strategy to work in their families to prevent risky sexual activity, drug use, and violent behavior. Building upon this theory and the literature on risk and protective factors, SCT is guided by a logic model (see Figure 10.1). The program features activities designed to provide teens with opportunities to contribute to their families, to acquire the skills needed to take advantage of those opportunities, and to increase parental monitoring, reduce harsh parenting, and use reward and recognition in order to promote bonding. The figure illustrates that SCT seeks specifically to improve positive family management skills (while simultaneously diminishing family conflict and rewards for negative behaviors) and increase parental confidence to influence children. By implementing family management skills, SCT leads to improved family management and greater child compliance with parental beliefs and expectations. Note that many of the family dynamics considered to be the proximal outcomes of SCT are risk and protective factors for adolescent problem behavior noted earlier.

Structure of SCT

Staying Connected with Your Teen® is a universal (Tier 1) prevention program for families with children 12 to 17 years old. It was designed to include both parents and teens and is delivered either through seven workshop sessions or as a self-directed program used at home. Table 10.1 summarizes the content of the seven sessions and how they address SDM constructs.

The program includes an interactive video or DVD and a workbook based on the social development strategy (Catalano & Hawkins, 1996; Hawkins & Weis, 1985). The 108-page family workbook is written at an 8th-grade reading level, and a 117-minute video in 18 sections features Latino, African American, and Caucasian families portrayed by professional actors.

In the group-administered format (PA), families meet with two group leaders for seven consecutive sessions, conducted once per week, in a convenient community location (e.g., local school). Sessions are 2–2.5 hours long, and youth attend the sessions with one or both of their parents. During the first 30–40 minutes of each session, families meet together and view the video components of the curriculum. Then parents and teens separate into different groups to practice specific skills for about 40–60 minutes. They

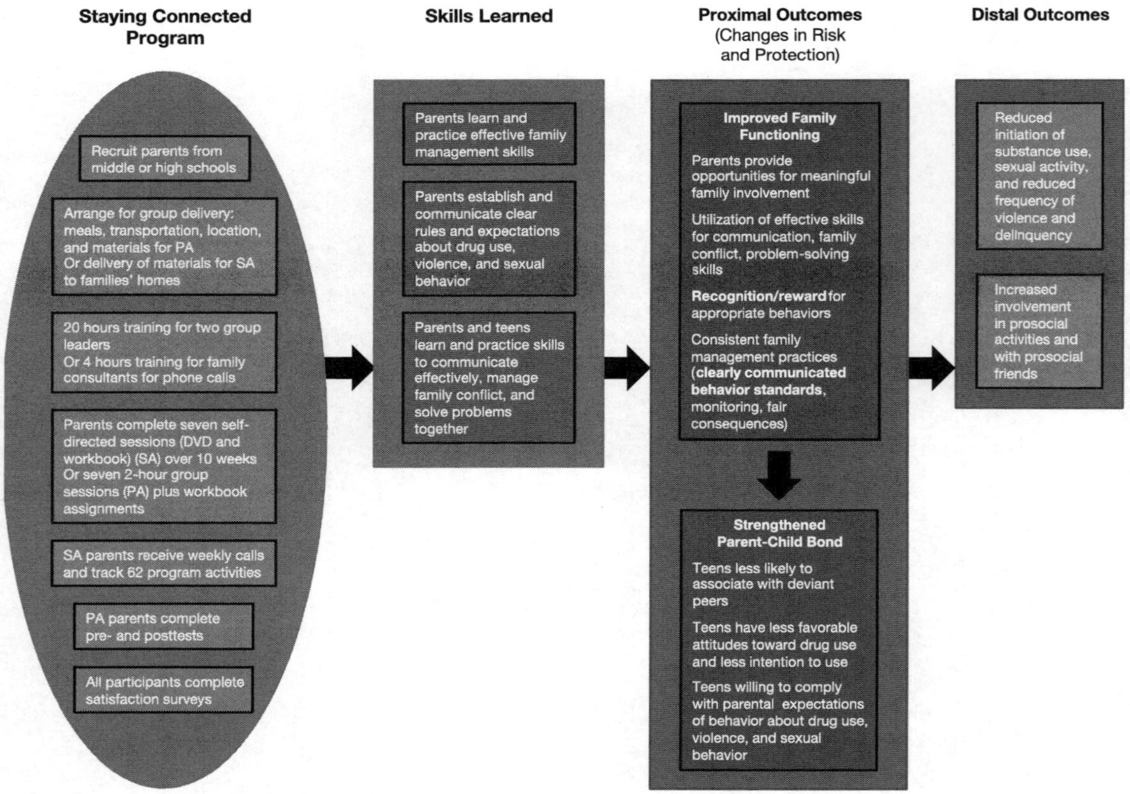

Staying Connected Program

- Recruit parents from middle or high schools
- Arrange for group delivery: meals, transportation, location, and materials for PA Or delivery of materials for SA to families' homes
- 20 hours training for two group leaders Or 4 hours training for family consultants for phone calls
- Parents complete seven self-directed sessions (DVD and workbook) (SA) over 10 weeks Or seven 2-hour group sessions (PA) plus workbook assignments
- SA parents receive weekly calls and track 62 program activities
- PA parents complete pre- and posttests
- All participants complete satisfaction surveys

Skills Learned

- Parents learn and practice effective family management skills
- Parents establish and communicate clear rules and expectations about drug use, violence, and sexual behavior
- Parents and teens learn and practice skills to communicate effectively, manage family conflict, and solve problems together

Proximal Outcomes
(Changes in Risk and Protection)

Improved Family Functioning

Parents provide opportunities for meaningful family involvement

Utilization of effective skills for communication, family conflict, problem-solving skills

Recognition/reward for appropriate behaviors

Consistent family management practices (**clearly communicated behavior standards**, monitoring, fair consequences)

Strengthened Parent-Child Bond

Teens less likely to associate with deviant peers

Teens have less favorable attitudes toward drug use and less intention to use

Teens willing to comply with parental expectations of behavior about drug use, violence, and sexual behavior

Distal Outcomes

Reduced initiation of substance use, sexual activity, and reduced frequency of violence and delinquency

Increased involvement in prosocial activities and with prosocial friends

FIGURE 10.1 Logic Model

TABLE 10.1 Program Components and SDM Constructs

Session	Program Components	SDM Construct Addressed
1) *Roles: Relating to your Teen*	Learn how the role of parenting changes as your child moves toward the teen years and undergoes physical, intellectual, social, and identity development	Opportunities for prosocial interaction; Positive family management skills; Skills for positive interactions
2) *Risks: Identifying and Reducing Them*	Education about multiple levels of risk factors; Videos to introduce risky behaviors and initiate dialogue; *Take Care of Yourself* to make objectives towards reaching goals	Opportunities for positive involvement; Positive family management; Communication and prosocial beliefs and standards
3) *Protection: Bonding to Strengthen Resiliency*	Education about the social development model; Families view videos to discuss teen involvement in risky behaviors; Discuss *Protective Factors* available to youth and family	Opportunities for positive involvement; Skills for positive interactions; Rewards for positive interactions; Perceived rewards/costs for antisocial interactions; Clear beliefs and standards; Family bonding
4) *Tools: Family Communication, and Decision Making, and Conflict Management*	Work to solve problems: How to use six "tools for parents": holding family meetings, choosing effective parenting styles, making family decisions, using good communication skills, managing anger and other feelings, and solving family problems	Positive family management; Skills for positive interactions (communication, managing family conflict, problem solving); Perceived rewards for positive interactions; Family bonding
5) *Involvement: Allowing Everyone to Contribute*	Explore youth contributions to family and community; Develop a list of life skills important to reaching youth goals; *Take Care of Yourself* to consider personal contributions and find ways to reward yourself for these	Opportunities for family involvement; Skills for positive interactions; Rewards for prosocial interactions; Family bonding
6) *Setting Family Policies on Health and Safety Issues*	Explore perceptions of their parents' expectations; *Rewards*: make a list identifying what the teen finds rewarding; *Establish a Family Policy* on a health and safety issue using the skills learned in this program; Develop a "*Behavior Contract*" together	Positive family management; Perceived opportunities for positive involvement; Skills for positive interactions; Rewards for positive interactions; Perceived rewards/costs for antisocial interactions; Clear beliefs and standards for behavior
7) *Supervising without Invading*	Create a *Personal Network Map* exploring teen's influences; View, discuss, and practice *Refusal Skills*; Use a *Family Meeting* to develop a supervision strategy; Write letters to one another sharing what you've learned and hopes for the future	Positive family management (monitoring); Skills for prosocial interactions; Perceived rewards for prosocial interactions; Perceived prosocial family bonding

return for the last 40 minutes to practice skills through structured family interaction tasks. At the end of each session, participants are reminded to practice at home, are asked to read and complete exercises from the SCT workbook, and are encouraged to review and continue to use tools provided in the session.

In order to address some of the challenges with recruitment and retention, a self-administered (SA) format was subsequently developed. Families who receive this mode receive the same DVD and workbook as the PA condition and are asked to complete the program activities within 10 weeks. They receive written instructions about how to use these materials, and a checklist of 62 key activities to conduct as a family (e.g., view video sections, do workbook exercise). A family consultant contacts the family by phone once a week to record completed activities, motivate families to use the materials with their teen, and help them integrate the skills and practices into their daily lives. Note that family consultant contacts do not substitute for full group sessions; rather, they are intended to monitor progress, provide brief guidance in using the materials, and reinforce continued program participation.

The structure of the SA modality is designed to overcome the logistic and other barriers to participation; an additional benefit is the reduced resources needed. For instance, we have shown that the direct costs[1] per participating family for SA are much lower than the traditional group format: $280 vs. $935 per family (Haggerty, Skinner, Catalano, Abbott, & Crutchfield, 2015). Also, family (phone) consultants require less parent training experience and less SCT-specific training. For example, in an efficacy trial described below, only group leaders were required to have prior experience teaching or conducting family-based trainings; family consultants were not. Group leaders also received considerably more training (20 hours) relative to their consultant counterparts (4 hours). The cost effectiveness of self-directed programs is an important benefit, especially for widespread dissemination.

Summary of the Research on Staying Connected With Your Teen®

This chapter summarizes the research that has been conducted to date on the Staying Connected with Your Teen® program. We briefly review a pilot study of group-administered SCT. Next, we discuss the results of a randomized clinical trial of SCT. The study is unique because (a) it contained multiple follow-up assessments (up to 8 years post-intervention); (b) participants were assigned to either the group or self-administered format and were compared to a no-intervention control condition, such that the effects of both modalities could be tested; and (c) it included equal numbers of White and Black families, which allowed for examination of outcomes by race. Finally, we describe efforts to disseminate SCT to an outpatient mental health/substance use treatment facility and to the child welfare system in Washington State.

Pilot

The group-administered SCT curriculum was developed with input from a series of focus groups with parents and teens across the country. The program was field tested using a randomized waitlist design which consisted of assignment of families with 8th-grade students to experimental (n = 35) and control (n = 31) conditions. Analyses at posttest revealed significant differences between the program and control groups in risk and protective factors targeted by the program. Specifically, as intended, those who were treated showed a significant increase in family bonding (Cohen's d = .46) and reductions in poor family management (e.g., guidelines and monitoring, Cohen's d = .75), family conflict (Cohen's d = .23), and attitudes favorable to substance use (Cohen's d = .41) compared to the waitlist control group. After being treated, waitlist controls showed similar changes (Pollard, 1998). The findings supported the logic model and led to the development of the self-directed program materials, setting the stage for a larger experimental efficacy trial.

Efficacy Trial

Three hundred thirty-one families were recruited through the Seattle Public Schools and were informed that the study sought to test a program to prevent teen behavior problems, such as drug and alcohol use, violence, and sexual activity. Families were eligible if they had a Black or White 8th grader living at home who spoke English as their primary language. The overall consent rate of 46% was similar to other universal family prevention studies (Spoth, Redmond, & Shin, 2001), but rates were higher for Black (55%) than White families (40%). Once recruited, the sample was stratified on race (168 White/163 Black) and gender (170 male/161 female) of the target child, and families were randomly assigned to one of three experimental conditions as follows: 107 self-administered (SA), 118 parent and youth group-administered (PA), and 106 no-program control. Families were paid up to $100 for participation in PA or SA. Comparisons at baseline found no significant differences on demographic characteristics or outcome variables by condition, indicating the integrity of randomization (see Haggerty, Skinner, MacKenzie, & Catalano, 2007). Analyses are based on an intent-to-treat design in which all participants assigned to a particular treatment condition are included, regardless of initiation or level of participation in the program. An exception to intent-to-treat analyses are tests of program effects on initiation into substance use or sex, since only those who had not initiated prior to the program could be included.

216 Kevin P. Haggerty et al.

TABLE 10.2 Race Differences in Sample Characteristics at Baseline

Characteristics	African American n = 163	European American n = 168	Total sample n = 331
Mean age of child	13.7 years	13.7 years	13.7 years
Mean number of household members	5.0	4.2★★	4.6
Mean income	$7,807	$21,970★★	$15,042
Education			
Parent high school diploma	78.9%	94.0%★★	86.6%
Parent college grad	13%	61.4%★★	37.6%
Single parent (no spouse or partner)	56.8%	24.4%★★	40.3%

★★ p < .01

Examination of race differences at baseline indicated significant differences in demographics (see Table 10.2). Black youth were more likely to be in single-parent families with larger households, and have lower per capita income and lower parent education compared to White youth, reflecting the population trends in Seattle. There were no significant race differences in prevalence of daily cigarette smoking, marijuana, heavy episodic drinking, other illegal drugs, or violence at baseline (Table 10.3). However, as previously published, significantly more Black teens reported sexual initiation, and had lower prevalence of past-30-day alcohol use at baseline than their White counterparts (Haggerty et al., 2007).

In adolescence, overall attrition of participants from the study was relatively low and there were no significant race differences in attrition through 10th grade. In the outcome follow-up study in young adulthood, attrition was 9% at age 20 and 16% at age 22. There were differences by race, with greater attrition among Black young adults of up to 24% at age 22 (Table 10.4) vs. 9% for White young adults. Due to the potential bias introduced by missing data, especially at age 22, we used multiple imputation (Graham, 2012) in most analyses. With the exception of structural equation modeling, analyses that include age 22 data utilize imputed data with the full sample.

Implementation fidelity

The PA intervention was guided by a structured written curriculum. Group leaders, who had prior clinical experience, received 20 hours of training on this content, as well as in implementation of standardized protocols. To assess implementation fidelity, each family session was independently observed and rated using a specific coding scheme developed for each session. In 20% of the sessions, two raters coded in order to assess inter-rater reliability; average agreement

TABLE 10.3 Means (SD) and Simple Race Differences in Substance Misuse, Violence, and Risky Sex

Outcome	Race	8th-grade baseline	8th-grade post	9th grade	10th grade	Age 20	Age 22
Daily smoking	White	1.79 (1.02)	2.40 (1.19)	7.30 (2.09)	9.12 (2.36)	22.11 (3.28)	20.37 (3.19)
	Black	2.49 (1.26)	2.49 (1.23)	6.58 (2.02)	7.45 (2.07)	18.14 (3.11)	26.15 (4.17)
Heavy episodic drinking[a]	White	1.79 (1.02)	2.39 (1.18)	10.52 (2.46)	14.62 (2.86)★	47.13 (3.97)★★★	54.14 (4.00)★★★
	Black	0.61 (0.60)	1.24 (0.88)	7.57 (2.17)	3.70 (1.49)	17.97 (3.14)	26.46 (4.12)
Marijuana	White	5.96 (1.83)	7.61 (2.10)	18.09 (3.06)	23.14 (3.37)	46.84 (3.93)	45.54 (4.01)
	Black	6.13 (1.88)	9.20 (2.27)	16.86 (2.96)	18.62 (3.11)	40.18 (4.12)	44.89 (4.61)
Marijuana heavy use (20+ occ/month)	White	0.006 (0.08)	0.006 (0.08)	0.012 (0.11)	4.21 (1.59)	15.30 (2.84)	14.00 (2.83)
	Black	0.00 (0.0)	0.00 (0.0)	0.013 (0.11)	4.06 (1.59)	16.42 (3.16)	23.59 (3.67)
Other illicit drugs	White	N/A	N/A	3.96 (1.55)	11.01 (2.52)★	37.87 (3.82)★★★	37.70 (3.85)★★
	Black	N/A	N/A	3.07 (1.35)	3.68 (1.48)	11.29 (2.54)	17.48 (3.58)
Violence	White	0.34 (0.07)	0.27 (0.06)★★	0.16 (0.11)★	0.19 (0.20)★	0.10 (0.02)★	0.09 (0.02)★
	Black	0.49 (0.08)	0.55 (0.10)	0.62 (0.11)	0.62 (0.11)	0.21 (0.03)	0.20 (0.04)
Inconsistent condom use	White	N/A	N/A	N/A	59.2★★	74.4	72.00
	Black	N/A	N/A	N/A	28.6	68.8	77.00
No. sexual partners	White	N/A	N/A	N/A	2.02 (2.57)	3.64 (8.9)	3.38 (4.2)
	Black	N/A	N/A	N/A	2.47 (2.51)	4.11 (10.51	3.21 (5.91)

★p < .05; ★★p < .01; ★★★p < .001
[a] Prior to age 20, the gender-specific measure (4/5) is not used.

218 Kevin P. Haggerty et al.

TABLE 10.4 Sample Size for Each Survey by Assigned Program Group and Race

Time of assessment	Program group	Total N	Whites N	Blacks N
8th grade	Parent admin (PA)	118	59	59
	Self-admin (SA)	107	53	54
	Control	106	56	50
10th grade	Parent admin (PA)	109	54	55
	Self-admin (SA)	93	45	48
	Control	101	53	48
Age 20	Parent admin (PA)	107	56	51
	Self-admin (SA)	98	51	47
	Control	95	53	42
Age 22	Parent admin (PA)	97	52	45
	Self-admin (SA)	89	49	40
	Control	89	51	38

between raters was high (93%). At the end of the 7 weeks, overall content covered per group ranged from 75.5% to 88.3%, with an average of 82.3%.

The SA program was supervised by an intervention coordinator and staffed by four family consultants who received 4 hours of training in the phone call protocols and the implementation of standardized protocols. In addition, they met weekly with the intervention coordinator to review cases, promote fidelity to the phone follow-up protocols, and ensure that families were contacted on a weekly basis. Family consultants contacted the family each week by phone, and based on a standard list of 62 activities, recorded which activities the family had completed that week. Families typically completed 5–7 tasks per week. Further, to minimize the potential impact of social desirability in responses, family consultants asked specific open-ended questions about the activities (e.g., How helpful was the activity for you as a parent? Why?). On average, families reported completing 46 (74%) tasks, ranging from 0 to 62 (SD = 21.48). For more information on program activities, facilitator training, or quality of program delivery in either format, see Haggerty et al. (2007).

Program initiation and exposure

Program initiation—whether families completed any portion of the program— was significantly higher for SA (92.5%) vs. PA (84.9%). Furthermore, there was no interaction between program modality and race, suggesting similar rates of initiation for Black and White families in each modality. Of those who initiated PA (n = 92), the mean number of sessions attended was 4.56. Among program initiators in the SA condition (n = 99), on average, family consultants made

Staying Connected With Your Teen® **219**

16.9 call attempts, resulting in 9.7 completed calls per family during the 10 weeks; phone calls lasted about 10.5 minutes per week. On average, White families completed 87% of the SA program activities and Black families completed 66%. Predictors of exposure to different levels or proportions of the program were of interest; however, due to differing methods of program delivery, comparisons could not be made across modalities (for more details, see Haggerty, MacKenzie, Skinner, Roberson et al., 2006). For the PA modality, program exposure was higher for White families, with 92% initiating participation compared to 78% of Black families ($p = .04$). In contrast, there were no race differences in exposure to the SA condition (although parents who reported engaging in any high-risk behavior had lower rates of exposure to SA). Overall, these results suggest that for Black families (and perhaps other minorities), self-administration may result in greater initiation and exposure to program content. Further analyses on characteristics predicting program initiation and exposure may be found in Haggerty, MacKenzie, Skinner, Harachi, and Catalano (2006).

Outcomes at 2-year follow-up

Key outcomes explored at the 2-year follow-up include more proximal risks, such as perceived harm of substance use and favorable attitudes toward substance use and intentions to use. Protective factors include observed measures of parental rewards for appropriate behavior. Problem behaviors include frequency of violent behavior, substance use and misuse (including initiation of drugs or sex), as well as inconsistent condom use and multiple sex partners.

Table 10.5 displays mean values in each treatment condition for the outcomes at 2-year follow-up for Black and White 10th graders. Tests of program effects were conducted using multiple regression, controlling for gender, age, household income, and baseline levels of the outcome. As reported in Haggerty et al. (2007), favorable attitudes towards substance use were significantly reduced at immediate posttest (8th grade) in the SA (Cohen's $d = 0.26$), but not PA (Cohen's $d = 0.09$) condition relative to controls. In 10th grade, 2 years after program implementation, favorable attitudes were significantly reduced in both the SA and PA conditions compared to controls (Cohen's $d = 0.39$ and 0.22, respectively). These effects were equally strong for Black and White participants. There were no significant program effects for either racial group on perceived harm of substance abuse at posttest or 10th grade (see Haggerty et al., 2007). In the control condition, parents' observed positive responses to appropriate teen behavior declined significantly from the 8th to the 10th grade ($z = -3.35, p = .01$), while parents in both program conditions maintained more stable levels of observed positive responses to appropriate behavior (SA $z = 1.88, p = .03$; PA $z = 2.36$, $p = .01$).

220 Kevin P. Haggerty et al.

TABLE 10.5 Means (SDs) for Treatment Outcomes, White and Black by Group

Outcome	Time of assessment	Program group	N	White Mean (SD)	Black Mean (SD)
Favorable SU attitudes	8th-grade post	Parent admin (PA)	118	1.39 (0.56)	1.38 (0.65)
		Self-admin (SA)	107	1.27 (0.46)	1.29 (0.56)
		Control	106	1.55 (0.71)	1.38 (0.48)
	10th grade	Parent admin (PA)	109	1.67 (0.63)	1.48 (0.81)
		Self-admin (SA)	93	1.59 (0.54)	1.41 (0.72)
		Control	101	1.94 (0.72)	1.69 (0.66)
Perceived harm of SU	8th-grade post	Parent admin (PA)	118	2.90 (0.76)	3.06 (0.96)
		Self-admin (SA)	107	3.14 (0.66)	3.07 (0.89)
		Control	106	2.91 (0.73)	3.10 (0.81)
	10th grade	Parent admin (PA)	109	2.80 (0.57)	2.79 (1.03)
		Self-admin (SA)	93	2.94 (0.52)	2.91 (0.81)
		Control	101	2.75 (0.68)	2.74 (0.73)
Drug/sex initiation[a]	10th grade	Parent admin (PA)	120	54.82	31.05
		Self-admin (SA)	86	56.11	31.32
		Control	124	54.84	59.56
Inconsistent condom use[b]	Age 20	Parent admin (PA)	118	76.54 (6.14)	79.24 (6.75)
		Self-admin (SA)	107	80.21 (6.28)	63.19 (7.85)
		Control	106	67.65 (7.20)	67.93 (8.21)
Inconsistent condom use[b]	Age 22	Parent admin (PA)	118	68.17 (6.67)	64.43 (7.63)
		Self-admin (SA)	107	76.63 (6.45)	60.21 (9.01)
		Control	106	70.10 (7.13)	81.91 (7.16)
No. of sex partners[b]	Age 20	Parent admin (PA)	118	2.46 (0.27)	2.65 (0.62)
		Self-admin (SA)	107	2.32 (0.25)	2.86 (0.63)
		Control	106	2.18 (0.28)	2.74 (0.42)
No. of sex partners[b]	Age 22	Parent admin (PA)	118	2.48 (0.29)	2.73 (0.55)
		Self-admin (SA)	107	2.63 (0.32)	2.76 (0.67)
		Control	106	2.58 (0.40)	2.74 (0.45)

[a] Raw percentages
[b] Age 20 and 22 means are based on multiple imputations used in analyses. Standard deviations indicate the variability across imputations.

Drug use, sex, and violence at 10th grade

The dichotomous variable for initiation into sex or drug use was regressed on program condition, race, gender, and chronological age. In 10th grade, there were no treatment main effects on initiation of drugs or sex; however, race-by-program-condition interactions were observed at trend levels for both treatment conditions (SA $p = .06$; PA $p = .08$). In both cases, the program reduced initiation for Black teens relative to Black teens in the control group,

Staying Connected With Your Teen® **221**

but not for White teens compared to their counterparts in the control group (Haggerty et al., 2007). Black teens experienced similar reductions in initiation of drugs/sex relative to controls in both treatment conditions (SA OR = .31; PA OR = .25). Although no program effects on the frequency of violent behavior were observed at posttest, by 10th grade, analyses revealed that SA reduced violence among Black teens (Cohen's d = .45) but not White teens (Cohen's d = .02; Haggerty et al., 2007).

Outcomes at ages 20 and 22

In young adulthood, we explored the influence of family management problems, family conflict, observed negative rewards for behavior, and observed rewards for positive behavior on drug use frequency. Structural equation modeling was used to model direct and indirect effects of the program on drug use frequency (using multivariate weighted least squares; see Haggerty et al., 2013 for more details). At age 20, we found that the SA condition had no direct effects on the drug use frequency for either race, but did have a small total indirect effect for White young adults (β = −.28, p = .06) through family stressors and adolescent drug use. The PA condition had a small but significant direct effect on drug use frequency for both Black and White young adults (β = −.04, p < .01). In addition, there was a significant indirect effect of PA for White (β = −.25, p = .04) and a marginally significant indirect effect of PA for Black (β = −.07, p = .05) young adults through the family factor variable. At age 22, the same model was estimated and no significant race differences were detected in direct or indirect effects on drug use frequency. The total indirect effects for PA were just significant (β = −.19, p = .05), indicating that, overall, the group-administered approach continued to have some dampening effect on drug use frequency at age 22. It is noteworthy that the indirect effects of both conditions provide some support for the SCT logic model in young adulthood (age 20), not only in adolescence, as it was originally conceptualized.

Additionally, at the age 22 timeframe, logistic regressions were conducted to assess program and program-by-race effects on substance misuse, one substance at a time, from posttest to young adulthood. Clustering due to recruitment through schools was accounted for and controls were included for age, gender, and household income. Baseline levels of the outcome were included if measures were available (daily smoking, heavy episodic drinking, and marijuana use) but not included otherwise (heavy marijuana use and illegal drug use). No significant main effects for either program condition were found on drug use outcomes. Race-by-treatment interactions were likewise nonsignificant. Of interest, however, are the large race differences in heavy episodic drinking and illicit drug use in 10th grade and especially at ages 20 and 22. Table 10.5 demonstrates that, consistent with national population-based studies (Johnston, O'Malley, Bachman, & Schulenberg, 2013), fewer Black than White participants engaged in these behaviors. As explained above, these race differences are not attributable to program effects and persist in the face of demographic controls. As seen in Table 10.5, no further significant program effects have been found related to inconsistent condom use and multiple sex partners. Likewise, a test of program effects on the likelihood of self-reported violent behavior resulted in no significant effects.

Group- vs. Self-directed SCT

Overall, the efficacy study demonstrated that, despite significantly fewer resources invested in the SA program, both modalities of SCT impacted risk and protective factors for problem behavior such as positive family management, family conflict, favorable substance use attitudes, and intentions to use drugs and alcohol. The group mode may be somewhat more effective in preventing substance use into young adulthood, although no effects were observed on substance use during the adolescent or early adult years. This pattern potentially reflects a sleeper effect of the group-administered program. There were few effects of either modality on violent and sexually risky behaviors, which may indicate a need for more specific focus on situations and experiences directly involving these problem behaviors.

It is interesting, however, that where effects are observed for risky sex and violence, Black participants benefited more. This is true only for the SA program. Likewise, initiation of substance use or sex was reduced among Black (but not White) teens, but for this outcome both program formats were effective. Recall that we found no race differences in program initiation of either program modality, and no race difference in participating in the SA, but less participation of Black than White families in the PA. The patterns in outcomes and program initiation/exposure suggest that Black families may find self-administration especially beneficial. This finding is important in light of research demonstrating barriers to program recruitment and participation for minorities and low-income populations in the United States.

Dissemination

While efficacy trials under tightly controlled research conditions (such as the study described above) are essential to establish a program's effects on target outcomes, in order to understand whether similar outcomes can be replicated in real-world settings, effectiveness studies must be undertaken. Two such projects have been conducted with the self-administered modality of SCT.

SCT-SA with High-Risk Families

First, SCT-SA was introduced at a community (outpatient) mental health and substance use treatment agency with multiple facilities (branches) within the

Puget Sound region with the intention of testing the feasibility of providing light-touch prevention services to high-risk parents. SCT training and implementation was conducted as part of a waitlist controlled trial. However, even after the waitlisted branches conducted their recruitment and program participation, very few families completed the SCT-SA program. Overall, 302 families were offered SCT; 62 families consented to do the program, 48 began, but only 11 families completed 100% of the program. Given these extremely low participation rates, program effects could not be investigated; however, considerable effort was dedicated to an analysis of implementation barriers via multiple focus groups and surveys with staff and other stakeholders at the treatment facility (Haggerty et al., 2013).

Several important lessons can be learned from this experience. First, an in-depth assessment of the fit between clientele (i.e., potential program participants) and program requirements is critical. In focus groups, staff at the treatment agency expressed that the reading materials of the SA modality were inappropriate for their clients, and that motivating clients from a distance would be difficult. They further believed that their clients were often in "crisis mode," which necessitated a focus on more pressing survival concerns. Finally, staff stated that many youth were already engaged in problem behaviors; therefore, a prevention program such as SCT would be less beneficial than treatment. These staff concerns point to a second lesson: stakeholder buy-in for the program is crucial. Despite trainings and consultations with researchers, treatment staff were not particularly invested in a family-based prevention program, the self-directed modality, the nontraditional tasks required of them (e.g., phone follow-up), and various SCT activities. This may be due to their professional training and experience or the particular environment and requirements of the treatment agency. We noted that systemic support for recruitment, documentation, and implementation of SCT was missing. For instance, documentation of program activities (as well as other therapeutic endeavors) was cumbersome; the increased time and effort necessary for this component of the program likely created a barrier for many staff members. In sum, this experience leads us to believe that unlike the medical field, where treatment and prevention have been more smoothly integrated, in the mental health field additional planning and effort must be invested in order to reach a goal of integration.

SCT-SA with Foster Families

A second effort to disseminate SCT-SA has been conducted with foster families and youth in their care. Adolescents involved in the child welfare system have been shown to be at higher risk for problem behaviors than the general population (Havalchak, Roller White, & O'Brien, 2008; Pilowsky & Wu, 2006); thus, preventing such problems is an important goal. However, these adolescents have also been shown to have unique needs and experiences, such as greater exposure to trauma and acculturative stress in the unfamiliar environments in which they are placed. Thus, a "cultural" adaptation of SCT for foster families and youth was necessary.

Based on qualitative research with foster parents, youth, and child welfare staff (Storer, Barkan, Sherman, Haggerty, & Mattos, 2012), several key adaptations have been made to SCT using the ADAPT-ITT process (Wingood & DiClemente, 2008). Adaptations include activities that address (a) the stress that youth have experienced within their family of origin that led to them being placed outside of their home; (b) the stress associated with being placed into an unfamiliar family "culture," and often times with a family whose racial or ethnic culture is different from that of the youth; (c) their uncertainty about their current living situation and whether they will return to their family of origin or where they will find a permanent home; and (d) the added vulnerability associated with their developmental age, in this case, adolescence (Barkan et al., 2014). The important lesson we learned about stakeholder buy-in has been implemented in this setting, and the partnership with child welfare staff and clients has been instrumental to the successful adaptation of SCT within the public child welfare setting.

We are currently conducting a usability and feasibility trial of the adapted version of SCT called *Connecting*. Sixty foster families enrolled in the program were sent the materials, and received follow-up phone calls from a family consultant. Twenty-eight (88%) intervention group caregivers and 21 (75%) waitlist caregivers completed the posttest survey. Among those program participants, overall satisfaction with the program was high; 100% are very or somewhat satisfied. Satisfaction with the workbook/DVD is also strong (86%), as well as with the added digital stories (89%), and over two thirds of the participants indicate they will continue to use the program (69%). Families tended to use the program available to them. Nearly 65% (39) of those enrolled reported completing the program. Nearly all (75%) reported having read most or quite a bit of the *Connecting* workbook, 14% reported reading "some—about half," and 11% reported not having read much of the workbook. Ninety-six percent were "very" (89.3%) or "somewhat" (7.1%) satisfied with the family consultant they spoke with over the phone for the weekly calls. On average, we made 27 contact attempts and had an average of 7 completed family consultant check-ins. The average amount of time over 7 weeks spent on the phone with families was 79 minutes. Program dosage was measured by looking at video, activity, and overall program completion. The average program completion was 62%. On average, participants viewed 12 of 18 videos (66%) and completed 27 out of 44 (61%) of the activities. Overall, participants spent about 9 hours on the *Connecting* program. We are currently testing whether the adapted program has proximal impacts on family management practices, family conflict, family bonding, and favorable attitudes toward drug use and other risky behaviors in the short term. Preliminary findings from this feasibility (and therefore underpowered) study supported the logic model. Program participation led to better communication between teens and caregivers around monitoring and media use, teen participation in setting family rules, and decreased teen deviant attitudes.

Future Directions

As this chapter and others in the book have demonstrated, evidence-based family-centered programs offer great potential for preventing child and adolescent problems. Fundamentally, many of these programs share similarities in the family dynamics targeted and activities used to achieve outcomes. A systematic review of these program elements would be beneficial in order to clearly identify which are important for impacting key outcomes, and which can be eliminated from future programs (in the service of greater efficiency).

Self-directed family programs hold great promise for accessing more diverse and hard-to-reach families; however, more program development and rigorous outcomes testing is clearly needed as the field advances. Close attention should be paid to program components specific to self-administration (e.g., staff monitoring, ease of use of materials), which may prove critical to the success or failure of such programs. In addition, self-directed programs may not be suitable for all settings and populations; therefore, careful and systematic assessment is necessary, qualifying where and with whom such programs are best implemented. Finally, this format allows prevention scientists and practitioners to take advantage of the latest technologies in order to most flexibly and efficiently work with families. Little work has been conducted using, for instance, smart phones and mobile applications in this arena, but interventions in public health (e.g., Eng & Lee, 2013; Tomlinson, Rotheram-Borus, Swartz, & Tsai, 2013) suggest that this is a fruitful avenue to pursue.

Note

1   Costs for both modalities include: participant and other (e.g., consultant, group) materials, phone calls, incentive payments (as part of randomized clinical trial), scheduling and facilities coordination, and supervision of group leaders and family consultants. In SA, other costs include: family consultant training, cost of family calls, and postage. In PA, costs include: leader training, session preparation and delivery, overhead for group meeting space, dinners/snacks for participants, childcare for siblings, and leader travel.

References

Barkan, S. E., Salazar, A. M., Estep, K., Mattos, L. M., Eichenlaub, C., & Haggerty, K. P. (2014). Adapting an evidence based parenting program for child welfare involved teens and their caregivers. *Children and Youth Services Review, 41*, 53–61.

Bauman, K. E., Ennett, S. T., Foshee, V. A., Pemberton, M., & Hicks, K. (2001). Correlates of participation in a family-directed tobacco and alcohol prevention program for adolescents. *Health Education and Behavior, 28*, 440–461.

Biglan, A., & Metzler, C. W. (1998). A public health perspective for research on family-focused interventions. In R. S. Ashery, E. B. Robertson, & K. L. Kumpfer (Eds.), *Drug abuse prevention through family interventions*. NIDA Research Monograph No. 177 (pp. 430–458). Rockville, MD: National Institute on Drug Abuse, U.S. Department of Health and Human Services.

Catalano, R. F., Fagan, A. A., Gavin, L. E., Greenberg, M. T., Irwin, C. E., Ross, D. A., et al. (2012). Worldwide application of the prevention science research base in adolescent health. *The Lancet, 379*, 1653–1664.

Catalano, R. F., Haggerty, K. P., Hawkins, J. D., & Elgin, J. (2011). Prevention of substance use and substance use disorders: The role of risk and protective factors. In Y. Kaminer & K. C. Winters (Eds.), Clinical manual of adolescent substance abuse treatment (pp. 25–63). Washington, DC: American Psychiatric Publishing.

Catalano, R. F., & Hawkins, J. D. (1996). The social development model: A theory of antisocial behavior. In J. D. Hawkins (Ed.), *Delinquency and crime: Current theories* (pp. 149–197). New York: Cambridge University Press.

Eng, D. S., & Lee, J. M. (2013). The promise and peril of mobile health applications for diabetes and endocrinology. *Pediatric Diabetes, 14*, 231–238.

Farrington, D. P., & Welsh, B. C. (2002). Family-based crime prevention. In L. W. Sherman, D. P. Farrington, B. C. Welsh, & D. L. MacKenzie (Eds.), *Evidence-based crime prevention* (pp. 22–55). London: Routledge.

Fleming, C. B., Marchesini, G., Haggerty, K. P., Hill, K. G., & Catalano, R. F. (2012). The importance of high completion rates: Evidence from two longitudinal studies of the etiology and prevention of problem behaviors. Unpublished manuscript.

Foxcroft, D., Ireland, D., Lister-Sharp, D., Lowe, G., & Breen, R. (2003). Longer-term primary prevention for alcohol misuse in young people: A systematic review. *Addiction, 98*, 397–411.

Gorman-Smith, D., Tolan, P. H., Henry, D. B., & Leventhal, A. (2002). Predictors of participation in a family-focused preventive intervention for substance use. *Psychology of Addictive Behaviors, 16*(4 Suppl.), S55–S64.

Graham, J. W. (2012). *Missing data: Analysis and design*. New York: Springer.

Haggerty, K. P., Fleming, C. B., Lonczak, H. S., Oxford, M. L., Harachi, T. W., & Catalano, R. F. (2002). Predictors of participation in parenting workshops. *The Journal of Primary Prevention, 22*, 375–387.

Haggerty, K. P., & Kosterman, R. (2012). Helping parents prevent problem behavior. *Better: Evidence-Based Education, 4*(3), 22–23.

Haggerty, K. P., MacKenzie, E. P., Skinner, M. L., Harachi, T. W., & Catalano, R. F. (2006). Participation in "Parents Who Care": Predicting program initiation and exposure in two different program formats. *The Journal of Primary Prevention, 27*, 47–65.

Haggerty, K. P., MacKenzie, E. P., Skinner, M. L., Roberson, K. C., Harachi, T. W., & Catalano, R. F. (2006). Self-administered parenting programs to promote adolescent behavioral health: A review and promising developments. Unpublished manuscript.

Haggerty, K. P., McGlynn-Wright, A., & Klima, T. (2013). Promising parenting programs for reducing adolescent problem behaviors. *Journal of Children's Services, 8*, 229–243.

Haggerty, K. P., Skinner, M. L., Catalano, R. F., Abbott, R. D., & Crutchfield, R. D. (2015). Long-term effects of Staying Connected with Your Teen® on drug use frequency at age 20. *Prevention Science*, 16, 538–549.

Haggerty, K. P., Skinner, M. L., MacKenzie, E. P., & Catalano, R. F. (2007). A randomized trial of Parents Who Care: Effects on key outcomes at 24-month follow-up. *Prevention Science*, 8, 249–260.

Havalchak, A., Roller White, C., & O'Brien, K. (2008). *The Casey Young Adult Survey: Findings over three years*. Seattle, WA: Casey Family Programs.

Hawkins, J. D., Catalano, R. F., & Miller, J. Y. (1992). Risk and protective factors for alcohol and other drug problems in adolescence and early adulthood: Implications for substance abuse prevention. *Psychological Bulletin, 112*, 64–105.

Hawkins, J. D., & Weis, J. G. (1985). The social development model: An integrated approach to delinquency prevention. *The Journal of Primary Prevention, 6*, 73–97.

Heinrichs, N., Bertram, H., Kuschel, A., & Hahlweg, K. (2005). Parent recruitment and retention in a universal prevention program for child behavior and emotional problems: Barriers to research and program participation. *Prevention Science, 6*, 275–286.

Herrenkohl, T. I., Lee, J. O., & Hawkins, J. D. (2012). Risk versus direct protective factors and youth violence: Seattle Social Development Project. *American Journal of Preventive Medicine. Special issue: Protective factors for youth violence perpetration: Issues, evidence, and public health implications, 43*(2 Suppl. 1), S41–S56.

Johnston, L. D., O'Malley, P. M., Bachman, J. G., & Schulenberg, J. E. (2013). Demographic subgroup trends among adolescents for forty-six classes of licit and illicit drugs, 1975–2012 (Monitoring the Future Occasional Paper No. 79). Ann Arbor, MI: Institute for Social Research.

Kumpfer, K. L., & Alvarado, R. (2003). Family-strengthening approaches for the prevention of youth problem behaviors. *American Psychologist, 58*, 457–465.

Offord, D. R. (2000). Selection levels of prevention. *Addictive Behaviors, 25*, 833–842.

Pilowsky, D. J., & Wu, L. T. (2006). Psychiatric symptoms and substance use disorders in a nationally representative sample of American adolescents involved with foster care. *Journal of Adolescent Health, 38*, 351–358.

Pollard, J. A. (1998). Final report on NIDA SBIR grant #DA07435, Risk Focused Family Training for Drug Use Intervention. Seattle, WA: Developmental Research and Programs.

Rehm, J., Mathers, C., Popova, S., Thavorncharoensap, M., Teerawattananon, Y., & Patra, J. (2009). Global burden of disease and injury and economic cost attributable to alcohol use and alcohol-use disorders. *Lancet, 373*, 2223–2233.

Skinner, M. L., Haggerty, K. P., & Catalano, R. F. (2009). Parental and peer influences on teen smoking: Are White and Black families different? *Nicotine & Tobacco Research, 11*, 558–563.

Spoth, R., Redmond, C., Hockaday, C., & Shin, C. Y. (1996). Barriers to participation in family skills preventive interventions and their evaluations: A replication and extension. *Family Relations: Journal of Applied Family and Child Studies, 45*, 247–254.

Spoth, R. L., Redmond, C., & Shin, C. (2001). Randomized trial of brief family interventions for general populations: Adolescent substance use outcomes 4 years following baseline. *Journal of Consulting and Clinical Psychology, 69*, 627–642.

Storer, H. L., Barkan, S. E., Sherman, E. L., Haggerty, K. P., & Mattos, L. M. (2012). Promoting relationship building and connection: Adapting an evidence-based parenting program for families involved in the child welfare system. *Children and Youth Services Review, 34*, 1853–1861.

Tomlinson, M., Rotheram-Borus, M. J., Swartz, L., & Tsai, A. C. (2013). Scaling up mHealth: Where is the evidence? *PLoS Med, 10*, e1001382.

Wingood, G. M., & DiClemente, R. J. (2008). The ADAPT-ITT model: A novel method of adapting evidence-based HIV interventions. *JAIDS Journal of Acquired Immune Deficiency Syndromes, 47*(Suppl. 1), S40–S46.

11

FAMILIES OVERCOMING UNDER STRESS (FOCUS)

A Family-Centered Preventive Intervention for Families Facing Trauma, Stress, and Adversity: Implementation with Military Families

Patricia Lester, Lee Klosinski, William Saltzman, Norweeta Milburn, Catherine Mogil, and William Beardslee

Background on Military Children and Families: The Impact of Wartime Service

Over a decade of war in Afghanistan and Iraq has defined a rapidly evolving set of challenges for military families and their children. It is estimated that about 4 million children and adolescents have had a parent serve in the military since 9/11; many of these have spent much of their childhood with at least one parent leaving and returning in the context of danger. Some children have experienced the hardships of parental injury, illness, and even loss (for review, see Holmes, Rauch, & Cozza, 2013). With an increased risk for combat-related mental health problems such as Post Traumatic Stress Disorder (PTSD) and Traumatic Brain Injury (TBI) as well as physical injuries in their families and extended communities, military children and families face unique and often sustained stressors that may influence child well-being over time in ways that are not yet well understood.

Despite the limitations in longitudinal research with military children and families affected by wartime deployments, a rapidly expanding body of research has consistently documented increased social, emotional, behavioral, and academic risk associated with parental wartime military service for children across developmental periods, as well as the direct and indirect reverberations of heightened stress across the family system (Lester and Flake, 2013). Further, parental combat-related mental health problems have been associated with disruptions in parenting and family relationships, as well as increased psychological health symptoms in children (Gewirtz, Forgatch, & Wieling, 2008; Lester,

230 Patricia Lester et al.

Leskin et al., 2010; Lester, Petersen et al., 2010). As in other contexts of early adversity, family-level interactions have been identified as mediators of children's ability to adapt and thrive in the context of military life stressors (for review, see Paley, Lester, & Mogil, 2013).

Using a framework that is informed by the larger field of developmental systems research, emerging research with military families has been informed by an understanding of processes that predict individual- and family-level resilience in the context of adversity (Luthar, 2006; Masten 2001, 2013; Zelazo, 2013). Consistent family-level processes characterize families that demonstrate resilience in the face of trauma or significant stressors: open and effective communication, an ability to express and regulate emotions, collaborative problem solving, and the capacity to construct a shared understanding of stressful or traumatic experiences – an activity often supported by shared beliefs or values (Saltzman, Lester, Beardslee, Layne, & Nash, 2011; Walsh, 2006).

War has often accelerated advancements in medical and behavioral health care in part due to urgent need, advances in technology, mobilization of resources, and sustained national attention. An all-volunteer, professional military with prolonged, multiple deployments, and significant changes in wartime duties, demographics, communication technologies, and combat injuries have created unprecedented tests for the resilience of service members, their families, and the systems that support them (Tanielian & Jaycox, 2008). These challenges highlight a cultural, political, and scientific convergence around the significant potential of preventive interventions for promoting psychological health for military members and their families.

The Department of Defense (DOD) and Department of Veterans Affairs (VA) have increasingly highlighted the needs of military and veteran families as a national public health priority (MacDermid Wadsworth et al., 2013). A notable example includes the evolution of the US military's own understanding of the role and needs of the military family. In particular, the concept of military preparedness or "readiness" has been expanded to include the well-being of families. While originally understood as the ability of service members to carry out their service duties, the current wars have increasingly highlighted the important role of families in the readiness of service members to perform their duties, underscoring the relevance of psychological well-being across the family system for national security. By 2010, "health-of-the-force" became a priority of the Joint Chiefs of Staff and expanded beyond military preparedness to a national moral obligation to service members and the families who serve alongside of them: "Our core responsibility is to win wars while caring for our people and their families" (Chairman of the Joints Chief of Staff, 2010, p. 30). Recognizing the importance of the health of military families for military readiness has opened up new opportunities for the development of effective behavioral health prevention strategies for military and veteran families, and has brought a national scientific and political spotlight to the need for more rigorous science to inform program development and implementation (IOM, 2014).

In this context, the field of prevention science can provide relevant guidance. In particular, family-centered approaches to prevention in the context of adversity have consistently demonstrated effectiveness in promoting psychological health and mitigating stress in children and adults in other populations (National Research Council [NRC] and IOM, 2009a, 2009b; Spoth, Kavanagh, & Dishion, 2002). Family-based prevention science has demonstrated that parenting and family processes influence child well-being over the course of development (NRC, 2009a). Interventions that provide psychoeducation and developmental guidance and build skills that support effective parent–child relationships can provide the scaffolding for behavioral and emotional regulation in children (NRC, 2009a, 2009b; Spoth et al., 2002). Research also indicates that approaches to family-centered prevention and treatment are likely to be more engaging and culturally acceptable than individual interventions across multiple contexts (Kumpfer, Alvarado, Smith, & Bellamy, 2002; NRC, 2009a, 2009b). Relevant to the national public health challenge facing the DOD and VA, there has been increasing rigor in efforts to implement and disseminate effective evidence-based interventions widely in order to have a population-level impact on psychological health (Biglan, Flay, Embry, & Sandler, 2012; NRC, 2009a). The importance of data-driven implementation and dissemination practices has been further underscored by the prevention and evidence-based practice priorities of the 2010 Patient Protection and Affordable Care Act (Fiese, Rhodes, & Beardslee, 2013; Howell, Golden, & Beardslee, 2013).

This chapter provides a description of the theoretical and research foundations of Families OverComing Under Stress (FOCUS), a family-centered preventive intervention developed to enhance individual and family resilience and to mitigate psychological distress associated with adverse or traumatic events, including military deployments and/or combat-related injuries. Developed from the common core elements of established family-centered interventions and customized specifically for military and veteran families, FOCUS has been implemented broadly in the context of this evolving public health challenge. In this chapter, we describe the theoretical and research foundations and development of the FOCUS intervention. Second, we describe the family resilience framework used to inform the FOCUS model, using the specific translation of military family stressors associated with deployment, reintegration, and injury challenges. Third, we describe the large-scale implementation of the FOCUS intervention for military families as a public health response to an urgent national need through the use of a partnered, data-driven implementation platform, and present effectiveness outcomes from this implementation process. We share potential implications of strategies for design and diffusion of evidence-based practices in rapidly evolving, real-world contexts, and describe ongoing research with this model.

Theoretical and Research Foundations of a Trauma-Informed, Family-Centered Preventive Intervention

Consistent with a developmental systems and social ecological framework, the FOCUS intervention model builds upon developmental and intervention research that identifies the mutual influences among individuals within families and between families and broader social contexts (Bronfenbrenner, 1977a, 1977b, 1986). FOCUS was developed to build upon the findings of the foundational research that a family-centered preventive intervention targeting youth outcomes could also improve adjustment in parents and families (Lester et al., 2011). Consistent with these foundational interventions, the FOCUS model (Figure 11.1) is designed to improve individual adjustment of parents and children as well as functioning within and across relationships (parent–parent, parent–child, sibling–sibling) with the expectation that improvements in one area will reverberate throughout the entire family (Lester et al., 2011; MacDermid Wadsworth et al., 2013).

FOCUS was developed from two evidence-based, family-centered preventive interventions shown to enhance child well-being in the context of parental medical and mental health problems (Beardslee, Gladstone, Wright, & Cooper, 2003; Beardslee & Knitzer, 2003; Beardslee, Wright, Gladstone, & Forbes, 2007;

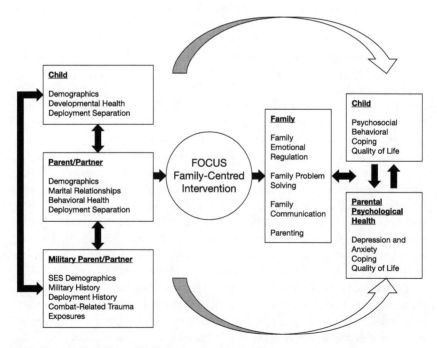

FIGURE 11.1 Underlying FOCUS Theoretical Model

Rotheram-Borus, Lee, Gwadz, & Draimin, 2001), as well as a third intervention for children and parents affected by wartime exposures (Layne et al., 2008). Comprised of prevention scientists that had overseen the original foundational research, the FOCUS team conducted a rigorous review of each intervention's protocols and research, developing consensus on shared contributing structures, processes, and core elements of the FOCUS intervention.

The first foundational intervention was designed to strengthen children and families in which a parent is depressed (Beardslee et al., 2003, 2007; Beardslee & Knitzer, 2003). This manualized preventive intervention (known as both "Family Talk" and Clinician-Based Cognitive Psychoeducational Intervention [CBCPI]) was developed to enhance resilience and reduce risk in children by increasing positive parent–child interactions, and to increase the understanding of depression within the family (Beardslee, 1984; Beardslee & Wheelock, 1994; Beardslee et al., 2003). The intervention provides psychoeducation about mood disorders, communication skills, and developmental guidance for parents, and opens a dialogue within families about the effects of parental depression. Parents are helped to build resilience in their children through encouraging prosocial skills and supportive relationships outside the home. The clinician-facilitated condition consisted of eight sessions, including separate meetings with parents and children and a family meeting in which the parents lead a discussion of the illness and of positive steps that can be taken to promote healthy functioning in the children. The interventionist helps the family to link the material to the family's own unique illness experience. The core processes and elements of CBCPI/Family Talk contributing to the development of FOCUS include the structural framework of delivery (eight-session model, parents-only, youth-only, and entire family sessions), development of a family narrative, delivery of context-specific psychoeducation, development of family/parent communication skills, and support of family resilience processes (routines, support, prosocial interactions).

CBCPI has undergone a randomized controlled trial with depressed parents and their children with findings that the intervention is effective both short-term and long-term in changing attitudes, behaviors, and interactions in these families and in reducing the long-term risk of mental health problems among children (Beardslee et al., 2003). This intervention has received the highest ratings within the SAMHSA National Registry of Evidence Based Programs and Practices (www.nrepp.samhsa.gov/), and has been successfully replicated both nationally and internationally (Podorefsky, McDonald-Dowdell, & Beardslee, 2001; D'Angelo et al., 2009).

The second foundational intervention contributing to FOCUS is "Project TALC (Teens and Adults Learning to Communicate)" a family-centered preventive intervention delivered to parents with HIV and their adolescent children in youth-only, parent-only, and conjoint multi-family groups. Parents who had been in the intervention condition showed benefits in psychosocial

234 Patricia Lester et al.

adjustment, reduced risk for substance misuse, and improved coping over time, while youth also showed improved well-being across several important domains of adjustment over time, including fewer anxiety and depressive symptoms, fewer risk-taking behaviors, greater school attendance, and reduced early childbearing (Lee, Lester, & Rotheram-Borus, 2002; Lester, Rotheram-Borus, Elia, Elkavich, & Rice, 2008; Rotheram-Borus et al., 2001; Rotheram-Borus, Lee, Lin, & Lester, 2004).

Core intervention elements of TALC include: 1) developmental guidance and education regarding parental illness; 2) learning and practicing positive cognitive behavioral coping skills at the individual and family level (emotional regulation, communication, problem solving, and goal setting); and 3) development of positive parenting practice and family routines. Core processes and elements contributing to FOCUS include: interactive delivery across family systems (interactive in-session and at-home activities to learn and practice skills); skill development, including affect identification and emotional regulation, goal setting, communication, and problem solving; and development of positive parenting practices and family routines.

Because the FOCUS model was designed for use with families affected by significant stress and/or traumatic exposure, a third trauma-focused intervention for children and parents was reviewed to augment the intervention for a trauma-exposed population. Utilizing trauma-informed psychoeducation and skills to manage the impact of traumatic reminders, this group intervention was found to reduce youth psychological health symptoms in a randomized trial in Bosnia Herzegovina (Layne et al., 2008). The FOCUS intervention has integrated trauma-informed psychoeducation and cognitive behavioral skill building (including managing trauma and loss reminders) from this program (Saltzman, Lester et al., 2009).

The FOCUS intervention was customized for the specific challenges and cultural context for military-connected families facing multiple deployment and transitional stress (Beardslee et al., 2011; Lester et al., 2011; Saltzman et al., 2011). The intervention team modified the key processes to respond to the needs of military families and culture through rigorous assessment of risk and resilience processes in military families (Lester, Leskin et al., 2010; Lester, Petersen et al., 2010), as well as through an iterative process that included focus groups with military providers, families, and children. The model was manualized with initial pilot delivery with active duty families (Saltzman, Lester et al., 2009). This process informed the refinement of the intervention's core elements and delivery protocols for military families.

As a manualized preventive intervention program, FOCUS is delivered in eight sessions to parents and children aged 4–17 in individual families, including parent-only, child-only, and family sessions. Figure 11.2 provides the structural framework for the intervention model, including identification of the core elements of FOCUS.

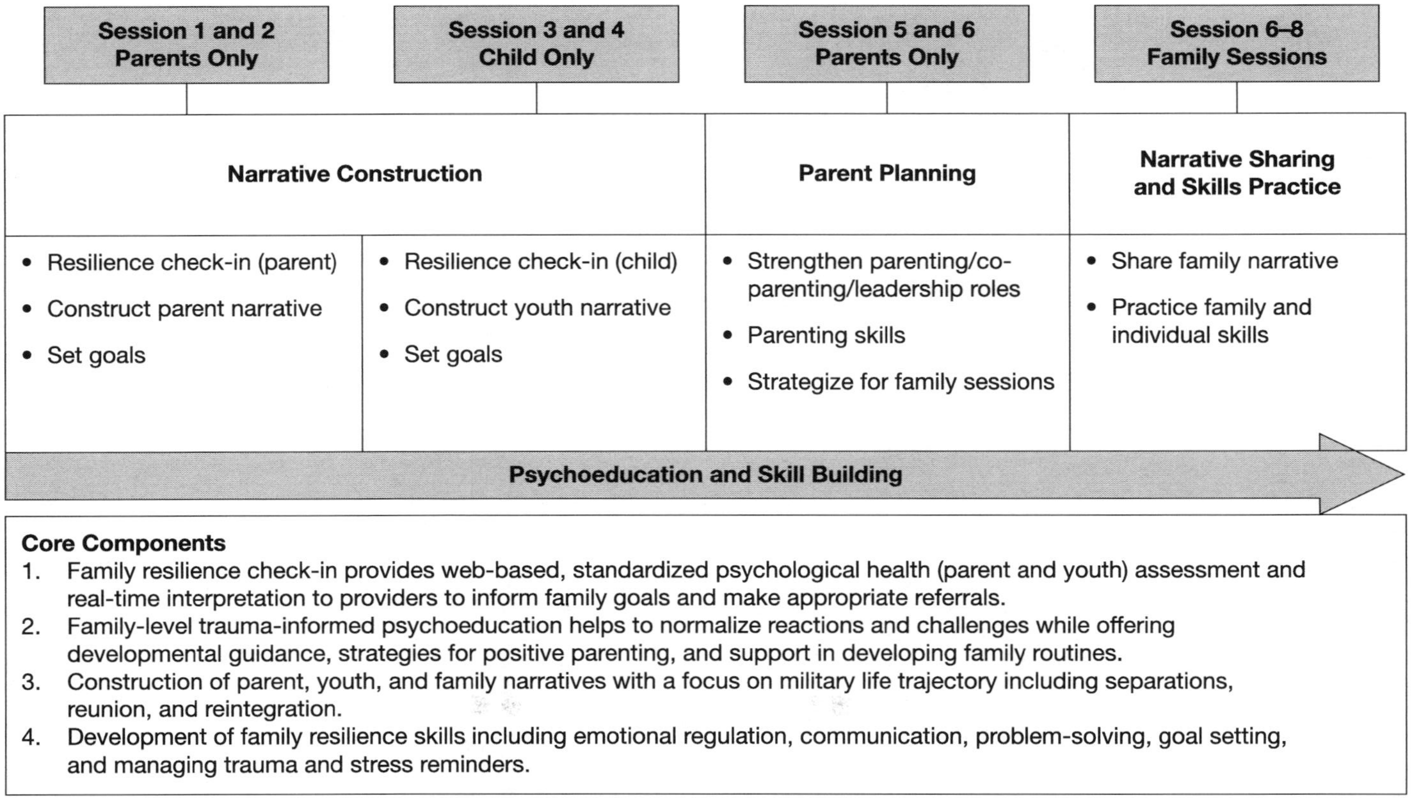

Session 1 and 2 Parents Only	Session 3 and 4 Child Only	Session 5 and 6 Parents Only	Session 6–8 Family Sessions

Narrative Construction		Parent Planning	Narrative Sharing and Skills Practice
• Resilience check-in (parent) • Construct parent narrative • Set goals	• Resilience check-in (child) • Construct youth narrative • Set goals	• Strengthen parenting/co-parenting/leadership roles • Parenting skills • Strategize for family sessions	• Share family narrative • Practice family and individual skills

Psychoeducation and Skill Building

Core Components

1. Family resilience check-in provides web-based, standardized psychological health (parent and youth) assessment and real-time interpretation to providers to inform family goals and make appropriate referrals.

2. Family-level trauma-informed psychoeducation helps to normalize reactions and challenges while offering developmental guidance, strategies for positive parenting, and support in developing family routines.

3. Construction of parent, youth, and family narratives with a focus on military life trajectory including separations, reunion, and reintegration.

4. Development of family resilience skills including emotional regulation, communication, problem-solving, goal setting, and managing trauma and stress reminders.

FIGURE 11.2 FOCUS Preventive Intervention for Military Families and Children

236 Patricia Lester et al.

Family Resilience Check-in

The first core element within the FOCUS intervention includes a web-based "Family Resilience Check-in" integrated within a customized cloud-based data management system used to support implementation quality control/quality improvement, collect assessment data, and provide real-time feedback to providers, clinical supervisors, and families (described previously in Lester, Leskin et al., 2010; measures included in Table 11.1).

At intake, completion, and follow-up intervals, parents and children complete standardized assessments in the waiting room setting (via laptops or iPad tablets) related to psychosocial adjustment. The system provides interpreted feedback to providers based on standardized scores, translates this to specific psycho-education and skills development goals, and indicates the need for referrals or crisis intervention (Lester et al., 2011, 2012). Specifically, providers are immediately alerted to both areas of strength/positive functioning and to risk for psychological disorder and/or suicide by an automatically generated color-coded continuum that is embedded throughout the intervention educational materials and activities. This process supports change by helping providers and families to better address specific challenges and also reinforces the unique strengths of the individuals in the family. Conducting follow-up remote

TABLE 11.1 Measures

Measures	*Reference*
Parent Measures	
McMaster Family Assessment Device (FAD)	Epstein et al., 1983
Brief Symptom Inventory 18 (BSI 18)	Derogatis, 2000
PTSD Checklist – Military/Civilian (PCLM/C)	Weathers et al., 1993
UCLA Grief Screening Questionnaire	Layne et al., 2008
FOCUS Impact Rating Scale – Parent	Adapted from Beardslee et al., 1992
FOCUS Satisfaction Rating	Saltzman et al., 2009
Parent Report on Child Strength and Difficulties Questionnaire/Parent (SDQ)	Goodman & Scott, 1999
Child/Adolescent Measures	
Kidcope	Spirito et al., 1988
Children's Depression Inventory (CDI)	Kovacs, 1985
Multidimensional Anxiety Scale for Children (MASC)	March, 1998
Strength and Difficulties Questionnaire (SDQ) – Youth Version	Goodman & Scott, 1999
FOCUS Satisfaction Rating	Saltzman et al., 2009
Provider Measures	
Global Assessment of Functioning (GAF) – Adult	APA, 2000
Global Assessment of Functioning (GAF) – Child	APA, 2000

Families OverComing Under Stress (FOCUS) **237**

check-ins helps to monitor goal attainment, support referrals, and identify the need for booster sessions or other services in the community.

Psychoeducation and Developmental Guidance

The FOCUS intervention provides developmentally appropriate parent and child education about: a) stress reactions, including helping the family to identify reminders that trigger unhelpful responses, and linking specific stress reactions to disruptions in family cohesion, communication, routines, and parenting activities; b) effective management of family routines and roles; c) development of positive parenting practices; and d) guidance about child development and common stress reactions. Education may cover many topics including developmental guidance, understanding symptoms and behaviors associated with diagnoses, navigation of systems of care, and advocating for family needs.

Construction of Narrative Timelines

During the initial set of parent-only and child-only sessions, parents and children construct graphic narratives of major family milestones and stressful events, with particular attention to separation and reunions. These narratives are shared during the final sessions attended by the entire family. The narrative timeline activity supports self- and family-level reflection on shared experiences, as well as sharing of individual perceptions of past and present experiences. Sharing perspectives helps families to clarify misunderstandings and address cognitive distortions/misattributions that may interfere with a shared sense of meaning. The narrative activity enables families to support one another more effectively and to value their strengths even in the context of adversity (Beardslee et al., 2013; Saltzman et al., 2013).

Skills Training

FOCUS utilizes skills training processes, activities, and content from the three foundational interventions to develop and practice individual and family-level skills designed to promote resilience, including: a) emotional regulation using tools and activities such as a feeling thermometer that each member of the family learns to employ in order to support affect identification, communicate about emotions, and develop and practice skills that support parent and child behavioral and emotional regulation; b) problem-solving techniques that support the family's ability to face challenges in a clear, step-by-step manner; c) communication skills to develop the ability to express experiences and assert preferences while also appreciating those of another person, as well as supporting effective parent–child communication, clear limit setting, and stable care routines; d) managing stress, trauma, or loss reminders, which supports parents

238 Patricia Lester et al.

and children in recognizing and planning for the impact of stress reminders or behavioral triggers resulting from exposure to stress, trauma, or loss; and e) goal setting to support parents and children in setting achievable goals, both individually and as a family.

Using a Family Resilience Framework for Military Families during Wartime

FOCUS draws upon a model of family resilience informed by family systems and social ecological framework that identifies the protective role of specific family-level processes (Walsh, 2006). Within the FOCUS model, core intervention elements are designed to enhance these processes by identifying existing family strengths and difficulties and then training family members on specific psychoeducation, skills, and practices that support enhanced family and individual resilience in the context of traumatic or stressful exposures (Lester, Petersen et al., 2010; Saltzman et al., 2011; Walsh, 2006).

We define resilience as a dynamic process within a system that encompasses positive adaptation (and not merely the absence of pathology or dysfunction) within the context of significant adversity (Luthar, 2006; Masten, 2013). While early conceptions of resilience focused on the role of individual traits contributing to childhood hardiness or "invulnerability" (Rutter, 1985), subsequent longitudinal studies have permitted more in-depth analyses of resilient processes, highlighted the importance of early caregiving relationships as predictors of child resilience when exposed to hardship, trauma, or loss, and emphasized the importance of families and the broader ecological contexts surrounding the child (Sroufe, 2005; Werner, 1993). In particular, these studies have demonstrated that children's outcomes in the face of adverse events are significantly mediated by the quality of parenting and the caregiving environment (for review, see Masten, 2004).

Longitudinal research on resilience has evolved from a focus on indicators of risk and resilience to the clarification of specific mechanisms of action that may support or undermine resilient functioning (Layne et al., 2007, 2009; Luthar, 2006; Rutter, 2006). Converging clinical and epidemiological research has identified five interrelated sets of family processes theorized to serve as risk mechanisms for families exposed to stressful circumstances, and these appear amenable to change via a relatively brief intervention (Luthar, 2006; Walsh, 2006).

As an applied example, these risk mechanisms are described briefly below in the context of challenges faced by military families in the context of wartime service (Lester, Leskin et al., 2010). Each risk mechanism is followed by a description of family processes theorized to function as mechanisms of family resilience. Taken together, these mechanisms of risk and resilience provide a useful framework to appreciate the role of the FOCUS intervention as adapted specifically for military families. A resilience model that focuses on positive adaptation in the face of stress and ongoing difficulties is well suited to the needs of the military family experiencing multiple wartime deployments and living with the impact of postwar trauma and loss (Lester, Leskin et al., 2010; Saltzman et al., 2013).

Mechanisms of Risk for Military Families during Wartime

Incomplete Understanding of the Impact of Wartime Separations and Combat-Related Stress and Injuries, and Inaccurate Developmental Expectations

A large number of returning service members and their spouses experience distress and clinically significant levels of depression and anxiety (Eaton et al., 2008; Lester, Petersen et al., 2010). Research has described specific ways in which parental psychological disturbance impairs marital, parental, and, ultimately, family functioning (Galovski & Lyons, 2004; Palmer, 2008). For example, parents with even sub-clinical levels of post-traumatic stress may have difficulty tolerating everyday household stressors, reacting with anger or aggression or by psychologically or physically distancing themselves from family activities (Galovski & Lyons, 2004). On the positive side, research has shown that providing a family member with information on the nature, cause, and specific manifestations of deployment and reintegration challenges can enable a spouse to be more flexible and understanding (Renshaw, Rodriques, & Jones, 2008) and for children to recognize that neither their parent's condition nor related family problems are their fault (Beardslee, 2002). Similarly, parents who are knowledgeable about expected reactions to stress in children of different ages are better able to avoid worrying unnecessarily about transient child stress reactions and respond appropriately to more serious or persistent behaviors (Rosenheck, 1986).

Impaired Family Communication

When a family is repeatedly separated, with one parent in a war zone and the rest of the family at home negotiating a very different daily reality, significant discrepancies in experience and missed opportunities for parent–child connections can result (Lester, Petersen et al., 2010; MacDonald, Chamberlain, Long, & Flett, 1999). Bridging these gaps requires specific communication skills and attitudes that may be particularly undermined when a parent experiences emotional numbing or avoidance related to post-traumatic stress or depression (Lincoln, Swift, & Shorteno-Fraser, 2008). The disruption of open and emotionally responsive communication across the family frequently impairs marital, co-parenting, and parent–child relationships, which in turn may spill over to a child's daily experiences and diminish the family's capacity to provide timely and appropriate support to each other (Cozza, Chun, & Polo, 2005; Sherman et al., 2005). The result of impaired communication can be a reduced sense of family closeness, warmth, and support—each of which has been identified as a vital component of family resilience processes (Walsh, 2006, 2007).

Impaired Parenting Practices

Impaired parenting practices are among the most potent predictors of poor child adaptation (Gewirtz et al., 2008). Researchers and clinicians have identified linked reactions within families that may undermine parenting practices in the context of stress. For example, a parent with post-traumatic stress may have disrupted sleep and heightened arousal and irritability that contribute to increases in spousal and family conflict and result in parental inability to maintain positive parenting practices (Galovski & Lyons, 2004; Lester, Leskin et al., 2010). Families contending with the care of an injured parent frequently experience "resource depletion" in terms of parental time, patience, and ability to maintain consistent care routines (Cozza et al., 2005). Risk may also be increased when a traumatized or anxious parent adopts more rigid, coercive, or authoritarian styles of parenting (Saltzman, Layne, & Steinberg, 2002).

Disrupted Family Organization

Resilient families have been often characterized by a flexible structure that balances strong parental leadership with the capacity to accommodate change even during stressful or disruptive family experiences (Kelley, Herzog-Simmer, & Harris, 1994). Less resilient families may be either overly rigid or chaotic, providing either too much or too little structure (Walsh, 2006).

Derailment of the Family's Guiding Belief Systems

A family's ability to make sense of a stressful or traumatic experience and endow it with meaning is central to the adaptive functioning of its members (Antonovsky, 1998). This capacity is aided by adherence to a common set of beliefs or transcendent values (Patterson & Garwick, 1994; Walsh, 2006). A threat to foundational family beliefs may thus be seen as a potential threat to a family's overall resilient functioning.

Mechanisms of Resilience in Military Families

Just as stress and adversity can initiate negative cascades within families that undermine adjustment, positive chain reactions can be strategically set in motion to enhance individual and family resilience (Rutter, 1999). In this section, we

Families OverComing Under Stress (FOCUS) **241**

describe how the FOCUS intervention's core elements have been designed to enhance adaptive family processes that support both individual and family resilience processes.

Providing Accurate, Developmentally Appropriate Information

In helping family members understand the impact of deployment separation, parental distress, and injury on children, clinicians can help families anticipate, address, and reduce expectable disruptions. Among these are excessively blaming the service member for symptoms directly related to PTSD, TBI, or the emotional sequelae of any identifiable physical or psychological injury. It is also important to help the service member desist from excessive self-blame and to help the children to better understand a parent's symptom-driven reactions and sometimes confusing or inappropriate behavior as manifestations of the injury and not due to anything they have done (Beardslee & Knitzer, 2003). Once provided with appropriate developmental guidance, family members may also be in a better position to discriminate between benign and problematic reactions to stress and change (Mogil et al., 2010).

Supporting Open and Effective Communication

Resilient families have been characterized by the ability to have direct, clear, consistent, and honest communication, and the capacity to tolerate open expression of emotion (Walsh, 2003, 2006). These capacities are especially important for families experiencing stress and change, given that unclear, distorted, or vague communication can rob family members of the essential tools for successfully adapting to challenges. Moreover, when parents withhold or "put a happy face" on communications about serious or difficult issues, they leave blanks that children fill in, often with their worst imaginings (Greene, Anderson, Hetherington, Forgatch, & DeGarmo, 2003). As such, it is important to work within the personal and cultural framework of each family and help them to find appropriate ways to invite sharing of a wide range of feelings and extend a tolerance for differences and the expression of strong emotions (Bowen, 1978; Walsh, 2006).

Enhancing Individual and Family Skills

In addition to effective communication, additional skill sets and coping strategies can help families anticipate, plan for, and mitigate the impact of stressful events, which can improve child adjustment (Saltzman, Lester et al., 2009; Spoth et al., 2002). Within the FOCUS intervention, these core skills include affect identification and emotional regulation, collaborative goal setting and problem solving, and managing trauma and loss reminders. For optimal utility, it is important that these skills be taught and practiced at both the individual and family level. For example, family members can be trained to collectively manage stress by identifying and anticipating stressful situations, monitoring idiosyncratic expressions of distress among different family members, and providing appropriate support in a timely and developmentally appropriate manner; they can be given structured opportunities to practice collaborative goal setting and problem solving; and they can work as a team to identify combat and deployment reminders and develop strategies to minimize disruptive reactions.

Developing Effective and Coordinated Parent Leadership

Parents should be supported to provide clear and consistent leadership for their family unit in order to clarify roles and reduce uncertainty during stressful times. As noted previously, parental distress and psychopathology may result in impaired forms of parenting that lead to reduced parental availability, limited engagement and monitoring, inconsistent care routines and discipline, and, in many cases, disruptive or problematic child behavior. Various tools may promote consistent and coordinated parental leadership in accordance with a co-parenting model. Co-parenting refers to a set of values and practices that lead to a co-equal and mutually supportive approach to parenting. In order to effectively co-parent, parents must learn to communicate clearly with each other, support each other, and collaboratively negotiate childrearing decisions and disagreements, along with family roles and duties (Feinberg, 2002). Movement towards effective co-parenting is often facilitated by parents' conjoint sharing of their personal narratives and guided exercises to align parenting efforts (Saltzman, Babayan, Lester, Beardslee, & Pynoos, 2009).

Developing Shared Family Understanding

After one or more wartime deployments, disparate experiences and problematic interpretations often occur between a service member and his or her family. Children often have difficulty understanding these experiences and have questions or concerns they are hesitant to raise with their parents, often resulting in misattributions about the meaning of events or their parent's actions. Bridging these gaps in understanding and clarifying questions and misattributions help to restore family closeness during the reintegration period (Palmer, 2008; Sherman et al., 2005). Unfortunately, there are numerous factors that may interfere with this process, including parental distress and/or injuries, limited communication skills, and constraining family or cultural expectations. By providing a family with a structured and safe forum for individual members to share experiences, reactions, fears, and ongoing concerns, and to then collectively craft a family narrative, a number of critical family processes and capabilities can be developed in service of improved adaptation and resilience.

Framework for Large-Scale Dissemination of FOCUS for Military Families

In 2008, the US Navy Bureau of Medicine and Surgery (BUMED) contracted with the UCLA Semel Institute to implement the FOCUS intervention program as the FOCUS Project (www.focusproject.org) at seven US Navy and Marine Corps installations in the United States and Japan. Based on successful initial implementation, the program was expanded and received support from the US Department of Defense (DOD) Office of Community and Family Policy to provide FOCUS services to US Army and Air Force families at selected sites. By 2014, FOCUS was being delivered at 24 active duty installations.

Military installations are designed as inclusive, self-contained systems of care for service members and their families. The public health framework used to implement FOCUS leveraged this unique design. The self-contained nature of the base facilitated implementation of a comprehensive continuum of approaches to reach military families. The FOCUS implementation for military families was imagined and implemented as a suite of services from universal to selective and indicated prevention, consistent with the preventive behavioral health model supported by the NRC & Institute of Medicine (2009a). The closed service ecology of the military installation readily supported this strategy of implementation as a continuum of less intensive to more intensive prevention suite of services using the FOCUS model core elements through group-level briefs, psychoeducational workshops, interactive skill building groups for adults and children, family and provider consultations, and the eight-session FOCUS intervention with individual families.

Developed in close partnership with military communities (providers, leaders, family members), the FOCUS implementation plan was conceptualized to decrease potential stigma associated with accessing and receiving a behavioral health preventive intervention, with the goal of supporting the overall well-being of the family, rather than addressing an identified problem or illness. FOCUS was identified as a non-clinical prevention program designed to support resilience within the family through education and skills training. Further, the "suite of services" all emphasized the goal of strengthening the family as a unit, as well as co-parenting and parent–child relationships. Interventionists were identified as "Resiliency Trainers." Structurally, participation in FOCUS was not noted in a service member's service or medical record and participation was voluntary and confidential. Wherever possible, services were located in a neutral community setting, not near mental health services. FOCUS offices were decorated to be "child-friendly" and maintained family-friendly evening and weekend hours.

The multi-site facet of FOCUS implementation posed an array of challenges around staff administrative and intervention model training and supervision at a range of different military installations (e.g., international and national; service

244 Patricia Lester et al.

branch cultural differences; urban and rural). FOCUS intervention training utilizes a "learning collaborative" training model that allows for practitioners from multiple organizations to join together and engage both initial training and ongoing learning and supervision. This learning collaborative framework was applied to training and ongoing education and development of staff, with the goal of building a community of expertise across geographically distributed installation sites.

While the foundations of the FOCUS model had been identified as evidence-based interventions, the adaption of FOCUS for military families had not undergone a standard biomedical validation model at the time of implementation due to the urgency of the public health need. Further, the rapidly evolving nature of challenges facing the military during wartime mandated that we be responsive to emerging and often unanticipated needs (such as types of injury, wartime duties), as well as differences in needs (service branches and regional differences). We adopted a continuous quality improvement model, which has been identified as a strategy to promote data-driven innovation with the design and diffusion of evidence-based practices (Rotheram-Borus, Swendeman, & Chorpita, 2012; Chorpita, Daleiden, & Weisz, 2005). The implementation plan included the use of a data-monitoring infrastructure to support real-time monitoring of system-wide factors vital to successful implementation, including monitoring outreach and marketing, tracking participation across tiers of services, participant engagement and retention, and referral tracking into and out of the program. Program data monitoring also required an integration of family and provider assessment to inform intervention delivery and referrals, session-level reporting to monitor model fidelity, and immediate reporting to ensure continuous quality improvement and control cycles. A collaborative team involving computer programmers, intervention designers and model supervisors, evaluation methodologists, and operations managers developed a HIPAA-secure, cloud-based assessment and data management platform by modifying a commercially available management platform (SalesForce) and survey tool (Survey Gizmo). Its capacity includes the ability to track all family outreach and marketing activities, manage contacts (family, community, providers, organizations), conduct real-time family-level screening and feedback, monitor fidelity to the FOCUS core elements at the session, family, and provider level, and track detailed referrals into and out of the program, insuring continuous evaluation of the program's effectiveness and supporting the programs responsiveness to emerging community needs (Beardslee et al., 2013).

A number of needs were identified through this monitoring process, including the need for intervention modifications for military families who either did not have children or did not have children in the defined age group. As described previously (Beardslee et al., 2013), the intervention team adapted the four core elements to couples, wounded warrior families and couples, and for families with very young children (aged 3–4). Additionally, the demands of geographical separation and high mobility underscored the need for remote delivery platforms, including an interactive, animated, web-based program with games, activities, and educational resources (www.focusworld.org), a mobile app for families with on-line skill-building games, resilience check-in surveys and feedback, and parent resources (http://nfrc.ucla.edu/focus-on-the-go), as well as through a remote in-home, provider-led video teleconferencing delivery platform (Beardslee et al., 2013).

Evidence of Effectiveness: FOCUS Project Evaluation for Military Families

Between 2008 and 2013, the FOCUS Project service implementation has delivered a family-centered suite of prevention services to over 500,000 military children, spouses/partners, service members, providers, leadership, and community members (Beardslee et al., 2011; Defense Centers of Excellence, 2010, 2013; Lester et al., 2013).

We report here on the effects of the most intensive of the suite of services delivered through this service project: the FOCUS family preventive intervention for military parents and children that is delivered at the individual family level. From the outset, this intervention has been evaluated within a quality improvement frame using a pre-test/post-test longitudinal design with follow-ups at exit, 1 month, and 4 to 6 months post-intervention. Outcome data from multiple sources (parent-self, parent/child, child-self, and provider report) have been collected to ensure that the intervention was having the desired effects as a service program, as well as to inform ongoing quality control/quality improvement processes. Standardized psychosocial adjustment measures were collected to identify psychological health risk in parents and children, to inform appropriate referrals, and to personalize intervention delivery (education and skill enhancement at the family level). Notably, these participant- and provider-report outcomes are integrated with a larger web-based program management system that enables linking of intervention process data (such as outreach, referral, attendance, fidelity monitoring) with individual and family outcomes.

These data were collected as an ongoing evaluation of the FOCUS prevention educational services program that was accessible to *all* military families with children aged 4–17 who expressed interest in participating and who were not experiencing active domestic violence or child abuse. Because this was implemented as a service program available to support military families affected by wartime deployments in an urgent climate of high operational tempo, a randomization of families to intervention and control conditions was not feasible. From the initial period of implementation of the FOCUS Project, Lester and colleagues (2012) reported a triangulated (child self-report, parent self-report, parent child-report, provider report) assessment including 488 families (742 parents and 873 children) with pre, post, and longitudinal outcomes for 331 families who completed the eight-session intervention. In brief, primary measures included the Brief Symptom Inventory (BSI) for parents and the Strengths and Difficulties Questionnaire (SDQ) completed at 1 and 4 to 6 months post-intervention, as well as the McMaster Family Assessment Device (FAD) and other parent and child report measures for program entry and exit (Derogatis, 2000; Goodman & Scott, 1999; Epstein, Baldwin, & Bishop, 1983). Intervention providers completed the Global Assessment of Functioning (GAF) at baseline and follow-up for both adults and children (APA, 2000). Parents were also asked to rate their perceptions of change and overall satisfaction with the program; child and parent psychological health outcomes were monitored pre- and post-intervention and at 1 month and 4 to 6 months follow-up using the Strength and Difficulties Questionnaire (SDQ), Parent Report Version for child outcomes (Goodman & Scott, 1999). A complete battery of the intervention outcome measures is provided in Table 11.1.

In terms of intervention effects, change scores across BSI domains identified showed significant reductions in anxiety and depressive symptoms for both civilian parents and service member parents. GAF rating for overall functioning was also significantly improved. Notably, the parents' scores at the clinically significant levels for anxiety and depression decreased by half. For child psychological health outcomes, change scores showed significant reductions of total difficulties in scores for boys and girls across all age groups (preschool, school age, and adolescents) and significant and meaningful reductions in number of children falling in the clinically significant range in conduct problems, emotional symptoms, and total difficulties. On self-reported coping assessment (Kidcope), children aged 7–17 reported greater use of positive coping strategies in the areas of emotional regulation, problem solving, cognitive restructuring, and increased use of social support (Spirito, Starke, & Williams, 1988). Emotion regulation, problem solving, and cognitive restructuring were specific strategies taught through the intervention.

Lester et al. (2013) also reported on the relationships of distress among family members and pathways of program impact on child development using structural equation modeling with a subsample of 280 families (505 children). This study demonstrated that among younger children, boys were more likely to have distress than older children and girls. At a family level, greater distress in the service member parent predicted increased numbers of visits attended in the intervention, and number of sessions attended predicted more positive changes in the FAD, which in turn predicted greater improvement in child adjustment at 4–6 month follow-up. Individual components of the FAD that were most influential included affective involvement, problem solving, and communication, which are dimensions targeted by the intervention. Thus, our path model confirmed our theoretically targeted intervention (Epstein et al., 1983).

Additionally, the contributions from this intervention's implementation evidence have been highlighted as positive examples of rigorous evaluation designs for service program implementation in recent reports from the IOM (2013) and *The Future of Children* (Lester & Flake, 2013).

Evaluation Challenges and Opportunities Going Forward

The challenges of both meeting the needs of families and evaluating the FOCUS family intervention without a randomized design are considerable, but in our view, this situation is not uncommon in designing and disseminating interventions to respond rapidly to real-world salient needs. Threats to internal validity cannot be fully ruled out with the pre-test/post-test repeated measures longitudinal design. Nonetheless, the intervention effect sizes that have been obtained thus far in evaluating the intervention have supported that clinically significant effects are clearly sustained over time, suggesting that the intervention is efficacious. More recently, as our work has evolved, two randomized trials of variations of the FOCUS intervention are underway—one an adaptation for combat-injured families that includes a standard care control arm, and one for families with young children, with a web-based parenting information-only control condition.

In the future, more systematic evaluations of the multiple levels of FOCUS are needed, including the less intense interventions ("suite of services"), to determine their effectiveness. In addition, another question that warrants further investigation is for whom, and under what circumstances, does the FOCUS intervention work? Addressing this question would allow us to adapt the intervention more fully to the unique needs of different groups. For example, understanding how cultural and ethnic factors influence intervention uptake is important. Greater research is also needed to adequately characterize both the systems in which this and other interventions are implemented and what contributes to effective intervention within these different systems. Overall, family-based preventions have proved cost effective and valuable, but increased cost-benefit data are needed for these approaches, particularly for families at risk, such as military and veteran families.

Access to Program and Training

Training in the FOCUS intervention and family of adapted interventions (e.g. Couples, Wounded Warrior Families) is available through the UCLA Nathanson Family Resilience Center Training Institute (NFRC; nfrc.ucla.edu). This training model was put forth by the Institute for Healthcare Improvement and has been used within SAMHSA and its National Child Traumatic Stress Network for dissemination of evidence-based practices (IHI, 2003).

For the FOCUS Project dissemination with military families, interventionist training starts as a distance process supported by pre-training through the NFRC on-line learning center. Pre-training consists of a 20-hour curriculum that includes on-line independent learning through reading, video demonstrations, expert presentations, and knowledge checks. Content includes the background of the population and adversity (such as combat-related post-traumatic stress, physical injuries, and child reactions regarding separations), the intervention model, review of the intervention manual and on-line session demonstrations, and important cultural considerations for diverse target populations. This allows trainees to adequately prepare for an intensive, interactive face-to-face training utilizing modeling videos and interactive activities.

The interventionist is assigned an experienced mentor to provide peer guidance through regular phone meetings, as well as a Master Trainer (licensed clinical psychologist) to provide guidance regarding the pre-training process. The in-person training includes the application of core elements and key characteristics of FOCUS through guided role plays. Following the in-person training, practitioners return to their delivery site, where they join an experienced interventionist to co-facilitate delivery until they have demonstrated competency in each intervention session. The supervision covers both care of families and direction in negotiating the complex network of military command and service providers.

Further, the on-line progress notes are reviewed for proper utilization of the real-time screening platform, documentation of delivery process, fidelity checks, and appropriate referral and follow-up. Until certified, providers receive ongoing model supervision from a Master Trainer to ensure fidelity to the model as well as sharing of best practices and lessons learned. In this collaborative learning framework, focus is on skill acquisition in intervention delivery, as well as the identification and sharing of implementation experiences at the specific military installation. Together, this results in a continuous improvement process that reduces the gap between actual practice and best practices (Rotheram-Borus et al., 2012).

Training utilizes video- and tele-conferencing capability in the form of weekly model supervision and agency consultation calls. The NFRC on-line learning center supports ongoing training in advanced topics, sharing of best practices, and mutual inter-agency support. In this platform, we use video demonstrations of both basic and advanced skills, share documents and intervention materials, and host forums for practitioners to post questions and get ideas about recruitment, outreach, and implementation from other agencies. To prepare staff to work with their local communities, the training describes differences between and within each service branch and includes material about the specific military installations, differences in deployment experiences and cycles, and community norms and values. The shared training experience leads to a strong *esprit de corps* and provides a basis for ongoing dialogue via the on-line learning center platform. Central to the training strategy is provision of core supervisory support, both as-needed and on a regular basis, as well as

Families OverComing Under Stress (FOCUS)

continued training relevant to emerging science, community issues, and quality improvement. In addition to ensuring effective intervention delivery, model supervisors are consulted to problem-solve about such implementation matters as finding office space, building relationships, and networking.

Lessons Learned for Family Prevention from the FOCUS Intervention

FOCUS and its foundational interventions are grounded in the larger field of research on family preventive interventions, and consistent with other interventions in this volume, it has been developed with attention to the use of assessment-driven protocols, emphasis on psychoeducation and developmental guidance, learning and practicing cognitive and behavioral coping skills that promote emotional and behavioral regulation, and the development of positive parenting practices and parent–child relationships. However, perhaps distinct from the other models, which identify child outcomes as primary targets of prevention, the FOCUS framework proposes a theoretical model that frames the reverberating impact of stress, trauma, or adversity as potentially disruptive to any combination of individuals and relationships within the family system. Thus, FOCUS specifically targets both adult and child psychosocial adjustment through core elements that are designed to reduce individual (parent and child) psychological health symptoms directly as well as through enhanced parenting and family-level processes; this intervention addresses stress at the level of the family unit, rather than addressing a specific individual's risk or symptoms, such as youth with behavioral problems. The observation that long-term improvements were seen in both parents and youth in the foundational intervention provides support for this framework, as does the longitudinal outcomes from the large-scale service implementation (Rotheram-Borus et al., 2004; Lester et al., 2012). Additionally, because FOCUS was adapted for families affected by deployment-related experiences, such as separation in the context of danger, and combat-related traumatic exposures, the model includes trauma-informed education and cognitive behavioral management skills that are typically not included in family preventive interventions (Saltzman, Lester et al., 2009).

The design and dissemination of FOCUS highlights specific challenges and opportunities for integrating the advancements in family prevention and implementation science in the context of urgent public health challenges, and perhaps for rethinking approaches to traditional biomedical validation models for intervention development. Through an integrated web-based data management platform, the implementation and scaling of FOCUS within the US military provides an example of a successful "disruptive innovation," one which highlights the potential of continuous data monitoring for applying the broad knowledge base developed within prevention science to respond to a rapidly moving public health target. We would propose that the lessons learned

250 Patricia Lester et al.

from the design and diffusion of FOCUS for military families can also help to advance approaches to the development and implementation of family-centered prevention programs in civilian populations.

References

American Psychiatric Association. (2000). *Diagnostic and statistical manual of mental disorders* (4th ed., text revision). Washington, DC: American Psychiatric Association.

Antonovsky, A. (1998). The sense of coherence: An historical and future perspective. In H. McCubbin, E. Thompson, A. Thompson, & J. Fromer (Eds.), *Stress, coping, and health in families: Sense of coherence and resiliency* (pp. 3–20). Thousand Oaks, CA: Sage.

Beardslee, W. R. (1984). Familial influences in childhood depression. *Pediatric Annals, 13*(1), 32–36.

Beardslee, W. R. (2002). *Out of the darkened room: Protecting the children and strengthening the family when a parent is depressed* (1st ed.). Boston, MA: Little, Brown and Company.

Beardslee, W. R., Gladstone, T. R. G., Wright, E. J., & Cooper, A. B. (2003). A family-based approach to the prevention of depressive symptoms in children at risk: Evidence of parental and child change. *Pediatrics, 112*, e119–e131.

Beardslee, W. R., Klosinski, L. E., Saltzman, W., Mogil, C., Pangelinan, S., McKnight, C. P., & Lester, P. (2013). Dissemination of family-centered prevention for military and veteran families: Adaptations and adoption within community and military systems of care. *Clinical Child and Family Psychology Review, 16*(4), 394–409.

Beardslee, W. R., & Knitzer, J. (2003). Strengths-based family mental health services: A family systems approach. In K. Maton, C. Schellenbach, B. Leadbeater, & A. Solarz (Eds.), *Investing in children, youth, families, and communities: Strengths-based research and policy* (pp. 157–171). Washington, DC: American Psychological Association.

Beardslee, W. R., Lester, P., Klosinski, L., Saltzman, W., Woodward, K., Nash, W. et al. (2011). Family-centered preventive intervention for military families: Implications for implementation science. *Prevention Science, 12*(4), 339–348.

Beardslee, W. R., Salt, P., Porterfield, K., Rotherberg, P. C., Van De Velde, P., Swatling, S. et al. (1992). Comparison of preventive interventions for families with parental affective disorder. *Journal of the American Academy of Child & Adolescent Psychiatry, 32*(2), 254–263.

Beardslee, W. R., & Wheelock, I. (1994). Children of parents with affective disorders; Empirical findings and clinical implications. In W. M. Reynolds & H. P. Johnston (Eds.), *Handbook of depression in children and adolescents* (pp. 463–479). New York: Plenum.

Beardslee, W. R., Wright, E. J., Gladstone, T. R. G., & Forbes, P. (2007). Long-term effects from a randomized trial of two public health preventive interventions for parental depression. *Journal of Family Psychology, 21*(4), 703–713.

Biglan, A., Flay, B. R., Embry, D. D., & Sandler, I. N. (2012). The critical role of nurturing environments for promoting human well-being. *American Psychologist, 67*(4), 257.

Bowen, M. (1978). *Family therapy in clinical practice*. New York: Jason Aronson.

Bronfenbrenner, U. (1977a). Toward an experimental ecology of human development. *American Psychologist, 32*(7), 513–531.

Bronfenbrenner, U. (1977b). Lewinian space and ecological substance. *Journal of Social Issues, 33*(4), 199–212.

Bronfenbrenner, U. (1986). Ecology of the family as a context for human development. *Developmental Psychology, 22*, 723–742.

Chairman of the Joints Chief of Staff (CJCS). (2010). Chairman of the Joints Chief of Staff Guide to the Chairman's Readiness System. Retrieved from http://www.dtic. mil/cjcs_directives/cdata/unlimit/g3401.pdf

Chorpita, B. F., Daleiden, E. L., & Weisz, J. R. (2005). Identifying and selecting the common elements of evidence-based interventions: A distillation and matching model. *Mental Health Services Research, 7*, 5–20.

Cozza, S., Chun, R. S., & Polo, J. A. (2005). Military families and children during operation Iraqi Freedom. *Psychiatric Quarterly, 76*(4), 371–378.

D'Angelo, E. J., Llerena-Quinn, R., Shapiro, R., Colon, F., Rodriguez, P., Gallagher, K., & Beardslee, W. R. (2009). Adaptation of the Preventive Intervention Program for Depression for use with predominantly low-income Latino families. *Family Process, 48*(2), 269–291.

Derogatis, L. R. (2000). *Brief Symptom Inventory 18.* Minneapolis, MN: National Computer Systems Pearson.

Eaton, K. M., Hoge, C. W., Messer, S. C., Whitt, A. A., Cabrera, O. A., McGurk, D. et al. (2008). Prevalence of mental health problems, treatment need, and barriers to care among primary care-seeking spouses of military service members involved in Iraq and Afghanistan deployments. *Military Medicine, 173*(11), 1051–1056.

Epstein, N. B., Baldwin, L. M., & Bishop, D. S. (1983). The McMaster Family Assessment Device. *Journal of Marital and Family Therapy, 9*, 171–180.

Feinberg, M. E. (2002). Coparenting and the transition to parenthood: A framework for prevention. *Clinical Child and Family Psychology Review, 5*, 173–195.

Fiese, B. H., Rhodes, H. G., & Beardslee, W. R. (2013). Rapid changes in American family life: Consequences for child health and pediatric practice. *Pediatrics, 132*(3), 552–559.

Galovski, T. E., & Lyons, J. (2004). The psychological sequelae of exposure to combat violence: A review of the impact on the veteran's family. *Aggression and Violent Behavior: A Review Journal, 9*, 477–501.

Gewirtz, A., Forgatch, M., & Wieling, E. (2008). Parenting practices as potential mechanisms for child adjustment following mass trauma. *Journal of Marital and Family Therapy, 34*(2), 177–192.

Goodman, R., & Scott, S. (1999). Comparing the Strengths and Difficulties Questionnaire and the Child Behavior Checklist: Is small beautiful? *Journal of Abnormal Child Psychology, 27*, 17–24.

Greene, S. M., Anderson, E., Hetherington, E. M., Forgatch, M. S., & DeGarmo, D. S. (2003). Risk and resilience after divorce. In F. Walsh (Ed.), *Normal family processes* (pp. 96–120). New York: The Guilford Press.

Holmes, A. K., Rauch, P. K., & Cozza, S. J. (2013). When a parent is injured or killed in combat. *The Future of Children: Military Children and Families, 23*(2), 143–162.

Howell, E., Golden, O., & Beardslee, W. (2013). Emerging opportunities for addressing maternal depression under Medicaid. Urban Institute. Retrieved from http://www.urban.org.

Institute for Healthcare Improvement. (2003). *The breakthrough series: IHI's collaborative model for achieving breakthrough improvement.* IHI Innovation Series white paper. Boston.

IOM (Institute of Medicine). (2013). *Returning home from Iraq and Afghanistan: Assessment of readjustment needs of veterans, service members, and their families.* Washington, DC: The National Academies Press.

IOM (Institute of Medicine). (2014). *Preventing psychological disorders in service members and their families: An assessment of programs.* Washington, DC: The National Academies Press.

Kelley, M., Herzog-Simmer, P., & Harris, M. (1994). Effects of military-induced separation on the parenting stress and family functioning of deploying mothers. *Women in the Navy, 6,* 125–138.

Kovacs, M. (1985). The Children's Depression Inventory. *Psychopharmacology Bulletin, 21,* 995-998.

Kumpfer, K. L., Alvarado, R., Smith, P., & Bellamy, N. (2002). Cultural sensitivity in universal family-based prevention interventions. *Prevention Science, 3*(3), 241–244.

Layne, C. M., Beck, C. J., Rimmasch, H., Southwick, J. S., Moreno, M. A., & Hobfoll, S. E. (2009). Promoting "resilient" posttraumatic adjustment in childhood and beyond: "Unpacking" life events, adjustment trajectories, resources, and interventions. In D. Brom, R. Pat-Horenczyk, & J. Ford (Eds.), *Treating traumatized children: Risk, resilience, and recovery* (pp. 13–47). New York: Routledge.

Layne, C. M., Saltzman, W. R., Poppleton, L., Burlingame, G. M., Pasalic, A., Durakovic, E. et al. (2008). Effectiveness of a school-based group psychotherapy program for war-exposed adolescents: A randomized controlled trial. *Journal of the American Academy of Child & Adolescent Psychiatry, 47,* 1048–1062.

Layne, C. M., Warren, J., Watson, P., & Shalev, A. (2007). Risk, vulnerability, resistance, and resilience: Towards an integrative conceptualization of posttraumatic adaptation. In M. M. Friedman, T. M. Keane, & P. A. Resick (Eds.), *Handbook of PTSD: Science and practice* (pp. 497–520). New York: Guilford.

Lee, M. B., Lester, P., & Rotheram-Borus, M. J. (2002). The relationship between adjustment of mothers with HIV and their adolescent daughters. *Clinical Child Psychology and Psychiatry, 7*(1), 71–84.

Lester, P., & Flake, E. (2013). How wartime military service affects children and families. *The Future of Children: Military Children and Families, 23*(2), 121–142.

Lester, P., Leskin, G., Woodward, K., Saltzman, W., Nash, W., Mogil, C. et al. (2010). Wartime deployment and military children: Applying prevention science to enhance family resilience. In S. M. Wadsworth & D. Riggs (Eds.), *Risk and resilience in US military families.* New York: Springer.

Lester, P., Mogil, C., Saltzman, W., Woodward, K., Nash, W., Leskin, G. et al. (2011). FOCUS (families overcoming under stress): Implementing family-centered prevention for military families facing wartime deployments and combat operational stress. *Military Medicine, 176*(1), 19–25.

Lester, P., Peterson, K., Reeves, J., Knauss, L., Glover, D., Mogil, C. et al. (2010). The long war and parental combat deployment: Effects on military children and at-home spouses. *Journal of the American Academy of Child and Adolescent Psychiatry, 49*(4), 310–320.

Lester, P., Rotheram-Borus, M. J., Elia, C., Elkavich, A., & Rice, E. (2008). TALK: Teens and adults learning to communicate. In C. W. LeCroy (Ed.), *Evidence-based treatment manuals for children and adolescents* (pp. 170–285). New York: Oxford University Press.

Lester, P., Saltzman, W., Woodward, K., Glover, D., Leskin, G., Bursch, B. et al. (2012). Evaluation of a family centered prevention intervention for military children and families facing wartime deployments. *American Journal of Public Health, 102* (Suppl 1): S48–54.

Lester, P., Stein, J. A., Saltzman, W., Woodward, K., MacDermid, S. W., Milburn, N. et al. (2013). Psychological health of military children: Longitudinal evaluation of a family centered prevention program to enhance family resilience. *Military Medicine, 178*(8), 838–845.

Lincoln, A., Swift, E., & Shorteno-Fraser, M. (2008). Psychological adjustment and treatment of children and families with parents deployed in military combat. *Journal of Clinical Psychology, 64*, 984–992.

Luthar, S. S. (2006). Resilience in development: A synthesis of research across five decades. In D. Cicchetti & D. J. Cohen (Eds.), *Developmental psychopathology: Risk, disorder, and adaptation* (pp. 740–795). New York: Wiley.

MacDermid Wadsworth, S., Lester, P., Marini, C., Cozza, S, Sornborger, J., Strouse, T., & Beardslee, W. (2013). Approaching family-focused systems of care for military and veteran families. *Military Behavioral Health, 1*, 1–10.

MacDonald, C., Chamberlain, K., Long, N., & Flett, R. (1999). Posttraumatic stress disorder and interpersonal functioning in Vietnam War veterans: A meditational model. *Journal of Traumatic Stress, 12*(4), 701–707.

March, J. (1998). *Manual for the Multidimensional Anxiety Scale for Children (MASC).* Toronto: Multi-Health Systems.

Masten, A. S. (2001). Ordinary magic: Resilience processes in development. *American Psychologist, 56*(3), 227–238.

Masten, A. S. (2004). Regulatory processes, risk, and resilience in adolescent development. *Annals of the New York Academy of Sciences, 1021*, 310–319.

Masten, A. S. (2013). Risk and resilience in development. In P. D. Zelazo (Ed.), *Oxford handbook of developmental psychology: Self and other* (Vol. 2, pp. 579–607). New York: Oxford University Press.

Mogil, C., Paley, B., Doud, T., Havens, T., Moore-Tyson, J., Beardslee, W., & Lester, P. (2010). Families OverComing Under Stress (FOCUS) for early childhood: Building resilience for young children in high stress families. *Journal of Zero to Three, 31*(1): 10–16.

National Research Council & Institute of Medicine. (2009a). *Preventing mental, emotional, and behavioral disorders among young people: Progress and possibilities.* Washington, DC: National Academies Press.

National Research Council & Institute of Medicine. (2009b). *Depression in parents, parenting and children: Opportunities to improve identification, treatment, and prevention efforts.* Washington, DC: The National Academies Press.

Paley, B., Lester, P., & Mogil, C. (2013). Family systems and ecological perspectives on the impact of deployment on military families. *Clinical Child and Family Psychology Review, 16*(3), 245–265.

Palmer, C. (2008). A theory of risk and resilience factors in military families. *Military Psychology, 20*, 205–217.

Patterson, J. M., & Garwick, A. W. (1994). Levels of family meaning in family stress theory. *Family Process, 33*, 287–304.

Podorefsky, D. L., McDonald-Dowdell, M., & Beardslee, W. R. (2001). Adaptation of preventive interventions for a low-income, culturally diverse community. *Journal of the American Academy of Child and Adolescent Psychiatry, 40*, 879–886.

Renshaw, K. D., Rodriques, C. S., & Jones, D. H. (2008). Psychological symptoms and marital satisfaction in spouses of Operation Iraqi Freedom veterans: Relationships

254 Patricia Lester et al.

with spouses' perceptions of veterans' experiences and symptoms. *Journal of Family Psychology, 22*(3), 586–594.

Rosenheck, R. (1986). Impact of posttraumatic stress disorder of World War II on the next generation. *Journal of Nervous and Mental Disease, 174*(6), 319–327.

Rotheram-Borus, M. J., Lee, M. B., Gwadz, M., & Draimin, B. (2001). An intervention for parents with AIDS and their adolescent children. *American Journal of Public Health, 91*(8), 1294–1302.

Rotheram-Borus, M. J., Lee, M., Lin, Y. Y., & Lester, P. (2004). Six year intervention outcomes for adolescent children of parents with HIV. *Archives of Pediatrics & Adolescent Medicine, 158,* 742–748.

Rotheram-Borus, M. J., Swendeman, D., & Chorpita, B. (2012). Disruptive innovations for designing and diffusing evidence-based interventions. *American Psychologist, 67,* 463–476.

Rutter, M. (1985). Resilience in the face of adversity: Protective factors and resistance to psychiatric disorder. *British Journal of Psychiatry, 147,* 598–611.

Rutter, M. (1999). Resilience concepts and findings: Implications for family therapy. *Journal of Family Therapy, 21*(2), 119–144.

Rutter, M. (2006). Promotion of resilience in the face of adversity. In A. Clarke Stewart & J. Dunn (Eds.), *Families count: Effects on child and adolescent development* (pp. 26–52). New York: Cambridge University Press.

Saltzman, W. R., Babayan, T., Lester, P., Beardslee, W. R., & Pynoos, R. S. (2009). Family-based treatment for child traumatic stress: A review and report on current innovations. In D. Brom, R. Pat-Horenczyk, & J. D. Ford (Eds.), *Treating traumatized children: Risk, resilience and recovery* (pp. 240–254). New York: Routledge/Taylor & Francis.

Saltzman, W. R., Layne, C. M., Steinberg, A. M., Arslanagic, B., & Pynoos, R. S. (2002). Developing a culturally-ecologically sound intervention program for youth exposed to war and terrorism. *Child and Child Psychiatric Clinics of North America, 12,* 319–342.

Saltzman, W. R., Lester, P., Beardslee, W. R., Layne, C. M., & Nash, W. P. (2011). Mechanisms of risk and resilience in military families: Theoretical and empirical basis of a family-focused resilience enhancement program. *Clinical Child and Family Psychology Review, 14*(3), 213–230.

Saltzman, W. R., Lester, P., Pynoos, R., Mogil, C., Green, S., Layne, C. M. et al. (2009). *FOCUS for military families: Individual family resiliency training manual* (2nd ed.). Unpublished manual, UCLA.

Saltzman, W. R., Pynoos, R. S., Lester, P., Layne, C. M., & Beardslee, W. R. (2013). Enhancing family resilience through family narrative co-construction. *Clinical Child and Family Psychology Review, 16*(3), 294–310.

Sherman, M. D., Zanotti, D. K., & Jones, D. E. (2005). Key elements in couples therapy with veterans with combat-related posttraumatic stress disorder. *Professional Psychology: Research and Practice, 36*(6), 626–633.

Spirito, A., Stark, L. J., & Williams, C. (1988). Development of a brief coping checklist for use with pediatric populations. *Journal of Pediatric Psychology, 13,* 555–574.

Spoth, R. L., Kavanagh, K., & Dishion, T. (2002). Family-centered preventive intervention science: Toward benefits to larger populations of children, youth, and families. *Prevention Science, 3,* 145–152.

Sroufe, L. A. (2005). Attachment and development: A prospective, longitudinal study from birth to adulthood. *Attachment and Human Development, 7,* 349–367.

Tanielian, T., & Jaycox, L. (2008). *Invisible wounds of war*. Santa Monica, CA: RAND Corporation.

Walsh, F. (2003). Family resilience: A framework for clinical practice. *Family Process, 42*(1), 1–18.

Walsh, F. (2006). *Strengthening family resilience* (2nd ed.). New York: Guilford Press.

Walsh, F. (2007). Traumatic loss and major disasters: Strengthening family and community resilience. *Family Process, 46*(2), 207–227.

Weathers, F., Litz, B., Herman, D., Huska, J., & Keane, T. (1993, October). The PTSD Checklist (PCL): Reliability, validity, and diagnostic utility. Paper presented at the Annual Convention of the International Society for Traumatic Stress Studies, San Antonio, TX.

Werner, E. E. (1993). Risk, resilience, and recovery: Perspectives from the Kauai longitudinal study. *Development and Psychopathology, 5*, 503–515.

Zelazo, P. D. (2013). Developmental psychology: A new synthesis. In P. D. Zelazo (Ed.), *The Oxford handbook of developmental psychology. Vol. 1: Body and mind* (pp. 3–12). New York: Oxford University Press.

12

CULTURAL AND GENDER ADAPTATIONS OF EVIDENCE-BASED FAMILY INTERVENTIONS

Karol L. Kumpfer, Catia Magalhães, Jing Xie, and Sheetal Kanse

This chapter will review culturally and gender-adapted evidence-based family prevention and intervention programs. The growing ethnic populations in the USA and other Western countries have created the need for the development and evaluation of culturally adapted programs. The rapid spread worldwide of Western youth culture has also made effective parenting more critical to youth outcomes in non-Western cultures, requiring an extension of the evidence base for family programs to include populations in Asia, the Americas and Africa.

Research also points out that these problem behaviors are growing among teenage girls and women (Kumpfer, 2014), creating a demand for programs specifically tailored to their needs. The increase in delinquency and substance abuse in girls began in the United States in the mid-1990s with a desire among young girls to be liberated from sex role stereotypes and to be able to engage in the same "adult" behaviors exhibited by boys (Kumpfer, Alvarado, & Whiteside, 2003). The question of how best to prevent problem behaviors in girls and whether the existing evidence-based prevention programs were effective for girls was initially raised in the late 2000s (Kumpfer, Smith, & Summerhays, 2008). To find out if the current programs were as effective for girls as for boys, the authors conducted a survey for the United Nations Office on Drugs and Crime (UNODC) in Vienna. The survey concluded that most program developers had never conducted a gender analysis. Of the few that had done so and published their results, all of the family-based programs were effective for both girls and boys, but the youth-only programs primarily worked only for boys and not for girls (Kumpfer, 2014; Kumpfer & Magalhães, in press). Given the paucity of research on these topics, this chapter will end with recommendations for further research on the effectiveness of family-based programs for different ethnic populations and genders.

Cultural Adaptations of Family-Based Programs

The Need for Cultural Adaptation of Evidence-Based Family Programs

Effectiveness research involves the implementation and outcome evaluation of programs in different contexts and with new populations, including new cultures (i.e., type 2 translational research; Ferrer-Wreder, Adamson, Kumpfer, & Eichas, 2012). Effectiveness research can also involve controlled replication studies of family-based programs in new populations whose utility has already been established for a particular sample in an efficacy trial (Valentine et al., 2011).

Many practitioners doubt the value of using evidence-based programs (EBPs) developed for different cultures or in other countries, because they believe effective programs must be developed locally using principles of effective prevention. This chapter stresses that "principles of effective prevention", while useful in designing new programs, do not in themselves guarantee that a prevention program works. Proof is reserved for programs tested in multiple randomized controlled trials and field trials with different populations and replicated by independent research teams. The best programs are those with the largest effect sizes and not just those with statistically significant results. It is our belief that culturally adapting and testing existing EBPs is the best way to create effective prevention programs that will work for diverse ethnicities, cultures, or countries.

The resistance to adopting EBPs from other countries often arises because of the perceived difficulties of adapting them to new cultures or new situations. Many manualized evidence-based programs have been criticized as being too rigid and inflexible. This is partially by design, given that the first mandate for replication in prevention science is to maintain fidelity by implementing the program exactly as written. Resistance to such strict replications often resulted in poorer outcomes with different cultures. Program developers with experience in dissemination research have argued against this rigid interpretation of "fidelity" (Kumpfer et al., 2012a; Mazzucchelli & Sanders, 2010), stressing that delivering a program with fidelity does not mean inflexible delivery. Every EBP can be locally and culturally adapted within bounds, as long as core content (i.e., the themes and structure of program sessions) is left intact. Learning the boundaries between desirable cultural adaptation and undesirable structural modification should be part of training and supervision. Implementers should be encouraged to work collaboratively with program developers, supervisors, and families to adapt programs to the unique needs and situational context while preserving the program's core content.

The evidence-based family programs presented in this book were, for the most part, developed in the United States and tested in randomized controlled trials (RCTs) funded by federal government research agencies within the National Institutes of Health (NIMH). Only one program, Triple P, was developed in another English language country—Australia. Consequently, until recently, few of these family programs had been translated into other languages or culturally adapted, and even fewer were evaluated in RCTs for efficacy in non-English-speaking and non-Western cultures. Program developers were also mainly of Western cultural roots. Though some EBPs are in use in different countries, these culturally adapted versions have rarely been evaluated for effectiveness or efficacy. For example, many have only non-experimental pre- and post-test designs. Because of the lack of information on the extent and effectiveness of dissemination and evaluation of these evidence-based family programs in non-Western cultures, a review of program results will be presented in this chapter.

More Ethnic Minority Families Need Family Services

Worldwide, families are increasingly mobile and moving to new communities or countries in search of work and a better life for themselves (Kumpfer, Pinyuchon, Baharudin, Nolrajsuwat, & Xie, in press). This increase in refugee and immigrant families has created an increasing need for effective prevention and treatment services in far-flung locations around the world.

In the United States, ethnic minorities now comprise 37% of the US population; by 2060, due to the higher birthrates and immigration rates of minority families, particularly Latin and Asian families (CDC, 2013; US Census Bureau, 2012), minority families are expected to grow to 57% of the population and become the majority. Unfortunately, these minority families rarely seek prevention and treatment services, except when mandated by the courts because of suspected child abuse, drug abuse, or crime. In more traditional non-Western cultures, fear of bringing shame on the family by divulging family problems, as well as a belief that problems should be solved within the family, often deters at-risk families from seeking help. Insufficient family resources to pay for services are also an issue for many minority families. Lack of trained family services workers who are from minority cultures and speak their language compounds the problem. This is changing rapidly, however, as more ethnic students are graduating from Western universities in these fields with a desire to help families in their own countries or within their own cultures in this country.

Lack of culturally tailored family programs for minorities

Research suggests that it is difficult to engage minority families because most programs do not fit their culture and are not taught in their primary language (Biglan & Metzler, 1999; McLean & Campbell, 2003; Watson, 2005). Participation of ethnic families can be as low as 10% in family programs (Kumpfer, Alvarado, Smith, & Bellamy, 2002). Most universal prevention programs are developed for the general American population, focusing mostly on White, middle-class values that could be culturally inappropriate and not address the needs of ethnic families. For example, traditional ethnic families often favor family systems change approaches for prevention (see Van Ryzin and Fosco, this volume) as compared to individual change approaches, because their cultural values stress interconnection, reciprocity, and filial responsibility as contrasted with the Western value of individual achievement (Boyd-Franklin, 2001; Kumpfer et al., 2002). Thus, family-based interventions could be more appealing, and potentially more effective, for minority families if they were appropriately adapted for minority cultures.

Because of growing minority populations in this country and other Western countries, ethnic families will need increased attention from services providers, policy makers, and government funding agencies to identify and prevent behavioral health problems. Majority families in countries outside of the United States also need access to effective parenting and family programs. The simplest way to provide these effective family services is to culturally adapt proven evidence-based parenting and family programs rather than starting from scratch. Starting with a proven program increases the chances for success. Unfortunately, few governments are willing to invest the funds to conduct randomized controlled trials to determine the efficacy of newly adapted programs. Although early cultural adaptations have not been able to improve outcomes significantly, they have dramatically increased the attendance and retention of minority families (Kumpfer et al., 2002), which is a key first step in creating a significant public health impact.

To more fully realize a significant public health impact, however, the field must move beyond simple language translation of EBPs; unfortunately, it is often unclear what sorts of cultural adaptations are required. Given the high costs of program development and evaluation, the paucity of research on the cost/benefit of culturally adapted programs is unsurprising. To make family-based programs work better for minority families, the field requires more research on the primary family issues in minority cultures, as well as a better understanding by Western family program developers of cultural and family traditions, health disparities, and existing culturally appropriate and effective family services in minority communities.

Specific risk and protective factors in ethnic families

Making family interventions more effective for ethnic families requires understanding their most salient risk and protective factors. Testing of etiological or causal models for major adolescent problems (e.g., substance abuse, delinquency, school failure, teen pregnancy) has been conducted using structural equation models (SEM) on large data sets of general populations of youth (Ary, Duncan, Biglan, Metzler, Noell, & Smolkowski, 1999) and for each major ethnic population of youth in the USA (Center for Substance Abuse

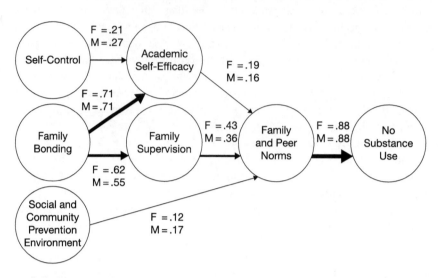

FIGURE 12.1 Social Ecology Model of Substance Abuse by Gender (Males/Females)

Prevention, 2000; Kumpfer et al., 2003; Sales, Sambrano, Springer, & Turner, 2003). As shown in Figure 12.1, the strongest pathway to poorer adolescent development is through the family (e.g., family bonding or parent/child attachment, supervision, and communication of positive family values and norms). The latter set of variables (i.e., values and norms) was merged into a latent construct representing parent/peer influence, which was the final pathway predicting a variety of problem behavior. It was equally powerful for different ethnic groups and for girls and boys (Sales et al., 2003). Family bonding and parental supervision, however, have a slightly greater impact on minority youth and also on girls' choice of substance-using or non-using friends. Behavioral and emotional self-control had a slightly larger role among boys, possibly because boys seem more prone to difficulties in this area. Girls were more influenced by their academic performance and self-efficacy than boys. The community and neighborhood environment has a greater influence on minority youth as well as on boys.

A similar model was tested for school failure, delinquency, and teen pregnancy as well as alcohol and drug use, with similar results (Ary et al., 1999). The authors found that low parental supervision had a greater influence on adolescent girls' alcohol and drug use than on boys'. Also, in a sample of African-American youth, Fothergill and Ensminger (2006) found that school bonding was a stronger protective factor for boys than for girls.

These tested theoretical models provide suggestive evidence that minority youth have similar risk and protective factors, but the strength of these factors varies somewhat by ethnic group and gender. For example, minority youth and girls are slightly more influenced by family protective factors than are non-minority boys, and girls seem to be more dependent on a positive relationship with their parents and friends to define their self-worth. In contrast, girls appear to be slightly less influenced by their community environment than are boys, but minority youth of both genders are more influenced by the community environment. These models supported the notion that many of the core family protective factors are similar for minority and Euro-Western families, including parent/child attachment, supervision or monitoring, and communication of family values and expectations.

Outside of these models, research has identified other key risk and protective factors. A key family risk factor found in ethnic minority families is increased differential generational acculturation, which can lead to increased family conflict and negatively impact family relationships (Rodnium, 2007). Other major ethnic minority family risk factors include discrimination, increased poverty, and parents working more than one job, implying a lack of time with children (Kumpfer, Magalhães, & Kanse, in press). Commonly identified protective factors include religiosity, family connectedness, and the presence of extended family members to provide emotional and fiscal support (Domenech Rodríguez & Bernal, 2012). Additional youth protective factors to be stressed in culturally adapted family prevention programs include maintaining cultural pride and family traditions and learning multicultural competencies, which support better psychological and academic adjustment (Beauvais & Trimble, 2006; Berkel et al., 2010; Guilamo-Ramos, 2009).

Acculturation among minority groups

Acculturation stress and differential generational acculturation are major family risk factors for minority families (Rodnium, 2007). Acculturation is "the extent to which individuals have maintained their culture of origin or adapted to the larger society" (Phinney, 1996, p. 921). This mainly pertains to families who immigrate to countries with different majority cultures and have to learn a new language and new rules for behavior. The level of acculturation among minority populations depends on many factors such as age, circumstances, socio-economic status, the reasons for immigration, length of stay, location of residence, and exposure to the new host culture in work or community activities (Farver, Bhadha, & Narang, 2002). Assimilation into the new culture is always much more difficult for families who are isolated or only associate with members of their own culture. Because education is generally mandatory, children in immigrant or refugee families typically assimilate much faster than their parents or grandparents. Immigrant parents are torn between retaining their original cultural identities or accepting and assimilating into the dominant host culture (Inman, Howard, Beaumont, & Walker, 2007). Previous research among Hispanic immigrants suggested that acculturation stress, deviation from the original cultural norms (e.g., daily contacts and social interaction with family and friends), language barriers, lower self-esteem, social isolation, boredom, and loneliness can result in increased alcohol consumption among immigrants (Gonzalez-Guarda, Ortega, Vasquez, & De Santis, 2010).

Because children generally assimilate more quickly than their parents to the majority culture (which is called "differential generational acculturation"), increased family conflict arising due to the clash of cultural values can alienate children from their parents and lead to children's developmental problems (e.g., delinquency, substance abuse, anxiety, depression, suicidal tendencies, violence, and prostitution; Dow, 2011; Farver et al., 2002; Feldman & Rosenthal, 1993). In our own research, Structural Equations Modeling (SEM) was used on youth self-report survey data to test the Social Ecology Model (Kumpfer et al., 2003) in four areas of Thailand with youth in retention and correctional facilities. Differential generational acculturation (i.e., adapting to Western culture as compared to maintaining traditional Thai culture) was found to be a major risk factor leading to increased family conflict, which then reduced family protective factors such as family bonding, supervision, and communication of positive family values and influence (Rodnium, 2007). Youth most in favor of adopting Western cultural values and behaviors were most prone to delinquency and drug use.

An additional risk factor in this context is role reversal, which occurs when children can speak the new language much more proficiently and must act as the mediator between the parents and the majority culture, taking on some aspects of the parental role. These youth then tend to reject parental authority and feel that their parents are "old fashioned". The risk posed by differential acculturation, as well as the other culture-specific issues documented above, call for clear models or frameworks that can be used to adopt existing family-based programs for minority populations.

Cultural Adaptation Models or Frameworks

Cultural adaptations of evidence-based family programs are needed to serve the growing minority population and to attract and engage more minority families (Biglan & Metzler, 1999; Kumpfer et al., in press). There is consequently a need for models or ideas on how to best culturally adapt family-based programs. Models for cultural adaptation have been proposed by a number of prevention researchers, namely Bernal, Ferrer-Wreder, Kumpfer, and others. In general, there are two types of cultural adaptation frameworks: those that inform *what* to modify in the intervention content and those that inform *how* to conduct the adaptation process (Ferrer-Wreder, Sundell, & Mansoory, 2012). The Ecological Validity Model (EVM) by Bernal, Bonilla, and Bellido (1995) is an example of *what* to adapt in eight domains: language, persons, metaphors, content, concepts, goals, methods, and context. A similar content model is the cultural sensitivity model, which distinguishes deep structure versus surface structure adaptations of program content (Resnicow, Soler, Braithwaite, Ahluwailia, & Butler, 2000).

The second set of frameworks focus on the *process* of adaptation, where decisions about when to adapt, how to adapt, and which stakeholders should be involved in the process are outlined. A number of frameworks fall into this category and vary in how prescriptive they are (i.e., whether they have a set of a priori steps that guide the process) and whether they are focused on the adaptation of one specific EBP. Several of these models have been described elsewhere (e.g., Bernal & Domenech Rodríguez, 2012); generally, they recommend adaptations to be informed by the expertise of program developers, past experience with similar populations, key stakeholders (e.g., funding project officers, members of local service delivery organizations), and members of the new population. They recommend the use of formative research methods such as focus groups and interviews, as well as formal outcome evaluations of the adapted intervention (Cabassa & Baumann, 2013; Domenech Rodríguez & Bernal, 2012). Unfortunately, many cultural adaptations are done informally "on the spot" by implementers to make the program concepts more understandable and acceptable to participants. Because of lack of time and failure to appreciate the need for replication, these informal adaptations are rarely documented sufficiently to enable outsiders to understand exactly what was delivered (unless the entire program was videotaped).

Kumpfer and UNODC steps to cultural adaptation

Kumpfer and associates (2012b) have developed over the past twenty years a recommended system for culturally adapting their Strengthening Families Program (SFP). These steps have been found to result in outcomes similar to or better than the original outcomes. The key is not to do any major adaptations before the program has been piloted with the new population. Also critical is that the implementers are from the participant population and understand cultural differences. Adaptations of content are recommended rather than modifications of program structure that would include shortening the number of sessions or lesson length, moving the topics or sessions around, or eliminating the basic format (i.e., parents and youth attend initial classes separately and then come together as a family). Participants from minority cultures sometimes object to experiential role plays as just "not done in our culture". However, they generally discover that, once given permission to do the role plays in a safe and non-judgmental setting, they actually enjoy these "fun and games" that are so critical to practicing new parenting and communication behaviors.

Cultural adaptation teams are encouraged to follow the steps to implementation and cultural adaptation found to produce the most effective outcomes, described in the recent UNODC publication (UNODC, 2009) and in journal

264 Karol L. Kumpfer et al.

publications (Kumpfer, Pinyuchon, de Melo, & Whiteside, 2008; Kumpfer, Magalhães, & Xie, 2012). These steps include: 1) conduct a local family needs assessment; 2) review EBP family programs and select the best program for age, ethnicity, and risk level of families (e.g., universal, selective, or indicated prevention); 3) create a cultural adaptation team, including family members, implementer (or group leader in the SFP), and the original program developer; 4) translate into the local language; 5) implement at first with minimal cultural adaptation; 6) make gradual cultural changes based on input from the adaptation team (e.g., culturally appropriate stories, songs); 7) test the adapted program with multiple replications; 8) conduct annual pre- and post-test evaluations to determine if the evolving cultural adaptations are making the program better or worse by comparing to the appropriate SFP age norms for the original program; 9) make adjustments as needed by adding or dropping new cultural adaptations; and 10) disseminate to similar cultural groups if the outcome evaluations show it to be as effective as the original SFP.

Family Programs with Cultural Adaptations

Many family-based programs have done at least one implementation in another country requiring language translations and evaluations of new programs outcomes. However, few of these programs document or disseminate a formal process of cultural adaptation. The family-based programs with the highest number of culturally adapted implementations include the SFP, which has been found effective for five major ethnic groups in the USA (Kumpfer et al., 2002) and 35 countries (Kumpfer, Pinyuchon, Baharudin, Nolrajsuwat, & Xie, in press), Triple P from Australia (to date in 25 countries), Incredible Years (three major US ethnic groups and in 22 countries), Parent Management Training— Oregon (in six countries), and Family Matters (in three countries). Several of these most widely disseminated family programs and their cultural adaptation processes are discussed in their own chapters in this book.

Indicated family prevention or treatment programs

Several indicated family-based prevention or treatment programs for higher risk youth with diagnosed behavioral health problems have been implemented internationally but not included in this book; hence, their cultural adaptations are discussed briefly below:

- *Multisystemic Therapy for Delinquents and Substance Abusing Youth* is an intensive family- and community-based treatment for juvenile offenders who have committed serious offences and their families. Most of the treatment is conducted in the home. It has been implemented internationally in 12 countries.

Cultural and Gender Adaptations **265**

- *Multidimensional Family Therapy* is a manual-driven intervention with specific assessment and treatment modules for drug abusing youth. MDFT helps the youth develop more effective coping and problem-solving skills for better decision making and helps the family improve interpersonal functioning as a protective factor against substance abuse and related problems. MDFT has language and cultural adaptations for five countries.

There are other parent training programs with cultural adaptations, such as Bavolek's *Nurturing Program*, the first parent training program for child maltreatment adapted for Hispanics and the military; Miller-Hyle's *Dare To Be You*, implemented with Navajos, Hispanics, and Whites; Schinke's web-delivered *Mothers and Daughters Program* with separate versions for Hispanic, African American, and Asian families; McDonald's *Families and Schools Together* (FAST) being disseminated by the UNODC to developing countries from a compendium of evidence-based family programs (UNODC, 2010); and Brody's *Strong African American Families* (SAAF) adapted from SFP 10–14 (see Brody, this volume).

The Strengthening Families Program (SFP)

Multiple age and cultural adaptations of the SFP have been found robust in producing positive outcomes when implemented for new populations outside the United States (Kumpfer, Pinyuchon et al., 2008). The UN Office on Drugs and Crime (UNODC) is disseminating SFP to developing countries in four regions of the world (Balkans, Central America, Brazil, and Southeast Asia), along with the Pan American Health Organization (PAHO) in Latin America, the International Rescue Committee (IRC) for refugees, and many international governments. An RCT study funded by the Thai government found that if both mothers and fathers attend, compared with only mothers, the outcomes are improved significantly (Pinyuchon, 2010). The outcome effectiveness results in Serbia with about 350 families have been excellent (Malouf, 2014). A survey of implementers of SFP and other evidence-based substance abuse prevention programs in Europe (Burkhart, 2013) found unanimous belief that SFP can be culturally adapted with excellent outcomes if implemented with fidelity and the recommended steps to SFP cultural adaptations are followed (Kumpfer, Pinyuchon et al., 2008; Kumpfer, Magalhães et al., 2012; UNODC, 2009).

Within the United States, culturally specific SFP versions for five major ethnic populations (Hispanic/Latino, African American, Pacific Islander/Hawaiian, Asian, and American Indian) were initially developed and evaluated in five separate 5-year phase-in studies using federal grants. The trials reported 40% better recruitment and retention for the culturally adapted versions, but overall the SFP outcomes were not a significant improvement compared to the non-culturally adapted SFP implemented with the same types of families (Kumpfer et al., 2002). Although we have no direct evidence, we can speculate about the reasons for this lack of improvement. Perhaps, given the robust program design and content of SFP, the additional cultural adaptations didn't add much except to increase attendance. We should not downplay the significant enhancements to recruitment and retention; we continue to recommend cultural adaptations for SFP and other family-based programs even if they do nothing more than increase family engagement. However, the time and cost of continuously updating culturally specific versions for each different age, risk level, or specific target populations has prompted the SFP developers as well as those for other EBPs to move to culturally sensitive, multi-ethnic versions rather than multiple culturally specific versions. A culturally sensitive SFP manual includes unique graphics for each ethnic group and changes names and examples as well, but the additional cultural tailoring and local language translation is done in the way the group leaders explain and present the SFP family skills.

Another issue is that a culturally specific version may not be specific enough for different ethnic subgroups and may still need considerable local adaptation even for White families, such as isolated Appalachian families (Marek, Brock, & Sullivan, 2006). None of the major categories of ethnicity in the US (e.g., Hispanic, Asian, American Indian, African American, Pacific Islanders) are homogeneous cultures, but differ in family traditions, values, historical and local issues in child raising, and language variations. For example, even among Hispanic families there is no uniform Spanish language to use for translations because each culture has different words for concepts. About five different language translations of SFP into Spanish (Mexican, Argentinian, Columbian, Puerto Rican, and El Salvadorian) were tried in an attempt to find a universally acceptable Spanish to most Hispanic and Latino families. However, each time the local Hispanic families would complain about inappropriate language in the manuals. For Asian and Pacific Islander families, it was clear that different language translations were needed in addition to local adaptations for each country and cultural group. For American Indians, several tribe-specific SFP versions were developed with funding by particular tribes, but these specific versions couldn't be used with other tribes; as a result, only the richest tribes could afford their own culturally specific version of SFP.

The SFP developers recently moved to a culturally sensitive SFP curriculum for each of the different age groups (SFP 3–5, 6–11, 12–16, 7–17, and new 0–3) by producing manuals that were free of any cultural-specific material. The new gold standard practice is for each SFP implementation team to use the culturally sensitive curricula as a starting point and to follow the recommended steps for cultural adaptation presented earlier and recommended by the UNODC Guidelines (UNODC, 2009) to make their own cultural adaptations over time using feedback from local families. In this scenario, cultural adaptations by culturally sensitive group leaders then became a mandated element of fidelity. At the very least, surface structure content should be altered to suit local cultural mores (i.e., incorporating songs, music, foods, games, and stories that reflect local culture). The involvement of consultants from the local population is essential for success, along with the approval of the program developer for any changes outside of these minor alterations. However, the SFP developers stress that, beyond these types of changes, implementation should closely adhere to the manual content, session order, and theoretical underpinnings in order to maintain fidelity and achieve similar outcomes to those obtained previously.

International SFP outcome results

Replications of SFP in randomized control trials (RCTs) and quasi-experimental studies in different countries (Canada, Ireland, the United Kingdom, Netherlands, Spain, Thailand, and Italy) with different cultural groups by independent evaluators have found SFP to be an effective program in reducing multiple risk factors for later alcohol and drug abuse, mental health problems, and delinquency by increasing family strengths, children's social competencies, and improving parenting skills (Kumpfer et al., 2002; Kumpfer & Johnson, 2007; Onrust & Bool, 2006; Orte, March, Ballester, &Touza, 2007). For summary of SFP outcomes from foreign studies see Kumpfer and associates (2012a).

Among the 13 countries in Europe that have culturally adapted and evaluated SFP are four that have one to five years of pre-to-post-test outcome results conducted independently by researchers: Orte et al. (2007) at the University of the Balearic Islands, Spain; Onrust and Bool (2006) at Trimbos Institute in Utrecht, Netherlands; Kimber (2005) at the Karolinska Institute in Stockholm, Sweden; and Foxcroft, Allen, and Coombes (2005; Coombes, Allen & Foxcroft, 2012) at Oxford Brookes University, United Kingdom. These studies were all non-experimental or quasi-experimental designs, but their positive results suggest that SFP can be culturally adapted and replicated in other countries with positive results. The Spanish and Irish results have been excellent, with even slightly higher effect sizes for the outcomes than the SFP US norms, possibly because they were implemented with higher risk families.

Excellent results have also been found in other countries (Portugal, Ireland, Northern Ireland, Italy, France, Slovenia, and Austria) with semi-independent replications where the implementing agencies have sent their data to the Strengthening Families Foundation, the SFP-recommended evaluation team that includes Dr. Kumpfer, the program developer and evaluator. These have all been quasi-experimental pre-to-post-test designs with a comparison to the norms for that country or the SFP international norms. In addition, the agencies used the recommended SFP testing instruments. Portugal and the Azores have implemented *SFP 6–11 Years* (see Kumpfer et al., earlier in this volume) and have excellent outcomes using the standardized SFP instruments. Norway has been implementing the *SFP 6–11 Years* and *SFP 10–14 Years* version, as has the United Kingdom.

268 Karol L. Kumpfer et al.

A multi-county quasi-experimental evaluation of an Irish cultural adaptation of *SFP 12–16 Years* for *indicated* youth in Ireland (Kumpfer, Xie, & O'Driscoll, 2012) has produced some of the largest effect sizes (Cohen's d = .50 to 1.11). These effect sizes were about 20% larger than the comparison group (US) SFP norms, possibly because the families were so needy and alcohol use rates were higher at pre-test. All 21 measured teen, parent, and family outcomes were significantly improved in the 288 families. They used a unique collaborative recruitment and staffing model that included probation services, local drugs task forces, schools, garda (police), and substance abuse treatment agencies. Each agency sending a staffing member was allowed to reserve 2 to 3 slots for families on their waiting lists for family services.

Reduced SFP effectiveness when not culturally adapted or implemented with fidelity

When local implementers do not address issues of cultural differences, program effectiveness can be attenuated. For example, a NIDA-funded RCT of the standard SFP among 715 primarily high-risk African Americans in the Washington, DC region still found good results but reduced effect sizes, recruitment, and retention compared to other SFP RCTs (Gottfredson et al., 2006), likely due to the lack of appropriate cultural adaptations.

Program modifications that go beyond language to change format and length can reduce program fidelity and overall effectiveness. An unfortunate Swedish modification of the 7-session *SFP 10–14 Years* resulted in non-significant outcomes (Skärstrand, Larsson, & Andreasson, 2008). To save money after making expensive new videos, they eliminated all but two of the weekly family sessions and some of the parenting classes at night. Meals, incentives for homework completion, and babysitting were also not offered, reducing parent attendance to only 33% of the families. School teachers offered a longer SFP, with more drug education classes, to their full classroom of students, thus increasing the possibility of an "iatrogenic" effect described by Dishion and Mauricio (this volume) when implementers are not skillful in maintaining control over the youth. This natural experiment demonstrated that a critical core component of SFP's success is bringing the family together to improve communication and relationship quality by eating together, learning the same family skills, and playing games and role plays together to practice their new interaction skills.

Gender Adaptations of Family Programs

Need for Gender-Adapted Family EBP Intervention

Despite more effective prevention programs, behavioral health problems including delinquency, crime, teen pregnancy, eating disorders, depression, and substance use in girls have increased more than for boys worldwide beginning with a dramatic increase in the United States in 1992 (Kumpfer, 2014). Traditionally, girls in Western countries have used alcohol, tobacco, and drugs less than boys; however, the gender gap has almost disappeared in the US and other developed countries (Kumpfer & Magalhães, in press). This gender gap is related to a complex interaction of genetic and environmental causes. The consequences have been costly to governments, with increased numbers of women needing drug treatment, many of them mothers who are losing their children to foster care. Also the social, emotional, and health consequences for their children are tremendous, particularly in the light of recent epigenetic research stressing the need for nurturing parenting to prevent the phenotypic expression of inherited diseases (Jirtle, 2010; Brody et al., 2010, 2012).

Genetic risks

The increase in girls' substance abuse is occurring despite research suggesting that men appear to have twice as high a genetic risk of alcohol dependency compared to women, according to early twin adoption studies conducted in Sweden, Denmark, and the USA (Pickens et al., 1991). These genetic risks help to explain why addiction appears to be a "family disease" with children of parents with substance use disorders at much higher genetic risk (Kumpfer & Johnson, 2009). Recently, several gene variants have been identified related to increased risk for depression, anxiety, substance abuse, delinquency, and HIV risk, namely one or two short alleles of the 5-HTTLPR serotonin transporter gene or the 7-repeat dopamine gene (Brody et al., 2010, 2012). These are found in 40% of White and 60% of Asian groups. Nurturing parenting has been found to reduce occurrence of these behavioral health diagnoses in mice or children with these genes (Jirtle, 2010; Champagne, 2010). There is also recent epigenetic research suggesting that gene/environment interactions due to maternal stress can cause changes in genes *in utero* that may be passed into the next generation (Champagne, 2010). Since genetic risk has not changed drastically in girls, the recent increase in substance use prevalence in girls is more likely due to the significant changes in social environments, such as reductions in parental involvement and major changes in social roles for girls and women.

Environmental risks

The increases in girls' behavioral health problems worldwide are likely to be related to the export of Western values through movies, music, and clothing, and adolescent freedoms for girls that include more violent behavior, sexualization, and positive norms toward drinking and drug use (Kumpfer, Magalhães, & Kanse, in press). With increased access to jobs, affluence, and social freedoms, young girls have begun to behave more like boys, including their vices. Kumpfer,

Smith, and Summerhays (2008) called this the "Virginia Slims Effect" related to sexual and social role liberation.

In many societies, girls are being exposed to media and societal pressures to conform to an unrealistically thin body ideal (Reel & Beal, 2009; Sypeck, Gray, & Ahrens, 2004). Significantly more females than males begin using tobacco and drugs because they believe it helps them to stay thin (Califano, 2001). In the USA, the use of amphetamines among Caucasian girls is linked to the desire to lose weight (NCASA, 2003). In addition, substance use and disordered eating can co-occur. Research suggests that one in six students have admitted to restricting caloric intake in order to amplify the effects of alcohol (Cofsky, 2012). In one study (Burke, Cremeens, Vail-Smith, & Woolsey, 2010), the 30% of students that restricted calories also reported binge drinking. Girls who combine disordered eating with binge drinking are more at risk for violence, risky sexual behavior, alcohol poisoning, substance abuse, and chronic diseases later in life, such as cirrhosis of the liver (Baker, Mitchell, Neale, & Kendler, 2010).

Reduced poverty and parental controls, with more parents working more hours, are likely contributing to these increases in behavioral health problems in girls more than boys (Annenberg Institute of School Reform, 2009). Another important risk factor is the increasing divorce rates in modern society and the loss of fathers in girls' lives (Kumpfer & Magalhães, in press). According to the Social Ecology Model shown earlier (Kumpfer et al., 2003), girls are slightly more influenced by their parents than are boys in terms of parent/child relationship quality and monitoring. Also, peer pressure may be more strongly associated with drinking for girls than it is for boys (Donovan, 2002). When several of a girl's closest friends smoke or drink, they are more than seven times more likely to smoke and drink, whereas boys are only three times more likely (Barber, Bolitho, & Bertrand, 1999). Finally, early maturing girls who have older friends appear to be at an elevated risk for substance misuse, truancy, delinquency, and sexual activity (Caspi, Lynam, Moffitt, & Silva, 1993; Lanza & Collins, 2002).

High rates of comorbidity exist between substance use and depression in girls (Kloos, Weller, Chan, & Weller, 2009). Substance abusing girls are more likely to be depressed, and, likewise, depression leads to increased substance abuse, reduced self-esteem, and increased suicide attempts for girls (Kloos et al., 2009). More girls than boys (as young as the 6th grade) believe in self-medicating powers of alcohol to reduce depression, anger, or frustration, even before they begin to drink. Girls who believe that drinking alcohol reduces depression or helps them deal with negative thoughts and feelings report more alcohol use them those who do not (CASA, 2003). Other drugs such as ecstasy and marijuana are also used by girls to reduce depression (Kumpfer & Magalhães, in press).

Sexual abuse also appears to be a strong risk factor for girls and women, possibly due to the higher prevalence of victimization. On average, at least one in three women is beaten, coerced into sex, or otherwise abused by an intimate partner in the course of her lifetime (United Nations, 2008). Higher percentages

(55% to 95%) of women as compared to men in drug treatment facilities were sexually abused as a child (Kumpfer & Bays, 1995). In the USA, the prevalence of sexual abuse was reported to be 60% for incarcerated female and 20% for male adolescents (Dembo et al., 2000). Finally, youth who misuse alcohol, marijuana, or drugs are at increased risk of victimization, with female substance users at particularly elevated risk of sexual assault (Testa & Livingston, 2009).

For these reasons, more effective prevention and treatment programs for girls and women are needed. Unfortunately, the prevention field has not conducted much research to determine how to design more effective prevention programs and policies for adolescent females. Also, the etiological causal factors are complex and research on girls is lacking. A gender-attentive approach would implement gender-specific strategies for girls that address their specific risk factors for behavioral and health issues.

Effectiveness of Family-Based Programs for Boys and Girls

A survey of evidence-based prevention programs conducted for a UNODC gender guideline (Kumpfer & Magalhães, in press) revealed 13 family-based programs that worked for girls. Of the seven generic evidence-based family programs that had done a gender analysis, all reported equally effective results for girls and boys and one reported better results for girls (i.e., Multidimensional Treatment Foster Care). In addition, all six gender-specific family-based programs reported positive results for girls.

Gender-specific family-based programs

Very few of the evidence-based family programs have developed gender-specific versions for girls, partially because the need to do so was only recently discovered. Of the three gender-specific programs, randomized control trials of a mother–daughter substance use prevention program delivered through CDs or internet showed good results for reducing HIV risk and alcohol and drug use among inner city Hispanic, African American, and Asian American girls (Fang & Schinke, 2013; Schinke, Cole, & Fang, 2009; Schinke, Fang, Cole, & Cohen-Cutler, 2011; Schwinn, Schink, & Di Noia, 2010). Two gender and ethnic adaptations of *SFP 6–11 Years* targeting mothers and daughters also reported positive results for Hawaiians (Kameoke, 1996) and Hispanic mothers and daughters (Alvarado, 1996).

A recent gender analysis of a large SFP normative database of over 4,000 families from SFP groups worldwide found that SFP is equally effective for girls as for boys and in some cases even more effective for girls despite lower base rates of risk factors, possibly because girls are more influenced by family relationships (Magalhães, 2013). Finally, a recent gender analysis of *SFP 12–16*

Years with high-risk adolescents in Ireland found SFP to be equally effective for adolescent girls as for boys (Mahoney, Kumpfer, Xie, & Cofrin Allen, 2014).

The general positive results of family-based programs are consistent with both the brief discussion above regarding vulnerability and resilience factors that are particular to girls, as well as with other general reviews of the effectiveness of family-based programs (Kumpfer, 2014; Petrie, Bunn, & Byrne, 2007). In particular, family-based strategies are generally effective for both boys and girls (Kumpfer et al., 2003; Petrie et al., 2007), while school-based and community-based programs are often not as effective for girls.

Recommended Gender Adaptations

Enhancing existing EBPs to be even more effective for girls would require that program developers take into account girls' unique needs. Specific recommendations for making prevention programs more effective for girls include:

1. In general, topics to include in adolescent females programming should include dealing with stress, depression, and body image, and improving relations and communication with parents and significant others.
2. Girls need developmentally appropriate positive models and practice of skills such as conflict negotiation, drug refusal skills, and social assertiveness.
3. Program modules on dating, the meaning of love and sexual relationships, protection from date rape, unwanted pregnancy, and sexually transmitted diseases would be helpful for girls. Program design could include: a) separate activities for boys and girls, focusing on knowledge and skill development around open cross-gender communication; and b) opportunities for mixed-gender group discussions that could promote both skill development and greater shared understanding of these issues.
4. Given the importance of abuse, and particularly sexual abuse, as a significant risk factor in the development of substance abuse disorders, especially among girls and women, programs to prevent such abuse and, particularly, to support the victims and to address post-traumatic stress disorders appear to be essential (United Nations, 2008).
5. Gender-specific prevention programs should include opportunities for relationship building between girls and adult female role models and should incorporate the everyday realities of women's and girls' lives, including opportunities for girls to debunk societal and media pressures to engage in health compromising behaviors.
6. Effective gender-specific programs should be culturally tailored to address the unique needs of girls and women from varying races, ethnicities, and social classes. For example, two gender and ethnic adaptations of *SFP 6–11 Years* targeting mothers and daughters reported positive results for Hawaiians (Kameoke, 1996) and Hispanic mothers and daughters (Alvarado, 1996).

Recommendations for Future Research and Practice

The majority of substance abuse prevention programs that are not family-based are not as effective in reducing behavioral health problems in adolescent girls as in boys, possibly because these programs are not designed specifically to address the unique needs of girls. Most prevention programs are developed for universal school-based populations of both girls and boys, so they do not attend to important gender differences in the etiology of behavioral and health problems. In the prevention of substance abuse, this includes the differing pathways for girls' initiation and continued use of substances as well as the differences in the kinds of substance used and the effects of those substances. Therefore, it is important to encourage researchers with epidemiological or etiological data to conduct separate gender analyses to enhance our current understanding of the precursors of substance use among girls (Kumpfer, Smith et al., 2008). These models should be comprehensive and include family, peer, community, and school processes, and should consider both risk and protective factors (e.g., stress, depression and anxiety, social roles, assertiveness, social competencies). In addition, secondary data analyses should be conducted on prevention program data sets to determinate the factors that influence program effectiveness for girls as compared to boys (Kumpfer, 2014).

Because family-based programs appear to be the most effective in preventing behavioral health problems in both boys and girls (Foxcroft, Ireland, Lister-Sharp, Lowe, & Breen, 2003; Foxcroft & Tsertsvadze, 2012; Kumpfer, 2014; Kumpfer & Hansen, 2014; Miller & Hendrie, 2008), more funds should be allocated for dissemination of proven programs to high-risk populations of girls. More cost-effective ways of dissemination such as DVD, web, mail-out booklets, and smart phone apps should be developed, tested, and compared to the more costly group or individual family delivery. Professional training and continuing education programs for prevention specialists should include training in family-based programs as well as better specification of the practices associated with improved gender outcomes. Identifying and specifying which aspects of girls' development and girls' patterns of substance use/abuse must be incorporated into a program in order for it to be considered "gender-specific" is another critical element in addressing the growing problems with girls' substance use (Kumpfer, Smith et al., 2008).

Conclusion

To improve engagement and program efficacy, evidence-based family prevention programs should consider adaptations for both culture and gender. Culturally adapted prevention programs do increase enrollment and retention in family interventions, but it is not clear yet if they always improve outcomes. Cultural adaptation can be achieved for the least cost by hiring and training implementers

274 Karol L. Kumpfer et al.

from the same cultural group, who can make the language and cultural improvements even "on the spot" in interacting with families. Generic culturally sensitive family programs that have video clips or graphics that represent the major ethnic groups would be the next step in cultural adaptation.

At this point, there is insufficient research evidence or published articles to conclude whether most prevention programs are as effective for girls as for boys. A recent gender subgroup analysis of a large SFP normative database of over 4,000 families from agencies worldwide did find that the traditional 14-session SFP is equally effective for girls as for boys (Kumpfer, 2014; Magalhães & Kumpfer, 2014). In some cases, SFP was even more effective for girls despite lower base rates of risk factors, possibly because girls are more influenced by family relationships. Although this finding is laudable, the degree of effectiveness for girls as compared to boys for other evidence-based prevention programs should be investigated. In particular, parenting and family interventions with the potential to have greater protective impact on girls should publish their gender-by-program interaction analyses. Component or mediational analyses are also needed to determine which aspects of the interventions contribute to effectiveness for the two genders. Additionally, we do not know if making evidence-based programs more gender-specific would strengthen outcomes for girls. Cultural adaptation research does suggest that enrollment and retention can increase dramatically with adaptations (UNODC, 2009) and this might conceivably apply also in the case of gender.

References and Further Reading

Alvarado, R. (1996). Evaluation of the Strengthening Hispanic Mothers and Daughters Program. (Evaluation report submitted to SAMHSA Center for Substance Abuse Prevention). Unpublished manuscript.

Annenberg Institute of School Reform (2009). *Annual Report*. Providence, RI: Annenberg Institute of School Reform, Brown University.

Ary, D.V., Duncan, T. E., Biglan, A., Metzler, C. W., Noell, J. W., & Smolkowski, K. (1999). Developmental model of adolescent problem behavior. *Journal of Abnormal Child Psychology*, 27(2), 141–150.

Baker, J. H., Mitchell, K. S., Neale, M. C., & Kendler, K. S. (2010). Eating disorder symptomatology and substance use disorders: Prevalence and shared risk in a population based sample. *International Journal of Eating Disorders*, 43, 648–658.

Barber, J. G., Bolitho, F., & Bertrand, L. D. (1999). Intrapersonal versus peer group predictors of adolescent drug use. *Children and Youth Services Review*, 21(7), 565–579.

Bauman, K. E., Ennett, S. T., Foshee, V. A., Pemberton, M., King, T. S., & Koch, G. G. (2000). Influence of a family-directed program on adolescent cigarette and alcohol cessation. *Prevention Science*, 1(4), 227–237.

Beauvais, F., & Trimble, J. E. (2006). The effectiveness of alcohol and drug abuse prevention among American-Indian youth. *Handbook of Drug Abuse Prevention*, 393–410.

Cultural and Gender Adaptations 275

Berkel, C., Knight, G. P., Zeiders, K. H., Tein, J. Y., Roosa, M. W., Gonzales, N. A. et al. (2010). Discrimination and adjustment for Mexican American adolescents: A prospective examination of the benefits of culturally-related values. *Journal of Research on Adolescence, 20*, 893–915.

Bernal, G., Bonilla, J., & Bellido, C. (1995). Ecological validity and cultural sensitivity for outcome research: Issues for the cultural adaptation and development of psychosocial treatments with Hispanics. *Journal of Abnormal Child Psychology, 23*(1), 67–82.

Bernal, G. E., & Domenech Rodríguez, M. M. (2012). *Cultural adaptations: Tools for evidence based practice with diverse populations.* Washington, DC: American Psychological Association.

Biglan, A., & Metzler, C. (1999). A public health perspective for research on family-focused interventions. In R. Ashery, E. Robertson, & K. Kumpfer (Eds.), *Drug abuse prevention through family interventions* (National Institute of Drug Abuse Research Monograph on family-focused prevention research). Rockville, MD: National Institute on Drug Abuse.

Boyd-Franklin, N. (2001). Reaching out to larger systems. In interventions with multicultural families (Part 2). *The Family Psychologist, 17*(3), 1–4.

Brody, G. H., Chen, Y.-f., Kogan, S. M., Murry, V. M., & Brown, A. C. (2010). Long-term effects of the Strong African American Families program on youths' alcohol use. *Journal of Consulting and Clinical Psychology, 78*(2), 281–285.

Brody, G. H., Chen, Y.-f., Kogan, S. M., Yu, T., Molgaard, V. K., DiClemente, R. J., & Wingood, G. M. (2012). Family-centered program to prevent substance use, conduct problems, and depressive symptoms in Black adolescents. *Pediatrics, 129*(1), 108–115.

Burke, S., Cremeens, J., Vail-Smith, K., & Woolsey, C. (2010). Drunkorexia: Calorie restriction prior to alcohol consumption among college freshman. *Journal of Alcohol & Drug Education, 54*(2), 17–34.

Burkhart, G. (2013). *North American drug prevention programmes: Are they feasible in European cultures and contexts?* European Monitoring Center for Drugs and Drug Addiction (EMCDDA) http://www.emcdda.europa.eu/publications/thematicpapers/north-american-drug-prevention-programmes.

Cabassa, L., & Baumann, A. (2013). A two-way street: Bridging implementation science and cultural adaptations of mental health treatments. *Implementation Science, 8*, doi:10.1186/1748-5908-8-90.

Califano, J. A. (2001). Food for thought: Substance abuse and eating disorders. Paper presented at the National Center on Addiction and Drug Abuse (CASA) at Columbia University Conference, New York.

CASA. (2003). *The formative years: Pathways to substance abuse among girls and young women ages 8–22.* New York: CASA.

Caspi, A., Lynam, D., Moffitt, T. E., & Silva, P. A. (1993). Unraveling girls' delinquency: Biological, dispositional, and contextual contributions to adolescent misbehavior. *Developmental Psychology, 29*, 19–30.

Centers for Disease Control and Prevention (CDC). (2013). *Asian American populations.* Retrieved from http://www.cdc.gov/minorityhealth/populations/REMP/asian.html.

Center for Substance Abuse Prevention (2000). *Final report: The national cross-site evaluation of high-risk youth programs* (ORC MACO, 4.18-4.22). Local: EMT Associates.

Chamberlain, P., Price J. M., Reid, J. B., Landsverk, J., Fisher, P. A., & Stoolmiller, M. (2006). Who disrupts from placement in foster and kinship care? *Child Abuse and Neglect, 30*, 409–424.

Champagne, F. A. (2010). Epigenetic influence of social experiences across the lifespan. *Developmental Psychobiology, 52*(4), 299–311.

Coombes, L., Allen, D. M., & Foxcroft, D. H. (2012). An exploratory pilot study of the Strengthening Families Programme 10–14 (UK). *Drugs: Education, Prevention, and Policy, 19*(5), 387–396.

Cofsky, L. (2012). Drunkorexia: A prevalent disorder on college campuses. *The Daily Pennsylvanian.* Retrieved from http://www.thedp.com/r/17f289d6.

Dembo, R., Wothke, W., Shemwell, M., Pacheco, K., Seeberger, W., Rollie, M., & Schmeidler, J. (2000). A structural model of the influence of family problems and child abuse factors on serious delinquency among youths processed at a juvenile assessment center. *Journal of Child and Adolescence Substance Abuse, 10*(1), 17–31.

Domenech Rodríguez, M. M., & Bernal, G. (2012). Bridging the gap between research and practice in a multicultural world. In G. Bernal & M. M. Domenech Rodriguez (Eds.), *Cultural adaptations: Tools for evidence-based practice with diverse populations* (pp. 265–287). Washington, DC: American Psychological Association Press.

Donovan, J. E. (2002). Gender differences in alcohol involvement in children and adolescents: A review of the literature. In J. M. Howard, S. E. Martin, P. D. Mail, M. E. Hilton, & E. D. Taylor (Eds.). *Women and alcohol: Issues for prevention research: NIAAA research monograph no. 32* (NIH Pub. No. 96-3817, pp. 133–162). Bethesda, MD: US Department of Health and Human Services.

Dow, H. D. (2011). The acculturation processes: The strategies and factors affecting the degree of acculturation. *Home Health Care Management & Practice, 23*(3), 221–227.

Fang, L., & Schinke, S. P. (2013). Two-year outcomes of a randomized, family-based substance use prevention trial for Asian American adolescent girls. *Psychology of Addictive Behaviors, 27*(3), 788–798.

Farver, J. A. M., Bhadha, B. R., & Narang, S. K. (2002). Acculturation and psychological functioning in Asian Indian adolescents. *Social Development, 11*(1), 11–29.

Feldman, S. S., & Rosenthal, D. A. (1993). Culture makes a difference . . . or does it? A comparison of adolescents in Hong Kong, Australia, and the USA. In R. Silbereisen & E. Todt (Eds.), *Adolescence in context.* New York: Springer.

Ferrer-Wreder, L., Adamson, L., Kumpfer, K. L., & Eichas, K. (2012). Advancing intervention science through effectiveness research: A global perspective. *Child and Youth Care Forum, 41*, 109–117.

Ferrer-Wreder, L., Sundell, K., & Mansoory, S. (2012). Tinkering with perfection: Theory development in the intervention cultural adaptation field. *Child and Youth Care Forum, 41*, 149–171.

Fothergill, K. E., & Ensminger, M. E. (2006). Childhood and adolescent antecedents of drug and alcohol problems: A longitudinal study. *Drug and Alcohol Dependence, 82*, 61–76.

Foxcroft, D., Allen, D., & Coombes, L. (2005). Adaptation and Implementation of SFP 10–14 Years for U.K. Abstract submitted to Society for Prevention Research, San Antonio, May 2005. School of Health and Social Care, Oxford Brookes University, Oxford, UK.

Foxcroft, D. R., Ireland, D., Lister-Sharp, D. J., Lowe, G., & Breen, R. (2003). Longer-term primary prevention for alcohol misuse in young people: A systematic review. *Addiction, 98*, 397–411.

Foxcroft, D. R., & Tsertsvadze, A. (2012). Universal alcohol misuse prevention programmes for children and adolescents: Cochrane systematic reviews. *Perspectives in Public Health, 132*, 128–134.

Gonzalez-Guarda, R. M., Ortega, J., Vasquez, E., & De Santis, J. (2010). La maneha negra: Substance abuse, violence and sexual risks among Hispanic males. *Western Journal of Nursing Research*, *32*(1), 128–148.

Gottfredson, D., Kumpfer, K., Polizzi-Fox, D., Wilson, D., Puryear, V., Beatty, P., & Vilmenay, M. (2006). The Strengthening Washington D.C. Families Project: A randomized effectiveness trial of family-based prevention. *Prevention Science*, 7, 57–74.

Guilamo-Ramos, V. (2009). Maternal influence on adolescent self-esteem, ethnic pride and intentions to engage in risk behavior in Latino youth. *Prevention Science*, *10*, 366–375.

Henggeler, S. W. (1997). The development of effective drug abuse services for youth. In J. A. Egertson, D. M. Fox, & A. I. Leshner (Eds.), *Treating drug abusers effectively* (pp. 253–279). New York: Blackwell.

Inman, A. G., Howard, E. E., Beaumont, R. L., & Walker, J. A. (2007). Cultural transmission: Influence of contextual factors in Asian Indian immigrant parents' experiences. *Journal of Counseling Psychology*, *54*(1), 93.

Jirtle, R. (2010). Epigenetic mechanisms on gene expression. Plenary session I, Annual Conference of the Society for Prevention Research. Denver, Colorado (June 2, 2010).

Johnson, K., Strader, T., Berbaum, M., Bryant, D., Bucholtz, G., Collins, D. et al. (1996). Reducing alcohol and other drug use by strengthening community, family, and youth resiliency: An evaluation of the Creating Lasting Connections program. *Journal of Adolescent Research*, *11*(1), 36–67.

Kameoke, V. A. (1996). *The effects of a family-focused intervention on reducing risk for substance abuse among Asian and Pacific-island youths and families: Evaluation of the Strengthening Hawaii's Families Project*. Honolulu: University of Hawaii, Social Welfare Evaluation and Research Unit.

Kerr, D., Leve, L. D., & Chamberlain, P. (2009). Pregnancy rates among juvenile justice girls in two RCTs of Multidimensional Treatment Foster Care. *Journal of Consulting and Clinical Psychology*, 77, 588–593.

Kimber, B. (2005). Cultural adaptation and preliminary results of the Strengthening Families Program 6–11 in Sweden. Paper presented at Society for Prevention Research, San Antonio, TX, full report at Department of Public Health Sciences, Karolinska Institutet, Stockholm, Sweden.

Kloos, A., Weller, R., Chan, R., & Weller, E. (2009). Gender differences in adolescent substance abuse. *Current Psychiatric Reports*, *11*(2), 120–126.

Knowlton, J., Noe, T., Collins, D., Strader, T., & Bucholtz, G. (2000). Mobilizing church communities to prevent alcohol and other drug abuse: A model strategy and its evaluation. *Journal of Community Practice*, *7*(2), 1–27.

Kumpfer, K. L. (2014). Family-based interventions for the prevention of substance abuse and other impulse control disorders in girls. *ISRN Addiction*, *2014*, Article ID 308789.

Kumpfer, K. L., Alvarado, R., Smith, P., & Bellamy, N. (2002). Cultural sensitivity and adaptation in family-based prevention interventions. *Prevention Science*, *3*(3), 241–246.

Kumpfer, K. L., Alvarado, R., & Whiteside, H. O. (2003). Family-based interventions for substance abuse prevention. *Substance Use and Misuse*, *38*(11–13), 1759–1789.

Kumpfer, K. L., & Bays, J. (1995). Child abuse and alcohol and other drug abuse. In J. H. Jaffe (Eds.), *The encyclopedia of drugs and alcohol* (pp. 217–222). New York: Macmillan.

Kumpfer, K. L., & Hansen, W. (2014). Family-based prevention programs. In L. Scheier & W. Hansen, *Parenting and Teen Drug Use*, Ch. 8. Oxford: Oxford University Press.

Kumpfer, K. L., & Johnson, J. (2007). Strengthening family interventions for the prevention of substance abuse in children of addicted parents. *Adicciones, 11*(1), 1–13.

Kumpfer, K. L., & Johnson, J. L. (2009). Enhancing positive outcomes for children of substance-abusing parents, In B. Johnson (Ed.), *Addiction medicine: Science and practice*. New York: Springer.

Kumpfer, K., & Magalhães, C. (in press). *Gender guidelines on substance abuse prevention among adolescent females and males*. Vienna, Austria: United Nations Office on Drugs and Crime.

Kumpfer, K. L., Magalhães, C., & Kanse, S. (in press). Family structure, culture, and family-based interventions for health promotion. In M. Korin (Ed.), *The handbook of health promotion for children and adolescents*. New York: Springer.

Kumpfer, K. L., Magalhães, C., & Xie, J. (2012a). Cultural adaptations of evidence-based family interventions to strengthen families and improve children's outcomes. *European Journal of Developmental Psychology, 9*(1), 104–116.

Kumpfer, K. L., Pinyuchon, M., de Melo, A., & Whiteside, H. (2008). Cultural adaptation process for international dissemination of the Strengthening Families Program (SFP). *Evaluation and Health Professions, 31*(2), 226–239.

Kumpfer, K. L., Pinyuchon, M., Baharudin, R., Nolrajsuwat, K., & Xie, J. (in press). Evidence-based parenting education in the Asian and Pacific Region. In J. Ponzetti (Ed.), *Evidence-based parenting education: A global perspective*, Chapter 18. New York: Routledge.

Kumpfer, K. L., Smith, P., & Summerhays, J. (2008). A wake-up call to the prevention field: Are prevention programs for substance use effective for girls? *Substance Use and Misuse, 43*(8), 978–1001.

Kumpfer, K. L., Xie, J., & O'Driscoll, R. (2012b). Effectiveness of a culturally adapted Strengthening Families Program 12–16 Years for high risk Irish families. *Child and Youth Care Forum, 41*, 173–195.

Lanza, S. T., & Collins, L. M. (2002). Pubertal timing and the onset of substance use in females during early adolescence. *Prevention Science, 3*, 69–81.

Liddle, H. A., Dakof, G. A., Henderson, C. E., & Rowe, C. L. (2011). Implementation outcomes of Multidimensional Family Therapy-Detention to Community: A reintegration program for drug-using juvenile detainees. *International Journal of Offender Therapy and Comparative Criminology, 55*, 587–604.

Liddle, H. A., Dakof, G. A., Parker, K., Diamond, G. S., Barrett, K., & Tejeda, M. (2001). Multidimensional Family Therapy for adolescent drug abuse: Results of a randomized clinical trial. *Journal of Drug and Alcohol Abuse, 27*(4), 651–688.

Liddle, H. A., Rowe, C. L., Dakof, G. A., Henderson, C. E., & Greenbaum, P. E. (2009). Multidimensional family therapy for young adolescent substance abuse: Twelve-month outcomes of a randomized controlled trial. *Journal of Consulting and Clinical Psychology, 77*, 12–25.

Magalhães, C. (2013). *Effectiveness of the Strengthening Families Program 6–11 Years among US Portuguese immigrant families and families in Portugal compared to SFP norms* (PhD dissertation). University of Lisbon, Lisbon.

Magalhães, C., & Kumpfer, K. L. (2014). Effectiveness of the SFP 6–11 Years for Portuguese girls and boys. Paper presented at European Society of Prevention Research, Palma, Mallorca, Spain, 17 October.

Mahoney, C., Kumpfer, K., Xie, J., & Cofrin Allen, K. (2014). Effectivenesed of SFP 12–16 Years in high risk Irish youth. Paper presented at the European Society for Prevention Research annual conference, Palma, Mallorca, Spain, October, 2014.

Malouf, W. (2014). Implementing family skills pilots in South East Europe: Infrastructures needed, cost implications, value added and lessons learned. Paper presented at the 5th International Conference of the European Society for Prevention Research (EUSPR), Palma, Mallorca, Spain, October 2014.

Marek, L., Brock, D., & Sullivan, R. (2006). Cultural adaptations to a family life skills program: Implementation in rural Appalachia. *Journal of Primary Prevention, 27*(2), 113–133.

Mazzucchelli, T. G., & Sanders, M. R. (2010). Facilitating practitioner flexibility within an empirically supported intervention: Lessons from a system of parenting support. *Clinical Psychology: Science and Practice, 17*, 238–252.

McLean, C. A., & Campbell, C. M. (2003). Locating research informants in a multiethnic community: Ethnic identities, social networks and recruitment methods. *Ethnicity and Health, 8*(1), 41–61.

Miller, T. A., & Hendrie, D. (2008). *Substance abuse prevention: Dollars and cents: A Cost-benefit analysis.* DHHS Pub. No. 07-4298. Rockville, MD: Center for Substance Abuse Prevention (CSAP), SAMHSA.

National Center on Addiction and Substance Abuse (NCASA). (2003). The formative years: Pathways to substance abuse among girls and young women ages 8–22, Report February 2003.

Ogden, T., & Halliday-Boykins, C. A. (2004). Multisystemic treatment of antisocial adolescents in Norway: Replication of clinical outcomes outside of the US. *Child & Adolescent Mental Health, 9*(2), 77–83.

Onrust, S., & Bool, M. (2006). *Evaluatie van de Cursus Gezin aan Bod: Nederlandse versie van het Strengthening Families Program (SFP) [Evaluation of Cursus Gezin aan Bod: The distribution.* Dutch adaptation of the Strengthening Families Program (SFP)]. Utrecht, the Netherlands: Trimbos Institute.

Orte, C., March, M., Ballester, L., & Touza, C. (2007, May). Results of a family competence program adapted for Spanish drug abusing parents (2005–2006). Poster presented at the 15th Annual Conference of the Society for Prevention Research, Washington, DC.

Petrie, J., Bunn, F., & Byrne, G. (2007). Parenting programmes for preventing tobacco, alcohol or drugs misuse in children <18: A systematic review. *Health Education Research, 22*, 177–191.

Phinney, J. (1996). When we talk about American ethnic groups, what do we mean? *American Psychologist, 51*, 917–918.

Pickens, R. W., Svikis, D. S., Mcgue, M., Lykken, D. T., Heston, L. L., & Clayton, P. J. (1991). Heterogeneity in the inheritance of alcoholism: A study of male and female twins. *Archives of General Psychiatry, 48*, 19–28.

Pinyuchon, M. (2010). *The effectiveness of father involvement in the Strengthening Thai Families Program.* Paper at NIDA International Forum, Scottsdale. AZ, June 12, 2010.

Reel, J. J., & Beal, K. (2009). *The hidden faces of eating disorders.* Reston, VA: AAPHERD.

Resnicow, K., Soler, R., Braithwaite, R. L., Ahluwalia, J. S., & Butler, J. (2000). Cultural sensitivity in substance use prevention. *Journal of Community Psychology, 28*, 271–290.

Rodnium, J. (2007). Causes of delinquency: The Social Ecology Model for Thai Youth. Unpublished dissertation, Department of Health Promotion and Education, University of Utah, Salt Lake City.

Sales, E., Sambrano, S., Springer, F. J., & Turner, C. (2003). Risk, protection, and substance use in adolescents: A multi-site model. *Journal of Drug Education, 33*(1), 91–105.

Sanders, M. R. (1999). Triple P positive parenting program: Towards an empirically validated multilevel parenting and family support strategy for the prevention of behaviour and emotional problems in children. *Clinical Child and Family Psychology Review, 2*, 71–90.

Sanders, M. R., & Kirby, J. N. (2012). Consumer engagement and the development, evaluation and dissemination of evidence-based parenting programs. *Behavior Therapy Journal, 10*, doi:10.1016/j.beth.2011.01.005.

Sanders, M., Calam, R., Durand, M., Liversidge, T., & Carmont, S. A. (2008). Does self-directed and web-based support for parents enhance the effects of viewing a reality television series based on the Triple P–Positive Parenting Programme? *Journal of Child Psychology and Psychiatry, 49*, 924–932.

Sanders, M. R., Turner, K. M. T., & Markie-Dadds, C. (2002). The development and dissemination of the Triple P—Positive Parenting Program: A multilevel, evidence-based system of parenting and family support. *Prevention Science, 3*, 173–189.

Schaeffer, C. M., & Borduin, C. M. (2005). Long-term follow-up to a randomized clinical trial of multisystemic therapy with serious and violent juvenile offenders. *Journal of Consulting and Clinical Psychology, 73*(3), 445–453.

Schinke, S. P., Cole, K. C., & Fang, L. (2009). Gender-specific intervention to reduce underage drinking in early adolescent girls: Test of a computer-mediated Mother-Daughter Program. *Journal of Studies on Alcohol Drugs, 70*, 70–77.

Schinke, S. P., Fang, L., Cole, K. C., & Cohen-Cutler, S. (2011). Preventing substance abuse among Black and Hispanic adolescent girls: Results from a computer-delivered, mother-daughter intervention approach. *Substance Use and Misuse, 46*(1), 35–45.

Schwinn, T. M., Schinke, S. P., & Di Noia, J. (2010). Preventing drug abuse among adolescent girls: Outcome data from an internet-based intervention. *Prevention Science, 11,* 24–32.

Skärstrand, E., Larsson, J., & Andreasson, S. (2008). Cultural adaptation of the Strengthening Families Programme to a Swedish Setting. *Health Education, 108*, 287–300.

Sypeck, M. F., Gray, J. J., & Ahrens, A. H. (2004). No longer just a pretty face: Fashion magazines' depictions of ideal female beauty from 1959 to 1999. *International Journal of Eating Disorders, 36*, 342–347.

Testa, M., & Livingston, J. (2009). Alcohol consumption and women's vulnerability to sexual victimization: Can reducing women's drinking prevent rape? *Substance Use and Misuse, 44*(9–10), 1349–1376.

United Nations (2008). *Depth study on violence against women, 2006.* Electronic document http://www.un.org/en/women/endviolence/pdf/VAW.pdf.

United Nations Office on Drugs and Crime (2009). *Guide to implementing family skills training programmes for drug abuse prevention.* Vienna, Austria: United Nations Office on Drugs and Crime. Electronic document https://www.unodc.org/documents/prevention/family-guidelines-E.pdf.

United Nations Office on Drugs and Crime (2010). *Compilation of evidence-based family skills training programmes.* Vienna, Austria: United Nations Office on Drugs and Crime. Retrieved from http://www.coe.int/t/dg3/children/corporalpunishment/positive%20parenting/UNODCFamilySkillsTrainingProgrammes.pdf.

US Census Bureau (2012). *America's families and living arrangements: 2012.* Retrieved from http://www.census.gov/hhes/families/data/cps2012.html.

Valentine, J. C., Biglan, A., Boruch, R. F., Castro, F. G., Collins, L. M., Flay, B. R. et al. (2011). Replication in prevention science. *Prevention Science, 12*, 103–117.

Watson, J. (2005). *Active engagement: Strategies to increase service participation by vulnerable families.* Ashfield: New South Wales: Centre for Parenting & Research.

Webster-Stratton, C. (1994). Advancing videotape parent training: A comparison study. *Journal of Consulting and Clinical Psychology, 62*(3), 583–593.

Webster-Stratton, C., Reid, M., & Stoolmiller, M. (2008). Preventing conduct problems and improving school readiness: Evaluation of the Incredible Years Teacher and Child Training Programs in high-risk schools. *Journal of Child Psychology and Psychiatry, 5,* 471–488.

13

FAMILY-CENTERED PREVENTION FOR RURAL AFRICAN AMERICANS

The Strong African American Families Program (SAAF), the Strong African American Families–Teen Program (SAAF–T), and the Adults in the Making Program (AIM)

Gene H. Brody

Overview

Historically, residing in rural communities in the southern United States has protected African American preadolescents and adolescents from the use of alcohol and other drugs. Recent epidemiological data, however, indicate that African American youths in rural areas use these substances at rates equal to or exceeding those of youths in densely populated inner cities (National Center on Addiction and Substance Abuse, 2000). Escalation of alcohol use has prognostic significance for rural African American youths' educational and occupational opportunities and attainment, involvement with the criminal justice system, and physical health (Centers for Disease Control and Prevention, 2000). Prevention programs designed to deter alcohol use are scarce in the rural South. These circumstances, and the resulting need for prevention programming, led to the development of the Strong African American Families (SAAF) program for preadolescents, the Strong African American Families–Teen (SAAF–T) program for adolescents, and the Adults in the Making (AIM) program for emerging adults. These family-centered prevention programs were developed, implemented, and tested in longitudinal, randomized efficacy trials. Evaluations of these programs confirmed their efficacy in preventing the use of alcohol and other drugs for 2 years or longer (Brody, Murry, Kogan, Gerrard, Gibbons, & Molgaard, 2006; Brody, Chen, Kogan, Smith, & Brown, 2010; Brody et al., 2012). In this chapter, I describe (a) the process of translating etiological research into the prevention programs developed at the Center for Family Research (CFR) of the University of Georgia, (b) each program and the research that verified its efficacy, (c) the ways in which CFR family-centered

Prevention for Rural African Americans **283**

prevention trials were used to test Gene × Environment (G×E) hypotheses, and (d) exploratory research that illustrates the potential benefits of CFR family-centered drug use prevention programs for health outcomes that are tied to the chronic diseases of aging.

Type I Translational Research and the Development of Prevention Programs at the Center for Family Research

An influential report from the Institute of Medicine (IOM; 1994) outlined challenges for preventing mental health problems among youths and established a paradigm for prevention research in general. Recently updated (O'Connell, Boat, & Warner, 2009), this model has sponsored a heightened focus on the translation of longitudinal developmental research to intervention development, program evaluation in randomized trials, and the formulation of effective dissemination strategies to achieve public health impact. As specified by the IOM, the preventive intervention development cycle begins with a definition of a target problem based on demographic and epidemiological information. The second phase involves the use of developmental, epidemiological, and longitudinal research to articulate an etiological model of the problem's development and the specific protective and risk factors involved in that process (Kellam & Van Horn, 1997). The protective and risk factors that can be modified are identified as proximal targets for prevention programming.

Longitudinal Developmental Research with Rural African American Families

For more than 25 years, scientists at CFR have been conducting systematic investigations of rural African American family life. More than 4,000 families, the majority of whom live in or close to poverty, have taken part in this research. Longitudinal developmental studies that CFR researchers implemented have examined models of family and contextual processes associated with self-regulation, psychological adjustment, academic and social competence, and drug use among rural African American children, adolescents, and young adults; studies also have examined protective-stabilizing factors that moderate the effects of risk on child and adolescent development, enabling youths to avoid negative developmental trajectories.

Empirical Basis for Translating Protective Caregiving into a Prevention Target for Rural African American Families

On the basis of the tenets of the IOM model, processes that demonstrate protective capacities by promoting development or reducing risk and are malleable—that is, amenable to change through prevention programming—are

284 Gene H. Brody

candidates for translation. In this section, I review findings that support the translation of protective caregiving into components of preventive interventions designed specifically for rural African American families. As youths grow and mature, the exact form of protective caregiving changes to insure that parenting behaviors continue to be age appropriate. These behaviors are defined in detail in the sections describing CFR prevention programs.

Two types of findings support the design of preventive interventions for rural African American families; they concern buffering models and mediational analyses. Buffering effects occur when people who are exposed to similar adverse experiences differ in their outcomes. These models are used to identify variables that operate to reduce the impact of risk factors, particularly for persons experiencing high levels of adversity. My colleagues and I hypothesized that protective caregiving practices, such as emotional support, would buffer youths from contextual disadvantages and the risk factors that covary with them. Mediational analyses specify how a risk or protective process affects a distal outcome by identifying intermediate processes in the pathway. For example, self-regulation could mediate the influence of protective caregiving on youth outcomes, such as the use of alcohol and other drugs.

Buffering Properties of Protective Caregiving

In resilience research (Luthar, 2006), variables that moderate the influence of contextual disadvantage are called "protective-stabilizing" because protective processes contribute to stable youth functioning despite the presence of risk. Demonstrating that protective caregiving could buffer risks that African American youths in the rural South commonly experience, such as exposure to dangerous neighborhoods, poorly organized classrooms, and racial discrimination, would further buttress our decision to translate protective caregiving practices into prevention programs.

Three sets of studies from our research program examined protective-stabilizing effects of protective caregiving. The first set examined the possibility that residence in rural neighborhoods characterized by high unemployment rates and pervasive poverty could increase children's risk for physiological indicators of stress (Brody, Lei, Chen, & Miller, 2014), affiliation with deviant peers (Brody et al., 2001), development of conduct problems (Brody, Ge et al., 2003), and development of cognitions that increase the likelihood of substance use (Cleveland, Gibbons, Gerrard, Pomery, & Brody, 2005). We also tested the protective-stabilizing hypothesis that protective caregiving would buffer these adverse neighborhood effects and found that youths residing in disadvantaged neighborhoods whose caregivers used high levels of protective caregiving displayed fewer physiological indicators of stress, affiliated less with deviant peers, displayed fewer conduct problems, and evinced fewer risk cognitions than did those in similar neighborhoods whose caregivers used few protective practices (Brody, Chen et al., 2012).

Using a three-wave longitudinal design (Brody, Chen et al., 2006; Brody, Kogan, & Chen, 2012; Brody, Lei, Chae et al., 2014), we found that heightened levels of protective caregiving reduced the likelihood that African American youths who reported racial discrimination would develop conduct problems or depressive symptoms. The results indicated that (a) increases in perceived discrimination were linked positively with the development of conduct problems, depressive symptoms, and indicators of physiological stress; and (b) the impact of perceived discrimination on the outcome variables was reduced when youths received relatively high levels of protective caregiving. The protective-stabilizing effects were strong, as indicated by the effect size (Jaccard, Dittus, & Gordon, 1996); the effect size of the coefficient for the association between perceived discrimination and youth outcomes in the "low" protective caregiving group was three times as large as the coefficient for the "high" group, supporting the inclusion of positive parenting skills in prevention programs.

Mediation Evidence

Mediational analyses permitted assessment of the mechanisms through which protective caregiving affected youths' development. Empirical analyses revealed that protective caregiving practices consistently forecast high levels of youth self-regulation, academic achievement, social competence, and avoidance of affiliations with deviant peers, along with low levels of externalizing and internalizing problems, low levels of substance use, and disinterest in antisocial self-presentation. Consistent with the conceptual underpinnings of the research program, the links between rural African American parents' protective caregiving and youths' outcomes were consistently mediated through the association of caregiving with self-regulation. Support for the pathway from protective caregiving to self-regulation to youths' development of competence and positive adjustment emerged consistently from both contemporaneous (Brody & Flor, 1997, 1998; Wills, Ainette, Mendoza, Gibbons, & Brody, 2007) and longitudinal (Brody, Dorsey, Forehand, & Armistead, 2002; Brody & Ge, 2001; Brody, Kim, Murry, & Brown, 2003, 2004, 2005; Kim & Brody, 2005) analyses.

Community Partnership Processes

At the outset of the CFR's etiological and prevention science research programs, little longitudinal, ecologically informed research on child and youth development had been conducted in rural African American communities. This lack of studies can be attributed, in part, to challenges in recruiting and retaining participants in these communities. Fear, mistrust, and lack of knowledge regarding research and those who conduct it play critical roles in dissuading parents from participating in public health, developmental, and prevention research (Corbie-Smith, Thomas, Williams, & Moody-Ayers, 1999). Participation in research is an unfamiliar experience for most families, children, and adolescents; it can be a particularly ambiguous and anxiety-provoking experience for rural African Americans. Given this context, it was imperative that CFR create partnerships with representatives of the population from which samples were drawn to (a) establish the good faith and credibility of our intentions, and (b) develop research protocols that were acceptable to the participants and with which they were comfortable. Two partnership mechanisms were implemented to facilitate these goals: the community liaison system, and the use of focus groups to provide ongoing feedback on research activities, questions, and findings.

Community Liaison Network

The retention of over 90% of the participants in the CFR longitudinal epidemiological studies and randomized prevention trials is attributable to the establishment of a community liaison network. Community liaisons are residents of the counties in which the study families live and act as contacts between CFR and the communities. They are selected on the basis of their reputations in their communities and the extent of their community social contacts. This network has been invaluable in establishing credibility with study participants. The liaisons review study protocols prior to implementation and make suggestions for improving them. The liaisons work with the CFR recruitment coordinator to enroll families and then remain in contact with participating families, tracking the addresses and phone numbers of participants who move. The community liaisons' roles were expanded during the implementation of CFR prevention programs, with the liaisons and the prevention coordinator working together to facilitate families' engagement. Families taking part in prevention programming were contacted between sessions to identify and solve any problems that might interfere with attendance at the next session.

Focus Groups

Scientists at CFR routinely consult focus groups of rural African American community members for feedback about measures and methodology. For example, in our initial focus group work (Brody & Stoneman, 1992), we were concerned about accurate assessment because most instruments used to evaluate family processes and individual outcomes were developed for use with, and were standardized on, middle-class European American families. Focus groups composed of 20–40 community members evaluated the measures that we planned to use. Each member rated every instrument on a Likert-type scale ranging from 1 (*not appropriate* for rural African American families) through 3 (*appropriate*) to 5 (*very appropriate*). Instruments that attained a mean rating of 3.5 or higher were used in the studies. The group members also reviewed every item on each scale for wording clarity and relevance to rural African Americans.

Item wording was changed and items were deleted in response to their feedback. Similar protocols were used as additional studies were initiated.

Focus groups also provide feedback regarding research models, longitudinal epidemiological studies, prevention models, prevention topics, program content, and protocols for collecting biological data. Proposed conceptual and prevention models are presented to focus group members, whose feedback increases the models' ecological sensitivity and cultural validity. For example, a focus group of rural African American community members urged CFR researchers to include the role of the African American church in the conceptual scheme of a longitudinal study concerning competence-promoting influences in rural African American children's lives. Accordingly, church and religious influences were included in the model, operationalized, and assessed. Several analyses have confirmed the importance of the church and religious faith to individual and family well-being among rural African Americans (Brody & Flor, 1998; Brody, Stoneman, & Flor, 1996a, 1996b).

The Structure of the Prevention Programs

Culturally and ecologically valid *family skills training* programs were developed for rural African American preadolescents, adolescents, and emerging adults. The family skills training approach integrates individual youth skill building, parenting skills training, and family interaction training (Kumpfer & Alvarado, 2003). Family skills training was selected based on several considerations. It was particularly attractive to the rural families who participated in focus groups. Evidence also suggests that the integration of youth, caregiver, and family curricula may produce better outcomes than does targeting only youths or only caregivers in prevention programming (Foxcroft, Ireland, Lister-Sharp, Lowe, & Breen, 2003; Spoth, Redmond, Trudeau, & Shin, 2002). The family skills format has also outperformed parent-only interventions in facilitating protective caregiving (Spoth, Redmond, & Shin, 1998). This model also permits program implementation by facilitators who, although trained to conduct the intervention, do not have postsecondary education or clinical certification. Few African Americans in rural areas have these credentials.

These programs are designed to accommodate groups of 8 to 13 families. Caregivers and youths attend a structured program that is composed of weekly 2-hour meetings: seven meetings for SAAF, six meetings for AIM, and five meetings for SAAF–T. In the first hour, caregivers and youths meet separately; in the second hour, families practice the skills they learned in their separate sessions in a joint caregiver–youth session. Youth and caregiver sessions have parallel content during most meetings, with the family session providing reinforcement and skills practice. Because the family skills approach is highly structured, a detailed curriculum manual is used and all activities are timed. Program content for the caregivers' sessions is delivered by narrators on DVDs

288 Gene H. Brody

that also depict family interactions illustrating targeted behaviors. DVDs are used in some youth sessions, showing age-appropriate models discussing typical high-risk situations and ways of dealing with temptation and peer pressure issues. Structured activities, games, role-playing, and group discussions are also part of the youth sessions. Group leaders facilitate activities, guide group discussions, organize role-playing and other interactive activities, and answer participants' questions. Leaders are provided with materials designed to help them correctly execute the session protocol; these materials include an outline of each session, a checklist of the materials necessary for each activity, the specific theme of each task, and forms for in-session notes. This carefully structured approach standardizes much of the content and facilitates fidelity in implementation.

The Strong African American Families Prevention Trial

An Overview of the SAAF Randomized Trial

Participants in the original SAAF randomized prevention trial were African American youths (mean age at pretest = 11.2 years) and their primary caregivers, who resided in rural Georgia. Families in this area live in small towns and communities in which poverty rates are among the highest in the nation and unemployment rates are above the national average (Proctor & Dalaker, 2003). The intervention group included 369 families, and the control group included 298 families. Families were oversampled into the intervention to ensure that at least 350 would take part in SAAF. From lists that schools provided, 11-year-old African Americans residing in nine rural counties were randomly selected. Their families were contacted and invited to participate; the recruitment rate of 64% exceeds rates commonly reported for prevention trials. Recruitment procedures are described in detail in Brody, Murry et al. (2004). Of the recruited families, 85% completed pretest, posttest, and four long-term follow-up assessments, the last of which took place 5.4 years after the pretest. To preserve the random nature of the group assignments, the analyses included all families in the intervention condition who completed all assessments regardless of the number of prevention sessions they actually attended, a procedure called an intent-to-treat analysis.

At each data collection point, one home visit lasting 2 hours was made to each family. Field researchers administered self-report questionnaires to caregivers and youths in an interview format. At the same time that the intervention families participated in seven 2-hour prevention sessions, the control families received three leaflets via postal mail; the leaflets dealt with development in early adolescence, stress management, and suggestions for encouraging children to exercise. Caregivers in the prevention condition were taught involved–vigilant parenting, which includes the consistent use of nurturant–involved parenting along with high levels of monitoring and control, adaptive racial socialization strategies, strategies for communication about sex, and the establishment of clear expectations about alcohol use. Program content for the youth sessions focused on the importance of caring family relationships and compliance with household rules, peer pressure and resistance efficacy strategies, and development of a positive racial identity.

Testing the Validity of SAAF's Theoretical Underpinnings

The SAAF causative model includes the hypotheses that (a) participation in the intervention would increase protective caregiving and youth intrapersonal protective processes, and (b) intervention-induced changes in youth self-regulation would be mediated through the intervention's effects on involved–vigilant parenting. As hypothesized, parents in SAAF reported greater changes from pretest to posttest in involved–vigilant parenting than did control parents (β = .33, p < .01), and youths in SAAF demonstrated greater changes in intrapersonal protective processes than did control youths (β = .23, p < .01). Of particular interest was the finding that, in control families, both parent and youth protective processes declined, whereas the same processes increased in families randomly assigned to participate in SAAF. Thus, across the relatively short period of 7 months that separated the pretest and posttest, protective processes among control families began to wane during a developmental period when youths begin to spend more time away from home and with peers. A hypothesis was tested that changes in involved–vigilant parenting would mediate the effect of treatment condition on changes in youth protective factors. The analyses met all of Baron and Kenny's (1986) criteria for mediation.

SAAF Efficacy

In addition to evaluating effects on alcohol use, we ran a test to determine whether SAAF-induced increases in youth protective factors from the pretest to posttest assessments would mediate the influence of SAAF on alcohol use at the first long-term follow-up (Brody, Murry et al., 2006). Our results revealed that, compared with adolescents in the control condition, fewer SAAF participants initiated alcohol use, and those who did increased their use at a slower rate over time. The analysis also confirmed the proposed mediational hypothesis: Youth self-regulation at posttest, with pretest levels controlled, were associated with decreases from pretest to long-term follow-up in youth alcohol use, and the impact of group assignment was not significant in the presence of SAAF-induced increases from pretest to posttest in youth protective factors. These results confirmed findings from the CFR longitudinal developmental research program regarding the etiological processes that forecast youth alcohol use

290 Gene H. Brody

(Brody, Ge, Katz, & Arias, 2000; Gibbons, Gerrard, Cleveland, Wills, & Brody, 2004; Wills, Yaeger, & Sandy, 2003). The second analysis addressed SAAF's continuing efficacy more than 5 years after program participation (Brody, Chen, Kogan, Murry, & Brown, 2010). The results showed that, 65 months after the pretest, youths who participated in SAAF reported drinking half as often during the previous month than did those in the control condition.

The Strong African American Families–Teen (SAAF–T) Prevention Trial

SAAF–T builds on other family-centered intervention programs—particularly SAAF—that have been found to enhance parent and youth competence while inhibiting substance use, delinquent activity, and other co-occurring problems among youths in elementary school and middle school (Brody, Murry et al., 2004; Kumpfer, Alvarado, & Whiteside, 2003; Leigh & Stahl, 1993). For broad public health impact, however, family-centered prevention programs must be available for youths at all developmental stages. Unfortunately, no family-centered prevention programs for rural African American adolescents had been developed and tested, despite epidemiologic research that highlights the emergence and escalation of substance use, conduct problems, and depressive symptoms around the time of high school entry (Brody, Chen, & Kogan, 2010; O'Connell et al., 2009). The development of these problems could be addressed with timely intervention. The development and evaluation of SAAF–T was designed to meet the need for family-centered prevention programs for adolescents in general and for African American adolescents in particular. Participants in the trial included 502 African American families in rural Georgia; in each family, an adolescent who was 16 years of age at recruitment (51% girls) and the adolescent's primary caregiver (in most cases the biological mother) provided data.

Overview of Trial

Researchers made one visit lasting 2 hours to each family at each assessment. The time from pretest to long-term follow-up averaged 22 months. When completing pretest measures, families had not yet been assigned to SAAF–T or the control group. Data on adolescents' conduct problems, substance use, substance use problems, and depressive symptoms were obtained via self-report at ages 16 years (pretest) and 17 years 10 months (long-term follow-up) from all adolescents taking part in the study.

Adolescents and their families were randomly assigned to either SAAF–T or the attention control program. The use of an attention control group is unique in evaluations of the efficacy of family-centered interventions. Typically, control groups in such evaluations receive either no treatment or minimal information.

Prevention for Rural African Americans **291**

These designs do not control for nonspecific factors, such as social support from intervention trainers and other group members, which arguably could be responsible for observed intervention effects. To provide a more stringent efficacy evaluation, all families, whether assigned to SAAF–T or the attention control condition, attended a five-session, 10-hour group prevention program held at community facilities.

The SAAF–T program followed the structure of the SAAF program, including separate caregiver and adolescent skill-building curricula and a family curriculum presented during 1-hour concurrent training sessions and a 1-hour family session. During the implementation of SAAF–T, the attention control group participated in a family-centered intervention designed to promote healthful behaviors among adolescents by encouraging good nutrition, exercise, and informed consumer behavior. The school-based FUEL program was adapted into the five-session family skills format used in SAAF–T. The result was a program structurally similar to SAAF–T that we named Fuel for Families (FF).

In SAAF–T, caregivers were taught developmentally appropriate use of monitoring and control, adaptive racial socialization approaches that included guidance for dealing with discrimination, establishment of clear norms and expectations about adolescent substance use, provision of academic support, and cooperative caregiver-adolescent problem solving. Adolescents were taught the importance of having and following household rules, strategies to use when encountering racism, the importance of academic success, goal formation, and strategies for attaining educational and occupational goals. Most importantly, optional training on safer sex practices, particularly condom use, was provided. To preserve the random nature of the group assignments, data analyses included all families regardless of the number of program sessions they attended, an intent-to-treat analysis. Both SAAF–T and FF families attended an average of four of the five program sessions.

SAAF–T Efficacy

The analyses for changes in the frequencies of conduct problems, substance use, and substance use problems revealed consistent results. SAAF–T participation caused significant and robust prevention effects (all $ps < .001$), such that participation in SAAF–T, compared with participation in the attention control program, was associated with a 36% decrease ($100*[1 - e^{-0.442}]$) in the frequency of conduct problems, a 32% decrease in substance use ($100*[1 - e^{-0.637}]$), and a 47% decrease ($100*[1 - e^{-0.442}]$) in substance use problems. With socioeconomic risk, gender, and pretest depression levels controlled, SAAF–T participants experienced fewer depressive symptoms over time than did attention control participants ($p < .01$). SAAF–T participants evinced a 4.5% decrease in depressive symptoms relative to participants in the attention control program.

292 Gene H. Brody

The Adults in the Making (AIM) Prevention Trial

The transition from adolescence to emerging adulthood involves pervasive contextual and social role changes that can increase young people's involvement in health-risk behaviors, including marijuana use, excessive drinking, and sexual intercourse while using substances (Kogan et al., 2008; Schulenberg, Sameroff, & Cicchetti, 2004). The stress that this transition engenders is particularly salient for risk behavior trajectories among emerging adult populations who confront sociodemographic stressors (French, Finkbiner, & Duhamel, 2002). For example, after leaving high school, rural African American emerging adults confront environments that provide minimal opportunities and resources for employment or continuing education to help them embark on beneficial life paths. Some who see no pathway to adequate subsistence or attainment of life goals may cope by drinking excessively, using marijuana, or having sexual intercourse (Fergus & Zimmerman, 2005). Not all emerging adults, however, evince increases in risk behaviors when they confront sociodemographic and contextual stressors that include opportunity limitations.

The AIM program was designed to buffer the negative impact of life stress and contextual stress (e.g., racial discrimination, conflicted family relationships, deviant companions) on rural African Americans and to prevent increases in risk behavior by increasing the provision of family-based buffering processes such as emotional and instrumental support, vocational coaching and advocacy, and racial socialization. The curriculum was informed by studies of protective processes demonstrating that, despite challenging circumstances, many rural African Americans display positive psychological adjustment and low levels of risk behavior across adolescence (Brody, Murry et al., 2004; Vazsonyi, Trejos-Castillo, & Young, 2008). These studies indicate that protective caregiving contributes to low levels of internalizing problems, externalizing problems, and substance use among rural African American adolescents (Brody & Ge, 2001).

Vocational coaching and advocacy is another key element of effective support for rural African American emerging adults (Kogan & Brody, 2010). Vocational coaching includes talking to young adults about future jobs and education, helping them plan, and instilling confidence for pursuing their plans (O'Brien & Fassinger, 1993; Rainey & Borders, 1997). Parents' vocational support is linked with adolescents' vocational aspirations and achievements, career decisiveness, commitment, and self-efficacy (Ferry, Fouad, & Smith, 2000; Hargrove, Creagh, & Burgess, 2002). Protective family processes also include continuing racial socialization that includes strategies for dealing with discrimination. Thus, my colleagues and I predicted that AIM would reduce the impact of life stressors on increases in risk behaviors.

Overview of the AIM Trial

Participants were 347 African American students in the last 2 years of secondary school (M age = 17.7 years) who resided in six rural counties in Georgia. The AIM program consists of six consecutive weekly meetings, held at community facilities and structured in the same manner as SAAF and SAAF–T. Parents and youths receive 12 hours of prevention training. Parents in the prevention condition were taught to provide developmentally appropriate emotional and instrumental support, to provide ongoing racial socialization that included strategies for dealing with discrimination, to provide occupational and educational mentoring, to promote autonomy and adult responsibility, and to encourage responsible decisions about risk behaviors. Youths in the prevention condition were taught to develop a future orientation, to plan to meet goals, to identify people in their communities who could help them attain goals, to cope with barriers and racial discrimination, and to formulate self-care strategies.

AIM Efficacy

Latent growth modeling (LGM) was used to test the efficacy of AIM (Brody, Chen, Kogan, Smith et al., 2010; Brody, Yu, Chen, Kogan, & Smith, 2012). Contextual risk, a composite formed from family conflict, affiliation with deviant companions, and exposure to racial discrimination, was regressed on the intercept of alcohol use (alcohol use prevalence at pretest); participation in AIM, contextual risk, and the AIM × contextual risk interaction were regressed on the slope of alcohol use. Contextual risk was positively associated with the intercept of alcohol use, indicating that participants who experienced high levels of contextual risk were likely to report alcohol use at the beginning of the study. A significant AIM × contextual risk interaction predicted the slope of alcohol use. As predicted, the interaction suggests that participants in the control group who experienced high levels of contextual risk were more likely than AIM participants to increase their alcohol use over time. No significant differences between the control and AIM groups emerged for alcohol use when contextual risk was low.

Using Randomized Prevention Trials to Test Gene × Environment Hypotheses

Randomized prevention trials provide a unique opportunity to test hypotheses about the interaction of genetic predispositions with contextual processes to create variations in phenotypes over time. Such transactions are termed Gene × Environment (G×E) interactions (Shanahan & Hofer, 2005). Typically, G×E interactions have been studied using epidemiological research designs in which interactions among genotypes and environmental risk factors are observed at one point in time or as they unfold over time. This approach has some limitations, the most notable of which involves difficulty in determining whether an observed environmental effect is causal or results from unmeasured variables. Through the implementation of randomized prevention trials, a causal relationship between an environmental manipulation and the alteration of a phenotype can be identified, and the likelihood that genetic status moderates the environmental effect of the prevention program can be determined. An additional advantage of this approach is that, because the environmental variable is randomized, prevention trials control for gene–environment correlations that can masquerade as G×E interactions (Rutter, 2005).

Theoretical support for this research was derived from a differential susceptibility hypothesis (Belsky, Bakermans-Kranenburg, & van IJzendoorn, 2007). This hypothesis posits that genetic polymorphisms influence the extent to which individuals respond to environmental contexts, with some individuals primed by their genes to be more sensitive or adaptable than others. Van IJzendoorn, Bakermans-Kranenburg, and Ebstein (2011) and Bakermans-Kranenburg and van IJzendoorn (2014) have published meta-analyses supporting this conjecture. The results showed that children and adolescents carrying specific alleles in the serotonin and dopaminergic systems were more sensitive to both positive and negative environmental influences. Applied to CFR research, youths assigned randomly to a prevention condition who carry a putative sensitivity allele would be expected to be more responsive than other youths to intervention-induced changes in protective practices. This sensitivity, in turn, would be expected to result in a decrease in youths' substance use over time.

G×E findings

Several studies from CFR have provided initial evidence of the utility of randomized controlled trials in circumventing the issues inherent in epidemiological G×E studies. In the SAAF randomized trial, Brody, Beach, Philibert, Chen, and Murry (2009) found that the intervention was particularly efficacious for children carrying 1 or 2 copies of the serotonin transporter short allele at the 5-HTTLPR, protecting them from initiation and escalation of risk behaviors. These short alleles are not rare but occur in about 40% of Caucasians, 50% of African Americans, and 60% of Asians. Genetic risk was determined by using simple saliva tests. Other research has shown SAAF's efficacy to be genetically moderated by the 7-repeat version of the dopamine receptor-4 gene (*DRD4*). Beach, Brody, Lei, and Philibert (2010) demonstrated that preadolescents who carried the 7-repeat version of *DRD4* and were assigned to SAAF evinced considerably less drug use across 2 years than did youths with the same genotype who were assigned to the control group. Finally, Brody, Yu, Chen, and Miller (2014) found that African American adolescents carrying the 7-repeat allele of *DRD4* benefited most from SAAF–T.

Finally, my colleagues and I conducted a study using data pooled from the SAAF and SAAF–T trials to create a more powerful sample with which to extend knowledge about G×E hypotheses (Brody, Chen, & Beach, 2013). The study was designed to answer two questions. First, do common variations in the dopaminergic genes (*DRD2, DRD2/ANKK1, TaqI A,* and *DRD4*) and GABAergic genes (*GABRG1* and *GABRA2*) forecast increases in alcohol use for youths assigned randomly to the pooled control condition? Presumably, youths in the control condition represent normative alcohol use patterns and therefore provide an opportunity to determine whether putative risk/sensitivity genes for alcohol use are actually associated with increases in use across 2 years. Second, can participation in efficacious prevention programming moderate the risk that dopaminergic and GABAergic genes confer for increases in youths' alcohol use across 2 years? Prior to this study, evaluations of prevention program efficacy in moderating genetic risk have been limited by their reliance on single genetic loci (predominantly *DRD4*), despite the likelihood that many youths carry multiple risk-conferring loci (Rutter, 2005). This study was unique in combining data from two large prevention trials involving more than 900 youths to test hypotheses about gene × prevention interactions.

The results revealed that dopaminergic and GABAergic candidate genes forecast increases in alcohol use across 2 years. This finding established the validity of these genes' designation as conferring risk/sensitivity because each gene forecast increases in alcohol use. Second, the risk conferred by the six genes was moderated by participation in a prevention program. Youths who carried the risk variations of the dopaminergic and GABAergic genes who were assigned to the control condition evinced more alcohol use over time than did (a) those who were assigned to the prevention condition, or (b) those assigned to either condition who carried the non-risk genetic variant. Of the six significant gene × prevention interactions, three remained significant ($p < .05$) after significance levels were adjusted for multiple comparisons: *GABRG1,* Block 2; *GABRA2,* Block 1; and *DRD2.* The results support Belsky et al.'s (2007) differential susceptibility hypothesis in which variants of specific genes, including dopaminergic and GABAergic genes, are proposed to render individuals more susceptible to the surrounding environment, whether it is characterized by high positivity or high risk. The finding that, after exposure to the protective processes that the prevention programs offered, carriers of risk/sensitivity genes evinced less alcohol use over time than did similar youths in the control condition supports differential susceptibility predictions. These results extended the existing literature to previously unstudied genes. The finding that participation in prevention moderated genetic risk and the retention of significance by three of those genes after controls for multiple comparisons were applied supports the importance of prevention efforts and the explanatory value of differential susceptibility theory.

New Explorations: Health Benefits of Participation in CFR Family-Centered Prevention Programs

As children from low-SES families mature, they continue to experience health problems at rates that are substantially higher than those of their more advantaged peers. Low-SES youths show a heightened prevalence of obesity, insulin resistance, and asthma (Chen, Matthews, & Boyce, 2002; Goodman, Daniels, & Dolan, 2007; Singh, Siahpush, & Kogan, 2010; Wright & Subramanian, 2007). These conditions appear to act as precursors of chronic diseases associated with aging. When they reach the later stages of life, persons who grew up in low-SES families show excessive morbidity and mortality from stroke, coronary heart disease, some cancers, and chronic lung diseases (Galobardes, Lynch, & Smith, 2004, 2008; Galobardes, Smith, Jeffreys, & McCarron, 2006; Galobardes, Smith, & Lynch, 2006). These associations are typically independent of SES in adulthood, suggesting that childhood disadvantage can leave a biological "residue" with long-term health consequences.

Despite these trends, not all low-SES children have, or go on to develop, health problems (Chen & Miller, 2012). Evidence suggests that a subset of youths develop resilience to the health consequences of low-SES environments if they receive high-quality parenting. One study followed rural adolescents across 3 years and found that disadvantage was associated with increasing allostatic load, a composite indicator of cardiometabolic risk. These trends, however, were absent in low-SES youths whose mothers were rated as highly responsive to their needs (Evans, Kim, Ting, Tesher, & Shannis, 2007). Similar patterns have emerged in retrospective studies of adults. One such study found that low childhood SES was associated with heightened prevalence of metabolic syndrome at midlife (Miller, Lachman et al., 2011). Again, however, this effect was offset by nurturing parenting. Participants who reported that they grew up in nurturant low-SES families had metabolic risks identical to those of participants from higher-SES households. A third study explored the relation of maternal nurturance to inflammation, a process central to the pathogenesis of many health problems that pattern by SES (Libby, Ridker, Hansson, & Leducq Transatlantic Network on Atherothrombosis, 2009; Miller, Chen, & Parker, 2011; Nathan & Ding, 2010). Among participants who grew up in low-SES families, maternal nurturance was associated with better regulation of inflammation.

Can Participation in SAAF Reduce Inflammation?

The findings regarding the protective benefits of nurturant parenting are provocative. To the extent that they reflect a causal process in which nurturant parenting offsets some of the health risks associated with childhood disadvantage, they have theoretical implications for a number of research domains, including those focused on social disparities, early origins of disease, and resilience to adversity. Causal inferences, however, cannot easily be gleaned from existing studies because their observational designs are prone to residual confounding and reverse directionality errors. We navigated around these interpretational problems by conducting secondary analyses of SAAF (Miller, Brody, Yu, & Chen, 2014). The endpoint was low-grade inflammation, a process that underlies many health problems to which low-SES youths are vulnerable. When youths reached age 19, peripheral blood was collected to quantify six cytokines that orchestrate inflammation. Youths who participated in the intervention had significantly less inflammation according to all six indicators than did controls (all p values < 0.001; effect sizes in Cohen's d units ranged from -0.69 to -0.91). Mediation analyses suggested that improved parenting was partially responsible for the intervention's benefits. Inflammation was lowest among youths who received more nurturant-involved parenting, and less harsh-inconsistent parenting, as a consequence of the intervention. These findings have theoretical implications for research on resilience to adversity and the early origins of disease. If substantiated, they may also highlight a strategy for practitioners and policymakers to use in ameliorating social and racial health disparities.

Protective Effect of SAAF on Stress Hormones

A growing body of research has tested the hypothesis that family emotional climate during childhood and adolescence may contribute to chronic diseases later in life (Chen & Miller, 2012). The *risky family model* offers a psychosocial account of the impact that stress during childhood exerts on health (Repetti, Taylor, & Seeman, 2002). It posits that some families confer risk for later health problems by producing emotionally cold, nonsupportive rearing environments in which primary caregivers evince elevated depressive symptoms and low self-esteem. Such rearing environments are hypothesized to influence the development of the body's stress response systems such as the sympathetic nervous system (SNS), calibrating the way in which it responds to threats across the life course.

The SNS enables people to mount biobehavioral responses, such as fight or flight, which mobilize bodily resources to cope with threats. Everyday SNS activity is typically indexed by overnight urinary concentrations of the system's hormonal end products, the catecholamines epinephrine and norepinephrine. Although SNS responses can be adaptive for managing short-term threats, considerable research with animal models suggests that such responses can take a physiological toll on affected organs if frequent, prolonged, or both (Manuck, Marsland, Kaplan, & Williams, 1995; Sloan, Capitanio, & Cole, 2008). The impact of chronic hormonal surges from the SNS may accumulate with time, leading to multisystem dysregulation that contributes to health problems (Reuben, Talvi, Rowe, & Seeman, 2000).

Our analysis was designed to advance understanding of the association between risky family processes and SNS activity by testing two hypotheses with youths who took part in SAAF. The first hypothesis proposed that youths assigned randomly to the control condition who, at age 11, were living with a primary caregiver who reported psychological dysfunction—defined as relatively high levels of depressive symptoms and low self-esteem—or provided nonsupportive parenting would evince relatively high catecholamine levels at age 20. This study also tested the hypothesis that, among youths exposed to nonsupportive parenting or low caregiver functioning, random assignment to SAAF would be associated with relatively low catecholamine levels at age 20. As mentioned earlier, in observational studies, enhancing parental warmth, involvement, and communication have buffered youths from the effects of stress on biological regulatory systems (Chen & Miller, 2012). Evaluations of SAAF confirmed its efficacy in enhancing these protective parenting practices (Brody, Kogan, & Grange, 2012). To test these hypotheses, primary caregivers provided data on their own depressive symptoms and self-esteem at baseline, when youths were 11.2 years of age, and youths provided data on their receipt of nonsupportive parenting. When the youths were 20 years of age, indicators of SNS activity, the catecholamines epinephrine and norepinephrine, were assayed from their overnight urine voids. The results revealed that parental psychological dysfunction and nonsupportive parenting forecast elevated catecholamine levels for youths in the control condition, but not for those in the SAAF condition. The demonstration that a prevention program can induce reduction of catecholamine levels is important from both theoretical and public health perspectives, because it shows that the developmental progression from family risk factors to heightened sympathetic nervous system activity is not immutable.

Protective Effects of AIM on Telomere Length

To understand how social environments and psychological processes impact aging, researchers seek to identify biomarkers that provide a window into social environments' associations with longevity. Telomere length (TL) appears to be such a marker. Telomeres, the protective caps at the tips of chromosomes, shorten with age; this shortening predicts both disease and longevity (Blackburn, 2005; Epel, 2009). TL may be viewed from a life-span approach because it reflects, in part, the cumulative number of cell divisions that have occurred and the long-term biochemical environment. Many studies find a negative association between age and TL (Monaghan & Haussmann, 2006), but substantial variation in TL exists among age-matched individuals. This suggests that factors other than chronological age affect telomere shortening. Reduction in TL has been associated contemporaneously with the presence of subclinical cardiovascular disease, cancer, stroke, diabetes, and autoimmune disease (Price, Kao, Burgers, Carpenter, & Tyrka, 2013).

A growing body of research has demonstrated that telomeres appear to shorten with exposure to chronic stress via the biological indicators of stress exposure such as oxidative, endocrine, inflammatory, and other processes (Aviv, 2008). Studies have found financial stress (Epel et al., 2004), strain associated with caregiving (Kiecolt-Glaser et al., 2011), perceived overall stress (Bauer, Jeckel, & Luz, 2009), and exposure to violence (Shalev et al., 2013) to be associated with diminished TL. This suggests that TL may be useful in determining how psychosocial stress is associated with biological aging at the cellular level. Consistent with suggestions that the chronic diseases of aging originate in biological processes occurring at earlier stages of development (Shonkoff, Boyce, & McEwen, 2009), studies have examined possible associations between childhood adversity and TL. Adverse childhood events that have been found to be associated retrospectively with TL include maltreatment, trauma, parental death, familial mental illness, and parental unemployment. Four of these retrospective studies found that adults who recalled childhood adversity had shorter TL than did controls (Kananen et al., 2010; Kiecolt-Glaser et al., 2011; O'Donovan et al., 2011; Tyrka et al., 2009), and one study did not replicate this association (Glass, Parts, Knowles, Aviv, & Spector, 2010). The sole prospective study found that cumulative exposure to violence was associated with heightened telomere erosion in children across ages 5 to 10 years (Shalev et al., 2013). In our analyses, my colleagues and I sought to extend existing research by examining prospective associations between nonsupportive parenting and TL.

Nonsupportive parenting places children and adolescents at risk through high levels of conflict and low levels of warmth and emotional support. Two hypotheses were tested with participants in the AIM trial. The first hypothesis proposed that youths who, at age 17, received highly nonsupportive parenting would evince shorter TL at age 22. The second hypothesis proposed that adolescents who, at age 17, were assigned to the intervention condition and who received highly nonsupportive parenting would at age 22 evince longer TL than youths in the control condition, indicating less cellular stress. To test these hypotheses, we used the primary caregivers' pretest data on nonsupportive parenting. When the youths were age 22, TL was assayed from a blood draw. The results indicated that (a) high levels of caregiver-reported nonsupportive parenting were associated with diminished TL, and (b) young adults experiencing these risks who were assigned to the control condition evinced shorter TL than did those assigned to AIM who were exposed to the same parenting risk. This demonstration of program-induced maintenance of TL is important from a theoretical viewpoint because it shows that the developmental progression from a risky family factor to TL is not immutable. From a public health perspective, the results suggest that developmentally appropriate interventions designed to enhance supportive parenting practices can buffer the effects of receipt of nonsupportive parenting on TL.

Some Reflections on Prevention and Health

The SAAF, SAAF–T, and AIM trials were not designed with health outcomes in mind. Consequently, we did not collect blood samples or overnight urine voids before the trials that could be used to determine whether the intervention and control groups' inflammation profiles, catecholamine levels, and telomere lengths changed differentially over time. At study entry, the prevention and control groups were similar in terms of SES, parenting quality, mental health, and lifestyle. These findings are consistent with the possibility that the groups began the trial with similar inflammation profiles. Nevertheless, until both pretest and posttest data are available, conclusions about intervention programs' capacity to bring about changes in biomarkers must be viewed as tentative. Despite these limitations, to the extent that they are substantiated in future research, these results may provide a strategy for narrowing some of the racial and social disparities in health apparent in the United States (Braveman, Cubbin, Egerter, Williams, & Pamuk, 2010; Williams, 2012), particularly those conditions originating in childhood (Berenson, Srnivasan, & the Bogalusa Heart Study Group, 2005; Lynch & Smith, 2005). Childhood poverty has increased steadily in the United States in recent years, and this trend has been especially pronounced in rural, African American communities (Addy, Engelhardt, & Skinner, 2013). When added to existing social and racial disparities, this trend has the potential to worsen significantly Americans' health, to increase health care costs even more (Woolf, Aron, National Research Council, & Institute of Medicine, 2013), and to limit the country's ability to develop its human capital (Knudsen, Heckman, Cameron, & Shonkoff, 2006) in the coming decades. Thus, family interventions, such as those presented here, with the capacity to ameliorate these disparities, could pay long-term social, public health, and economic dividends for this country (Heckman, 2006; Shonkoff et al., 2009).

Acknowledgements

The research reported in this chapter was supported by Award Number R01 AA012768 from the National Institute on Alcohol Abuse and Alcoholism, Awards Numbers R01 DA021736, R01 DA019230, and P30 DA027827 from the National Institute on Drug Abuse, and Award Number R01 HD030588 from the National Institute of Child Health and Human Development.

References

Addy, S., Engelhardt, W., & Skinner, C. (2013). *Basic facts about low-income children: Children under 18 years, 2011.* New York: Columbia University, National Center for Children in Poverty.

Aviv, A. (2008). The epidemiology of human telomeres: Faults and promises. *Journals of Gerontology: Series A. Biological Sciences and Medical Sciences, 63A*, 979–983.

Bakermans-Kranenburg, M. J., & van IJzendoorn, M. H. (2014). The hidden efficacy of interventions: Gene × environment experiments from a differential susceptibility perspective. *Annual Review of Psychology, 66.* Advance online publication. doi:10.1146/annurev-psych-010814-015407.

Baron, R. M., & Kenny, D. A. (1986). The moderator–mediator variable distinction in social psychological research: Conceptual, strategic, and statistical considerations. *Journal of Personality and Social Psychology, 51,* 1173–1182.

Bauer, M. E., Jeckel, C. M. M., & Luz, C. (2009). The role of stress factors during aging of the immune system. *Annals of the New York Academy of Sciences, 1153,* 139–152.

Beach, S. R. H., Brody, G. H., Lei, M.-K., & Philibert, R. A. (2010). Differential susceptibility to parenting among African American youths: Testing the *DRD4* hypothesis. *Journal of Family Psychology, 24,* 513–521.

Belsky, J., Bakermans-Kranenburg, M. J., & van IJzendoorn, M. H. (2007). For better *and* for worse: Differential susceptibility to environmental influences. *Current Directions in Psychological Science, 16,* 300–304.

Berenson, G. S., Srnivasan, S. R., & the Bogalusa Heart Study Group. (2005). Cardiovascular risk factors in youth with implications for aging: The Bogalusa Heart Study. *Neurobiology of Aging, 26,* 303–307.

Blackburn, E. H. (2005). Telomeres and telomerase: Their mechanisms of action and the effects of altering their functions. *FEBS Letters, 579,* 859–862.

Braveman, P. A., Cubbin, C., Egerter, S., Williams, D. R., & Pamuk, E. (2010). Socioeconomic disparities in health in the United States: What the patterns tell us. *American Journal of Public Health, 100*(S1), S186–S196.

Brody, G. H., Beach, S. R. H., Philibert, R. A., Chen, Y.-f., & Murry, V. M. (2009). Prevention effects moderate the association of 5-HTTLPR and youth risk behavior initiation: Gene × environment hypotheses tested via a randomized prevention design. *Child Development, 80,* 645–661.

Brody, G. H., Chen, Y.-f., & Beach, S. R. H. (2013). Differential susceptibility to prevention: GABAergic, dopaminergic, and multilocus effects. *Journal of Child Psychology and Psychiatry, 54,* 863–871.

Brody, G. H., Chen, Y.-f., & Kogan, S. M. (2010). A cascade model connecting life stress to risk behavior among rural African American emerging adults. *Development and Psychopathology, 22,* 667–678.

Brody, G. H., Chen, Y.-f., Kogan, S. M., Murry, V. M., & Brown, A. C. (2010). Long-term effects of the Strong African American Families program on youths' alcohol use. *Journal of Consulting and Clinical Psychology, 78,* 281–285.

Brody, G. H., Chen, Y.-f., Kogan, S. M., Smith, K., & Brown, A. C. (2010). Buffering effects of a family-based intervention for African American emerging adults. *Journal of Marriage and Family, 72,* 1426–1435.

Brody, G. H., Chen, Y.-f., Kogan, S. M., Yu, T., Molgaard, V. K., DiClemente, R. J., & Wingood, G. M. (2012). Family-centered program to prevent substance use, conduct problems, and depressive symptoms in Black adolescents. *Pediatrics, 129,* 108–115.

Brody, G. H., Chen, Y.-f., Murry, V. M., Ge, X., Simons, R. L., Gibbons, F. X. et al. (2006). Perceived discrimination and the adjustment of African American youths: A five-year longitudinal analysis with contextual moderation effects. *Child Development, 77,* 1170–1189.

Brody, G. H., Dorsey, S., Forehand, R., & Armistead, L. (2002). Unique and protective contributions of parenting and classroom processes to the adjustment of African American children living in single-parent families. *Child Development, 73,* 274–286.

302 Gene H. Brody

Brody, G. H., & Flor, D. L. (1997). Maternal psychological functioning, family processes, and child adjustment in rural, single-parent, African American families. *Developmental Psychology, 33*, 1000–1011.

Brody, G. H., & Flor, D. L. (1998). Maternal resources, parenting practices, and child competence in rural, single-parent African American families. *Child Development, 69*, 803–816.

Brody, G. H., & Ge, X. (2001). Linking parenting processes and self-regulation to psychological functioning and alcohol use during early adolescence. *Journal of Family Psychology, 15*, 82–94.

Brody, G. H., Ge, X., Conger, R. D., Gibbons, F. X., Murry, V. M., Gerrard, M., & Simons, R. L. (2001). The influence of neighborhood disadvantage, collective socialization, and parenting on African American children's affiliation with deviant peers. *Child Development, 72*, 1231–1246.

Brody, G. H., Ge, X., Katz, J., & Arias, I. (2000). A longitudinal analysis of internalization of parental alcohol-use norms and adolescent alcohol use. *Applied Developmental Science, 4*, 71–79.

Brody, G. H., Ge, X., Kim, S. Y., Murry, V. M., Simons, R. L., Gibbons, F. X. et al. (2003). Neighborhood disadvantage moderates associations of parenting and older sibling problem attitudes and behavior with conduct disorders in African American children. *Journal of Consulting and Clinical Psychology, 71*, 211–222.

Brody, G. H., Kim, S., Murry, V. M., & Brown, A. C. (2003). Longitudinal direct and indirect pathways linking older sibling competence to the development of younger sibling competence. *Developmental Psychology, 39*, 618–628.

Brody, G. H., Kim, S., Murry, V. M., & Brown, A. C. (2004). Protective longitudinal paths linking child competence to behavioral problems among African American siblings. *Child Development, 75*, 455–467.

Brody, G. H., Kim, S., Murry, V. M., & Brown, A. C. (2005). Longitudinal links among parenting, self-presentations to peers, and the development of externalizing and internalizing symptoms in African American siblings. *Development and Psychopathology, 17*, 185–205.

Brody, G. H., Kogan, S. M., & Chen, Y.-f. (2012). Perceived discrimination and longitudinal increases in adolescent substance use: Gender differences and mediational pathways. *American Journal of Public Health, 102*, 1006–1011.

Brody, G. H., Kogan, S. M., & Grange, C. M. (2012). Translating longitudinal, developmental research with rural African American families into prevention programs for rural African American youth. In R. B. King & V. Maholmes (Eds.), *The Oxford handbook of poverty and child development* (pp. 553–570). New York: Oxford University Press.

Brody, G. H., Lei, M.-K., Chae, D. H., Yu, T., Kogan, S. M., & Beach, S. R. H. (2014). Perceived discrimination among African American adolescents and allostatic load: A longitudinal analysis with buffering effects. *Child Development, 85*, 989–1002.

Brody, G. H., Lei, M.-K., Chen, E., & Miller, G. E. (2014). Neighborhood poverty and allostatic load in African American youth. *Pediatrics, 134*, 1–8.

Brody, G. H., Murry, V. M., Gerrard, M., Gibbons, F. X., Molgaard, V., McNair, L. D. et al. (2004). The Strong African American Families program: Translating research into prevention programming. *Child Development, 75*, 900–917.

Brody, G. H., Murry, V. M., Kogan, S. M., Gerrard, M., Gibbons, F. X., Molgaard, V. et al. (2006). The Strong African American Families program: A cluster-randomized prevention trial of long-term effects and a mediational model. *Journal of Consulting and Clinical Psychology, 74*, 356–366.

Brody, G. H., & Stoneman, Z. (1992). Child competence and developmental goals among rural Black families: Investigating the links. In I. E. Sigel, A. V. McGillicuddy-DeLisi & J. J. Goodnow (Eds.), *Parental belief systems: The psychological consequences for children* (2nd ed., pp. 415–431). Hillsdale, NJ: Erlbaum.

Brody, G. H., Stoneman, Z., & Flor, D. L. (1996a). Family wages, family processes, and youth competence in rural married African American families. In E. M. Hetherington & E. A. Blechman (Eds.), *Stress, coping, and resiliency in children and families* (pp. 173–188). Hillsdale, NJ: Erlbaum.

Brody, G. H., Stoneman, Z., & Flor, D. L. (1996b). Parental religiosity, family processes, and youth competence in rural, two-parent African American families. *Developmental Psychology, 32*, 696–706.

Brody, G. H., Yu, T., Chen, E., & Miller, G. E. (2014). Prevention moderates associations between family risks and youth catecholamine levels. *Health Psychology*. Advance online publication. doi:10.1037/hea0000072.

Brody, G. H., Yu, T., Chen, Y.-f., Kogan, S. M., & Smith, K. (2012). The Adults in the Making program: Long-term protective stabilizing effects on alcohol use and substance use problems for rural African American emerging adults. *Journal of Consulting and Clinical Psychology, 80*, 17–28.

Centers for Disease Control and Prevention. (2000). Youth risk behavior surveillance—United States, 1999. *Morbidity and Mortality Weekly Report, 49*.

Chen, E., Matthews, K. A., & Boyce, W. T. (2002). Socioeconomic differences in children's health: How and why do these relationships change with age? *Psychological Bulletin, 128*, 295–329.

Chen, E., & Miller, G. E. (2012). "Shift-and-persist" strategies: Why low socioeconomic status isn't always bad for health. *Perspectives on Psychological Science, 7*, 135–158.

Cleveland, M. J., Gibbons, F. X., Gerrard, M., Pomery, E. A., & Brody, G. H. (2005). The impact of parenting on risk cognitions and risk behavior: A study of mediation and moderation in a panel of African American adolescents. *Child Development, 76*, 900–916.

Corbie-Smith, G. M., Thomas, S. B., Williams, M. V., & Moody-Ayers, S. (1999). Attitudes and beliefs of African Americans toward participation in medical research. *Journal of General Internal Medicine, 14*, 537–546.

Epel, E. S. (2009). Telomeres in a life-span perspective: A new "psychobiomarker"? *Current Directions in Psychological Science, 18*, 6–10.

Epel, E. S., Blackburn, E. H., Lin, J., Dhabhar, F. S., Adler, N. E., Morrow, J. D., & Cawthon, R. M. (2004). Accelerated telomere shortening in response to life stress. *Proceedings of the National Academy of Sciences of the USA, 101*, 17312–17315.

Evans, G. W., Kim, P., Ting, A. H., Tesher, H. B., & Shannis, D. (2007). Cumulative risk, maternal responsiveness, and allostatic load among young adolescents. *Developmental Psychology, 43*, 341–351.

Fergus, S., & Zimmerman, M. A. (2005). Adolescent resilience: A framework for understanding healthy development in the face of risk. *Annual Review of Public Health, 26*, 399–419.

Ferry, T. R., Fouad, N. A., & Smith, P. L. (2000). The role of family context in a social-cognitive model for career-related choice behavior: A math and science perspective. *Journal of Vocational Behavior, 57*, 348–364.

304 Gene H. Brody

Foxcroft, D. R., Ireland, D., Lister-Sharp, D. J., Lowe, G., & Breen, R. (2003). Longer-term primary prevention for alcohol misuse in young people: A systematic review. *Addiction, 98*, 397–411.

French, K., Finkbiner, R., & Duhamel, L. (2002). *Patterns of substance use among minority youth and adults in the United States: An overview and synthesis of national survey findings.* Fairfax, VA: Department of Health and Human Services.

Galobardes, B., Lynch, J. W., & Smith, G. D. (2004). Childhood socioeconomic circumstances and cause-specific mortality in adulthood: Systematic review and interpretation. *Epidemiologic Reviews, 26*, 7–21.

Galobardes, B., Lynch, J. W., & Smith, G. D. (2008). Is the association between childhood socioeconomic circumstances and cause-specific mortality established? Update of a systematic review. *Journal of Epidemiology and Community Health, 62*, 387–390.

Galobardes, B., Smith, G. D., Jeffreys, M., & McCarron, P. (2006). Childhood socioeconomic circumstances predict specific causes of death in adulthood: The Glasgow student cohort study. *Journal of Epidemiology and Community Health, 60*, 527–529.

Galobardes, B., Smith, G. D., & Lynch, J. W. (2006). Systematic review of the influence of childhood socioeconomic circumstances on risk for cardiovascular disease in adulthood. *Annals of Epidemiology, 16*, 91–104.

Gibbons, F. X., Gerrard, M., Cleveland, M. J., Wills, T. A., & Brody, G. H. (2004). Perceived discrimination and substance use in African American parents and their children: A panel study. *Journal of Personality and Social Psychology, 86*, 517–529.

Glass, D., Parts, L., Knowles, D., Aviv, A., & Spector, T. D. (2010). No correlation between childhood maltreatment and telomere length. *Biological Psychiatry, 68*, e21–e22.

Goodman, E., Daniels, S. R., & Dolan, L. M. (2007). Socioeconomic disparities in insulin resistance: Results from the Princeton School District Study. *Psychosomatic Medicine, 69*, 61–67.

Hargrove, B. K., Creagh, M. G., & Burgess, B. L. (2002). Family interaction patterns as predictors of vocational identity and career decision-making self-efficacy. *Journal of Vocational Behavior, 61*, 185–201.

Heckman, J. J. (2006). Skill formation and the economics of investing in disadvantaged children. *Science, 312*, 1900–1902.

Institute of Medicine. (1994). *Reducing Risks for Mental Disorders: Frontiers for Preventive Intervention Research.* Washington, DC: National Academies Press.

Jaccard, J., Dittus, P. J., & Gordon, V. V. (1996). Maternal correlates of adolescent sexual and contraceptive behavior. *Family Planning Perspectives, 28*, 159–165.

Kananen, L., Surakka, I., Pirkola, S., Suvisaari, J., Lönnqvist, J., Peltonen, L. et al. (2010). Childhood adversities are associated with shorter telomere length at adult age both in individuals with an anxiety disorder and controls. *PLoS ONE, 5*, Article e10826.

Kellam, S. G., & Van Horn, Y. V. (1997). Life course development, community epidemiology, and preventive trials: A scientific structure for prevention research. *American Journal of Community Psychology, 25*, 177–188.

Kiecolt-Glaser, J. K., Gouin, J.-P., Weng, N.-P., Malarkey, W. B., Beversdorf, D. Q., & Glaser, R. (2011). Childhood adversity heightens the impact of later-life caregiving stress on telomere length and inflammation. *Psychosomatic Medicine, 73*, 16–22.

Kim, S., & Brody, G. H. (2005). Longitudinal pathways to psychological adjustment among Black youth living in single-parent households. *Journal of Family Psychology, 19*, 305–313.

Knudsen, E. I., Heckman, J. J., Cameron, J. L., & Shonkoff, J. P. (2006). Economic, neurobiological, and behavioral perspectives on building America's future workforce. *Proceedings of the National Academy of Sciences of the USA, 103*, 10155–10162.

Kogan, S. M., & Brody, G. H. (2010). Linking parenting and informal mentor processes to depressive symptoms among rural African American young adult men. *Cultural Diversity and Ethnic Minority Psychology, 16*, 299–306.

Kogan, S. M., Brody, G. H., Gibbons, F. X., Murry, V. M., Cutrona, C. E., Simons, R. L. et al. (2008). The influence of role status on risky sexual behavior among African Americans during the transition to adulthood. *Journal of Black Psychology, 34*, 399–420.

Kumpfer, K. L., & Alvarado, R. (2003). Family-strengthening approaches for the prevention of youth problem behaviors. *American Psychologist, 58*, 457–465.

Kumpfer, K. L., Alvarado, R., & Whiteside, H. O. (2003). Family-based interventions for substance use and misuse prevention. *Substance Use and Misuse, 38*, 1759–1787.

Leigh, B. C., & Stahl, R. (1993). Substance use and risky sexual behavior for exposure to HIV: Issues in methodology, interpretation, and prevention. *American Psychologist, 48*, 1035–1045.

Libby, P., Ridker, P. M., Hansson, G. K., & Leducq Transatlantic Network on Atherothrombosis. (2009). Inflammation in atherosclerosis: From pathophysiology to practice. *Journal of the American College of Cardiology, 54*, 2129–2138.

Luthar, S. S. (2006). Resilience in development: A synthesis of research across five decades. In D. Cicchetti & D. J. Cohen (Eds.), *Developmental psychopathology: Vol. 3. Risk, disorder, and adaptation* (2nd ed., pp. 739–795). Hoboken, NJ: Wiley.

Lynch, J. W., & Smith, G. D. (2005). A life course approach to chronic disease epidemiology. *Annual Review of Public Health, 26*, 1–35.

Manuck, S. B., Marsland, A. L., Kaplan, J. R., & Williams, J. K. (1995). The pathogenicity of behavior and its neuroendocrine mediation: An example from coronary artery disease. *Psychosomatic Medicine, 57*, 275–283.

Miller, G. E., Brody, G. H., Yu, T., & Chen, E. (2014). A family-oriented psychosocial intervention reduces inflammation in low-SES African American youth. *Proceedings of the National Academy of Sciences of the USA, 111*, 11287–11292.

Miller, G. E., Chen, E., & Parker, K. J. (2011). Psychological stress in childhood and susceptibility to the chronic diseases of aging: Moving toward a model of behavioral and biological mechanisms. *Psychological Bulletin, 137*, 959–997.

Miller, G. E., Lachman, M. E., Chen, E., Gruenewald, T. L., Karlamangla, A. S., & Seeman, T. E. (2011). Pathways to resilience: Maternal nurturance as a buffer against the effects of childhood poverty on metabolic syndrome at midlife. *Psychological Science, 22*, 1591–1599.

Monaghan, P., & Haussmann, M. F. (2006). Do telomere dynamics link lifestyle and lifespan? *Trends in Ecology and Evolution, 21*, 47–53.

Nathan, C., & Ding, A. (2010). Nonresolving inflammation. *Cell, 140*, 871–882.

National Center on Addiction and Substance Abuse. (2000). *No place to hide: Substance abuse in mid-size cities and rural America.* New York: Columbia University.

O'Brien, K. M., & Fassinger, R. E. (1993). A causal model of the career orientation and career choice of adolescent women. *Journal of Counseling Psychology, 40*, 456–469.

O'Connell, M. E., Boat, T., & Warner, K. E. (2009). *Preventing mental, emotional, and behavioral disorders among young people: Progress and possibilities.* Washington, DC: National Academies Press.

306 Gene H. Brody

O'Donovan, A., Epel, E., Lin, J., Wolkowitz, O., Cohen, B., Maguen, S. et al. (2011). Childhood trauma associated with short leukocyte telomere length in posttraumatic stress disorder. *Biological Psychiatry, 70*, 465–471.

Price, L. H., Kao, H.-T., Burgers, D. E., Carpenter, L. L., & Tyrka, A. R. (2013). Telomeres and early-life stress: An overview. *Biological Psychiatry, 73*, 15–23.

Proctor, B. D., & Dalaker, J. (2003). *Poverty in the United States: 2002* (Current Population Reports, P60-222). Washington, DC: US Census Bureau.

Rainey, L. M., & Borders, L. D. (1997). Influential factors in career orientation and career aspiration of early adolescent girls. *Journal of Counseling Psychology, 44*, 160–172.

Repetti, R. L., Taylor, S. E., & Seeman, T. E. (2002). Risky families: Family social environments and the mental and physical health of offspring. *Psychological Bulletin, 128*, 330–336.

Reuben, D. B., Talvi, S. L. A., Rowe, J. W., & Seeman, T. E. (2000). High urinary catecholamine excretion predicts mortality and functional decline in high-functioning, community-dwelling older persons: MacArthur Studies of Successful Aging. *Journals of Gerontology: Series A. Biological Sciences and Medical Sciences, 55A*, M618–M624.

Rutter, M. L. (2005). Environmentally mediated risks for psychopathology: Research strategies and findings. *Journal of the American Academy of Child and Adolescent Psychiatry, 44*, 3–18.

Schulenberg, J. E., Sameroff, A. J., & Cicchetti, D. (2004). The transition to adulthood as a critical juncture in the course of psychopathology and mental health. *Development and Psychopathology, 16*, 799–806.

Shalev, I., Moffitt, T. E., Sugden, K., Williams, B., Houts, R. M., Danese, A. et al. (2013). Exposure to violence during childhood is associated with telomere erosion from 5 to 10 years of age: A longitudinal study. *Molecular Psychiatry, 18*, 576–581.

Shanahan, M. J., & Hofer, S. M. (2005). Social context in gene–environment interactions: Retrospect and prospect. *Journals of Gerontology: Series B. Psychological Sciences and Social Sciences, 60B*(Suppl. 1), 65–76.

Shonkoff, J. P., Boyce, W. T., & McEwen, B. S. (2009). Neuroscience, molecular biology, and the childhood roots of health disparities: Building a new framework for health promotion and disease prevention. *Journal of the American Medical Association, 301*, 2252–2259.

Singh, G. K., Siahpush, M., & Kogan, M. D. (2010). Rising social inequalities in US childhood obesity, 2003–2007. *Annals of Epidemiology, 20*, 40–52.

Sloan, E. K., Capitanio, J. P., & Cole, S. W. (2008). Stress-induced remodeling of lymphoid innervation. *Brain, Behavior, and Immunity, 22*, 15–21.

Spoth, R. L., Redmond, C., & Shin, C. (1998). Direct and indirect latent-variable parenting outcomes of two universal family-focused preventive interventions: Extending a public health-oriented research base. *Journal of Consulting and Clinical Psychology, 66*, 385–399.

Spoth, R. L., Redmond, C., Trudeau, L., & Shin, C. (2002). Longitudinal substance initiation outcomes for a universal preventive intervention combining family and school programs. *Psychology of Addictive Behaviors, 16*, 129–134.

Tyrka, A. R., Price, L. H., Gelernter, J., Schepker, C., Anderson, G. M., & Carpenter, L. L. (2009). Interaction of childhood maltreatment with the corticotropin-releasing hormone receptor gene: Effects on hypothalamic-pituitary-adrenal axis reactivity. *Biological Psychiatry, 66*, 681–685.

Van IJzendoorn, M. H., Bakermans-Kranenburg, M. J., & Ebstein, R. P. (2011). Methylation matters in child development: Toward developmental behavioral epigenetics. *Child Development Perspectives, 5*, 305–310.

Vazsonyi, A. T., Trejos-Castillo, E., & Young, M. A. (2008). Rural and non-rural African American youth: Does context matter in the etiology of problem behaviors? *Journal of Youth and Adolescence, 37*, 798–811.

Williams, D. R. (2012). Miles to go before we sleep: Racial inequities in health. *Journal of Health and Social Behavior, 53*, 279–295.

Wills, T. A., Ainette, M. G., Mendoza, D., Gibbons, F. X., & Brody, G. H. (2007). Self-control, symptomatology, and substance use precursors: Test of a theoretical model in a community sample of 9-year-old children. *Psychology of Addictive Behaviors, 21*, 205–215.

Wills, T. A., Yaeger, A. M., & Sandy, J. M. (2003). Buffering effect of religiosity for adolescent substance use. *Psychology of Addictive Behaviors, 17*, 24–31.

Woolf, S. H., Aron, L., National Research Council, & Institute of Medicine (Eds.). (2013). *U.S. health in international perspective: Shorter lives, poorer health.* Washington, DC: National Academies Press.

Wright, R. J., & Subramanian, S. V. (2007). Advancing a multilevel framework for epidemiologic research on asthma disparities. *Chest, 132*(5 Suppl), 757S–769S.

14

THINKING SYSTEMATICALLY FOR ENDURING FAMILY CHANGE

Gregory M. Fosco, Brian Bumbarger, and Katharine T. Bamberger

Introduction

The family-centered prevention programs described in the previous chapters underscore (1) the importance of family systems and other theories for guiding the development of family-centered preventive programs; (2) the efficacy of such well-designed and theoretically informed programs for significantly improving outcomes for both children and parents; and (3) the robust, population-level public health benefits that can accrue from disseminating family-based programs that can simultaneously effect a wide range of risk outcomes by improving core aspects of family functioning. In addition to carefully considering change at the individual and family systems levels, the previous chapters demonstrate that there are important macro- and systems-level challenges to overcome before these types of programs can achieve their optimal reach and impact—to improve outcomes for whole populations over generations. The programs described in this volume have been uniquely successful at addressing many of these barriers, especially regarding dissemination, and in a few cases have achieved impressive scale. In many respects, the programs described in previous chapters can be viewed as the first generation of evidence-based family-centered prevention programs; they can serve as a guidepost for the development of the next generation of programs that will achieve even greater impact and scale, and do so more quickly and efficiently, and with larger effect sizes.

In this chapter, we discuss a number of the important challenges and potential barriers that remain, at both societal and family levels. At the societal level, this includes broad issues related to delivery and support capacity and infrastructure, which impact the reach and population-level impact that prevention programs can have (see Figure 14.1). At the family level, we discuss the importance of pushing the field toward testing the guiding theories of prevention programs

Thinking Systematically **309**

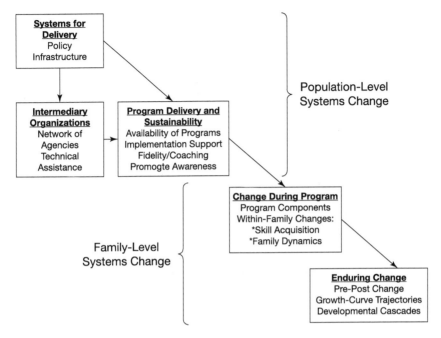

FIGURE 14.1 A Social-Ecosystems Model of Systems Change

by assessing both the prevention process *and* mechanisms that account for enduring changes for family and individual outcomes, which we think of as family-level systems change.

Population-Level Systems Change: Dissemination and Implementation of Evidence-Based Family Programs

Family systems theory and the evidence base for effective family-centered prevention can be considered recent innovations. As with any new technology or advancement, there has to be recognition of the incongruence with the larger culture or context when the innovation is first introduced. Consider the introduction of any important societal innovation: indoor plumbing, the automobile, television, the desktop computer, or e-mail. Each of these innovations was an exciting discovery, but without a supporting infrastructure, each would have been of limited use. All required a concomitant and complex infrastructure surrounding and supporting the innovation in order to take full advantage of the new technology (e.g., public water systems, highways and traffic signals, cable networks, LAN, and the internet). Thinking about the introduction of a generation of new family-focused prevention programs in the same way helps us to consider exactly what infrastructure is necessary and what systems change is required to take full advantage of this new "technology".

310 Gregory M. Fosco et al.

We can ask questions such as:

- What kind of prevention support and delivery systems are required?
- What policy and funding structures would be optimal?
- Who is responsible for developing this infrastructure?
- How can we measure and assess incremental change and improvement in this support and delivery infrastructure as part of the research agenda to assess the impact of these programs?

Systems for Delivery to Promote Dissemination and Adoption

A primary challenge relates to developing the necessary infrastructure to promote the adoption of effective family-based prevention programs by communities, including increasing demand and improving goodness of fit between programs and community-identified needs. As the evidence-based programs agenda has matured, there is increasing awareness of the need for improving communities' capacity to identify their unique service and programming needs and to support data-informed program selection. With increasing recognition and adoption of the public health risk-focused prevention paradigm (Hawkins, Catalano, & Arthur, 2002), more states and communities are implementing community-level risk-factor surveillance systems to empower the monitoring of risk and protective factors associated with or predictive of a wide range of health and behavior outcomes. These surveillance systems provide communities with the capacity to continually monitor underlying conditions across ecological domains (i.e. community, family, school, peer/individual) and at key developmental stages, and to promote informed decisions about the programs and strategies most likely to achieve population-level impact (Mrazek, Biglan, & Hawkins, 2007). Research has demonstrated that when communities have this surveillance and diagnostic capacity in place, they are more likely to adopt evidence-based programs, more likely to monitor implementation quality and implement with fidelity (i.e., less likely to make adaptations), more likely to achieve results across multiple health, education, and behavioral outcomes, and more likely to sustain programs beyond initial seed-funding (Feinberg, Jones, Greenberg, Osgood, & Bontempo, 2010; Tibbits, Bumbarger, Kyler, & Perkins, 2010; Rhoades, Bumbarger, & Moore, 2012). Having such diagnostic capacity can also help communities match program-targeted mechanisms to specific community needs or risk mechanisms, which can not only increase the likelihood of effectiveness but also create a better community fit and thus contribute to sustainability of program delivery (Cooper, Bumbarger, & Moore, 2013).

Quality in Program Delivery

Scale and quality of program delivery sometimes work in opposition. As dissemination and scale increase, so does the concern and challenge to maintain sufficient implementation quality and fidelity. Research has clearly established the correlation between high-quality implementation and better outcomes (Fixsen, Naoom, Blase, & Friedman, 2005; Durlak & DuPre, 2008), but there is continued call from practitioners and communities for greater sensitivity and adaptation to meet communities' cultural needs (Castro, Barrera, & Holleran Steiker, 2010). Although this demand for flexibility and tailored implementation must be recognized as valid and valuable, it should not be used to justify a laissez-faire approach in which practitioners are given carte-blanche to adapt theoretically well-defined programs at will. In fact, research has shown that as evidence-based programs (EBPs) go to scale, the majority of adaptation can be characterized not as thoughtful and proactive cultural tailoring, but more accurately as program "drift", which is reactive rather than proactive and likely to reduce program effectiveness (Moore, Bumbarger, & Cooper, 2013). Thus, the challenge is to maintain high-quality implementation as programs go to scale while still utilizing practitioners' indigenous knowledge and respecting local culture.

To address this challenge, the infrastructure for quality implementation must support capacity building within and across provider organizations to promote a *culture of excellence*. Among provider organizations, there is a need for a greater emphasis on and capacity to support workforce and leadership development and regular implementation monitoring and continuous quality improvement. Providers should be encouraged and supported to regularly reflect on the fundamental questions of "how well are we delivering prevention services?" and "what impact are we having on children and families?" Promoting this culture of excellence includes setting high standards for the workforce to whom we entrust the delivery of family-focused prevention programs. Perhaps as an artifact of historically naïve ideas about the simplicity of offering "parenting guidance", many family strengthening programs are still considered rather elementary, not requiring a particularly skilled or experienced workforce. It is not uncommon for entry-level human service workers with no specific training or experience, and without any minimum education requirements, to deliver these programs. Additionally, with very few exceptions, family-centered prevention programs are rarely delivered within an organizational context and culture of "clinical supervision". It is easiest to recognize this particular shortcoming of prevention delivery in comparison to some popular evidence-based therapeutic interventions, such as Multisystemic Therapy or Functional Family Therapy (Carr, 2000). In the case of both of these therapeutic interventions, implementers are required to be Master's level therapists, to have regular coaching and feedback from an experienced clinical supervisor, and to be certified through a structured training process. Both programs also have sophisticated national data infrastructure to support implementation quality and fidelity monitoring and the use of data feedback for continuous quality improvement. These models demonstrate the type of workforce and organizational

312 Gregory M. Fosco et al.

capacity that is required to scale programs while maintaining sufficient quality and fidelity, and stand in stark contrast to the way family-focused prevention programs are typically disseminated.

Quality in program dissemination and implementation also requires a fundamental shift in the conventional training paradigm for scaling programs. The traditional model for training practitioners typically does not reflect best practices in teaching adult learners or incorporate decades of effective diffusion of innovation theory. The conventional approach to training for dissemination is proving ineffective and insufficient at achieving the level of mastery necessary for practitioners to achieve high-quality implementation. In our experience supporting the replication of nearly 300 EBPs over the last decade, very often the certification training offered by program developers is the wrong training at the wrong time. Specifically, in the conventional training model, there is too much emphasis on the *mechanics and logistics* of program delivery and too little emphasis on practitioners' depth of knowledge and understanding of the *underlying theory of prevention and behavior change*—both generally and as it relates to the particular program. Practitioners often leave training with a detailed script to read but without the necessary skills to effectively process and respond when realities force them to go off-script during program delivery. This may be at least partially due to the ongoing "black box" nature of many programs, as research to date on prevention mechanisms and participant learning processes is scarce (for a more in-depth discussion of this issue, see the section below on Family-Level Systems Change). Careful work evaluating these processes would help practitioners understand how exactly a given program's core elements lead to fundamental changes in risk or protective factors, skills, knowledge, attitudes, or intentions that have been hypothesized to ultimately lead to both proximal and distal behavior change outcomes.

Finally, in the conventional training model, training takes place well before implementation—often without any follow-up coaching, supervision or peer support during implementation; this leads predictably to skill and knowledge loss between training and implementation. Shifting to a model that instead emphasizes ongoing coaching and support during implementation, as exemplified by many of the model programs in this volume, is likely to not only increase practitioners' engagement, understanding, and mastery, but will quite likely reduce program implementation costs, since the typical face-to-face, large group pre-implementation training is the costliest aspect of many family-centered prevention programs.

Program Sustainability

In addition to dissemination and implementation, *sustainability* is another significant challenge for achieving (and maintaining) the scale necessary to affect population-level public health improvement. Even the most effective family-focused prevention programs must work across multiple generations to achieve their full potential (Haskins, Garfinkel, & McLanahan, 2014; Weisz, 2014). The sustainability challenge is especially great for programs that are *both* family-focused and preventive, since this combination presents specific challenges to scale and sustainability. The robust effects of family-based prevention programs in impacting a wide range of developmental outcomes is a double-edged sword. On one hand, it allows multiple developmental and behavioral outcomes to be targeted simultaneously, encouraging buy-in from a broad cross-section of service delivery organizations. On the other hand, current funding models tend to encourage a singular focus, which allows a diffusion of responsibility for family-strengthening across multiple service systems, where systems and policymakers "pass the buck" on promoting (and funding) these programs to other systems that may also be impacted by such a program. Because government systems are not naturally inclined to collaboration, a service that is everyone's responsibility can easily become no one's responsibility. Likewise, while the theoretical and empirical evidence clearly supports primary prevention approaches (Offord, Kraemer, Kazdin, Jensen, & Harrington, 1998), the practical and fiscal realities of short-term budget cycles are in opposition to the delayed "payoff" of programs that sometimes operate decades or generations in advance, and for which the cause–effect relationship between program outcomes and systems savings is more difficult to demonstrate.

Recently, however, there has been some reason for optimism that we may overcome these policy and funding conundrums. First, a new generation of more sophisticated economic analyses is helping to better articulate the return-on-investment equation, especially for family-focused prevention, and the cost-savings are often astounding even when using intentionally conservative calculations (Aos, Lieb, Mayfield, Miller, & Pennucci, 2004; Crowley, Coffman, Feinberg, Greenberg, & Spoth, 2014). Second, the passage of the Affordable Care Act has established a mechanism (and important legislative precedent) for supporting primary prevention—including family strengthening—through the same managed-care system that has been used to successfully scale family-focused treatment/therapy (Koh & Sebelius, 2010). Third, pioneering new Social Impact Bond initiatives are facilitating private sector venture capital investment in evidence-based programs as a way to 'kick-start' these programs in public systems without the need for public seed funding (Liebman, 2013; Pew-MacArthur, 2014).

The exemplar programs described in this volume have served as "proof-of-concept" that well-designed and theoretically informed family-focused prevention can achieve significant results beyond the controlled environments of research trials. This has led to increasing interest from state and federal agencies to take such programs to scale. Appreciating the complexity of the multiple macro-system challenges described in this chapter, there is growing recognition of the potential role of *intermediary organizations* as part of the necessary infrastructure for achieving

314 Gregory M. Fosco et al.

scale. Representing an evolution of the traditional technical assistance provider, intermediaries facilitate productive interaction between researchers (including program developers and evaluators), policymakers (including funders and system leaders), and the practitioners and provider organizations responsible for program delivery. Wandersman and colleagues (2008) have described this interactive systems framework for promoting the dissemination and implementation of evidence-based practices (family-based and otherwise) and articulated the need for such intermediaries to function as a prevention support system. Intermediaries serve not only as technical assistance providers and knowledge brokers, but importantly connect these diverse stakeholder groups and facilitate the identification of barriers to dissemination and implementation, supporting cross-system problem-solving that might not otherwise be prioritized (Dymnicki, Wandersman, Osher, Grigorescu, Huang, & Meyer, 2014; Franks, 2010; Greenwood & Welsh, 2012). Some notable examples include Pennsylvania's Evidence-based Prevention and Intervention Support Center (EPISCenter) at Penn State University's Prevention Research Center (www.episcenter.psu.edu), the Connecticut Center for Effective Practice at the Child Health and Development Institute (www.kidsmentalhealthinfo.com), and the Centre for Effective Services in Ireland (www.effectiveservices.org). These intermediaries help to network practitioners, policymakers, and researchers; problem-solve barriers to the dissemination and high-quality implementation of evidence-based programs (family-focused and otherwise); and advance the research agenda to improve the efficiency and effectiveness of scaling evidence-based programs.

Family-Level Systems Change

Delivery and evaluation of family-based prevention programs, and the randomized controlled trial in particular, have historical roots in the medical model in which treatments are administered clinically to a patient. Accordingly, much of the research stemming from randomized controlled trials regards programs in a manner akin to giving a patient a medicine and comparing change in those who receive the medicine to those who did not. This approach overlooks the nuances of prevention programs and the reality that there are typically several distinct components to a given program, its delivery, and the processes by which families "absorb" the program components.

Indeed, change processes in family-based prevention programs reflect the intersection of family and developmental theory and prevention science. Building on strong theoretical foundations, family-based programs target specific dynamics and skills for change in an effort to promote protective factors and reduce risk factors in the service of improving the lives of the youth and families. Interestingly, this rich theory has largely been unevaluated within the context of prevention program evaluations that adhere closely to the gold-standard randomized controlled trial design in which random assignment to the

Thinking Systematically **315**

prevention program is associated with improvements in targeted outcomes. With a premium placed on distal outcomes, there is a relative dearth of research that directly evaluates the theoretical models that guide these programs. The absence of such research has created a "black box" in our understanding of the effects of prevention programs (Chen & Rossi, 1983); that is, when change occurs due to a prevention program, there is little knowledge of the process of change. This "black box" problem creates limitations to our scientific understanding of program effectiveness and causes real-world problems in terms of practitioners' ability to gain a deep conceptual understanding and achieve high-quality delivery of a prevention program.

In the following sections, we discuss change processes in prevention programs in two timescales. We focus first on the traditional approach to testing change processes following prevention programs, which we refer to as *enduring change processes*. This approach typically examines the degree of change that occurs from pre-test to post-test and how such change predicts long-term outcomes for families and youth. In this section, we review methods that have been used and future directions for research that can show how prevention programs elicit change in proximal program targets (e.g., family relationships) and the subsequent enduring effects on distal outcomes (e.g., child misbehavior).

Second, we discuss research, methods, and future directions for the study of how families change during the course of the prevention program itself. This approach, which we consider to be *change during prevention programs*, makes use of new evaluation frameworks such as "components analysis", where programs are decomposed into their constituent parts, as well as related within-family research methods.

Mechanisms of Enduring Changes

It is a humbling exercise to stop and think for a moment about the enduring effects of the prevention programs summarized in this volume. In a way, it is quite impressive that a program that provides only a few hours of support each week and lasts only a couple of months would have such lasting effects that are detectable *years* later. This improbable result underscores the absolutely incredible impact that these programs have and the value of targeting family functioning as a means of creating a lasting impact on the lives of youth. At the same time, such impressive effects also raise important scientific questions about *how* these programs evoke such changes and *why* they are sustained for years after a program concludes. Such scientific questions call for a synthesis of developmental, family, and prevention science.

Traditional pre-post mediation analysis

Historically, tests of program mediators have typically involved examining whether randomization to the prevention program is associated with proximal outcomes, such as parenting practices or relationship quality at post-test, and that this proximal outcome accounts for the program effects on distal outcomes (e.g., adolescent substance use, children's school readiness); essentially, this approach applies principles of statistical tests of mediation to the randomized controlled trial design. Discussions elsewhere have expanded on best practices in testing mediation in prevention and intervention trials (e.g., Kazdin, 2007; Sandler, Schoenfelder, Wolchik, & MacKinnon, 2011). At a basic level, such studies offer valuable insight into why prevention programs cause improvements in outcomes. Unfortunately, very few programs have been subjected to tests of the causal mechanisms of change (Liddle, 2004; Sandler et al., 2011). Although it is unusual to find tests of even one mediator, Kazdin (2007) points out that testing multiple mediators is an important direction for future research. Studies with multiple mediators would allow for tests of specificity in the mechanisms of change (i.e., is it one process or another, or both?) and would create opportunities for tests of alternative hypotheses. Such tests can provide evidence for specificity in program effects, which in turn can lend support to the theoretical model. For example, a family program might have a parent and youth session that targets parenting skills and youth cognitions, respectively, but it may be unclear whether both of these proximal outcomes account for long-term youth outcomes (e.g., conduct problems). Only by testing both potential mediators (parenting skills and youth cognitions) is it possible to know if each have unique effects, or if one process is accounting for these outcomes.

Alternative hypothesis testing is also an important direction for evaluating prevention programs. When prevention programs are evaluated within the theoretical framework from which they were developed, it is common to ignore other potential mechanisms that may also account for change. Suppose for a moment that a program was developed using a behavioral parent training approach for reducing child noncompliance, and that this program focused on parenting practices such as establishing clear expectations, positive reinforcement of appropriate behavior, and using effective consequences for misbehavior. One would expect that a study testing mediators of this parenting program would test an index of these key parenting practices learned during the program as the mechanism accounting for changes in children's noncompliant behavior. However, an alternative hypothesis, drawing on a different theoretical model, might be that in the context of more consistent and effective parenting, parent–child bonding also improves. It is then plausible that parent–child bonding may be an alternative pathway by which the parenting program effects changes on noncompliance. However, neglecting to test such alternative hypotheses makes it more likely that findings will support the theory that guides the program, but only because other theories are not considered as alternatives.

Building on pre–post mediation approaches, studies that use intensive longitudinal methods, such as daily diary or ecological momentary assessment approaches, have several advantages in comparison to retrospective self-report methods. First, intensive longitudinal methods minimize recall bias because of the frequency of assessment (Stone, Shiffman, Atienza, & Nebeling, 2007), which is especially important for mundane day-to-day behaviors (e.g., using praise to reinforce good behavior), and for accuracy in reporting on the intensity of experiences (e.g., conflict), both of which are poorly recalled retrospectively (Schwarz, 2007). Second, intensive longitudinal methods offer greater ecological validity of the assessment—especially in comparison with laboratory assessments—because they are conducted frequently and in the context in which events have occurred (Stone et al., 2007). Third, intensive longitudinal methods can be used to evaluate dynamic within-person processes, which provide greater specificity of temporal events than do global, retrospective accounts (Collins, 2006; Stone et al., 2007). Because of these advantages, intensive longitudinal data are better-suited to address certain specific kinds of research questions and test theories involving processes and change (Collins, 2006), and can have enhanced predictive validity (Kumar et al., 2013) when compared to traditional methods. Although data collection is "intensive", instruments are often brief, relevant to the participant's current experience, and require little summarization across prior experiences. As a result, this approach is highly feasible and typically perceived as unobtrusive by participants (Smyth & Heron, 2014).

A powerful application of intensive longitudinal methods is the measurement-burst design, which can be flexibly applied to a variety of evaluation designs, depending on the expected timescale or constructs of interest (Shiffman, 2007; Sliwinski, 2008). In a measurement-burst design, there are periods of intense measurement "bursts", such as 14 consecutive daily assessments, with periods in between these bursts (e.g., one burst per year). In a prevention program evaluation, this might be applied such that the first measurement burst occurs at pre-test and a subsequent burst occurs at post-test. Such approaches are better able to accurately track daily behavior (e.g., use of parenting strategies) and fluctuations in behavior or emotions from day to day (Shiffman, 2007; Sliwinski, 2008; Smyth & Stone, 2003). There are many other possibilities in terms of dynamics within families that unfold in mutually influential interactions over time (e.g., Schermerhorn, Chow, & Cummings, 2010), or even the degree to which family members influence others' feelings or stress (Almeida, 2005). Overall, intensive longitudinal methods have the potential to capture families as systems (Larson & Almeida, 1999), and consequently, capture change in the family system as the result of a family-based prevention program.

Developmentally informed approaches to mediation

Many family-based prevention programs also draw upon a developmental psychopathology framework in their design. Such programs might target developmentally sensitive periods that have long-lasting repercussions developmentally, such as early childhood programs. Other approaches target periods of

318 Gregory M. Fosco et al.

developmental transition (e.g., transition to school, transition into middle school, transitions following divorce). This same developmental framework can be applied to tests of program mechanisms. We highlight two major ways this can be done: developmental trajectory approaches, and developmental cascade model approaches.

Developmental trajectory approaches can be applied to the study of family or individual functioning that changes over a particular period of development, rather than limiting attention to a single post-test assessment. In these cases, latent growth curve modeling approaches (e.g., Duncan, Duncan, & Stryker, 2013) have been applied as a powerful strategy for evaluating the impact of family-based prevention programs on family or individual trajectories over time. For example, family-based programs implemented in early adolescence may be optimally timed for preventing adolescents from embarking on an escalating trajectory of substance use or problem behavior. Latent growth curve models, or growth mixture models, offer an assessment strategy that can identify the ways in which family-based programs can alter the developmental progression of problem behavior.

Similarly, family functioning may also correspond to a developmental trajectory perspective. For example, individual differences in family trajectories of parental monitoring and effective parenting practices have been identified in early adolescence (e.g., Dishion, Nelson, & Bullock, 2004). In this example, youth in families who experience rapid decreases in parental monitoring and involvement are at risk for substance use outcomes (e.g., Laird, Pettit, Bates, & Dodge, 2003). Thus, a prevention program would be effective if it helped families maintain their levels of parental monitoring and involvement over the years following the delivery of the program. Such nuanced theoretical models require appropriate design and analytic approaches. Using a latent growth curve modeling approach, it is possible to evaluate whether random assignment to a prevention or control group is associated with differences in rates of change in the proposed mediator over time. Following the parental monitoring and adolescent substance use example above, one would expect that participation in the prevention program would be associated with slower rates of decline in parental monitoring over time; in turn, slower rates of decline in monitoring over time would be associated with slower rates of escalation in substance use. In short, a program that prevented declines in monitoring would then place youth at reduced risk for later substance use. Some studies have used this approach with other family processes, such as family conflict (Van Ryzin & Dishion, 2012; Fosco, Van Ryzin, Stormshak, & Dishion, 2014) and family cohesion (Caruthers, Van Ryzin, & Dishion, 2014). More sophisticated bivariate growth modeling approaches could be used to test multiple mediators simultaneously, and within this multivariate framework, cross-lagged latent difference score modeling (McArdle, 2009) offers a powerful approach to explore the direction and timing of effects among potential mediators and between purported mediators and outcomes, acknowledging that processes of change may be reciprocal rather than exclusively unidirectional.

A second developmentally informed approach to mediation focuses on questions of how a prevention program might disrupt a developmental sequence toward long-term problematic adjustment. This perspective draws on a *developmental cascade* framework, which suggests that effects of individual functioning in one developmental period can set into motion a series of subsequent problems in other developmental periods (e.g., social problems in early childhood that continue into adulthood), expand into different developmental domains (e.g., behavioral problems leading to academic problems), and spill over into other developmental contexts (e.g., family dynamics predicting academic problems) (Dodge et al., 2009; Fosco & Feinberg, 2014; Masten & Cicchetti, 2010; Masten et al., 2005; Moilanen, Shaw, & Maxwell, 2010). Cascade processes may function in a unidirectional manner, or exhibit patterns of reciprocal influence over time (Masten & Cicchetti, 2010). Evaluating programs within a developmental cascade modeling framework can provide important insights into the degree to which program effects endure across developmental periods and the diffusion of program gains across domains and contexts.

Applications of developmental cascades to prevention programs can open up scientific inquiry to consider other influences on the long-term outcomes of youth in family-based prevention programs. Beyond program effects on targeted parenting skills or relationship enhancement, it is important to also think about broader systemic processes that might operate to support positive functioning, or that might, over time, work to erode the benefits from a prevention program. For example, the degree to which improvements in parenting practices are maintained over the long term may be explained by coparenting support processes (e.g., Feinberg, 2003). In families with strong coparenting support processes, positive parenting practices, such as praise for good behavior, may be easier to sustain within the family system. Moreover, from a family systems perspective, changes to any part of the family are thought to reverberate to other relationships in the family (Minuchin, 1985). This "ripple effect" may offer broader insight into change processes for programs that initially target a specific subset of the family system, such as parenting practices (Patterson, 2005), or it may broaden the range of program targets to maximize long-term maintenance. Of note, evidence is accruing to support the view that a parenting program designed to improve child behavior can have collateral benefits for parents' well-being and quality of life (Beach et al., 2008; DeGarmo, Patterson, & Forgatch, 2004; McEachern et al., 2013).

Cascade model approaches also offer unique insights into the long-term implications of a prevention program. For example, some programs may have long-term *indirect* effects on outcomes as a function of intermediary processes that warrant attention. Other programs may have "time-limited" effects because they do not alter the developmental sequence. This may be particularly relevant

Change During Prevention Programs

The other domain of family change processes is change *during* prevention programs. Surprisingly little is known about how change occurs over the course of program delivery. There are some exceptions to this found in early work on parenting interventions that highlighted therapist techniques (e.g., Patterson & Forgatch, 1985), but much of what we "know" about how change in families is elicited in a matter of weeks or months is derived from extensive hands-on experience and trial-and-error approaches as programs were developed over time. Unfortunately, much of this work has been relegated to the applied expertise that accumulates within research groups and has not been disseminated broadly to inform the field. Although much of this work has been conducted through a systematic and iterative development process, it is often the case that empirical evaluations of how change occurs during prevention programs remain unpublished. The current state of the field is one where established and emerging programs alike would benefit from careful application of recent methodological innovations that can capture change processes in exciting new ways.

Component analysis

Essentially, component analysis focuses on whether all components of a prevention program are contributing to program benefits experienced by individuals or families. Early examples include dismantling designs of therapeutic intervention packages in which different combinations of components are administered to subgroups for comparison (Kazdin, 2007). Even in the context of theory-driven programs, surprising results can emerge. A notable example is found in a now-classic study in which cognitive-behavioral therapy was subjected to a component analysis that compared the full therapy package to two components: behavioral activation, and treatment of automatic cognitions (Jacobson et al., 1996). This study yielded surprising results, which indicated that those who received the full therapy did not exhibit better outcomes than those that received only one of the components of the therapy. This study, and subsequent work, has stimulated growth in our understanding of the presumed processes underlying therapeutic changes in depression.

Recently, meta-analytic techniques have been applied to consider a component analysis approach to family-based prevention programs (e.g., Kaminski, Valle, Filene, & Boyle, 2008). Using this approach, prevention programs are decomposed into logical units, which can include units of content or curricula (e.g., family management, conflict resolution, self-regulation, managing peer influences), program modalities (e.g., whether the program was delivered in-person or remotely, whether it was delivered individually or in a group setting), and/or the presence or absence of specific instructional techniques (e.g., role playing). Subsequently, all prevention programs included in a meta-analysis are coded for the presence or absence (or, in some cases, the amount) of each component, and these codes are used to predict program outcomes across studies. In Kaminski et al. (2008), for example, the authors found that curricula focusing on positive parent–child interactions and the use of role-playing activities were two components that predicted increased efficacy among family-based prevention programs targeting behavioral problems in young children. This approach can also include analysis of moderation of effects, in which specific components are evaluated with regards to specific subgroups (e.g., boys vs. girls, low-risk vs. high-risk families), or when the potential for synergistic (i.e., interactive) relationships between components is tested. This type of research can not only help to address questions of *how* programs achieve their effects, but *for whom* they are most effective. The knowledge generated can, in turn, contribute to the goals outlined at the beginning of this chapter, i.e., to develop a new generation of prevention programs that can achieve effects more quickly and efficiently, and with larger effect sizes.

These meta-analytic and early component analysis approaches under-score the importance of evaluating the "active ingredients" of prevention programs. This goal requires a diversification of evaluation designs that can complement the gold-standard randomized controlled trial. If we consider the possibility that program components may vary in their effects, then it is possible that, although some components may function as expected, others may have no effect at all, while some components may even have a deleterious effect, reducing the overall potency of a prevention program (Collins, Murphy, Nair, & Stretcher, 2005). Perhaps more concerning is the reality that these nuances are obscured by the traditional randomized trial design in which the prevention program is evaluated as a whole, rather than by random assignment to various components of the program (Collins, Murphy, & Stretcher, 2007).

Recently, innovative applications of factorial experimental designs have emerged as a response to the need for systematic evaluation of prevention programs (Collins, Dziak, Kugler, & Trail, 2014). Through random assignment to the different combinations of program components, it is possible to identify which components have a desired effect on outcomes and to test interactive (e.g., synergistic) effects of program components, which allows the investigator to determine the optimal subset of components for program effectiveness with a particular population (Collins, Dziak et al., 2014). Beyond evaluating com-ponents of prevention programs, these factorial experimental methods have been applied in new ways to aid in the development and optimization of programs. The multiphase optimization strategy (MOST; e.g., Collins et al.,

322 Gregory M. Fosco et al.

2011; Collins, Murphy, & Stretcher, 2007) is a methodological framework that guides researchers in drawing on a theoretical model to identify a set of program components, which is then evaluated and refined through factorial experiments, resulting in the assembly of a program package for evaluation and ultimately dissemination (Collins et al., 2011).

Another emerging perspective in prevention science is the problem of heterogeneity of family needs as they engage in prevention programs; this is a serious consideration at all levels, but is particularly salient for universal-level prevention programs. There is growing recognition that families differ in their needs and responsiveness to prevention programs (Weissberg & Greenberg, 1998). Some families may have broad support needs, while other families' needs may be more narrowly supported by specific components of a program. This issue presents a challenge for programs delivered as a standardized curriculum and has led some program designers to use adaptive strategies that modify the curriculum based on the unique needs of a given family. However, evidence-based application of adaptive programs requires that careful attention is given to the key characteristics of an individual or family that are related to program response (i.e., the "tailoring variables") and to the empirically guided decision rules for how and when to adapt programs (Collins, Murphy, & Bierman, 2004). Sequential multiple assignment randomized trial (SMART) designs have arisen as a way of developing and evaluating adaptive programs (Murphy, 2005). Briefly, this approach helps identify the tailoring variables, decision rules, and corresponding optimal program component sets and sequences that will allow for an empirically guided adaptive approach (for reviews, see Collins, Nahum-Shani, & Almirall, 2014; Collins et al., 2007; Murphy, 2005).

Within-family change processes

Few studies have examined family change processes as they occur over the course of a prevention program. Some intervention or therapy programs are beginning to think about daily timescales in which change begins during therapy sessions, which is related to changes between therapy sessions, and ultimately accumulates to explain the treatment outcome (Gelo & Manzo, 2015). With regard to family-based prevention programs, family members may participate in exercises to learn new skills, or participate in relationship enhancement training or exercises, and it is the use of new skills, or changes to relationship quality, that generally account for change in outcomes. However, the ways in which family members implement skills at home, or the ways relationships change, are generally unclear. Intensive longitudinal methods offer a powerful tool for understanding change processes that occur during the program. By following participants intensively through the process of change, it is possible to see what they are doing that contributes to change (e.g., engaging in sessions, practicing skills), in addition to seeing the change itself as it occurs. Specific research questions related to within-family change that could be addressed with intensive longitudinal methods during programs include: how family members' behaviors in daily life change as they participate in a family program (i.e., tracking change in outcomes to determine the timescale, rate, and "shape" of change between pre-test and post-test); identifying micro-timescale mechanisms of change in functioning/outcomes, such as increasing or heightened day-to-day feelings of coparenting support from a partner as a mechanism of change toward sensitive parenting; and pinpointing cascades of change among family members, such as which family members change first, who and what changes next, and whether that differs by participants' engagement in the program, family interactional patterns, or other characteristics (Smyth & Stone, 2003). In sum, using intensive longitudinal methods during a prevention program allows for a close look at ordering and mechanisms of change in family members with temporal specificity that is not possible with pre–post or even measurement burst designs that miss this time period marking the beginning of change.

Conclusions

Efforts at developing strong evidence for family-based prevention programs have paid off. There are now several programs that have demonstrated robust effects in the lives of youth and their families. The field has progressed tremendously in the science of development, evaluation, and dissemination of evidence-based prevention programs; the chapters in this volume serve as a testament to this fact. Of course, much remains to be done. This chapter offers a guiding framework for future research across two levels: (1) change in family prevention programs and (2) change in systems of support and delivery of family prevention programs.

An important direction for future research is to further our understanding of change processes in family-based prevention programs, which requires rigorous evaluation of the enduring effects of these programs as well as the ways in which change unfolds during program delivery. The importance of evaluating program mechanisms is by no means a new idea. However, with innovations in methodology and the growing availability of long-term data from established family-based prevention trials, there is a vast array of new information to be gained from these approaches. Not only do studies of these mechanisms allow us to understand *how* and *why* a program works, but it opens up new realms of evaluation, including the breadth of public health impact and ways that we can bolster these effects through systematic maintenance of program effects for those who need it most. Because of the important role it serves, evidence supporting theorized mediators of a prevention program should be a key criterion for establishing a prevention program as evidence-based (Kazdin, 2007; Sandler et al., 2011). In this chapter, we offer guidance for conceptualizing and implementing such studies.

324   Gregory M. Fosco et al.

Moreover, we discuss new directions in both domains. We give attention to the importance of branching out in new directions to measure and analyze change, including intensive measurement approaches, such as daily diary, ecological momentary assessment, or dynamic systems approaches. Through intensive longitudinal methods, it is possible to gather information about processes and interactions at multiple points over time (i.e., in measurement-burst designs) in order to evaluate change in those family processes affected by family-based programs. There are many relevant questions that intensive longitudinal data can address to advance the knowledge of family processes and program effectiveness and potentially inform future prevention programs in order to optimize program effects.

It is important to note, however, that these programs are only useful to the extent to which they are introduced to the lives of those who can benefit from such services. Reaching those families most in need of prevention services will require a paradigm shift in how we design, staff, train, and fund governmental service delivery organizations. The current delivery model, which suffers from inadequate training, high staff turnover, program churn, and competition for funds among organizations that should (ideally) be cooperating, has resulted in inappropriate or insufficient services that are not able to address our most important public health challenges. Recent innovations such as Social Impact Bonds hold a great deal of promise, as do recent advances in health care that have arisen out of the Affordable Care Act, which is pushing medical care providers to think more holistically about family health. In response, many providers that have traditionally focused only on physical health have broadened their focus to consider the emotional and psychological well-being of the patient *and his or her family*. Clearly, the next horizon for the field of family-based prevention is to be found in contexts such as these—the family medical practice, the juvenile justice court, the correctional facility. By bringing our knowledge and expertise into these contexts, supported by properly trained and qualified practitioners, we can envision a future in which the promise of family-based prevention is fulfilled.

References

Almeida, D. M. (2005). Resilience and vulnerability to daily stressors assessed via diary methods. *Current Directions in Psychological Science, 14*(2), 64–68.

Aos, S., Lieb, R., Mayfield, J., Miller, M., & Pennucci, A. (2004). *Benefits and costs of prevention and early intervention programs for youth* (No. 04–07, p. 3901). Olympia, WA: Washington State Institute for Public Policy.

Beach, S. R., Kogan, S. M., Brody, G. H., Chen, Y. F., Lei, M. K., & Murry, V. M. (2008). Change in caregiver depression as a function of the Strong African American Families Program. *Journal of Family Psychology, 22*(2), 241.

Carr, A. (2000). Evidence-based practice in family therapy and systemic consultation. *Journal of Family Therapy, 22*(1), 29–60.

Caruthers, A. S., Van Ryzin, M. J., & Dishion, T. J. (2014). Preventing high-risk sexual behavior in early adulthood with family interventions in adolescence: Outcomes and developmental processes. *Prevention Science, 15*, 59–69.

Castro, F. G., Barrera Jr., M., & Holleran Steiker, L. K. (2010). Issues and challenges in the design of culturally adapted evidence-based interventions. *Annual Review of Clinical Psychology, 6*, 213–239.

Chen, H.-T., & Rossi, P. H. (1983). Evaluating with sense: The theory-driven approach. *Evaluation Review, 7*(3), 283–302.

Collins, L. M. (2006). Analysis of longitudinal data: The integration of theoretical model, temporal design, and statistical model. *Annual Review of Psychology, 57*, 505–528.

Collins, L. M., Baker, T. B., Mermelstein, R. J., Piper, M. E., Jorenby, D. E., Smith, S. S. et al. (2011). The multiphase optimization strategy for engineering effective tobacco use interventions. *Annals of Behavioral Medicine, 41*(2), 208–226.

Collins, L. M., Dziak, J. J., Kugler, K. C., & Trail, J. B. (2014). Factorial experiments: Efficient tools for evaluation of intervention components. *American Journal of Preventive Medicine, 47*(4), 498–504.

Collins, L. M., Murphy, S. A., & Bierman, K. L. (2004). A conceptual framework for adaptive preventive interventions. *Prevention Science, 5*(3), 185–196.

Collins, L. M., Murphy, S. A., Nair, V. N., & Strecher, V. J. (2005). A strategy for optimizing and evaluating behavioral interventions. *Annals of Behavioral Medicine, 30*(1), 65–73.

Collins, L. M., Murphy, S. A., & Strecher, V. (2007). The multiphase optimization strategy (MOST) and the sequential multiple assignment randomized trial (SMART): New methods for more potent eHealth interventions. *American Journal of Preventive Medicine, 32*(5), S112–S118.

Collins, L. M., Nahum-Shani, I., & Almirall, D. (2014). Optimization of behavioral dynamic treatment regimens based on the sequential, multiple assignment, randomized trial (SMART). *Clinical Trials, 11*, 426–434.

Cooper, B. R., Bumbarger, B. K., & Moore, J. E. (2013). Sustaining evidence-based prevention programs: Correlates in a large-scale dissemination initiative. *Prevention Science*, 1–13.

Crowley, D. M., Coffman, D. L., Feinberg, M. E., Greenberg, M. T., & Spoth, R. L. (2014). Evaluating the impact of implementation factors on family-based prevention programming: Methods for strengthening causal inference. *Prevention Science, 15*(2), 246–255.

DeGarmo, D. S., Patterson, G. R., & Forgatch, M. S. (2004). How do outcomes in a specified parent training intervention maintain or wane over time? *Prevention Science, 5*(2), 73–89.

Dishion, T. J., Nelson, S. E., & Bullock, B. M. (2004). Premature adolescent autonomy: Parent disengagement and deviant peer process in the amplification of problem behaviour. *Journal of Adolescence, 27*(5), 515–530.

Dodge, K. A., Malone, P. S., Lansford, J. E., Miller, S., Pettit, G. S., Bates, J. E., Schulenberg, J. E., & Maslowsky, J. (2009). A dynamic cascade model of the development of substance use onset. *Monographs of the Society for Research in Child Development, 74*(3), 1–120.

Duncan, T. E., Duncan, S. C., & Strycker, L. A. (2013). *An introduction to latent variable growth curve modeling: Concepts, issues, and application*. New York: Routledge Academic.

Durlak, J. A., & DuPre, E. P. (2008). Implementation matters: A review of research on the influence of implementation on program outcomes and the factors affecting implementation. *American Journal of Community Psychology, 41*(3–4), 327–350.

326 Gregory M. Fosco et al.

Dymnicki, A., Wandersman, A., Osher, D., Grigorescu, V., Huang, L., & Meyer, A. (2014). *Willing, able → ready: Basics and policy implications of readiness as a key component for implementation of evidence-based practices.* ASPE Issue Brief, Office of the Assistant Secretary for Planning and Evaluation, Office of Human Services Policy, United States Department of Health and Human Services.

Feinberg, M. E. (2003). The internal structure and ecological context of coparenting: A framework for research and intervention. *Parenting: Science and Practice, 3*(2), 95–131.

Feinberg, M. E., Jones, D., Greenberg, M. T., Osgood, D. W., & Bontempo, D. (2010). Effects of the Communities That Care model in Pennsylvania on change in adolescent risk and problem behaviors. *Prevention Science, 11*(2), 163–171.

Fixsen, D. L., Naoom, S. F., Blase, K. A., & Friedman, R. M. (2005). *Implementation research: A synthesis of the literature.* Tampa, FL: University of South Florida.

Fosco, G. M., & Feinberg, M. E. (2014). Cascading effects of interparental conflict in adolescence: Linking threat appraisals, self-efficacy, and adjustment. *Development and Psychopathology, 27*(1), 239–252.

Fosco, G. M., Van Ryzin, M. J., Stormshak, E. A., & Dishion, T. J. (2014). Putting theory to the test: Examining family context, caregiver motivation, and conflict in the Family Check-Up model. *Development and Psychopathology, 26*, 305–318.

Franks, R. (2010). *Role of the intermediary organization in promoting and disseminating best practices for children and youth.* Farmington: Connecticut Center for Effective Practice, Child Health and Development Institute.

Gelo, O. C. G., & Manzo, S. (2015). Quantitative approaches to treatment process, change process, and process-outcome research. In O. Gelo, A. Pritz, & B. Rieken (Eds.), *Psychotherapy research* (pp. 247–277). Vienna: Springer.

Greenwood, P. W., & Welsh, B. C. (2012). Promoting evidence-based practice in delinquency prevention at the state level. *Criminology & Public Policy, 11*(3), 493–513.

Haskins, R., Garfinkel, I., & McLanahan, S. (2014). Introduction: Two-generation mechanisms of child development. *The Future of Children, 24*(1), 3–12.

Hawkins, J. D., Catalano, R. F., & Arthur, M. W. (2002). Promoting science-based prevention in communities. *Addictive Behaviors, 27*(6), 951–976.

Jacobson, N. S., Dobson, K. S., Truax, P. A., Addis, M. E., Koerner, K., Gollan, J. K. et al. (1996). A component analysis of cognitive-behavioral treatment for depression. *Journal of Consulting and Clinical Psychology, 64*(2), 295.

Kaminski, J. W., Valle, L. A., Filene, J. H., & Boyle, C. L. (2008). A meta-analytic review of components associated with parent training program effectiveness. *Journal of Abnormal Child Psychology, 36*(4), 567–589.

Kazdin, A. E. (2007). Mediators and mechanisms of change in psychotherapy research. *Annual Review of Clinical Psychology, 3*, 1–27.

Koh, H. K., & Sebelius, K. G. (2010). Promoting prevention through the Affordable Care Act. *New England Journal of Medicine, 363*(14), 1296–1299.

Kumar, S., Nilsen, W., Abernethy, A., Atienza, A., Patrick, K., Pavel, M. et al. (2013). Mobile health technology evaluation: The mHealth evidence workshop. *American Journal of Preventive Medicine, 45*(2), 228–236.

Laird, R. D., Pettit, G. S., Bates, J. E., & Dodge, K. A. (2003). Parents' monitoring-relevant knowledge and adolescents' delinquent behavior: Evidence of correlated developmental changes and reciprocal influences. *Child Development, 74*, 752–768.

Larson, R., & Almeida, D. M. (1999). Emotional transmission in the daily lives of families: A new paradigm for studying family process. *Journal of Marriage and Family, 61*(1), 5–20.

Liddle, H. A. (2004). Family-based therapies for adolescent alcohol and drug use: Research contributions and future research needs. *Addiction, 99*(s2), 76–92.

Liebman, J. (2013). *Building on recent advances in evidence-based policymaking.* Washington, DC: The Brookings Institution.

Masten, A. S., & Cicchetti, D. (2010). Developmental cascades. *Development and Psychopathology, 22*(3), 491–495.

Masten, A. S., Roisman, G. I., Long, J. D., Burt, K. B., Obradović, J., Riley, J. R. et al. (2005). Developmental cascades: Linking academic achievement and externalizing and internalizing symptoms over 20 years. *Developmental Psychology, 41*(5), 733.

McArdle, J. J. (2009). Latent variable modeling of differences and changes with longitudinal data. *Annual Review of Psychology, 60*, 577–605.

McEachern, A. D., Fosco, G. M., Dishion, T. J., Shaw, D. S., Wilson, M. N., & Gardner, F. (2013). Collateral benefits of the family check-up in early childhood: Primary caregivers' social support and relationship satisfaction. *Journal of Family Psychology, 27*(2), 271–281.

Minuchin, P. (1985). Families and individual development: Provocations from the field of family therapy. *Child Development, 56*, 289–302.

Moilanen, K. L., Shaw, D. S., & Maxwell, K. L. (2010). Developmental cascades: Externalizing, internalizing, and academic competence from middle childhood to early adolescence. *Development and Psychopathology, 22*(3), 635–653.

Moore, J. E., Bumbarger, B. K., & Cooper, B. R. (2013). Examining adaptations of evidence-based programs in natural contexts. *The Journal of Primary Prevention, 34*(3), 147–161.

Mrazek, P. B., Biglan, A., & Hawkins, J. D. (2007). *Community-monitoring systems: Tracking and improving the well-being of America's children and adolescents.* Falls Church, VA: Society for Prevention Research.

Murphy, S. A. (2005). An experimental design for the development of adaptive treatment strategies. *Statistics in Medicine, 24*(10), 1455–1481.

Offord, D. R., Kraemer, H. C., Kazdin, A. E., Jensen, P. S., & Harrington, R. (1998). Lowering the burden of suffering from child psychiatric disorder: Trade-offs among clinical, targeted, and universal interventions. *Journal of the American Academy of Child & Adolescent Psychiatry, 37*(7), 686–694.

Patterson, G. R. (2005). The next generation of PMTO models. *The Behavior Therapist, 28*(2), 25–32.

Patterson, G. R., & Forgatch, M. S. (1985). Therapist behavior as a determinant for client noncompliance: A paradox for the behavior modifier. *Journal of Consulting and Clinical Psychology, 53*(6), 846–851.

Pew-MacArthur Results First Initiative (2014). *Evidence-based policymaking: A guide for effective government.* Washington, DC: The Pew Charitable Trusts.

Rhoades, B. L., Bumbarger, B. K., & Moore, J. E. (2012). The role of a state-level prevention support system in promoting high-quality implementation and sustainability of evidence-based programs. *American Journal of Community Psychology, 50*(3–4), 386–401.

Sandler, I. N., Schoenfelder, E. N., Wolchik, S. A., & MacKinnon, D. P. (2011). Long-term impact of prevention programs to promote effective parenting: Lasting effects but uncertain processes. *Annual Review of Psychology, 62*, 299–329.

Schermerhorn, A. C., Chow, S. M., & Cummings, E. M. (2010). Developmental family processes and interparental conflict: Patterns of microlevel influences. *Developmental Psychology, 46*(4), 869–885.

Schwarz, N. (2007). Retrospective and concurrent self-reports: The rationale for real-time data capture. In A. A. Stone, S. Shiffman, A. A. Atienza, & L. Nebeling (Eds.), *The science of real time data capture: Self-reports in health research* (pp. 11–26). New York: Oxford University Press.

Shiffman, S. (2007). Designing protocols for ecological momentary assessment. In A. A. Stone, S. Shiffman, A. A. Atienza, & L. Nebeling (Eds.), *The science of real time data capture: Self-reports in health research* (pp. 27–53). New York: Oxford University Press.

Sliwinski, M. J. (2008). Measurement-burst designs for social health research. *Social and Personality Psychology Compass, 2,* 245–261.

Smyth, J. M., & Heron, K. E. (2014). Ecological momentary assessment (EMA) in family research. In S. McHale, P. Amato, & A. Booth (Eds.), *Emerging methods in family research* (pp. 145–161). New York: Springer.

Smyth, J. M., & Stone, A. A. (2003). Ecological momentary assessment research in behavioral medicine. *Journal of Happiness Studies, 4,* 35–52.

Stone, A. A., Shiffman, S., Atienza, A. A., & Nebeling, L. (2007). Historical roots and rationale of ecological momentary assessment (EMA). In A. A. Stone, S. Shiffman, A. A. Atienza, & L. Nebeling (Eds.), *The science of real time data capture: Self-reports in health research* (pp. 3–10). New York: Oxford University Press.

Tibbits, M. K., Bumbarger, B. K., Kyler, S. J., & Perkins, D. F. (2010). Sustaining evidence-based interventions under real-world conditions: Results from a large-scale diffusion project. *Prevention Science, 11*(3), 252–262.

Van Ryzin, M. J., & Dishion, T. J. (2012). The impact of a family-centered intervention on the ecology of adolescent antisocial behavior: Modeling developmental sequelae and trajectories during adolescence. *Development and Psychopathology, 24,* 1139–1155.

Wandersman, A., Duffy, J., Flaspohler, P., Noonan, R., Lubell, K., Stillman, L. et al. (2008). Bridging the gap between prevention research and practice: The interactive systems framework for dissemination and implementation. *American Journal of Community Psychology, 41*(3–4), 171–181.

Weissberg, R. P., & Greenberg, M. T. (1998). Prevention science and collaborative community action research: Combining the best from both perspectives. *Journal of Mental Health, 7,* 479–492.

Weisz, J. R. (2014). Short-term treatment as long-term prevention: Can early intervention produce legacy effects? *American Journal of Psychiatry, 171*(6), 600–602.

INDEX

acculturation: defined 261; differential generational acculturation 262; in ethnic families 261–2

ADHD/ADD (Attention deficit disorders) 47, 49, 52, 54, 60, 61, 69, 154

Adolescent Transitions Program (ATP) 91–2

adolescents: behavioral problems, global rise in 43, 68; behavioral stages of problem behavior and substance abuse 87–90, *91*; comorbidity of substance abuse and depression, adolescent girls 270; delinquency and role of the family 86–7; delinquency in girls 256, 269; eating disorders and adolescent girls 270; environmental risks, girls 269–70; etiological studies, substance abuse 86–7; genetic risks, girls 269; increase peer group influence 87; limitations of science of adolescents and role of the family 90–1; parental monitoring, efficacy of 11; parental substance abuse as antecedent to adolescent substance abuse 87; reduction in behavioral problems 1–2; substance abuse and intervention outcomes, Family Check-up Model 99; substance abuse and parental monitoring 11, 87, 90, 95–6, 100–1; substance abuse and role of the family 86–7, 90, 209–10, 260, *260*; substance abuse, PROSPER Delivery System 163, 171–2; substance abuse, Staying Connected with Your Teen 216, **217**, 220–1; substance prevention, Strengthening Families Program 80–1, 165

Adults in the Making (AIM): development of 282; efficacy 293; prevention trial 292; session structure 287–8; trial overview 293

African Americans, rural USA: buffering properties, protective caregiving 284–5; community liaison network 286; family skills training programs, development of 287–8; focus groups 286; mediation evidence, protective caregiving 285; protective caregiving and preventative interventions, empirical basis for 283–4; recruitment and retention of parents 285–6; substance abuse 282; *see also* Adults in the Making (AIM); Strong African American Families (SAAF); Strong African American Families-Teen (SAAF-T)

American Psychological Association Task Force on Psychological Intervention Guidelines 8

antisocial behavior, childhood: parental monitoring processes and 5; proactive antisocial behavior 89; reactive antisocial behavior 89; as stage to adolescent substance abuse 87, 88–9

autism spectrum disorders 50, 61, 69, 154

330 Index

Bandura, A. 46, 72
behavioral parent training: avoiding coercive family processes 4; coding system, family-based programs 14; parental monitoring processes 5; positive family relationships 14
behavioral problems: antisocial behavior, childhood 5, 87, 88–9; conduct problem outcomes, PROSPER Delivery System 172–3; early-onset, risks of 3, 42, 43; efficacy of family-based prevention programs and 1–2; increase in adolescents 43, 68; role of familial processes 23–4; *see also* delinquency
Brestan, E.V. and Eyberg, S. M. 2
Building Strong Families study 26

Center for Family Research (CFR): community partnership processes 285–7; health benefits through prevention program participation 296–300; longitudinal development research, rural African American families 283; randomized trials and Gene x Environment hypotheses 293–5
change processes: alternative hypothesis testing 316; component analysis 320–2; developmental cascade framework 319–20; developmental trajectory approaches 318–19; developmentally informed approaches to mediation 317–20; within-family change processes 322–3; future research directions 323–4; intensive longitudinal methods 316–17; lack of research on 314–15; measurement burst design 317; mechanisms of enduring change 315; during prevention programs 320–3; traditional pre-post mediation analysis 315–17
Clinician-Based Cognitive Psychoeducational Intervention (CBCPI) 233
Cochran Reviews 2, 43
coding system, family-based programs 12–14, **13**
coercive family processes: avoidance of, Incredible Years Series 45; avoidance of, Parent Management Training - Oregon Model 116; avoidance of, Strengthening Families Program 72; parental monitoring processes and 5; as risk factors 4; and transition to parenthood 24

cognitive learning, modelling and self-efficacy theories 46, 72
community-based partnerships: difficulties in delivering 161; dissemination of evidence-based interventions 160–1; *see also* PROSPER Delivery System
conflict: family violence, Family Foundations (FF) 33, 35; parental and competent parenting 27–9; prevention program impacts 32
cost-benefit analyses: family-based prevention programs 2, 25, 313; PROSPER Delivery System 173; Staying Connected with Your Teen (SCT) 212–14; Strengthening Families Program 80–1; Triple-P program (Positive Parenting Program) 151; *see also* funding models
Cowan, C.P. and Cowan, P.A. 24, 26
cultural adaptations: Ecological Validity Model (EVM) 262–3; for ethnic families/sub-groups 258, 266; of evidence-based family programs 257–8; family recruitment challenges 258–9; family-based prevention programs 264; Incredible Years Series 264; international implementations family-based programs 264–5; international outcome results, Strengthening Families Program 267–8; lack of ethnically-tailored adaptations 258–9; models for 262–3; need for evaluation of 256; need for in evidence-based interventions 273–4; no adaptation and reduced effectiveness 268; Parent Management Training - Oregon Model 115, 117–18, 264; practitioners" cultural backgrounds 263, 266–7, 273–4; and program fidelity 257, 311; PROSPER Delivery System 176; role-playing 263; Strengthening Families Program 79, 265–7; Triple-P program (Positive Parenting Program) 139, 155, 264; UNODC steps for 263–4

Dare To Be You program 265
delinquency: adolescents and role of the family 86–7; increased, adolescent girls 256, 269; tests of SIL model, Parent Management Training - Oregon model 120–2, *121*
depression: comorbidity with substance abuse, adolescent girls 270; effects of, Family Check-Up Model 96, 97, 100;

Index **331**

effects of, Parent Management Training - Oregon Model 115; effects on, Family Foundations (FF) 27, 29, 31, 32, 33, 37; effects on, Incredible Years Series 61; maternal depression 6, 24; parental, military families 233
developmental cascade framework 319–20
developmental trajectory approaches 318–19
Dick, D.M. *et al* (2009) 90
disciplinary skills, childhood 11
Dishion, T.J. and Medici-Skaggs, N. 90–1
Dishion, T.J. *et al* (1988) 91

Ecological Validity Model (EVM) 262–3
elementary children: developmental needs of 69; effective family interventions, core components of 70–1; evidence-based programs for 70; risk factors for 69
epigenetics: gender-specific risk 269; parental monitoring and genetic risk emergence 68, 78, 90; randomized trials and Gene x Environment hypotheses 293–5
ethnic families: acculturation 261–2; cultural fit with family-based interventions 259; cultural pride maintenance 261; ethnic sub-groups and program adaptations 266; generational acculturation 261–2; lack of ethnically-tailored adaptations 258–9; monitoring impacts 260–1; need for family services 258; protective factors for 259–60; risk factors for 259–60, 262; *see also* African Americans, rural USA
evidence analyses: effective programs 9–10; efficacious programs 9; external validity 9; internal validity 9; randomized controlled trials (RCT) 9; randomized trials 9; ready for dissemination programs 9, 10; Standards Committee (SPR) 8–10

facilitators *see* practitioners
Families and Schools Together program 265
Family Check-Up Model: adapted and tailored approach 93–6, *95*; adolescent substance abuse, effects on 99; aggregation of youths into groups, disadvantages of 91–2; as behavioral parent training approach 5; effects on depression 96, 97, 100; Everyday

Parenting Curriculum (EPC) *93*; facilitators, role of 101, 102–3; implementation model 101–4; initial Adolescent Transition Program (ATP) 91–2; intervention outcomes from randomized trials 96–101; overview of 92–3, *92*; parental engagement 100; Three Domains of Family Management Skills *95*
Family Foundations (FF): adaptations of 35–6; delivery through childbirth education 29; distal outcomes 31–2; effects on maternal depression 32, 33; efficacy of 30–1; and family violence 33, 35; future dissemination options 37; group session format 29–30; implementation fidelity 33–4; implementation structure 29–30; key goals of 26–7; Logic Model *28*; as manualized program 29–30; for military families 36; online, interactive versions 36; openness to change and transition to parenthood 29; outreach and recruitment of parents 35; Positive coparenting, model of 27–8, 30; proximal intervention targets 27–8; proximal outcomes 31; results 31–3; role of facilitators and implementation 34–5; second randomized trial 33; as supportive environmental factor 32; sustainable funding models 37; for teen parents 36
Family Matters 264
family recruitment: cultural adaptations 258–9; Family Foundations (FF) 35; PROSPER Delivery System 174; rural African American families 285–6; Strengthening Families Program 74–5, 266
family relationships/attachment perspective: behavioral benefits of 6; contingent parental responsiveness 5–6
family skills training 6, 12
family systems programs: interdependency 6–7; whole-family approaches (family wholism) 7
"Family Talk" 233
family-based prevention programs: cost-benefit analysis 2, 25, 313; cultural adaptations 259, 264; delivery systems 310; development of 3–4; evidence research 8–10; federal resources for 25–6; implementation levels 8, 9;

332 Index

infrastructure requirements 309–10; international implementations of 264–5; key roles of 308; meta-analysis project, adolescent substance abuse 12–14, **13**; models of 4; overview of 1–2; program effects 26; program processes 10–14; program sustainability 312–14; quality in program delivery 310–12; role of intermediary organizations 313–14; scale-up and fidelity maintenance 310–11; social-economic model of systems change *309*; universal framework for 25; *see also* change processes

fidelity of implementation: and cultural adaptations 257, 268, 311; Family Foundations (FF) 33–4; Incredible Years Series 56; Multidimensional Treatment Foster Care (MTFC) 200; Parent Management Training - Oregon Model 118–19, 125–6; PROSPER Delivery System 169, 175; scale-up and maintenance of 310–11; Staying Connected with Your Teen (SCT) 216–18; Triple-P program (Positive Parenting Program) 147

FOCUS (Families OverComing Under Stress): coordinated parent leadership 242; customization of 234; deployment and reintegration challenges 239; developmental guidance 237; developmentally appropriate information provision 241; disrupted family organization and belief systems 240; evidence of effectiveness 245–7; family resilience check-in 236–7; family resilience measures **236**; foundational interventions 233–4; future directions 247; impaired family communication 239–40; impaired parenting practices 240; individual and family skills 241–2; lessons learned 249–50; as manualized program 234; model adaptation 244–5; narrative timeline construction 237; open and effective communication 241; overview of 231; practitioners' training 247–9; psychoeducation 237; resilience mechanisms 240–2; resilience model 238–9; risk mechanisms for military families 239–40; scale-up dissemination framework 243–5; shared family understanding 242; skills training processes 237–8; structural framework *235*; theoretical model 232–3, **232**

funding models: within family-based programs 313; future directions for, PROSPER Delivery System 179–80; lack of, Incredible Years Series 61; Parent Management Training - Oregon Model 127; sustainable, Family Foundations (FF) 37; *see also* cost-benefit analyses

gender adaptations: comorbidity of substance abuse and depression, adolescent girls 270; eating disorders, adolescent girls 270; environmental risk, adolescent girls 269–70; future research directions 273; gender-specific family-based programs 271–2; genetic risks and substance abuse, adolescent girls 269; need for evaluation of 256; need for in evidence-based interventions 268–9, 273–4; parental monitoring processes and girls 260–1, 270; recommended gender adaptations 272; sexual abuse, girls 270–1; social ecology model of substance abuse by gender *260*

Hallfors, D. *et al* (2001) 161

health: health benefits, future directions, Strong African American Families (SAAF) 300; health problems, low-SES children 296; HIV family-based intervention 233–4; inflammation reduction, Strong African American Families (SAAF) 296–7; protective effects on teomere length (longevity), Strong African American Families (SAAF) 298–9; stress hormone reduction, Strong African American Families (SAAF) 297–8; *see also* mental health problems

Implementation Science 187, 202–3

Incredible Years Series: ADVANCE parenting program 49–50; attachment focus 6; attention to positive behavior 48; *Attentive Parenting Program* 50; *Autism Program* 50; Baby program 47; BASIC (core) parent training 47–8, 51, 53, 56; child programs (Dinosaur Curricula) 50–1, 60; cultural adaptations 264; evidence (studies and reviews) 51–6; factors affecting intervention outcomes 55–6; fidelity in implementation 56;

future research directions 60–1; group leaders training and supervision 56–7, 61; group-based learning method 46–7; *Home-based Coaching Model* 47–8; lack of sufficient funding 61; Level 3 (selective/high risk populations) 57–9; Level 4 (indicated populations) 59–60; Level 5 (multiple risk factors) 60; Levels 1 & 2 (universal programs) 57–9; levels of intervention according to risk populations 57–9; Levels of Intervention Pyramid According to Popular Risk *58*; Logic Model *44*; overview of 43; Parenting Pyramid 48, *49*; Preschool program 47; program content 45; program methods 46–7; protocols, children 3-5 years 45; protocols, school age children 45; *School Readiness Program* 50; School-Age program 47; selective prevention populations 53; sequence of content delivery 48; sessions 47; standardized program content 56; tailored goals 48; Teacher Classroom Management Program (IY-TCM) 50, 54–5, 60; theoretical background 45; use of video vignettes 47
Institute of Medicine (IOM): classification of implementation levels 8; paradigm for prevention research 283; preventative intervention cycle 283; promotion of community-based interventions 160
interventionists *see* practitioners

Kazdin, A.E. 316
Kumpfer, K.L. and Alvarado, R. 2

Laird, R.D. *et al* (2008) 90
Lester, P. *et al* (2013) 246
Liddle, H.A. 11
Lochman, J.E. and van den Steenhoven, A. 11

Mazzucchelli, T.G. and Sanders, M.R. 148
McCord, J. 86–7
measurement burst design 317
mental health problems: within family-centered approaches 3; increase in adolescents 68; and Incredible Years Series 59–60; role of familial processes 23
military families: adaptation for, Parent Management Training - Oregon Model 117; Family Foundations (FF) for 36; family stressors 229; family-based prevention programs and 231; increased awareness of needs of 230–1; PROSPER Delivery System for 181; relevance of psychological well-being 230–1; research on 229–30; role of family-level interactions 230; *see also* FOCUS (Families OverComing Under Stress)
Miller, T. and Hendrie, D. 11–12, 80
Mothers and Daughters Program 265
Multidimensional Family Therapy 265
Multidimensional Treatment Foster Care (MTFC): CDT model utility results 195–8; Community Development Team (CDT) Model 190–1; fidelity monitoring 200; funding instability (outer context factor) 198–9; future research directions 203; implementation research 189–90; infrastructure development 201; overview of 186–7, 188–9; program certification protocol 202; R³ model (feedback for intervention quality) 200–1; randomized implementation trial design 191–3; scale-up opportunities 188; on-site infrastructure 201–2; Stages of Implementation Completion 193–5, **194**; *see also* scale-up of evidence-based practices
Multisystemic Therapy for Delinquents and Substance Abusing Youth 264–5

National Prevention Council 179
National Research Council 160
needs-intervention paradox 187, 190
Nurturing Program 265

obesity, efficacy of family-based programs 2

Palinkas, L.A. *et al* (2011) 197
Palinkas, L.A. *et al* (2013) 197
parent management skills 4
Parent Management Training - Oregon Model (PMTO): adaptations for diverse populations 115, 117–18; as behavioral parent training approach 5; cultural adaptations 264; delinquency, SIL model tests 120–2, *121*; evaluations of 114–15; fidelity in implementation 118–19, 125–6; funding models 127;

334 Index

implementation 122–3, 128; increasing the pool of practitioners 126–7; mediational modelling tests of 120; outcomes for youth 119–20; overview of 113–14; Positive parenting practices focus 116; practitioners' role 118; progenitor generation training (GI) 123–5; reviews and testings 119–20; session structure 117; social interaction learning (SIL) basis 115–16; tailored goals 116–17

parental monitoring processes: and adolescent girls 260–1, 270; adolescents and unsupervised time with peers 89; behavioral parent training 5; efficacy, adolescence 11; for ethnic families 260–1; gender impacts 260–1, 270; and genetic risk emergence 68, 78, 90; influence on adolescent substance abuse 11, 87, 90, 95–6, 100–1

Patterson, G. 4, 14, 45, 72, 113

peer groups: deviant peer association 121–2; and ethnic minority adolescents 261; increased influence of in adolescence 87; peer clustering and anti-social behavior/substance abuse 89–90; peer rejection 89

practitioners: certification process, progenitor generation Parent Management Training - Oregon Model 123–5; cultural background of 263, 266–7, 273–4; fidelity in implementation, Parent Management Training - Oregon Model 119; implementation support following training, Triple P program 149–50; increasing the pool of practitioners, Parent Management Training - Oregon model 126–7; Parent Management Training - Oregon Model 118; practitioner selection, Triple P program 143–4; practitioners' training, FOCUS 247–9; risks of 'expert models' 46–7; role of, Family Check-Up Model 101, 102–3; role of, Family Foundations (FF) 34–5; selection and training, Strengthening Families Program 81; training and accreditation, Triple P program 144–50; training and supervision, Incredible Years Series 56–7, 61; training requirements 311–12

prenatal prevention programs 7

program processes: lack of systematic research on 11; narrative reviews 10–11; program composition and delivery 11–12

Project TALC (Teens and Adults Learning to Communicate) 233–4

PROSPER Delivery System: for adolescent substance abuse 163, 171–2; assessments 170–1; capacity building 162–3; community teams 165–6; community-level challenges 174; conduct problem outcomes 172–3; Cooperative Extension System (CES) 162; coordination of prevention dissemination efforts 179; cost-benefit analysis 173; cultural adaptations 176; delivery to sub-populations 181; as evidence-based intervention 163; Extension Systems, adoption of 175–6; family recruitment challenges 174; fidelity monitoring 169, 175; financing models 169, 176–8; Four-Tiered Delivery System *162*; funding, future directions 179–80; future integration with primary care services 181; future streamlined delivery systems 180–1; implementation 170; needed policy changes 178; Network Team 161, 166–8; original family-focused programs 164; overview of 161–3; preventative intervention outcomes 171; Prevention Coordinators 166; protective factor outcomes 171; standardized program content 168; State Management Team 166; structured communication 168–9; substance use outcomes 171–2; sustainability, challenges to 175; system structure 165–8; Technical Assistance to Community-Level Impact Model *167*; use of school programs 163; *see also* Strengthening Families Program

protective caregiving: buffering properties of 284–5; mediation evidence 285; and preventative interventions, empirical basis for 283–4

psychosocial treatments 2

public heath paradox 23

recruitment challenges *see* family recruitment

Resilience Framework 72

resilience model, defined 238

Rogers, E.M. 162, 190, 196
role-playing: for certification of
progenitor training, Parent Management
Training - Oregon model 124; cultural
adaptations 263; within family
relationship/attachment programs 6;
within Incredible Years Series 46
Romney, S. *et al* (2014) 144

Sandler, I.N. *et al* (2011) 11
scale-up of evidence-based practices:
family-based prevention programs 210;
fidelity maintenance 310–11; FOCUS
(Families OverComing Under Stress)
243–5; importance of 186, 187–8;
inner context factors 188, 199–202;
needs-intervention paradox 187, 190;
outer context factors 188, 198–9
Smith, J.D. *et al* (2014) 101
Snyder, J. *et al* (2005) 89
Society for Prevention Research (SPR),
Standards Committee 8–10
Spoth, R.L. and Greenberg, M. 177–8
Spoth, R.L. *et al* (2013) 178
Stanton, M.A. and Shadish, W.R. 2
Staying Connected with Your Teen
(SCT): *Connecting* (adapted program)
224–5; cost-benefit analysis 212–14;
efficacy trial 215–16; foster families,
dissemination to 223–5; future directions
225; group- vs. self-directed outcomes
222; group-administered format (PA)
211–14; high-risk families, dissemination
to 222–3; implementation fidelity, PA
intervention 216–18; Logic Model 211,
212; means (SD) and simple race
differences in substance abuse **217**;
means (SD) for treatment outcomes
220; outcomes at ages 20 and 22 221–2;
outcomes at two-year follow-up 219–20;
program components and SDM
constructs **213**; program initiation and
exposure 218–19; race differences in
sample characteristics at baseline 216,
216; research overview 214–15; research
pilot 215; sample size for each survey by
assigned program group and race **218**;
self-administered format (SA) 214;
stakeholder buy-in 223, 224; structure of
211–14; substance abuse, 10th Grade
220–1; theoretical foundations of 210–11
Strengthening Families Program: 7-17
years DVD 75, 81–2; adaptations within

the USA 265–6; behavioral skills
training (special play "Child's Game")
74; cost-benefit analysis 80–1; cultural
adaptations 79, 263–4; dissemination
in developing countries 79, 265;
effectiveness evidence 79–80, 164–5;
effectiveness trials in the USA 77–8;
efficacy trials 76–7; and epigenetic
research 78; etiological theory 71;
future research directions 81–2;
gender analyses of 271–2; international
outcome results 267–8; Logic Model 72,
73; overview of 71; program models 74;
recruitment and retention of parents
74–5, 266; selection and training of
group leaders 81; session structure
164; SFP 10-14 164; short-term
objectives 72; substance abuse and
non-parenting of children 68–9;
theoretical background 71–2; as a
universal prevention program 75;
see also PROSPER Delivery System
Strong African American Families
(SAAF): cultural adaptations of
265; development of 282; effects on
depression 6; efficacy trials 289–90;
and epigenetic research 78; health
benefits, future directions 300; health
benefits, inflammation reduction
296–7; health benefits, protective
effects on teomere length (longevity)
298–9; health benefits, stress hormone
reduction 297–8; health problems,
low-SES children 296; randomized
trial overview 288–9; randomized
trials and Gene x Environment
hypotheses 293–5; session structure
287–8; tests for theoretical model
289
Strong African American Families-Teen
(SAAF-T): development of 282;
efficacy 291; prevention trial 290;
session structure 287–8; trial
overview 290–1
substance abuse: adolescent and
Strengthening Families Program 80–1,
165; adolescent behavioral stages of
87–90, *91*; adolescents, intervention
outcomes, Family Check-up Model 99;
adolescents, Staying Connected with
Your Teen 216, **217**, 220–1; adolescents
and role of the family 86–7, 90, 209–10,
260, *260*; African Americans, rural USA

336 Index

282; comorbidity with depression, adolescent girls 270; efficacy of family-based prevention programs and 2; family skills training and 11–12; increased, adolescent girls 256, 269; limitations of science of adolescents and role of the family 90–1; meta-analysis project on family-based programs 12–14, **13**; and non-parenting of children 68–9; parental monitoring, efficacy of 11, 87, 90, 95–6, 100–1; parental substance abuse as antecedent to adolescent use 87; social ecology model of substance abuse by gender *260*; *see also* Strengthening Families Program
Szapocznik, J. *et al* (1989) 7

teachers: delivery of the PROSPER Delivery System 163; Incredible Years Teacher Classroom Management Program (IY-TCM) 50, 54–5, 60; school-district co-leader, PROSPER Delivery System 165–6
transition to parenthood: and coercive family processes 24; high-risk families and prevention programs 23; and marital deterioration 24; and negative developmental cascades 24; and openness to change 24–5, 29; *see also* Family Foundations (FF)

Triple-P program (Positive Parenting Program): adequate population reach 153; capacity to go to scale 152–3; central training team 145; community-wide roll outs 142–3; continuing evolution of 153–5; cost-benefit analysis 151; cultural adaptations 139, 155, 264; dissemination of 140–2; engagement phase 142; evidence for Triple P 140; fidelity and technical support 146–7; implementation framework 141, *141*; implementation maintenance 147, 150; implementation planning 143–4; meta-analyses of 140; multi-level Triple P approach 8, 135–8, **136–7**; overview of 134–5; PASS model 149–50; policy implications 151–2; population outcomes 150–1; practitioner selection 143; program outcome assessments 148, **149**; site readiness process 144; supervision of providers 149–50; tailored goals 139; tailored program delivery 148; tailored training methods and target groups 145–6; target population 135; training process 144–5, 146

video-based modelling techniques: for collaborative learning 47; efficacy of 51; for support for learning new skills 46

Wandersman, A. *et al* (2008) 314